Rick Steves'

PORTUGAL

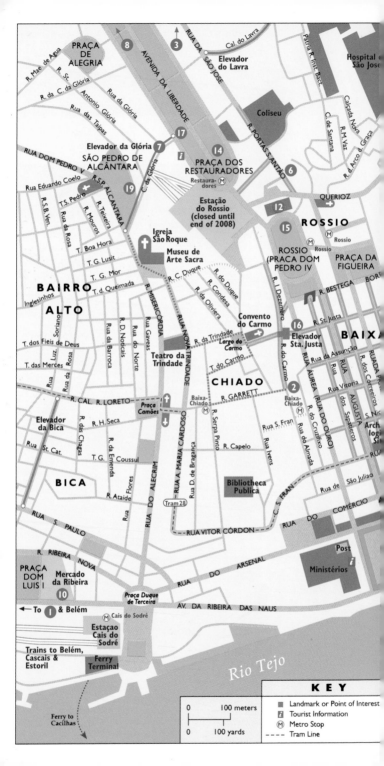

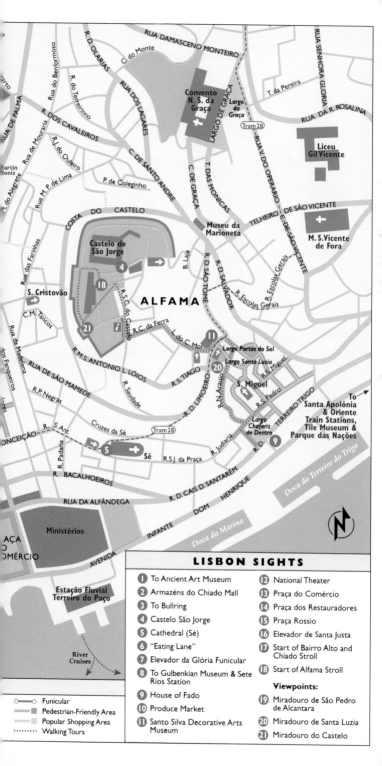

LISBON SIGHTS

1. To Ancient Art Museum
2. Armazéns do Chiado Mall
3. To Bullring
4. Castelo São Jorge
5. Cathedral (Sé)
6. "Eating Lane"
7. Elevador da Glória Funicular
8. To Gulbenkian Museum & Sete Rios Station
9. House of Fado
10. Produce Market
11. Santo Silva Decorative Arts Museum
12. National Theater
13. Praça do Comércio
14. Praça dos Restauradores
15. Praça Rossio
16. Elevador de Santa Justa
17. Start of Bairro Alto and Chiado Stroll
18. Start of Alfama Stroll

Viewpoints:

19. Miradouro de São Pedro de Alcântara
20. Miradouro de Santa Luzia
21. Miradouro do Castelo

○—○ Funicular
■ Pedestrian-Friendly Area
Popular Shopping Area
.... Walking Tours

Rick Steves'

PORTUGAL

AVALON
TRAVEL

CONTENTS

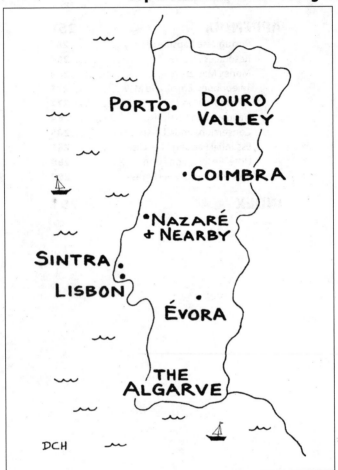

INTRODUCTION

Tucked into a far corner of the Continent, Portugal is Western Europe's least touristed country. Its relative isolation preserves a traditional culture of widows in black and fishermen mending nets. Along with the old, you'll find the modern, especially in the culturally rich capital of Lisbon and in the resort towns that rival Spain's (but feel more authentic). If your idea of travel includes friendly locals (who speak a bit of English), exotic architecture, windswept castles, and fresh seafood with chilled wine on a beach at sunset...you've chosen the right destination.

In recent years, Portugal has experienced economic success, thanks to its membership in the European Union. While Portugal is no longer a bargain basement for travelers, it's still a good budget option compared to the tourist-mobbed destinations of Northern Europe.

This book gives you all the information and suggestions necessary to wring the maximum value out of your limited time and money. Experiencing the culture, people, and natural wonders of Portugal economically and hassle-free has been my goal for three decades of traveling, guiding tours, and travel writing. With this book, I pass on to you the lessons I've learned.

Rick Steves' Portugal is a tour guide in your pocket, with a balanced, comfortable mix of big cities and cozy towns. It covers the predictable biggies, and mixes in a healthy dose of Back Door intimacy. You'll eat barnacles with green wine, recharge your solar cells in an Algarve fishing village, and wax nostalgic over bluesy fado singing.

To save time, maximize diversity, and avoid tourist burnout, I've been very selective. Rather than listing a string of mediocre Algarve beach towns, I focus on the top stops: Salema and Tavira.

The best is, of course, only my opinion. But after spending

Introduction

a third of my adult life exploring and researching Europe, I've developed a sixth sense for what travelers enjoy. Just thinking about the places featured in this book makes me want to hang out in a fado bar.

About This Book

This book is organized by destinations, each one a mini-vacation on its own, filled with exciting sights and convenient, affordable places to stay and eat. In the following chapters, you'll find this information:

Planning Your Time suggests a schedule with thoughts on how best to use your limited time.

Orientation includes tourist information, tips on public transportation, local tour options, helpful hints, and an easy-to-read map designed to make the text clear and your arrival smooth.

Self-Guided Walks take you through interesting neighborhoods, with a personal tour guide in hand.

Sights provides a succinct overview of Portugal's most important sights, arranged by neighborhood, with ratings:

    ▲▲▲—Don't miss.

    ▲▲—Try hard to see.

    ▲—Worthwhile if you can make it.

    No rating—Worth knowing about.

Sleeping describes my favorite hotels, from budget deals to splurges.

Eating serves up good-value restaurants, ranging from inexpensive take-out joints to fancier options.

Transportation Connections outlines your options for reaching nearby destinations by train, bus, and car.

The **appendix** is a traveler's tool kit, with a quick summary of Portugal's history, a handy packing checklist, recommended books and films, instructions on how to use the telephone, useful phone numbers, and the procedure for dealing with lost credit cards. You'll also find detailed information on driving and public transportation, a climate chart, a holiday and festival list, Portuguese survival phrases, and a hotel reservation form.

Study this book and put together the plan of your travel dreams. Then have a great trip! Traveling like a temporary local, and taking advantage of the information here, you'll enjoy the absolute most of every mile, minute, and dollar. As you travel the route I know and love, I'm happy that you'll be meeting some of my favorite Portuguese people.

PLANNING

Trip Costs

Five components make up your trip cost: airfare, surface transportation, room and board, sightseeing and entertainment, and shopping and miscellany.

Airfare: A basic round-trip flight from the US to Lisbon should cost $700–1,300 (cheaper in winter), depending on where you fly from and when you go. Smaller budget airlines provide bargain service from several European capitals to Lisbon (see "Cheap Flights" on page 283 for details). If you're adding Spain to your trip, consider saving time and money in Europe by flying "open jaw" (into one city and out of another; for instance, flying into Lisbon and out of Barcelona).

Surface Transportation: For a two-week whirlwind trip of all of my recommended destinations, allow $175 per person for second-class trains and buses or $600 per person (based on two people sharing) for a two-week car rental, gas, and insurance. Car rental or leases are cheaper if arranged from the US.

While train passes (generally designed to be purchased in your home country *before* arriving in Europe) are a convenience, they're a waste of money for a Portugal-only trip. It's cheaper to simply buy bus and train tickets as you go (see "Transportation," on page 277).

Room and Board: You can thrive in Portugal on $100 a day per person for room and board. This allows $15 for lunch, $5 for snacks, $30 for dinner, and $50 for lodging (based on two people splitting the cost of a $100 double room that includes breakfast; note that hotels outside of large cities are often less expensive). If you have more money, I've listed great ways to spend it. Students and tightwads can eat and sleep for $60 a day ($30 per bed, $30 for meals).

Sightseeing and Entertainment: Allow $3 to $6 per major sight (museums, churches), $2 to $3 for minor ones (climbing towers), and about $30 for splurge experiences (fado concerts, bullfights). An overall average of $12 a day works for most people. Don't skimp here. After all, this category is the driving force behind your trip—you came to sightsee, enjoy, and experience Portugal.

Shopping and Miscellany: Figure $1 per postcard, coffee, beer, and ice-cream cone. Shopping can vary in cost from nearly nothing to a small fortune. Good budget travelers find that this category has little to do with assembling a trip full of lifelong and wonderful memories.

When to Go

In peak season, May through September, sightseeing attractions are wide open. While it's not nearly as hot in Portugal as it is in Spain (except in the Alentejo region), an air-conditioned room is worth the splurge in summer.

Spring and fall offer the best combination of good weather, light crowds, long days, and plenty of tourist and cultural activities. In the off-season, roughly October through April, expect shorter hours, more lunchtime breaks at sights, and fewer activities. Confirm your sightseeing plans locally, especially when traveling off-season. For weather specifics, see the climate chart on page 285.

Sightseeing Priorities

Depending on the length of your trip, here are my recommended priorities. Assuming you're traveling by public transportation, I've taken geographical proximity into account.

3 days:	Lisbon, Sintra
6 days, add:	The Algarve (Salema and Tavira)
9 days, add:	Évora, Nazaré
11 days, add:	Sights near Nazaré, Coimbra
14 days, add:	Porto, Douro Valley

Travel Smart

Your trip to Portugal is like a complex play—easier to follow and really appreciate on a second viewing. While no one does the same trip twice to gain that advantage, reading this book before your trip accomplishes much the same thing.

Design an itinerary that enables you to visit the various sights at the best possible times. As you read this book, make note of festivals, seasonal closures, and the days sights are closed. For example, many museums and sights close on Mondays. Hotels are most crowded on Fridays and Saturdays, especially in resort towns.

Saturdays are virtually weekdays with earlier closing hours. Sundays have the same pros and cons as they do for travelers in the US: Sightseeing attractions are generally open; shops, banks, and markets are closed; public-transportation options are fewer; and city traffic is light. Rowdy evenings are rare on Sundays. Popular places are even more popular on weekends.

To give yourself a little rootedness, minimize one-night stands. It's worth a long drive after dinner to be settled into a town for two nights. People renting private rooms are also more likely to give a good price to someone staying more than one night.

Be sure to mix intense and relaxed periods in your itinerary. Every trip (and every traveler) needs at least a few slack days. Pace yourself. Assume you will return.

Know Before You Go

Your trip is more likely to go smoothly if you plan ahead.

Since **airline carry-on restrictions** are always changing, visit the Transportation Security Administration's website (www.tsa.gov/travelers) for an up-to-date list of what you can bring on the plane with you...and what you have to check. Remember to arrive with plenty of time to get through security.

Call your **debit and credit card companies** to let them know you'll be visiting Portugal, so that they'll accept (and not deny) your international charges. Confirm your daily withdrawal limit; consider asking to have it raised so you can take out more cash at each ATM stop.

Be sure that your **passport** is valid at least six months after your ticketed date of return to the US. If you need to get or renew a passport, it can take up to three months (for more on passports, see www.travel.state.gov).

Book your rooms in advance if you'll be traveling during peak season (July and August), any major holidays and festivals (see the appendix), and definitely for your first night.

If you're planning on **renting a car** in Portugal for more than a day or two, make arrangements before you leave the US. You can drive in Portugal with a valid US driver's license for up to six months.

Reread this book as you travel, and visit local tourist information offices. Upon arrival in a new town, lay the groundwork for a smooth departure; write down the schedule for the train or bus you'll take when you depart.

Plan ahead for banking, laundry, picnics, and Internet stops. Get online at Internet cafés or your hotel to research transportation connections, confirm events, check the weather, and get directions to your next hotel. Buy a phone card (or carry a mobile phone) and use it for reservations, reconfirmations, and double-checking hours.

Connect with the culture. Set up your own quest for the best cod dish, cloister, fado bar, custard tart, or whatever. Enjoy the hospitality of the local people. Slow down and ask questions—most locals are eager to point you toward their idea of the right direction. Keep a notepad in your pocket for organizing your thoughts. Wear your money belt, familiarize yourself with the currency, and learn a simple formula to quickly estimate rough prices in dollars. Those who expect to travel smart, do.

Portugal's Best Two-Week Trip By Car

Day	Plan	Sleep in
1	Arrive in Lisbon	Lisbon
2	Lisbon	Lisbon
3	Sintra side-trip by train, pick up car and drive to Salema in evening	Salema
4	Salema	Salema
5	Salema, side-trip to Cape Sagres	Salema
6	To Tavira via Lagos	Tavira
7	To Évora	Évora
8	To Nazaré via Óbidos	Nazaré
9	Nazaré	Nazaré
10	Near Nazaré (Alcobaça, Batalha, and Fátima), continue to Coimbra	Coimbra
11	Coimbra	Coimbra
12	To Douro Valley	Douro Valley
13	Douro Valley, end in Porto (could drop car)	Porto
14	Porto	Porto
15	Fly out of Porto; or drive or train back to Lisbon; or drive north to Santiago, Spain	

Try to avoid being in Lisbon (or Porto) on a Monday, when many major sights are closed (including Lisbon's Gulbenkian Museum, Museum of Ancient Art, National Tile Museum, Monastery of Jerónimos, Coach Museum, and Maritime Museum, as well as Sintra's Pena Palace). If you like big cities, Lisbon is worth an extra day. But if you're a beach-lover, leave Lisbon early and drive to Salema.

If, after touring Portugal, you're continuing to the Spanish destinations of Salamanca or Madrid, it's better to visit Porto and the Douro Valley before Coimbra.

While this itinerary is designed to be done by car, it can also be done by train and bus. If you're taking public transportation, stay three nights in Lisbon and catch a bus to Salema on the morning of the fourth day. Consider skipping Tavira, unless you're a beach connoisseur. From the Algarve, take the bus to

PRACTICALITIES

Red Tape: You need a passport—but no visa or shots—to travel in Portugal. Your passport must be valid for at least six months beyond the time you leave Portugal. Pack a photocopy of your passport in your luggage in case the original is lost or stolen.

Time: In Portugal—and in this book—you'll be using the

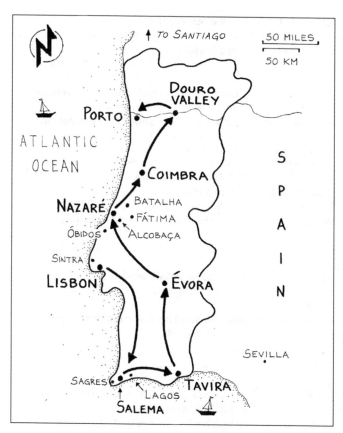

Évora (via Lagos) and spend a day and night, then take a bus to Nazaré (there's no direct service, so you have to go via Lisbon). See the sights near Nazaré by bus, using Nazaré as your home base. Take the train to Coimbra. Catch the bus or train to Porto and, using Porto as a home base, see the Douro Valley on a combination boat/train tour (or, with extra time, spend the night).

24-hour clock. It's the same through 12:00 noon, then keep going—13:00, 14:00, and so on. For anything past 12, subtract 12 and add p.m. (14:00 is 2:00 p.m.).

Though Portugal and Spain are neighbors, Portugal sets its clock one hour earlier than Spain and most of continental Europe. (This is always true, even during daylight saving time.) Portugal's time zone is the same as Great Britain's: generally five/eight hours

Just the FAQs, Please

Whom do I call in case of emergency?
In Portugal, dial 112 for medical or other emergencies.

What if my credit card is stolen?
Act immediately. See "Damage Control for Lost Cards," page 268, for instructions.

How do I make a phone call to, within, and from Portugal?
For detailed dialing instructions, refer to page 276.

How can I get tourist information about my destination?
Portugal has its own national tourist information office in the US (see page 264), as well as a network of local offices in virtually every city and town covered in this book. Note that Tourist Information is abbreviated **TI** in this book.

What's the best way to pack?
Light. For a recommended packing list, see page 287.

Does Rick have other resources that could help me?
For more on Rick's guidebooks, public television series, public radio show, website, guided tours, travel bags, and accessories, see page 264.

Are there any updates to this guidebook?
Check www.ricksteves.com/update for changes to the most recent edition of this book.

Can you recommend any good books or movies for my trip?
Sure. For suggestions, see pages 267–268.

ahead of the East/West Coasts of the US. The exceptions are the beginning and end of daylight saving time: Europe "springs forward" the last Sunday in March (two weeks after most of North America), and "falls back" the last Sunday in October (one week before North America). For a handy online time converter, try www.timeanddate.com/worldclock.

Business Hours: Some businesses in Portugal take an afternoon break (about 13:00–15:00). When it's 100 degrees in the shade, you'll understand why. The biggest museums stay open all day. Smaller ones often close for lunch. Small shops are usually open on Saturday only in the morning and are closed all day Sunday.

Watt's Up? Europe's electrical system is different from North America's in two ways: the shape of the plug (two round prongs) and the voltage of the current (220 volts instead of 110 volts). For your North American plug to work in Europe, you'll need an adapter, sold inexpensively at travel stores in the US. As for the voltage, most newer electronics or travel appliances (such as hair

Do I need to speak some Portuguese?
Many Portuguese people—especially those in the tourist trade, and in big cities—speak English. Still, you'll get better treatment if you learn and use the Portuguese pleasantries. For a list of phrases, see page 289.

Do you have information on driving, train travel, and flights?
Absolutely. See "Transportation" on page 277.

How much do I tip?
Relatively little. For tips on tipping, see page 269.

Will I get a student or senior discount?
Not likely. Discounts for sights are not listed in this book because they are generally limited to European residents and countries that offer reciprocal deals (the US does not). However, youths (under 18) and students (with International Student Identity Cards) often get discounts—but only by asking.

How can I get a VAT refund on major purchases?
See the details on page 270.

Does Portugal use the metric system?
Yes. A liter is about a quart, four to a gallon. A kilometer is six-tenths of a mile. I figure kilometers to miles by cutting them in half and adding back 10 percent of the original (120 km: 60 + 12 = 72 miles, 300 km: 150 + 30 = 180 miles). For more metric conversions, see page 285.

dryers, laptops, and battery chargers) automatically convert the voltage—if you see a range of voltages printed on the item or its plug (such as "110–220"), it'll work in Europe. Otherwise, you can buy a converter separately in the US (about $20).

News: Americans keep in touch in Europe with the *International Herald Tribune* (published almost daily via satellite throughout Europe). Every Tuesday, the European editions of *Time* and *Newsweek* hit the stands with articles of particular interest to travelers. Sports addicts can get their fix from *USA Today*. News in English will be sold only where there's enough demand: in bigger cities and tourist centers. Good websites include www.europeantimes.com and http://news.bbc.co.uk. Many hotels have CNN or BBC television channels available.

Theft Alert: Thieves target tourists throughout Portugal, especially in Lisbon. While hotel rooms are generally safe, thieves snatch purses, pick pockets, and break into cars. Use a money belt (a pouch with a strap that you buckle around your waist like a belt and wear under your clothes). Be on guard and treat any disturbance around you as a smoke screen for theft. Don't believe any "police officers" looking for counterfeit bills. When traveling by train, keep your backpack nearby and in sight. For tips for drivers, see the appendix.

MONEY

Banking

Throughout Europe, cash machines (ATMs) are the standard way for travelers to get local currency. Bring plastic—credit and/or debit cards—along with several hundred dollars in hard cash as an emergency backup. It's smart to bring two cards, in case one gets demagnetized or eaten by a temperamental machine. Travelers checks are a waste of time (long waits at slow banks) and a waste of money (in fees).

Banks are generally open Monday through Friday from 8:30 to 15:00. They charge outrageous, unregulated commissions for cashing a travelers check (can be up to $10). Shop around. Sometimes the hole-in-the-wall exchange offices offer better deals than the bank. Look for the rare American Express office. Better yet, use a cash machine.

Cash from ATMs

Portugal has readily available, easy-to-use, 24-hour ATMs with English instructions. Cash machines are called *Multibanco* (or *MB*), and are marked by a white sign with blue lettering. To withdraw money from your account, you'll need a debit card (ideally with a Visa or MasterCard logo for maximum usability), plus a PIN code. Know your PIN code in numbers; there are only numbers—no letters—on European keypads.

Before you go, verify with your bank that your card will work overseas, and alert them that you'll be making withdrawals in Europe; otherwise, the bank may not approve transactions if it perceives unusual spending patterns.

When using an ATM machine, try to take out large sums of money to reduce your per-transaction bank fees: Push the "other amount" button and ask for a higher amount (though this is not always possible). If the machine refuses your request, don't take it personally. Just try again and select a smaller amount.

Bank machines often dispense high-denomination bills, which can be difficult to break (especially at odd hours). My strategy: Request an odd amount of money from the ATM; or, if that doesn't work, go as soon as possible to a bank or a large store (such as a supermarket) to break the big bills.

Keep your cash safe. Thieves target tourists. A money belt provides peace of mind, allowing you to carry lots of cash safely. Don't

Exchange Rate

I list prices in euros for Portugal.

1 euro (€) = about $1.40

Just like the dollar, the euro is broken down into 100 cents. You'll find coins ranging from 1 cent to 2 euros, and bills from 5 euros to 500 euros. To roughly convert prices in euros to dollars, add 40 percent to Portuguese prices: €20 is about $28, €45 is about $63, and so on.

While the euro is the only official currency in Portugal, you might still see and hear locals quoting prices in the old currency, the *escudo,* especially in supermarkets and hotels. If you see a price in the thousands for an ordinary, affordable item, it's likely in *escudos* (for example, 5,000$, which can also be portrayed as 5,000$00).

waste time every few days tracking down a cash machine—withdraw a week's worth of money, stuff it in your money belt, and travel!

Credit and Debit Cards

For purchases, Visa and MasterCard are more commonly accepted than American Express. Just like at home, credit or debit cards work easily at larger hotels, shops, and restaurants, but smaller businesses prefer payment in local currency (in small bills—break large bills at a bank or larger store). Note that some receipts show your credit-card number; don't toss these thoughtlessly.

Using your credit and debit cards in Europe—whether for ATM withdrawals or purchases—can cost you additional "international transaction" fees (of up to 3 percent plus $5 per transaction), so it makes sense to ask your bank or credit-card company before your trip about these fees to avoid unpleasant surprises.

SIGHTSEEING

Sightseeing can be hard work. Use these tips to make your visits to Portugal's finest sights meaningful, fun, fast, and painless.

Set up an itinerary that allows you to fit in all your must-see sights. For a one-stop look at opening hours in the bigger cities—Lisbon and Porto—see the "At a Glance" sidebars. Most sights keep stable hours, but you can easily confirm the latest by calling the local TI.

All sights have rules, and if you know about these in advance, they're no big deal. Some important sights have metal detectors or conduct bag searches that will slow your entry.

At churches—which generally offer interesting art (usually free) and a cool, welcome seat—a modest dress code (no bare shoulders or shorts) is encouraged.

Some museums require you to check daypacks and coats. They'll be kept safely. If you have something you can't bear to part with, stash it in a pocket or purse. If you don't want to check a small backpack, carry it under your arm like a purse as you enter. From a guard's point of view, a backpack is generally a problem, while a purse is not.

Cameras are normally allowed, but not flashes or tripods (without special permission). Flashes damage oil paintings and distract others in the room. Even without a flash, a handheld camera will take a decent picture (or buy postcards or posters at the museum bookstore). Video cameras are usually allowed.

Many museums have special exhibits in addition to their permanent collection. Some exhibits are included in the entry price, while others come at an extra cost (which you may have to pay even if you don't want to see the exhibit).

Museums have bookstores selling postcards and souvenirs. Before you leave, scan the postcards and thumb through the biggest guidebook (or skim its index) to be sure you haven't overlooked something that you'd like to see.

Expect changes—paintings can be on tour, on loan, out sick, or shifted at the whim of the curator. To adapt, pick up any available free floor plans as you enter, and ask museum staff if you can't find a particular painting.

Many sights rent audioguides, which offer dry-but-useful recorded descriptions in English (about €5). If you bring along your own pair of headphones and a Y-jack, two people can sometimes share one audioguide and save. Guided tours in English (usually €6 and widely ranging in quality) are most likely to occur during peak season.

Some attractions have an on-site café or cafeteria (usually a good place to rest and have a snack or light meal). The WCs are generally free and clean.

Most sights stop admitting people 30–60 minutes before closing time, and some rooms close early (generally about 45 minutes before the actual closing time). Guards usher people out, so don't save the best for last.

Every sight or museum offers more than what is covered in this book. Use this information as an introduction—not the final word.

SLEEPING

Portugal offers some of the best accommodation values in Western Europe. Most places are government-regulated, with posted prices. While prices are low, street noise can be high. Always ask to see your room first. Check the price posted on the door, consider potential night-noise problems, ask for another room, or bargain down the price. You can request *com vista* (with a view) or *tranquilo* (quiet). In most cases, the view comes with street noise. Especially in resort areas, prices go way up in July and August. Most of the year, prices are soft.

In the interest of the smart use of your time, I favor hotels and restaurants handy to your sightseeing activities. Rather than list hotels scattered throughout a city, I describe my favorite couple of neighborhoods and recommend the best accommodations values in each, from $35 *quartos* to $320 suites.

All rooms have sinks with hot and cold water. Rooms with private bathrooms are often bigger and renovated, while the cheaper rooms without bathrooms often will be dingier and/or on the top floor. Any room without a bathroom has access to a bathroom on the corridor. Especially in private homes, where the boss changes the sheets, people staying several nights are most desirable. One-night stays sometimes cost extra.

For environmental reasons, towels are often replaced in hotels only when you leave them on the floor. In private accommodations and some cheap hotels, they aren't replaced at all, so hang them up to dry and reuse.

Before accepting a room, confirm your understanding of the complete price. You can usually save time by paying your bill the evening before you leave, instead of paying in the busy morning, when the reception desk is crowded with tourists who want to pay up, ask questions, or check in.

Types of Accommodations

Hotels: Hotel rooms are generally pleasant by American standards. Don't judge hotels by their bleak and dirty entryways. Landlords, stuck with rent control, often stand firmly in the way of hardworking hoteliers who'd like to brighten up their buildings.

Prepare for cool evenings if you travel in spring and fall. Summer can be extremely hot. Consider air-conditioning, fans, and noise (since you'll want your window open), and don't be shy about asking for ice at the fancier hotels. Many rooms come with mini-refrigerators (if it's noisy at night, unplug it).

Most hotel rooms with air-conditioners come with control sticks (like a TV remote, sometimes requires a deposit) that generally have the same symbols and features: fan icon (click to

Sleep Code

To help you easily sort through the listings, I've divided the rooms into three categories based on the price for a standard double room with bath:

$$$ **Higher Priced**
$$ **Moderately Priced**
$ **Lower Priced**

Prices listed in this book are per room, not per person. Hotels usually accept credit cards and include breakfast (unless otherwise noted); private accommodations rarely do either. Virtually all of my recommended accommodations are run by people who speak English; if they don't, I mention it in the listing.

When there is a range of prices in one category, that means the price fluctuates with the season; the prices and seasons are posted at or near the hotel desk. To give maximum information in a minimum of space, I use the following code to describe the accommodations.

S = Single room (or price for one person in a double).
D = Double or twin. Double beds are usually big enough for non-romantic couples.
T = Triple (often a double bed with a single).
Q = Quad (usually two double beds).
b = Private bathroom with toilet and shower or tub.
s = Private shower or tub only (the toilet is down the hall).

According to this code, a couple staying at a "Db-€90" hotel would pay a total of €90 (about $125) for a double room with a private bathroom.

toggle through wind power from light to gale); louver icon (choose steady air flow or waves); snowflake and sunshine icons (heat or cold, depending on season); clock ("O" setting: run X hours before turning off; "I" setting: wait X hours to start); and the temperature control (20° or 21° Celsius is the normal sleeping temperature).

Any regulated hotel will have a complaint book *(livro de rec-lamações)* checked by authorities. A request for this book will generally prompt the hotelier to solve your problem to keep you from writing a complaint.

Historic Inns: Portugal has luxurious, government-sponsored historic inns. These *pousadas* are often renovated castles, palaces, or monasteries, many with great views and stately atmospheres.

While full of Old World character, they often are run in a very sterile, bureaucratic way. These are pricey (doubles $130–320), but can be a good deal for younger people (30 and under) and seniors (60 and over), who often get discounted rates; for details, bonus packages, and family deals, see www.pousadas.pt.

Rooms in Private Homes *(Quartos):* In touristy areas, you'll typically find locals who've opened up a spare room to make a little money on the side. These rooms are usually as private as hotel rooms, often with separate entries. Especially in resort towns, the rooms might be in small, apartment-type buildings. Ask for a *quarto* (KWAR-too). They're less expensive than hotels ($35–70 for a double without breakfast) and usually offer a good experience.

Hostels and Campgrounds: Portugal has plenty of youth hostels and campgrounds, but considering the great bargains on other accommodations, I don't think they're worth the trouble and don't cover them in this book. Instead, I prefer simple, family-run hotels (listed as a *pensão* or *residencial*); they're easy to find, inexpensive, and, when chosen properly, a fun part of the Portuguese cultural experience. If you're on a starvation budget or just prefer camping or hosteling, plenty of information is available in the *Let's Go: Spain & Portugal* guidebook (see "Resources," page 266), through the national tourist office, and at local tourist information offices.

Making Reservations

Even though Easter, July, and August are often crowded, you can travel at any time of year without reservations. But given the high stakes and the quality of the gems I've found for this book, I'd recommend that you reserve your rooms in advance, particularly for Lisbon. Book several weeks ahead, or as soon as you've pinned down your travel dates. Note that some national holidays jam things up and merit your making reservations far in advance (see "Holidays and Festivals," page 284).

Some travelers make reservations as they travel, calling hotels a few days before their visit. If you prefer the flexibility of traveling without any reservations at all, you'll have greater success snaring rooms if you arrive at your destination early in the day. When you anticipate crowds, call hotels around 9:00 on the day you plan to arrive, when the hotel clerk knows who'll be checking out and just which rooms will be available.

To make a reservation in advance, contact hotels directly by email, phone, or fax. Email is the clearest and most economical way to make a reservation. In addition, many hotel websites now have online reservation forms. To ensure you have all the information you need for your reservation, use the form in this book's appendix (also at www.ricksteves.com/reservation).

I've taken great pains to list telephone numbers with

long-distance instructions (see "Telephones" in the appendix). Use the telephone and the convenient phone cards. Simple English is usually fine; most hotels listed are accustomed to English-only speakers. If phoning from the US, be mindful of time zones (see page 6).

When you request a room in writing for a certain time period, use the European style for writing dates: day/month/year. Hoteliers need to know your arrival and departure dates. For example, for a two-night stay in July I would request: "2 nights, arrive 16/07/09, depart 18/07/09." Consider in advance how long you'll stay; don't just assume you can extend your reservation for extra days once you arrive.

If you don't get a reply to your email or fax, it usually means the place is already fully booked. If you get a response that gives room availability and rates, it's not a confirmation. You must tell them that you want that room at the given rate.

Whether you reserve a few hours or a few months in advance, most hoteliers will trust you and hold a room until 16:00 (4:00 p.m.) without a deposit, though some will ask for a credit-card number. While you can email your credit-card information (I do), some people prefer to share that personal info via phone call, fax, or secure online reservation form (if the hotel has one on its website).

If you must cancel your reservation, it's courteous to do so with as much advance notice as possible (simply make a quick phone call or send an email). Hoteliers and *pensão* hosts lose money if they turn away customers while holding a room for someone who doesn't show up. Understandably, some hoteliers bill no-shows for one night. Hotels sometimes have strict cancellation policies (for example, you might lose a deposit if you cancel within two weeks of your reserved stay, or you might be billed for the entire visit if you leave early); ask about cancellation policies before you book. Again, don't let these people down—I promised you'd call and cancel as early as possible if for some reason you won't show up.

Always reconfirm your room reservation a few days in advance from the road. If you'll be arriving later than 16:00, let them know. Don't needlessly confirm rooms through the tourist office or Web services; they'll take a commission of up to 20 percent.

On the small chance that a hotel loses track of your reservation, bring along a hard copy of their emailed or faxed confirmation.

EATING

The Portuguese meal schedule is slightly later than in the US. Lunch *(almoço)* is the big meal, served between 12:30 and 14:00, while supper *(jantar)* is from about 19:30–21:30. You'll eat well in mom-and-pop restaurants for €10. For tips on tipping, see page

269. One of the most important things to remember when eating in Portugal is that if appetizers (olives, bread, butter, patés, and a veritable mini-buffet of other tasty temptations) are brought to your table before you order, they are not free. If you don't want them, push them to the side—you won't be charged for what you don't touch. But taking just one olive means you pay for the whole dish. Simple appetizers usually cost about €1 each, so it won't break the budget—just don't be surprised at extra charges on your bill. Most mom-and-pop restaurateurs will figure the bill in front of you, so everyone agrees on the final amount to be paid.

Eat seafood in Portugal. Fish soup *(sopa de peixe)* and shellfish soup *(sopa de mariscos)* are worth seeking out. *Caldo verde* is a popu-

lar vegetable soup. *Frango assado* is roast chicken; ask for *piri-piri* sauce if you like it hot and spicy. *Porco á Alentejana* is an interesting combination of pork and clams. Potatoes and greens are popular side dishes. Carbs never went out of style in Portugal—it's common to get both potatoes *and* rice with a meal. As in Spain, garlic and olive oil are big. *Meia dose* means half-portion (which is enough for one person), while *prato do dia* is the daily special.

For a quick snack, remember that cafés are usually cheaper than bars. Many cafés also double as lunch joints, which locals frequent. If you see a menu written on a paper tablecloth and taped in the window, you can be assured of a quick, home-cooked meal. Just don't expect fancy presentation (and be willing to sit at a table with someone—don't worry, it makes for great conversation).

Sandwiches *(sandes)* are everywhere. The Portuguese breakfast *(pequeno almoço)* is just coffee and a sweet roll, but due to the large expat English community, a full British "fry" is available in most touristy areas. A standard, wonderful local pastry is the custard tart, *pastel de nata* (called *pastel de Belém* in Lisbon's fancy suburb of the same name).

When you want the bill, say, *"Conta, por favor."*

Portuguese Drinks

For its size, Portugal is a major wine producer—145 million gallons in 2000. And Portuguese wines are cheap, decent, and distinctively fruity.

Vinho verde (VEEN-yoo VAIR-day) is light, refreshing, almost always white, and slightly fizzy. This "green wine" is actually golden in color, but "green" (young) in age—picked, made, and drunk within a year. *Alvarinho* grapes, from the northern Minho

Typical Portuguese Foods

bacalhau	dried and salted cod, served a reputed 365 different ways. It's arguably the national dish, but is definitely an acquired taste.
frango assado	roast chicken, commonly served with *piri-piri* hot sauce
porco á Alentejana	diced pork covered with clams, Portugal's unique contribution to world cuisine
sardinhas grelhadas	fresh sardines, grilled or barbecued

Soups and Stews (*Sopas*)

caldo verde	"green" soup of kale greens and potato puree
cataplana	seafood and potatoes cooked in a copper clamshell dish
caldeirada de peixe	like *cataplana,* but cooked in a casserole
sopa de mariscos	thick seafood soup
feijoada	pork and beans
arroz de mariscos	rice and mixed seafood stew (the "Portuguese paella")
sopa Alentejana	garlic soup with a poached egg, cilantro, and bread crumbs dropped in

Snacks

prego	steak sandwich
tosta mista	grilled ham and cheese sandwich
batatas fritas	potato chips

Desserts

You'll find various concoctions made from egg yolk and sugar, such as *barrigas de freiras* ("nuns' tummies") and *papos de anjo* ("angels' breasts").

pudim	flan
arroz doce	rice pudding with cinnamon
salame de chocolate	cookies and chocolate pressed together to look like salami when sliced
queque	muffin

region, are low-sugar and high-acid. After the initial fermentation, wine-makers introduce a second fermentation, whose by-product is carbon dioxide—the light fizz. They're somewhat bitter alone, but great with meals, especially seafood. The best are from Monaco Amarante and Aveleda, but the one on every menu is the perfectly acceptable Casal Garcia. If you like white *vinho verde*, you might enjoy the harder-to-find red version. It's dark in color, like a cabernet, but still fizzy and light in flavor, like a rosé—a unique combination.

The Dão region also produces fine red wines, mostly from the Mondego Valley between Coimbra, Guarda, and Viseu. They

 should sit for a year or two in the bottle before drinking. The Alentejo region (look for bottles labeled "Borba") is known for its quality red.

Madeira, made from grapes grown in volcanic soil in the Madeira Islands, is fortified and blended (as is port), and usually served as a sweet dessert wine. The English and George Washington both liked it ("Have some Madeira, m'dear"), though today's version is drier and less syrupy. A Madeira called *Sercial* is served chilled (like sherry) with almonds. If you find yourself drowning in choices, simply try a glass of the house wine *(vinho da casa)*.

If you like port wine, what better place to sample it than its birthplace, Port-ugal? (For a crash course on port wine, see page 232.) *Reserva* on the label means it's the best-quality port (and the most expensive). All bottles of port should have a *selo de garantia* (a seal of guarantee) issued by the Port Wine Institute.

Beer *(cerveja)* is also popular—for a small draft beer, ask for *uma imperial*. Freshly squeezed orange juice *(sumo de laranja)*, mineral water *(água mineral)*, and soft drinks are widely available. When ordering water, fizzy or not, you will always be asked, *"Fresco o natural?" Fresco* is chilled, and *natural* is room temperature. Coffee lovers enjoy a *bica*, the very aromatic shot of espresso so popular in Portugal.

These words will help quench your thirst:

água com/sem gás	water with/without bubbles
água da torneira	tap water
meia de leite	coffee with warm milk
galão	1/4 coffee, 3/4 warm milk served in a tall glass
chá	tea

How Was Your Trip?

Were your travels fun, smooth, and meaningful? If you'd like to share your tips, concerns, and discoveries, please fill out the survey at www.ricksteves.com/feedback. I value your feedback. Thanks in advance—it helps a lot.

vinho tinto	red wine
vinho branco	white wine
cerveja	beer
imperial	small draft beer
aguardente	firewater distilled from grape seeds, stems, and skins, with a kick like a mule
ginjinha	cherry liqueur, served at special bars in Lisbon and Óbidos

TRAVELING AS A TEMPORARY LOCAL

We travel all the way to Europe to enjoy differences—to become temporary locals. You'll experience frustrations. Certain truths that we find "God-given" or "self-evident," such as cold beer, ice in drinks, bottomless cups of coffee, hot showers, cigarette smoke being irritating, and bigger being better, are suddenly not so true. One of the benefits of travel is the eye-opening realization that there are logical, civil, and even better alternatives. A willingness to go local ensures that you'll enjoy a full dose of Portuguese hospitality.

If there is a negative aspect to the image Europeans have of Americans, it's that we are big, loud, aggressive, impolite, rich, superficially friendly, and a bit naive.

Americans tend to be noisy in public places, such as restaurants and trains. My European friends place a high value on speaking quietly in these same places. Listen while on the bus or in a restaurant—the place can be packed, but the decibel level is low. Try to remember this nuance, and soften your speaking voice as a way of respecting their culture.

While Europeans look bemusedly at some of our Yankee excesses—and worriedly at others—they nearly always afford us individual travelers all the warmth we deserve.

While updating my guidebooks, I hear over and over again that my readers are considerate and fun to have as guests. Thank you for traveling as temporary locals who are sensitive to the culture. It's fun to follow you in my travels.

Judging from all the happy feedback I receive from travelers who have used this book, it's safe to assume you'll enjoy a great, affordable vacation—with the finesse of an independent, experienced traveler.

Thanks, and happy travels! *Boa-viagem!*

BACK DOOR TRAVEL PHILOSOPHY
From *Rick Steves' Europe Through the Back Door*

Travel is intensified living—maximum thrills per minute and one of the last great sources of legal adventure. Travel is freedom. It's recess, and we need it.

Experiencing the real Europe requires catching it by surprise, going casual... "Through the Back Door."

Affording travel is a matter of priorities. (Make do with the old car.) You can travel—simply, safely, and comfortably—anywhere in Europe for $100 a day plus transportation costs. In many ways, spending more money only builds a thicker wall between you and what you came to see. Europe is a cultural carnival, and, time after time, you'll find that its best acts are free and the best seats are the cheap ones.

A tight budget forces you to travel close to the ground, meeting and communicating with the people, not relying on service with a purchased smile. Never sacrifice sleep, nutrition, safety, or cleanliness in the name of budget. Simply enjoy the local-style alternatives to expensive hotels and restaurants.

Extroverts have more fun. If your trip is low on magic moments, kick yourself and make things happen. If you don't enjoy a place, maybe you don't know enough about it. Seek the truth. Recognize tourist traps. Give a culture the benefit of your open mind. See things as different but not better or worse. Any culture has much to share.

Of course, travel, like the world, is a series of hills and valleys. Be fanatically positive and militantly optimistic. If something's not to your liking, change your liking. Travel is addictive. It can make you a happier American, as well as a citizen of the world. Our earth is home to six and a half billion equally important people. It's humbling to travel and find that people don't envy Americans. Europeans like us, but, with all due respect, they wouldn't trade passports.

Globe-trotting destroys ethnocentricity. It helps you understand and appreciate different cultures. Regrettably, there are forces in our society that want you dumbed down for their convenience. Don't let it happen. Thoughtful travel engages you with the world—more important than ever these days. Travel changes people. It broadens perspectives and teaches new ways to measure quality of life. Rather than fear the diversity on this planet, travelers celebrate it. Many travelers toss aside their hometown blinders. Their prized souvenirs are the strands of different cultures they decide to knit into their own character. The world is a cultural yarn shop, and Back Door travelers are weaving the ultimate tapestry. Join in!

PORTUGAL

Portugal is underrated. The country seems somewhere just beyond Europe—prices are a bit cheaper, and the pace of life is noticeably slower than in Spain. While the unification of Europe is bringing sweeping changes to Portugal, the traditional economy is based on fishing, cork, wine, and textiles.

Portugal isn't touristy—even its coastal towns lack glitzy attractions. The beach and the sea are enough, as they have been for centuries. They were the source of Portugal's seafaring wealth long ago, and are the draw for tourists today.

The locals, not jaded by tourists, will meet you with warmth—especially if you learn at least a few words of Portuguese, instead of launching into Spanish (see "Portuguese Survival Phrases" in the appendix).

Over the centuries, Portugal and Spain have had a love-hate, on-again-off-again relationship, but they have almost always

remained separate, each with their own distinct language and culture. The Portuguese seem humbler and friendlier than the Spanish. In Spain, if you ever feel like you can't do anything right, you'll find it's just the opposite in Portugal—you can't do anything wrong. Portugal is also more ethnically diverse than Spain, as it's inhabited by many people from its former colonies in Brazil, Africa, and Asia. The Portuguese continue to have a special affinity for their Brazilian cousins.

Portugal bucked the Moors before Spain did, establishing its present-day borders 800 years ago. A couple of centuries later, the Age of Discovery (1500–1700) made Portugal one of the world's richest nations.

Prince Henry the Navigator sponsored the voyages of explorers who traveled to Africa seeking a trade route to India. Bartolomeu Dias and Vasco da Gama, building upon the knowledge of previous generations, actually found the way. Portuguese-born Ferdinand Magellan, sailing under the auspices of Spain, was

Portugal Almanac

Official Name: It's República Portuguesa, but locals just say "Portugal."

Population: 10.6 million people. Most Portuguese are Roman Catholic (94 percent), with indigenous Mediterranean roots; there are a few black Africans from former colonies (less than 1 percent) and some Eastern Europeans.

Latitude and Longitude: 39°N and 8°W (similar latitude to Washington, D.C. or San Francisco).

Area: 35,000 square miles, which includes the Azores and Madeira, two island groups in the Atlantic which (distantly) guard the Straits of Gibraltar.

Geography: Portugal is rectangular, 325 miles long and 125 miles wide. (Indiana is a little shorter and wider.) The half of the country north of Lisbon is more mountainous, cool, and rainy. The south consists of rolling plains, hot and dry. Portugal has 350 miles of coastline.

Rivers: The major rivers, most notably the Tejo (or Tagus) River (600 miles long, spilling into the Atlantic at Lisbon) and the Douro (100 miles, running through wine country, ending at Porto), run east–west from Spain.

Best Skiing: Serra da Estrela, at 6,500 feet, is the highest point on the mainland, but Portugal's highest peak is Mt. Pico (7,713 feet) in the Azores.

Biggest Cities: Lisbon (the capital, 564,000 in the core, with 2.8 million in greater Lisbon), Porto (238,000 in the core, with 1.6 million total), and Coimbra (157,000 in the core, and 435,000 in the greater metropolitan area).

Economy: The Gross Domestic Product is $210 billion (similar to Indiana). The GDP per capita is $19,800 (Indiana's is

the first to undertake a voyage that successfully circumnavigated the globe (though he himself died en route).

A naval superpower for a century, Portugal established trading posts in Brazil and throughout Africa that eventually became colonies. The wealth that flowed into the country led to an explosion of the arts back home. (Now named the Manueline period—after King Manuel I—its finest architecture is in Lisbon, represented by Belém's tower and monastery.) But no country can corner the market on trade for long, and as with Spain, Portugal underwent a long decline.

Portugal endured the repressive regime of António de Oliveira Salazar and his successor Marcello Caetano, which occurred from 1932–1974—the longest dictatorship in Western European history. Salazar pumped money into fighting wars to hang on to the last of the country's African colonies. When Portuguese military officers

$29,000). Some major money-makers for Portugal are fish (canned sardines), cork, budget clothes and shoes, port wine, and tourism. A quarter of Portugal's foreign trade is with Spain. Though still 33 percent poorer than Europe's leaders, Portugal has improved considerably since joining the European Union in 1986 (then called the European Community), thanks to EU subsidies. One in 10 Portuguese still works in agriculture, 60 percent work in service jobs, and 30 percent in industry.

Government: The Prime Minister—currently the center-left Socialist José Sócrates—is the chief executive, having assumed power as the head of the leading vote-getting party in legislative elections. President Aníbal Cavaco Silva, elected in 2006, serves for a five-year term, commands the military, and can dissolve the Parliament when he sees fit (it's rarely done, but he has the power). There are 230 legislators, elected to four-year terms, making up the single-house Assembly. Regionally, Portugal is divided into 20 districts (Lisbon, Coimbra, Porto, etc.).

Flag: The flag is two-fifths green and three-fifths red, united by the Portuguese coat of arms—a shield atop a navigator's armillary sphere.

Soccer: The three most popular teams are Sporting Lisbon, Benfica (also from Lisbon), and FC Porto.

Senhor Average: The average Portuguese is 39 years old and will live 78 years. One in three Portuguese uses the Internet, one in three lives near either Lisbon or Porto, and slightly less than two in three own a car.

staged a coup in 1974, the locals were on their side (see sidebar on the Carnation Revolution, page 65). Portugal lost its colonies, but those former holdings—as well as the Portuguese—won their freedom.

Once the poorest European Union country in Western Europe, Portugal has worked hard to meet EU standards...and has enjoyed heavy EU investment. Poverty still exists in Portugal, particularly in the rural areas, though overall, the country has become more prosperous since joining the EU. New products are on the market, the infrastructure has improved, and Portugal is participating more in international politics.

With a rich culture, friendly people, affordable prices, and a salty setting on the edge of Europe, Portugal understandably remains a rewarding destination for travelers.

LISBON

Lisboa

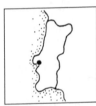

Lisbon is a ramshackle but charming mix of now and then. Vintage trolleys shiver up and down its hills, bird-stained statues mark grand squares, taxis rattle and screech through cobbled lanes, and well-worn people sip coffee in Art Nouveau cafés. It's a city of faded ironwork balconies, multicolored tiles, and mosaic sidewalks, of bougainvillea and red-tiled roofs with antique TV antennas. Men in suits and billed caps offer to "plastify" your documents, and Africans in traditional garb sell gemstones from handkerchiefs spread on sidewalks.

Lisbon, Portugal's capital, is the country's banking and manufacturing center. A port city on the yawning mouth of the Tejo River, Lisbon welcomes large ships to its waters and state-of-the-art dry docks. "Lisboa" (as locals call their city) comes from the Phoenician "Alis Ubbo," or "calm port."

While Romans and Moors originally populated Lisbon, the city's glory days were in the 15th and 16th centuries, when explorers such as Vasco da Gama opened new trade routes around Africa to India, making Lisbon one of Europe's richest cities. Portugal's Age of Discovery fueled rapid economic growth, which sparked the flamboyant art boom called the Manueline period—named after King Manuel I (r. 1495–1521). In the 17th and 18th centuries, the gold, diamonds, and sugarcane of Brazil (one of Portugal's colonies) made Lisbon even wealthier.

Then, on the morning of All Saints' Day in 1755, while most of the population was in church, a tremendous underwater earthquake occurred off the Portuguese coast. The violent series of tremors were felt throughout Europe as far away as Finland. Two-thirds of Lisbon was leveled. Fires started by cooking fires

Lisbon Overview

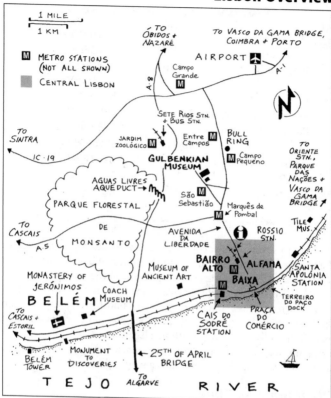

and church candles raged through the city, and a huge tsunami caused by the earthquake blasted the waterfront. Imagine a disaster similar to the Indian Ocean earthquake and tsunami of 2004 devastating Portugal's capital city. Of Lisbon's 270,000 people, it is estimated that the total death toll may have been close to 90,000. The earthquake's impact was profound, not only on Portugal but on all of Europe. (For more on this tragic event, see page 55.)

Under the energetic and eventually dictatorial leadership of Prime Minister Marquês de Pombal—who had the new city planned within a month of the quake—downtown Lisbon was rebuilt on a progressive grid plan, with broad boulevards and square squares. Remnants of Lisbon's pre-earthquake charm survive in Belém, the Alfama, and the Bairro Alto district. The bulk of your sightseeing will likely be in these neighborhoods.

As the Paris of the Portuguese-speaking world, Lisbon (pop. 564,000) is the Old World capital for some 100 million people whose origins stretch from Europe to Brazil to Africa to China.

Pronunciation Guide to Lisbon

Lisboa	leezh-BOH-ah
Rossio (main square)	roh-SEE-oo
Praça da Figueira (major square)	PRAH-sah dah fee-GAY-rah
Baixa (lower city)	BYE-shah
Alfama (hilly neighborhood)	al-FAH-mah
Bairro Alto (high town)	BYE-roh AHL-toh
Chiado (part of Bairro Alto)	shee-AH-doo
Belém (suburb with sights)	bay-LEHM
Tejo River	TAY-zhoo
rua (street)	ROO-ah

Immigrants from former colonies such as Mozambique and Angola have added diversity and flavor to the city, making it as likely that you'll hear African music as Portuguese fado these days.

But Lisbon's heritage survives. The city—with newly restored downtown squares and a hearty financial boost from the European Union—seems better organized, cleaner, and more prosperous and people-friendly than ever. With its elegant outdoor cafés, exciting art, stunning vistas, entertaining museums, a salty sailors' quarter, and a hill-capping castle, Lisbon is a world-class city.

Planning Your Time

For a two-week tour of Portugal, Lisbon is worth three days, including a day for a side-trip to Sintra. If you have an extra day, Lisbon has plenty to offer. Remember, many top sights are closed on Monday, particularly in Belém. Sintra's Pena Palace is also closed Monday.

Day 1: See Lisbon's three downtown neighborhoods. Start by touring Castle São Jorge at the top of the Alfama, and survey the city from the castle's viewpoint. Hike down to another fine viewpoint (Miradouro de Largo das Portas do Sol), then descend into the Alfama. Explore. Back in the Baixa ("lower city"), wander through the shops on your way to the major squares, Rossio and Praça da Figueira. Have lunch on the "eating lane" (Rua de Portas de Santo Antão), and walk to the funicular (nearby, at Praça dos Restauradores). Kick off the described self-guided walk through the Bairro Alto with a ride up the funicular. Joyride on a trolley. Art-lovers can then take a taxi or the Metro to the Gulbenkian Museum. Consider dinner at a fado show in the Bairro Alto or the Alfama.

Day 2: Trolley to Belém and tour the monastery, tower, and Coach Museum. Have lunch in Belém. Tour the Museum of Ancient Art, then spend the rest of your afternoon browsing through the Rossio, Bairro Alto, and Alfama neighborhoods.

Day 3: Side-trip to Sintra to tour the Pena Palace (closed Mon) and explore the ruined Moorish castle. (If you only have two days for Lisbon, it's possible, but extremely rushed, to substitute Sintra for the Museum of Ancient Art on the second afternoon.)

ORIENTATION

Downtown Lisbon is in a valley flanked by two hills along the banks of the Tejo River. At the heart sits the main square, **Rossio,** in the center of the valley (with Praça dos Restauradores and Praça da Figueira nearby). The **Baixa,** or lower city, stretches from Rossio to the waterfront. It's a flat, pleasant shopping area of grid-patterned streets and the pedestrian-only Rua Augusta. The **Alfama,** the hill to the east, is a colorful tangle of medieval streets, topped by Castle São Jorge. The **Bairro Alto** ("high town"), the hill to the west, has characteristic old lanes on the top and high-fashion stores along Rua Garrett (in the lower section called **Chiado**).

From Rossio, the **modern city** stretches north (sloping uphill) along wide Avenida da Liberdade and beyond (way beyond), where you find Edward VII Park, breezy botanical gardens, the bullring, and the airport. The suburb of **Belém,** home to several Age of Discovery sights, is three miles west of the city, along the waterfront.

Greater Lisbon has over two million people and some frightening sprawl, but for the visitor, the city can be a delightful small-town series of parks, boulevards, and squares. Focus on the three characteristic neighborhoods that line the downtown harborfront: the Baixa, the Bairro Alto, and the Alfama.

Tourist Information

Lisbon has several tourist offices, and additional information kiosks sprout around town late each spring. The main TIs are: at **Palacio Foz** at the bottom of Praça dos Restauradores (daily 9:00–20:00, overworked and tired staff, tel. 213-463-314; TI for rest of Portugal in same office, tel. 218-494-323 or 213-463-658); at the **"Ask Me Lisbon" center** on Praça do Comércio (daily 9:00–20:00, Internet access, tel. 210-312-810); and at the **airport** (daily 7:00–24:00, tel. 218-450-660). TI kiosks are at the **Santa Apolónia train station** (Tue–Sat 8:00–13:00, closed Sun–Mon, at the far end, by the lockers) and in front of the monastery in **Belém** (Tue–Sat 10:00–13:00 & 14:00–18:00, closed Mon, tel. 213-658-435).

For a handy city map, pick up a Carris or Cityrama tour

Central Lisbon

brochure or a free copy of the Lisbon city map (with helpful inset of town center) at a TI. To help make sense of the many public transportation options, ask for the in-depth *Public Transport Guide*, which shows bus, Metro, and trolley lines in amazing detail. And while you're at it, take some free English-language publications, such as the monthly *Follow Me Lisboa* (mainly cultural and museum listings) and *ConVida* (shopping, culture, and dining). For the most up-to-date lowdown on current exhibits, hip new bars and restaurants, and a concert schedule, you can't beat the monthly Portuguese-only *Agenda Cultural* (if you see a picture of something you like, ask your hotelier to translate—then go someplace most tourists miss). If you want a LisboaCard (described next), buy it at a TI. Two good websites are www.atl-turismolisboa.pt and www.portugalinsite.pt.

LisboaCard: This card covers all public transportation (including the Metro as well as trains to Sintra and Cascais) and free entrance to many museums (plus some Sintra sights and transportation). It also offers discounts on additional museums, city tours, and the Aero-Bus airport bus (described on page 33). You can buy this only at Lisbon's TIs (including the airport TI), not at participating sights. If you plan to museum-hop, the card is a good value, particularly for a day in Belém (covers your transportation and most sightseeing), but don't get the card for Sunday, when many sights are free until 14:00, or for Monday, when many sights are closed (24-hour card-€14.85, 48-hour-€25.50, 72-hour-€31, includes excellent explanatory guidebook). You choose the start date and time. While Lisbon's Shopping and Restaurant Cards are needlessly complicated, the LisboaCard is straightforward, and can save a frugal and busy sightseer 5 to 100 percent on many top attractions (over €25 if you visit all my listed sights). Be sure to carry the LisboaCard booklet with you when you sightsee; some discounts require coupons contained inside, plus it serves as a proof of purchase.

Arrival in Lisbon

Information on arriving in Lisbon by train, bus, and plane follows. If you're arriving by car, see "Driving in Lisbon," on page 96.

By Train

Lisbon has four primary train stations—Santa Apolónia (to Spain and most points north), Oriente (for the Algarve and Évora), Rossio; for Sintra, Óbidos, and Nazaré), and Cais do Sodré (for Cascais and Estoril).

If leaving Lisbon by train, see if your train requires a reservation (look for a boxed "R" in the timetable). For specifics on journeys, see "Transportation Connections," page 95.

Santa Apolónia Station covers international trains and nearly all of Portugal (except the south). It's located just east of

the Alfama. It has ATMs, a TI (by the lockers), and good bus connections to the town center (www.carris.pt). Bus #794 goes downtown to Praça do Comércio (as you exit the station, this bus stop is to your right across the street). Bus #759 goes to Rossio and Praça dos Restauradores, and #9, #90, and #746 continue up Avenida da Liberdade (as you exit the station, these bus stops are to your left along busy Avenida Infante Dom Henrique). A taxi from Santa Apolónia to any of my recommended hotels costs roughly €5.

All of Santa Apolónia Station's northbound trains stop at the **Oriente Station** (built for the World's Fair, Metro: Oriente).

Trains coming from West and South Portugal (including Évora and Lagos) also arrive at Oriente Station, crossing the 25th of April Bridge and dropping you in Lisbon proper.

Rossio Station, in the town center (and an easy walk from most recommended hotels), handles trains to Sintra (direct, 4/hr, 35 min) and to Óbidos and Nazaré (both require a transfer at Cacém; the bus is a better option for these destinations). And its all-Portugal ticket office on the ground floor sells long-distance and international train tickets to virtually everywhere except nearby destinations such as Sintra (Mon–Fri 7:00–20:00, closed Sat–Sun, cash only—see directions for buying tickets to Sintra on page 97).

If you're staying outside of Lisbon's City Center and day tripping to Sintra you could depart from the **Sete Rios Station,** just above the Metro stop Jardim Zoológico and next to the main bus station (for information on taking this rate, see page 98).

Cais do Sodré Station, on the waterfront just west of Praça do Comércio (Metro: Cais do Sodré), covers Cascais and Estoril (40 min, free with LisboaCard).

By Bus

Lisbon's efficient bus station is in the modern part of the city, several miles inland from the harbor, next to the Sete Rios Station. It has ATMs, a rack of schedules (near entrance/exit), a nifty computer that displays routes and ticket prices, and two information offices—one for buses within Portugal, the other for international routes (Intercentro booth).

If you plan to leave Lisbon by bus, you can almost always buy a ticket just a few minutes before departure, but you can also purchase it up to seven days in advance if you prefer the peace of mind.

To get from the bus station to downtown Lisbon, it's a €7 taxi ride or a short Metro trip on the blue line (to access Metro system from bus station, walk down and across to Sete Rios Station, then follow signs for Metro: Jardim Zoológico).

For national bus info, call 707-223-344. The EVA company handles the south and Rede Nacional de Expressos does the rest.

By Plane

Lisbon's easy-to-manage airport is five miles northeast of downtown, with ATMs and a 24-hour bank. While you're at the airport, take advantage of the all-Portugal tourist office, in the same place as the Lisbon TI (both open daily 7:00–24:00, tel. 218-493-689 or 218-491-323). For airport info, call 218-413-700.

Getting Downtown: You can take a 20-minute **taxi** ride (€10 fare if you get the metered rate—there is no legitimate "airport fee"). Just be sure that the cabbie turns the meter on. The airport

Lisbon

TI sells fixed-price taxi vouchers for €15 if you don't want to worry about possibly being overcharged.

There are also good **bus** connections into town. Buses #44, #45, and the Aero-Bus (#91) run frequently from the airport to Avenida da Liberdade, Praça dos Restauradores, Rossio, and Praça do Comércio. Bus #44 also connects the airport and Oriente Station (which has a Metro stop). Buses #44 and #45 are cheaper (€1.30), but the Aero-Bus is faster and more convenient (€3, 3/hr, 30 min, daily 7:45–20:45 in either direction, buy ticket on bus). Your ticket is actually a one-day Lisbon transit pass that covers bus, trolley, and funicular rides, but not the Metro. If you fly in on TAP airlines, show your boarding pass to get a free lift into town on the Aero-Bus (TAP tel. 707-205-700).

Helpful Hints

Theft Alert: Lisbon has piles of people doing illegal business on the street. While it's generally safe, if you're looking for trouble—especially after dark—you may find it. Pickpockets target tourists on the trolleys (especially #12E, #15E, and #28E) and on the subway system. Enjoy the sightseeing, but also be aware of your surroundings and always wear your money belt.

Pedestrian Warning: Sidewalks can be narrow in certain neighborhoods, and drivers are daring—cross the street with care. You'll see warnings painted at most crosswalks, alerting pedestrians to "stop to look and to be seen" and graphically showing the consequences of ignoring this advice.

Calendar Concerns: Tuesdays and Saturdays are flea- and food-market days in the Alfama's Campo de Santa Clara. National museums are free on Sunday (all day or until 14:00) and closed all day Monday. Bullfights take place irregularly throughout the summer, but mainly on Thursdays and Sundays (confirm schedule at TI, bullring, or ABEP kiosk—see page 83).

Money: ATMs are the way to go—they're all over Lisbon, as well as the rest of Portugal, and they give out the most euros per dollar. Banks offer fine rates, but charge outrageous fees (around €8) to change checks or cash (bank hours are generally Mon–Fri 8:30–15:00, closed Sat–Sun). American Express is outside the city center (Mon–Fri 9:30–13:00 & 14:30–18:30, closed Sat–Sun, in Top Tours office at Avenida Duque de Loule 108, Metro: Marquês de Pombal, tel. 213-194-190).

Laundry: Drop off clothes at centrally located **Lavandaria da Baixa** for next-day service (€4/kilogram, Mon–Fri 9:00–19:00, Sat 9:00–14:00, closed Sun, Rua dos Correeiros 105, tel. 916-421-054).

Internet Access: The TI has a list of the latest internet places. The handiest is **Portugal Telecom** (PTComunicações), on the northwest corner of Rossio near Rossio Station (daily 8:00–23:00, 25 terminals, pre-pay minimum €1/30 min). These similarly central places each have a few terminals: **"Ask Me Lisbon" center** on Praça do Comércio (€2/30 min) and **Western Union** on Praça da Figueira. All post offices, many public gathering places (especially malls and the airport), and many McDonald's offer Wi-Fi Internet access for a stiff fee (see www.ptwifi.pt for current list).

Post Office and Telephones: The post offices *(correios)* on Praça do Comércio (Mon–Fri only) and at Praça dos Restauradores 58 are modern and user-friendly (Mon–Fri 8:00–22:00, Sat–Sun 9:00–18:00). The **Portugal Telecom** office on Rossio, mentioned previously, sells phone cards, and has metered phones and card phones (daily 8:00–23:00).

Travel Agency: Agencies line the Avenida da Liberdade. For flights (but not train tickets), **Star Turismo** is handy and helpful (Mon–Fri 9:30–18:30, closed Sat–Sun, Praça dos Restauradores 14, southwest corner of square, tel. 213-245-240).

Getting Around Lisbon

A one-day pass—called 7 Colinas—that covers the Metro, funiculars, trolleys, and buses costs €3.85 (keep the card if you want to renew it for €3.35/day, five-day card-€14; sold at all Metro stations, Carris booth on Praça da Figueira, at left window of bullfight ticket kiosk at Praça dos Restauradores, and behind Elevador de Santa Justa). Buying a five-day card even for a three- to four-day stay can save you valuable time. Smart tourists buy tickets at automated ticket machines in all Metro stations (no long lines or language barrier, cards can also be recharged at Metro machines). To purchase the 7 Colinas pass at any Metro machine, follow these steps: press "7 Colinas Sale," then press "Joint CA/ML Ticket," followed by the amount of time you want the card to be valid (1 day or 5 days).

Note that the LisboaCard (see "Tourist Information," page 30) also covers Lisbon's public transportation and many museums, plus train rides to Sintra and Cascais.

By Metro

Lisbon's simple, fast subway stretches northward from the Baixa-Chiado Metro stop in two lines, green and blue, with yellow and red lines branching off. While not necessary for getting you around the historic downtown, the Metro is handy for trips to or from Rossio (Metro: Rossio or Restauradores), the Gulbenkian Museum (Metro: São Sebastião), the Chiado neighborhood (Metro: Baixa-Chiado), Colombo shopping mall (Metro: Colégio Militar/Luz), Parque das Nações and the Oriente train station

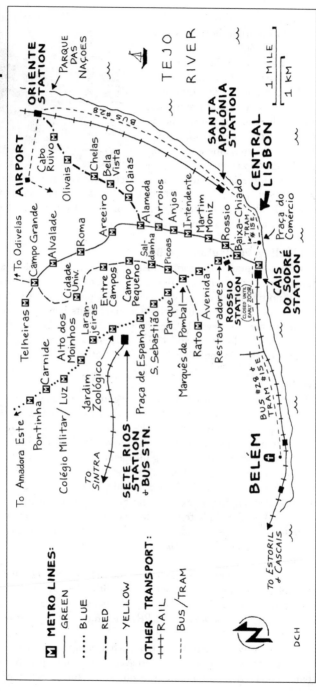

Lisbon's Public Transport

METRO LINES:
- GREEN
- BLUE
- RED
- YELLOW

OTHER TRANSPORT:
- +++ RAIL
- --- BUS/TRAM

DCH

(both at Metro: Oriente), and the long-distance bus station and Sete Rios Station (both at Metro: Jardim Zoológico).

Rides cost €0.75, and a one-zone 10-pack is €7.15 (covered by LisboaCard or use 7 Colinas bus/Metro pass described previously; runs daily 6:00–1:00 in the morning). Remember to validate your ticket in the machine and keep it until your trip is over—the ticket is required to exit the sliding doors. Metro stops are marked above ground with a red M. *Saída* means exit. You can find a Metro map at any Metro stop, on most city maps, in the TI's in-depth *Public Transport Guide*, or at www.metrolisboa.pt.

By Trolley, Funicular, and Bus

For fun and practical public transportation, use the trolleys and funiculars. If you buy your ticket from the driver, one ride costs €1.30 (no transfers), or you can use your 7 Colinas pass. Like San Francisco, Lisbon sees its trolleys as part of its heritage, and is keeping a few. Trolleys #12E (circling the Alfama), #28E (a scenic ride across the old town), and #15E (to Belém) are here to stay (also see "By Trolley" in the following "Tours" section).

By Taxi

Lisbon is a great taxi town. Cabbies are good-humored and (except for some at the airport) willing to use their meters. Rides start at €2, and you can go anywhere in the center for around €5. Decals on the window clearly spell out all charges in English. The most typical scam is the cabbie setting his meter at the high-price tariff. The meter should be at about €2 at the start and set to *Tarifa* 1 (Mon–Fri 6:00–21:00, including the airport) or *Tarifa* 2 (€2.50 drop rate; for nights, weekends, and holidays). If the meter reads *Tarifa* 3, 4, or 5, simply tell him to change it, unless you're going to Belém, which is considered outside the city limits of Lisbon (and has corresponding *Tarifa* 3 rates). *Tarifa* 5 is applied only for round-trips.

Cabs are generally easy to hail on the street (green light means available, lit number on the roof indicates it's taken). If you're having a hard time flagging one down, ask a local the location of the nearest taxi stand: *praça de taxi* (PRAH-sah duh taxi). They're all over the town center.

Especially if you're traveling with a companion, Lisbon's cabs are a cheap time-saver. For an average trip, couples save less than a dollar by taking public transportation, and spend an extra

15 minutes to get there—bad economics. If your time is limited, taxi everywhere.

TOURS

▲▲By Trolley

Lisbon's vintage trolleys, most from the 1920s, shake and shiver through the old parts of town, somehow safely weaving within

inches of parked cars, climbing steep hills, and offering sightseers breezy views of the city (rubberneck out the window and you die). As you board, pay the conductor (€1.30) or validate your 7 Colinas pass, take a seat, and watch the pensioners as they lurch by. Buses and trolleys usually share the same stops and routes. Signs for bus stops have just the bus number shown, while signs for trolley stops include an E for *eléctrico* before or after the route number. Remember that most pickpocketing in Lisbon takes place on trolleys, so enjoy the ride, but keep an eye on your belongings.

Trolley #28E is a Rice-A-Roni–style Lisbon joyride. (Don't confuse trolley #28E with bus #28 to Belém.) Trolley stops from west to east include Estrela (the 18th-century, late Baroque Estrela Basilica and Estrela Park—cozy neighborhood scene with pondside café and a "garden library kiosk"); the top of the Bica funicular (which drops steeply through a rough-and-tumble neighborhood to the riverfront); Chiado's main square (the café and "Latin Quarter"); Baixa (on Rua da Conceição between Augusta and Prata); the cathedral (Sé); Miradouro de Largo das Portas do Sol (the Alfama viewpoint); Campo de Santa Clara (flea market on Tue and Sat); and the pleasant and untouristy Graça district (with another excellent viewpoint).

Trolley #15E, while not usually vintage or pickpocket-free, whisks you efficiently from Praça da Figueira to Belém.

Trolley #12E (Circular Tour): For a colorful, 20-minute loop around the castle and the Alfama, catch this trolley on Praça da Figueira (departs every few minutes from the stop at closest corner of square to castle). The driver can tell you when to get out for the Miradouro de Largo das Portas do Sol (viewpoint) near the castle (about three-quarters of the way up the hill), or stay on the trolley and you'll be dropped back where you started.

Here's what you'll see on your self-guided tour: Leaving Praça da Figueira, you enter Largo de Martim Moniz—named for a knight who died heroically while using his body as a doorjamb to

Lisbon

Lisbon's Best Viewpoints
(*Miradouros* and Belvederes)

The first three are included in the self-guided walks descibed in this section:
- Miradouro de São Pedro de Alcântara (view terrace in Bairro Alto, at top of Elevador da Glória funicular; see "The Bairro Alto and Chiado Stroll," page 41)
- São Jorge Castle (on top of the Alfama; see photo above and "The Alfama Stroll," page 46)
- Miradouro de Largo das Portas do Sol (south slope of Alfama; see "The Alfama Stroll," page 46)
- Elevador de Santa Justa (Baixa)
- Monument to the Discoveries (Belém)
- Belém Tower (Belém)
- Cristo Rei (statue on hillside across the Tejo River)
- Edward VII Park (at north end of Avenida da Liberdade)
- Bica *miradouro* (atop the Bica funicular)

pry open the castle gate, allowing his Christian Portuguese comrades to get in and capture Lisbon from the Moors in 1147. The big, maroon-colored building capping the hill on the left was a Jesuit monastery until 1769, when the dictatorial Marquês de Pombal booted the pesky order out of Portugal and turned the building into the Hospital São Jose.

Turning right onto Rua de Cavaleiros, you climb through the atmospheric Mouraria neighborhood on a street so narrow that a single trolley track is all that fits. Notice how the colorful mix of neighbors who fill the trolley all seem to know each other. If the trolley's path is blocked and can't pass, lots of horn-honking and shouts from passengers ensue until your journey resumes. Look up the skinny side streets. Marvel at the creative parking and classic laundry scenes. This was the area given to the Moors after they were driven out of the castle and Alfama. Locals know it as the home of the legendary fado singer Maria Severa. The majority of residents these days are immigrant Asians, making this Lisbon's version of Chinatown.

At the crest of the hill (Largo Rodrigues de Freitas), you can get out to explore, eat at a cheap restaurant (see "Eating," page 90), or follow Rua de Santa Marinha to the Campo de Santa Clara flea market (Tue and Sat).

When you see the river, you're at Largo das Portas do Sol (Gates of the Sun), where you'll also see the remains of one of the seven old Moorish gates of Lisbon. The driver usually says *"castelo"* (cahzh-TAY-loo) at this point. Hop out here if you want to visit the Museu Escola de Artes Decorativas Portuguesas (see page 51), enjoy the most scenic cup of coffee in town, explore the Alfama, or tour the castle.

The trolley continues downhill past the fortress-like cathedral (on left) and into the Baixa (grid-planned Pombaline city). After a few blocks, you're back where you started.

By Bus and Tram

Carris City Bus and Tram Tours—Carris Tours offers a confusing array of bus and tram tours giving tired tourists a lazy overview of the city. While uninspiring and not cheap, they're handy and they operate daily year-round. They all start and end at Praça do Comércio, with trams on one side (in front of the TI) and open-top buses (near red info trolley) on the other.

Bus Tours: The **Tagus Tour** (which loops around west Lisbon) and the **Olisipo Tour** (which loops east) are double-decker, hop-on, hop-off bus tours: You can get off, tour a sight, and catch a later bus. Major stops on the Tagus Tour are the Museum of Ancient Art and Belém sights. Both tours stop at the Gulbenkian Museum (runs twice hourly March–Oct 9:15–20:15, fewer in winter). The major stops of the Olisipo Tour are at Parque das Nações and the National Tile Museum (runs hourly March–Oct 10:30–17:30, less in winter). Tours include audioguides and cost €14 apiece. For either tour, your ticket functions as a transit pass the rest of the day, covering trolleys, buses, and funiculars (but not the Metro, which is owned by a different company). You can't hop on and hop off between the two different tours.

Carris' **Sintra Tour** makes a swing around the scenic and historic peninsula (giving you an hour free in Sintra, but no Pena Palace visit) and all the way out to Cabo da Roca—which is frustrating to reach on your own, even if you have a car (€35, daily at 14:30, 4.5 hours, with a live three-language guide).

Tram Tours: Carris offers four tram tours, including the **Colinas Tour,** which takes you on a shiny red 1900s tramcar through the Alfama and the Bairro Alto. Scenic ride...sparse information (€17, 90-min tour with no stops and an audioguide narration most of the time, about 2/hr from 10:00–19:00 June–Sept, fewer off-season). The **Discovery Tour** goes around the Alfama and then on to Belém (€17, 2 hours, 3/day, live guide). A 48-hour ticket for €30 allows you to take all four tours. For more information, stop by their bright-red info trolley (northeast corner of Praça do Comércio, discount with LisboaCard, tel. 966-298-558).

By Boat

Tejo River Cruise—Crucero por el Tajo runs trips from the Terreiro do Paço dock off Praça do Comércio, cruising east to the Vasco da Gama Bridge and Parque das Nações, then west to Belém and back. You can buy a ticket at the small info kiosk directly in front of the large archway on Praça do Comércio (daily 11:00–12:30) or at the dock from 13:30 until departure (€20, discount with LisboaCard, 2 hours, April–Oct departure at 15:00, four-language narration includes English, drinks and WC on board; hop-on, hop-off option at Belém available on request; tel. 218-820-348).

On Foot

Walking Tour—Lisbon Walker offers excellent English-language walking tours through different districts downtown (focusing on the Baixa, Alfama, and Bairro Alto). Three Lisbon-loving locals tell fun stories about their hometown in four different walking routes. Tours vary depending on the day, but there is usually a 10:00 walk beginning at the northeast corner of Praça do Comércio—just across from the recommended Martinho da Arcada restaurant. Their newest tour focuses on Lisbon's history as a center for espionage (€15 per person, discount with LisboaCard, daily April–Oct, no reservations required, tel. 218-861-840, schedule online at www.lisbonwalker.com).

Local Guides—Because most sights don't come with audioguides, a local guide can be a big help. For a private guide, contact the Guides' Union (€85/4 hrs or half-day, €140/day, more on weekends, tel. 213-467-170). Also consider one of these local guides.

Claudia da Costa is a hardworking, reliable guide who really knows Lisbon well (mobile 965-560-216, claudiadacosta@hotmail.com). Two other good guides are Cristina Quental (mobile 919-922-480, anacristinaquental@hotmail.com) and Cristina Duarte (Mon–Fri: €92/half-day, €155/day; Sat–Sun: €137/half-day, €230/day; tel. 218-850-286, mobile 919-316-242, crisduarte@oninet.pt).

SELF-GUIDED WALKS

While Lisbon had its famous quake, there's nothing earth-shaking about most of its downtown sights. The charm of Lisbon is its people and the city itself, with hilltop views, ramshackle neighborhoods, and slices of urban life. The best way to explore Lisbon is like a local: See it on foot.

Ways to Get from the Baixa up to the Bairro Alto and Chiado

- Ride the Elevador da Glória funicular (a few blocks north of Rossio on Avenida da Liberdade) or walk alongside the tracks if the funicular isn't running.
- Walk up lots of stairs from Rossio (due west of the central column).
- Taxi to the Miradouro de São Pedro de Alcântara.
- Take the escalator at the Baixa-Chiado Metro stop.
- Catch trolley #28E from Rua da Conceição.
- Walk up Rua do Carmo from Rossio to Rua Garrett.
- Take escalators or elevators from the Armazéns mall to Rua Garrett.
- Take the Elevador de Santa Justa, which goes right by the Convento do Carmo and the Chiado.

The "Three Neighborhoods" Walk

You can see Lisbon's three downtown neighborhoods—the Bairro Alto, the Baixa, and the Alfama—in a single three-hour walk, linking together the two walks described next. Start with "The Bairro Alto and Chiado Stroll": From north of Rossio Station, take the Elevador da Glória funicular (or walk) up to the Bairro Alto and walk downhill to Café A Brasileira and Rua Garrett. From there, you can get to the beginning of "The Alfama Stroll" by catching trolley #28E across the Baixa and up the Alfama. At the Largo das Portas do Sol viewpoint (third stop past the cathedral), walk five minutes uphill to Castle São Jorge, where you can start the Alfama walk back down the hill to the Baixa. (To avoid the walk up to the castle altogether, take bus #37 from Praça da Figueira. It stops just a few feet in front of the castle gate.)

▲▲The Bairro Alto and Chiado Stroll

Rise above the Baixa on the funicular, Elevador da Glória, located near the obelisk at Praça dos Restauradores (€1.30, 6/hr, covered by 7 Colinas card or buy ticket from driver); you can also just walk up alongside the tracks. Leaving the funicular on top, turn right (go 100 yards, up a few steps into a park) to enjoy the city view from ❶ **Miradouro de São Pedro de Alcântara** (San Pedro Belvedere). The tile map guides you through the view, stretching from the twin towers of the cathedral (Sé, far right), to the ramparts of the castle birthplace of Lisbon (right), to another quaint, tree-topped viewpoint in Graça (directly across), to the skyscraper towers of the new city in the distance (on far left). The highlights of the park are a bust honoring a 19th-century local journalist (founder of Lisbon's

The Bairro Alto and Chiado Stroll

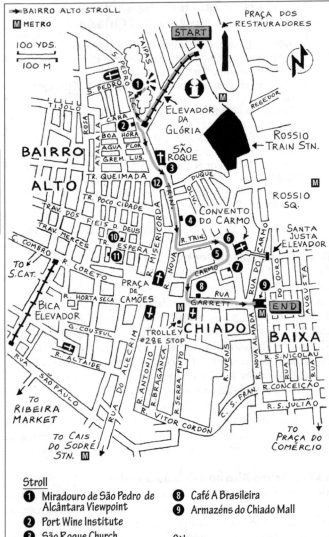

Stroll

1. Miradouro de São Pedro de Alcântara Viewpoint
2. Port Wine Institute
3. São Roque Church
4. Cervejaria da Trindade
5. Largo do Carmo
6. Convento do Carmo
7. Leitaria Académica Eatery
8. Café A Brasileira
9. Armazéns do Chiado Mall

Other

10. Canto do Camões Fado
11. Rest. Adega do Ribatejo Fado
12. Largo Trindade Coelho

first daily newspaper) and a statue of a charming, barefooted delivery boy. This district is famous for its writers, poets, publishers, and bohemians. (The walk continues downhill from here.)

• *Directly across the street from where you got off the Elevador da Glória is the...*

❷ **Port Wine Institute:** If you're into port (the fortified wine that takes its name from Porto, covered later in this book), you'll find the world's greatest selection at **Solar do Vinho do Porto** (run by the Port Wine Institute, Mon–Sat 11:00–24:00, closed Sun, WCs, Rua São Pedro de Alcântara 45, tel. 213-475-707, www .ivp.pt). The plush, air-conditioned, Old World living room holds leather chairs and cigar-smokers (it's not a shorts-and-T-shirt kind of place). On entering, you can order from a selection of over 300 different ports from €1 to €22 per glass, poured by an English-speaking bartender. (You may want to try only 150 or so, and save the rest for the next night.) Fans of port describe it as "a liquid symphony playing on the palate." Browse through the easy menu. Start white and sweet (cheapest), try spicy and ruby, then finish mellow and tawny—a *colheita* (single harvest) is particularly good. If port wine isn't your thing, they also have a nice selection of red wines from the Douro Valley, thought to be some of Portugal's finest. Appetizers *(aperitivos)* are listed in the menu with small photographs. Seated service can be slow and disinterested when it's busy. To be served without a long wait, go to the bar. For more on port, see page 232.

• *Follow the main street (Rua São Pedro de Alcântara) downhill a couple of blocks. Throughout this walk, look up and notice the fine tile work—both old and modern—on the buildings. When you reach the small square, Largo Trindade Coelho, on your left you'll see...*

❸ **São Roque Church:** Step inside, read the English description at the back of the right nave, and then sit on a pew in the middle to take it all in. Built in the 16th century, the church of St. Roque is one of Portugal's first Jesuit churches. The painted wood, false-domed ceiling is perfectly flat. The acoustics here are top-notch, important in a Jesuit church, where the emphasis is on the sermon. Notice all the numbered panels on the floor. These are tombs, nameless because they were for lots of people. They're empty now—the practice was stopped in the 19th century when parishioners didn't want plague victims rotting under their feet.

Survey the rich side chapels. The highlight is the Chapel of St. John the Baptist (left of altar, gold and blue lapis lazuli columns). It looks like it came right out of the Vatican. It did. Made in Rome out of the most precious materials, the chapel was the site of one papal Mass; then it was disassembled and shipped to Lisbon. Per square inch, it was probably the most costly chapel ever constructed in Portugal. Notice the mosaic floor (with the spherical symbol of Portugal) and the three paintings that are actually intricate, beautiful mosaics—a Vatican specialty, designed to avoid damage from candle smoke that would darken paintings. To the right, a glass case of relics is trying to grab your attention. The next chapel to the left features a riot of babies. Individual chapels are explained in the English leaflet available near the door (Mon–Fri 8:30–17:00, Sat–Sun 9:30–17:00).

The São Roque Museum, with some old paintings and church riches, is not as interesting as the church itself (€1.50, Tue–Sun 10:00–17:00, closed Mon).

• *Back outside in the church square, visit with the poor pigeon-drenched man (a statue to your friendly local lottery-ticket salesman—there are two lottery kiosks on this square; rustic WC underground), and continue (kitty-corner across the square) downhill along Rua Nova da Trindade. At #20, pop into...*

❹ **Cervejaria da Trindade:** The famous "oldest beer hall in Lisbon" is worth a visit for a look at the 19th-century tiles (see page 92). Once the refectory (dining hall) of a monastery, it became a brewery after the monks were expelled in 1834. If you're tired of all this history, continue downhill to Livraria Barateira at #16, Lisbon's biggest used bookstore, where you can sell this book.

• *Continue down the hill, where at the next intersection, signs point left to the ruined Convento do Carmo. Follow the inside trolley tracks downhill to the next square...*

❺ **Largo do Carmo:** On this square decorated with an old fountain, lots of pigeons, and jacaranda trees, police officers guard the headquarters of the National Guard. Famous among locals, this was the last refuge of the fascist dictator António Salazar's successor. The Portuguese people won their revolution in 1974, in a peaceful uprising called the Carnation Revolution. The name came when revolutionaries placed flowers in the guns of the soldiers, making it clear it was time for democracy here. For more information on the revolution, see page 65.

• *On Largo do Carmo, check out the ruins of...*

❻ **Convento do Carmo:** After the convent was destroyed by the 1755 earthquake, Marquês de Pombal (see sidebar on page 52) directed that the delicate Gothic arches of its church be left standing—supporting nothing but open sky—as a permanent reminder of that disastrous event (€2.50—or cheapskates can do a deep knee-bend at the ticket desk, sneak a peek, and crawl away; April–Sept Mon–Sat 10:00–18:00, Oct–March closes at 17:00, always closed Sun). The upper entrance to the Elevador de Santa Justa is down the trolley tracks to the right of the church, and has interesting views as well.

• *Kitty-corner from the ruins is a worthwhile eatery.*

Portugal's Two Greatest Poets

The Portuguese are justifiably proud of their two most famous poets, whose names, works, and memorials you may encounter on your travels.

Portugal's most important poet, **Luís de Camões** (1524–1580), was a Renaissance-age equivalent of the ancient Greek poet, Homer. Camões' masterpiece, *The Lusiads (Os Lusíadas)* tells the story of an explorer far from home. But instead of Odysseus, this epic poem describes the journey of Vasco da Gama, the man who found the route from Europe to India. Camões, who had sailed to Morocco to fight the Moors (where he lost an eye), to Goa (where he was imprisoned for debt), and to China (where he was shipwrecked), was uniquely qualified to write about Portugal's pursuit of empire on the high seas. For more on Camões, see page 72.

Fernando Pessoa (1888–1935) used multiple personas in his poetry. He'd take on the voice of a simple countryman and express his love of nature in free verse. Or he'd write as an erudite scholar, sharing philosophical thoughts in a more formal style. By varying his voice, he was able to more easily explore different viewpoints and truths. While Pessoa loved the classics—reading Milton, Byron, Shelley, and Poe—he was a true 20th-century bohemian at heart. Café A Brasileira, where he'd often meet with friends, has a statue of Pessoa outside. Today fado musicians still remember Pessoa, paying homage to him by putting his poetry into the Portuguese version of the blues.

❼ **Leitaria Académica,** a venerable little working-class place, hits the spot if you're hungry. Its tables spill out onto the breezy square. For €8, you can have one of their traditional specialties (Sr. Raul has an English cheat sheet), a salad, and a beverage.

• *Leave Largo do Carmo, walking a block slightly uphill on Travessa do Carmo. At the square, take a left on Rua Serpa Pinto, walking downhill to Rua Garrett, where—in the little pedestrian zone 50 yards uphill on the right—you'll find a famous old café across from the Baixa-Chiado Metro stop.*

❽ **Café A Brasileira,** reeking of smoke and Art Nouveau, is a 100-year-old institution for coffeehouse junkies. Drop in for a *bica* (Lisbon slang for an espresso) and a €1 *pastel de nata* custard tart—a local specialty. (WCs are in the basement, down the stairs near the entrance.) This café was the literary and creative soul of Lisbon in the 1920s and 1930s, when the country's avant-garde poets, writers, and painters would hang out here. The statue outside is of the poet Fernando Pessoa (see sidebar above), making him a perpetual regular at this café.

At the neighboring Baixa-Chiado (shee-AH-doo) Metro stop, a slick series of escalators whisks people effortlessly between Chiado Square and the Baixa. It's a free and fun way to survey a long, long line of Portuguese—but for now, we'll stay in the Chiado neighborhood. (If you'll be coming for fado in the evening, consider zipping up the escalator to get here—a recommended fado restaurant, Canto do Camões, is roughly three blocks away; see page 82.)

The **Chiado** district is popular for its shopping and theaters. Browse downhill on Rua Garrett, and notice its mosaic sidewalks, ironwork balconies, and fine shops. Peek into classy stores, such as the fabric-lover's paradise Paris em Lisboa (at #77, with a heavy dose of French style) or the venerable Bertrand bookstore (at #73, English books and a good guidebook selection in Room 5). The street lamps you see are decorated with the symbol of Lisbon: a ship, carrying the remains of St. Vincent, guarded by two ravens.

• *Rua Garrett ends abruptly downhill at the entrance of the big vertical mall. Don't bother walking down if you are planning on doing the Alfama stroll described next. Otherwise, continue to...*

❾ **Armazéns do Chiado:** This grand, six-floor shopping center connects Lisbon's lower and upper towns with a world of ways to spend money (daily 10:00–22:00, lively food court on sixth floor open daily 10:00–23:00—see page 93).

• *To end this walk, you have several options. Catch trolley #28E to the Alfama to connect with the next walk (stop is 100 yards away on Rua António Maria Cardoso); or walk down Rua do Carmo to reach Rossio (facing the mall entrance, it's the road downhill to your left); or enter the Armazéns mall. To get from the mall to the Baixa—the lower city— take the elevator (press 1) or the escalators down (you'll pass through the Sports Zone shop on the lower floors—exit through the ground level of the store). To get to the Metro from the Armazéns mall, exit through the lowest floor of the mall, turn right, and walk 50 yards to the Baixa-Chiado stop.*

▲▲The Alfama Stroll

Explore the Alfama, the colorful sailors' quarter that dates back to the age of Visigoth occupation, from the sixth to eighth centuries A.D. This was a bustling district during the Moorish period, and eventually became the home of Lisbon's fishermen and mariners (and of the poet Luís de Camões, who wrote, "Our lips meet easily, high across the narrow street"). The Alfama's tangled street plan is one of the few features of Lisbon to survive the 1755 earthquake. It helps make the neighborhood a cobbled playground of Old World color. Visit at the best time, during the busy mid-morning

The Alfama Stroll

① São Jorge Castle Gate
② Miradouro de São Jorge Viewpoint
③ Olisipónia Video Show
④ Largo do Contador Mor
⑤ Largo Santa Luzia
⑥ School of Portuguese Decorative Arts Museum
⑦ House of Fado and Portuguese Guitar Museum

market (Tue and Sat 8:00–15:00, on Campo de Santa Clara), or in the cooler hours in the late afternoon or early evening, when the streets teem with locals. Enjoy the grittiness now, before gentrification threatens to remove some of the traditional charm (along with a chunk of older residents) with promises that the *"Alfama vai ficar mais bonita"* (Alfama will look even better).

• *Start your walk at the highest point in town, São Jorge Castle. Get to the castle gate by taxi (€3) or by bus #37 from Praça da Figueira. (Trolleys #28E and #12E go to Largo Santa Luzia and Largo das Portas do Sol respectively, a few blocks below.)*

① São Jorge Castle Gate: Just inside the castle gate (on left) is a little statue of George, named for a popular saint in the 14th century. St. George (São Jorge; pronounced "sow ZHOR-zh")

Lisbon at a Glance

In Lisbon

▲▲▲**Gulbenkian Museum** Lisbon's best museum, featuring an art collection spanning 2,000 years, from ancient Egyptian to Impressionist to Art Nouveau. **Hours:** Tue–Sun 10:00–18:00, closed Mon.

▲▲**Museum of Ancient Art** Portuguese paintings from the 15th- and 16th-century glory days. **Hours:** Tue 14:00–18:00, Wed–Sun 10:00–18:00, closed Mon.

▲**House of Fado and Portuguese Guitar** Museum singing the story of Portuguese folk music. **Hours:** Tue–Sun 10:00–18:00, closed Mon.

▲**National Tile Museum** Tons of artistic tiles, including a panorama of pre-earthquake Lisbon. **Hours:** Tue 15:00–18:00, Wed–Sun 10:00–18:00, closed Mon.

Port Wine Institute Plush place selling tastes of the world's greatest selection of ports. **Hours:** Mon–Sat 11:00–24:00, closed Sun.

São Roque Church Fine 16th-century Jesuit church with false dome ceiling, chapel made of precious stones, and a less interesting museum. **Hours:** Mon–Fri 8:30–17:00, Sat–Sun 9:30–17:00.

São Jorge Castle Eighth-century bastion, first built by the Moors, with kingly views at the highest point in town. **Hours:** Daily March–Oct 9:00–21:00, off-season until 18:00.

Museu Escola de Artes Decorativas Portuguesas A stroll through aristocratic households richly decorated in 16th- to 19th-century styles. **Hours:** Mon–Sat 10:00–17:00, closed Sun.

---

hailed from Turkey and was known for fighting valiantly (he's often portrayed slaying a dragon). When the Christian noble Afonso Henriques called for help to eliminate the Moors from his newly founded country of Portugal, the Crusaders who helped him prayed to St. George...and won (castle entry-€5, 30 percent discount with LisboaCard, daily March–Oct 9:00–21:00, Nov–Feb 9:00–18:00, last entry 30 min before closing; free guided tours at 10:30, 11:30, 14:30, and 16:00—reserve at ticket office).

• Pick up your ticket and then follow the cobbles uphill past the first lanes of old Lisbon to the...

❷ **Miradouro de São Jorge (View Terrace):** Enjoy the grand

Elevador de Santa Justa A 150-foot-tall iron elevator offering a glittering city vista. **Hours:** Daily 7:00–21:00.

Cathedral (Sé) From the outside, an impressive Romanesque fortress of God; inside, not much. **Hours:** Daily 9:00–19:00.

In Belém
Note that all of these sights are closed on Monday.

▲▲▲Monastery of Jerónimos King Manuel's giant 16th-century, white limestone church and monastery, with remarkable cloisters and the explorer Vasco da Gama's tomb. **Hours:** May–Sept Tue–Sun 10:00–18:00, off-season until 17:00, closed Mon and during Sun Mass.

▲▲Coach Museum Dozens of carriages, from simple to opulent, displaying the evolution of coaches from 1600 on. **Hours:** Tue–Sun 10:00–18:00, closed Mon.

▲Monument to the Discoveries Giant riverside monument honoring the explorers who brought Portugal great power and riches centuries ago. **Hours:** May–Sept Tue–Sun 10:00–19:00, off-season until 18:00, closed Mon.

▲Belém Tower Consummate Manueline building with a worthwhile view up 120 steps. **Hours:** May–Sept Tue–Sun 10:00–18:30, off-season until 17:00, closed Mon.

Maritime Museum A salty selection of exhibits on the ships and navigational tools of the Age of Discovery. **Hours:** April–Sept Tue–Sun 10:00–18:00, off-season until 17:00, closed Mon.

view. The Tejo River is one of five main rivers in Portugal, four of which come from Spain. (Only the Mondego River, which passes

by Coimbra, originates in the Serra de Estrela inside Portuguese territory.) While Portugal and Spain generally have very good relations, the major sore point is the control of all this water. From here, you have a good view of the 25th of April Bridge, which leads to the Cristo Rei statue (described on page 64). Past the bridge, you can barely see the Monument to the Discoveries and the Belém Tower on a clear day.

Stroll inland along the **ramparts** for a more extensive view of Pombal's Lisbon (from Praça do Comércio on the water, the square and grid streets lead up to tree-lined Avenida de República and the big Edward VII Park capped with a large Portugal flag on the far right). Find places you know, such as the Elevador de Santa Justa (the Eiffel-style elevator in front of the ruined convent) and the sloping metal roof of the Rossio train station. After walking under the second arch, take a right and then a left to wander the grounds, then enter the actual inner castle (offering only a chance to climb up for more views; sometimes exhibitions are housed here).

The **castle** was first built by the Moors in the 11th century. After Portugal's first king, Afonso Henriques (whose statue stands on the view terrace), beat the Moors in the 12th century, the castle began its three-century-long stint as a royal residence. In the 16th century, the king moved, and the castle fell into ruins. What you see today was mostly rebuilt by the dictator Salazar in the 1960s (for more on Salazar, see page 63).

• *Heading back out past the café, you'll see...*

❸ **Olisipónia:** This high-tech, syrupy, English-language multimedia presentation, called Olisipónia after Lisbon's Roman name, offers two sweeping video overviews of the city's history. The video presentation at the Monument to the Discoveries in Belém is much better, but as a place to cool off from the Lisbon heat, Olisipónia gets two thumbs up. Next door, the Galería houses temporary art exhibits of questionable taste, but does so inside old jail cells. Arched brick ceilings combine with original stone walls and iron gates for a fun prison experience for kids of all ages.

• *Leave the castle. Across the ramp from the castle entrance/exit is the recommended restaurant Arco do Castelo (see "Eating," page 90). Facing the restaurant, go left, take your first right, and follow the striped lane downhill through...*

❹ **Largo do Contador Mor:** This small, car-clogged square contains the recommended restaurants A Tasquinha and Comidas de Santiago (see "Eating," page 90).

• *From there, pass another restaurant, Farol de Santa Luzia, to reach a superb Alfama viewpoint at...*

❺ **Largo Santa Luzia:** Currently undergoing a major makeover, this public spot is tentatively scheduled to reopen sometime in 2008. From this square (a stop for trolleys #12E and #28E), admire the panoramic view from the small terrace, Miradouro de Santa Luzia, where old-timers play cards amid lots of tiles. Find the wall of 18th-century tiles on the church's riverside façade; they show Praça do Comércio before the 1755 earthquake. The 16th-century

Royal Palace (on the left of tile work) was completely destroyed in the quake. Further on, another tile panel depicts the reconquest of Lisbon from the Moors by Afonso Henriques, mentioned earlier in this chapter. It was a nasty battle; Portuguese soldiers hired less-than-helpful mercenaries who abused city residents. Revered soldier Martim Moniz (mentioned on page 37) decided to give his life for the cause by holding the castle door open—with his body. Ouch. A Metro stop on the green line named for him is decorated with only his upper half. For an even better city view, hike around the church to the Largo das Portas do Sol catwalk. This is the place for the most scenic cup of coffee in town—at the Cerca Moura's café terrace (across the street from main café, daily 11:00–22:00, Largo das Portas do Sol 4).

• *Next door to Cerca Moura's main café on the square, you'll find the...*

❻ Museu Escola de Artes Decorativas Portuguesas (School of Portuguese Decorative Arts Museum): This museum offers a unique stroll through aristocratic households richly decorated in 16th- to 19th-century styles. The displays are nearly meaningless because of a lack of decent English descriptions. Visit only if you're a fan of the decorative arts (€5, 20 percent discount with LisboaCard, Mon–Sat 10:00–17:00, closed Sun, Largo das Portas do Sol 2, tel. 218-814-640, www.fress.pt).

• *From here, it's downhill all the way.*

Descending the Alfama: From Largo das Portas do Sol (near Cerca Moura's terrace bar), go down the stairs (Rua Norberto de Araújo, between the church and the cat-walk) into the Alfama. The old wall once marked the end of Moorish Lisbon. At the bottom of the wall, continue downhill, then turn left at the railing...and down more stairs.

Explore downhill from here until you end up on Rua de São Pedro, a main drag a few blocks below. The Alfama's urban-jungle roads are squeezed into tangled, confusing alleys—the labyrinthine street plan was designed to frustrate invaders trying to get up to the castle. What was defensive then is atmospheric now. Bent houses comfort each other in their romantic shabbiness, and the air drips with laundry and the smell of clams. Get lost. Poke aimlessly, peek through windows, buy a fish. Locals hang plastic water bags from windows to try to keep away the flies. Favorite saints decorate doors to protect families. St. Peter, protector of fishermen, is big in the Alfama. Churches are generally closed, since they share a roving priest. The rash of scaffolding you'll see throughout the

Pombal's Lisbon

In 1750, lazy King José I (r. 1750–1777) turned the government over to a minor noble, the Marquês de Pombal (1699–1782). Talented, ambitious, and handsome, Pombal was praised as a reformer, but reviled for his ruthless tactics. Having learned modern ways as the ambassador to Britain, he battled Church repression and promoted the democratic ideals of the Enlightenment, but enforced his policies with arrest and torture. He expelled the Jesuits to keep them from monopolizing the education system, put the bishop of Coimbra in prison, and broke off relations with the pope. When the earthquake of 1755 leveled the city, within a month Pombal had kicked off major rebuilding in much of today's historic downtown—featuring a grid plan for the world's first quake-proof buildings. In 1777, the king died and the controversial Pombal was dismissed.

Alfama is a sign of the local scramble to renovate and gentrify Old Lisbon with European Union funds before they run out.

The neighborhood here is tightly knit historically—families routinely sit down to communal dinners in the streets. Feuds, friendships, and gossip are all intense. When a woman loses her husband, she typically wears black for the rest of her life (though this is a tradition that's changing for the latest generation). The neighborhood hosts Lisbon's most popular outdoor party to St. Anthony on June 13. Imagine tables set up everywhere, bands playing, colorful plastic flowers strung across the squares, and all the grilled sardines *(sardinhas grelhadas)* you can eat.

If you see carpets hanging out to dry, it means a laundry is nearby. Because few homes have their own, every neighborhood has a public laundry and bathroom. In the early morning hours, the streets are traditionally busy with locals in pajamas, heading for the public baths. Today, young people are choosing to live elsewhere, lured by modern conveniences unavailable here.

• *Rua de São Pedro, the fish market and liveliest street around, leads left downhill to the square called Largo do Chafariz de Dentro and the...*

❼ **House of Fado and Portuguese Guitar:** This museum, rated ▲, tells the story of fado in English—push the buttons in each room for music. Don't miss Coimbra's male students' voices singing fado. Finish with a rest in a simulated fado bar, where you can watch old Alfama videos and hear the Billie Holidays of Portugal (30-min cycle includes crazy Portuguese bullfighting scenes). As you leave the fake fado bar, notice—on the wall by the door—the lyrics that were censored by the dictator Salazar (€2.50, 30 percent discount with LisboaCard, Tue–Sun 10:00–18:00, last entry 30 min before closing, closed Mon, Largo do Chafariz de Dentro, tel. 218-823-470). Two blocks uphill from this square is the recommended fado restaurant A Baiuca (see page 83).

• *To get back downtown from the fado museum, you can walk a block to the main waterfront drag (facing museum, go left around it) where Avenida Infante Dom Henrique leads back to Praça do Comércio downtown (a 15-min walk, plenty of taxis, bus stop to your left, all buses except #28 go to Praça do Comércio, bus #759 goes to Praça dos Restauradores; #9, #90, and #746 continue up Avenida de Liberdade).*

SIGHTS

Historic Downtown: The Baixa

Lisbon's sights, listed next, start at the waterfront and continue north through the city.

Praça do Comércio ("Trade Square")—At this riverfront square bordering the Baixa, ships used to dock and sell their goods.

Nicknamed "Palace Square" by locals, it was the site of Portugal's royal palace for 200 pre-earthquake years. Government ministries ring the square these days. It's also the departure point for city bus and tram tours, and the boat that cruises along the Tejo River. The area opposite the natural harbor was conceived as a residential neighborhood for the upper class, but they chose the suburbs. The statue is of King José I, the man who gave control of the government to the Marquês de Pombal, who rebuilt the city after the earthquake. The big arch is Pombal's attempt to restore Lisbon's Parisian-style grandeur.

The Baixa is the flat valley between two hills, sloping gently from Rossio to the water. After the disastrous 1755 earthquake, the neighborhood was rebuilt on a grid street plan. The former

maze of the Jewish Quarter was eliminated, but the area has many streets named for the crafts and shops historically found there. Its pedestrian streets, inviting cafés, bustling shops, and elegant old storefronts give the district a certain magnetism. City-government subsidies make sure the old businesses stay around, but modern ones find a way to creep in. I find myself doing laps in a people-watching stupor. Its delightful ambience for strolling reminds me of Barcelona's Ramblas.

The highlight of mosaic-decorated Rua Augusta is its grand arch, which stands near the river, framing the equestrian statue of King José I. After a massive restoration project, the arch's clock now ticks for the first time in decades.

Go on a cultural scavenger hunt in this easily navigated grid. Local artisans take over this area daily with hundreds of paintings of Lisbon's trademark trolleys. Shops usually reveal more than just what's for sale; 250-year-old building supports are visible in a number of window displays. For example, check out Farmácia Cortez (Rua de São Nicolau 93) and A Loja (Rua de Prata 229/231). Restaurants clamor for your attention along Rua da Prata. Bright orange-and-purple university housing (marked Z Zone) moves young people back into the neighborhood and keeps buildings occupied (on Rua dos Sapateiros, at the intersection with Rua de Conceição).

Check out the Roman objects on display in windows at Milenium BCP bank (Rua Augusta 84). For a more in-depth look, tour the **archaeological site** beneath the bank...but only if you're not claustrophobic or prone to back problems. Some areas have narrow access but are well worth the effort. Moorish-era ovens sit on Roman floor mosaics and give a surprising insight into Lisbon's earliest days (free guided visits in English, Thu at 17:00 and Sat at 12:00 and 17:00, reservations recommended, entrance at Rua dos Correeiros 9, tel. 213-211-700).

Notice the uniform and utilitarian Pombaline (named after the prime minister who rebuilt the city) architecture—its decoration is limited to wrought iron and tiles. In the years after the earthquake, Lisbon had to rebuild quickly, on a slim budget, and with a new focus on designing practical buildings that could withstand future quakes.

Cathedral (Sé)—The cathedral, just a few blocks east of Praça do Comércio, is not much on the inside, but its fortress-like exterior is a textbook example of a stark and powerful Romanesque fortress of God. Twin, castle-like, crenellated towers solidly frame an impressive rose window. Started in 1150, after the Christians retook Lisbon from the Moors, and built on the site of a mosque, it made a powerful statement: The *Reconquista* was here to stay.

The church is built on the site of the baptism of St. Anthony—another favorite saint of Portugal (locals appeal to him for help in finding a parking spot, a true love, and lost objects). Also, some of St. Vincent is buried here—legend has it that in the 12th century, his remains were brought to Lisbon on a ship guarded by two sacred black ravens, the symbol of the city.

The **cloisters** (€1 entry) are peaceful and an archaeological

The Lisbon Earthquake of 1755

At 9:40 in the morning on Sunday, November 1, All Saints' Day, an earthquake estimated to be close to 9.0 in magnitude rumbled through the city, punctuated by three main jolts. Its arrival came midway through Mass. Ten minutes later, thousands lay dead under the rubble.

Along the waterfront, shaken survivors scrambled aboard boats to sail to safety. They were met by a 20-foot wall of water, the first wave of the tsunami that rushed up the Tejo River. The ravaging water capsized ships, swept people off the docks, crested over the seawall, and crashed 800 feet inland.

After the quake, fires from overturned cooking fires and church candles ignited the city. They raged for five days, ravaging the downtown from the Bairro Alto across Rossio to the castle atop the Alfama.

Of Lisbon's 270,000 citizens, up to 90,000 may have perished. Besides leveling the city, the quake shook Portugal's moral and spiritual underpinnings. Had God punished Lisbon for the Inquisition killings they sanctioned on nearby Praça do Comércio?

On a secular note, this earthquake, one of the most violent in recorded history, was the first one studied methodically, marking the beginning of the science of seismology.

work-in-progress—they're now uncovering Roman ruins. The humble **treasury** is worthwhile only if you want to support the church and climb some stairs (church open daily 9:00–19:00; cloisters open Mon–Sat 14:00–19:00, until 18:00 off-season; treasury open Mon–Sat 10:00–17:00; on Largo da Sé, several blocks east of Baixa, take Rua da Conceição east, which turns into Rua de Santo António da Sé).

Elevador de Santa Justa—In 1902, a student of Gustav Eiffel built this 150-foot-tall iron elevator to connect the lower city with

the high town. You can ride the elevator for a fine city view, a cup of coffee, and a hill-free connection to the Largo do Carmo, walking underneath Gothic arches from the earthquake-damaged Convento do Carmo (€2.60 ticket, covered by 7 Colinas pass, daily 7:00–21:00).

Rossio—Lisbon's historic center, Rossio is still the city's bustling cultural heart. Given its elongated shape, historians believe it was a Roman racetrack 2,000 years ago. These days, cars do the loop instead of chariots. It's home to the colonnaded National Theater, a McDonald's, and street vendors who can shine your shoes, laminate your documents, and sell you cheap watches, autumn chestnuts, and lottery tickets. The column in the square's center honors Pedro IV—King of Portugal and Emperor of Brazil (many maps refer to the square as "Praça Dom Pedro IV," but locals always just call it Rossio, referring to the Neo-Manueline train station at one corner).

From Rossio, the pedestrian-only Rua Augusta slopes downhill through the Baixa to the waterfront. As you face the water, the Alfama is to your left, and the Bairro Alto is to your right. Pop into Pastelaria Suíça (on the east side of the square) and look out the other side onto adjoining Praça da Figueira, congested with buses, subways, taxis, trolleys, and pigeons leaving in all directions.

To the northeast of the square is the "eating lane," and at its mouth is the small square...

Largo de São Domingos—This square is busy with immigrants from Portugal's former African colonies. In the shadow of the Church of São Domingos, they hang out, trade news from home, and watch tourists go by. Lisbon's most classic *ginjinha* bar faces this square.

Liquid Sightseeing—*Ginjinha* (zheen-ZHEEN-yah) is a favorite Lisbon drink. The sweet liquor is made from the sour cherry–like

ginja berry, sugar, and grappa. It's sold for €1 a shot in funky old shops throughout downtown. Buy it with or without berries (*com elas* or *sem elas*—that's "with them" or "without them") and *gelada* (if you want it poured from a chilled bottle—very nice). In Portugal, when people are impressed by the taste of something, they say, *"Sabe melhor que nem ginjas"* ("It tastes even better than *ginja*"). The oldest *ginjinha* joint in town is a colorful hole-in-the-wall at Largo de São Domingos 8 (just off northeast corner of Rossio, at the beginning of the "eating lane"). If you hang around the bar long enough, you'll see them refill the bottle from an enormous vat. Another *ginjinha* bar is nearby on the "eating lane" itself, Rua das Portas de Santo Antão, next to #59 (just down the street from the recommended Casa do Alentejo restaurant).

Church of São Domingos—It's forgettable from the outside, but worthwhile if you don't want to pay for the Convento do Carmo (100 feet left of *ginjinha* stand, free, daily 7:30–19:00). The evocative inside—more or less rebuilt from the ruins left by the tragic 1755 earthquake—reminds visitors of that horrible All Saints' Day Sunday, when most of the city was at Mass and the earth rolled. Heavy stone church interiors like this collapsed on their congregations.

Take the small street behind the National Theater to the exuberant Rossio train station. Continue right to see...

Praça dos Restauradores—The monumental square is at the top end of Rossio and the lower end of Avenida da Liberdade (listed next). Its centerpiece, an obelisk, celebrates the restoration of Portuguese independence from Spain in 1640. (In 1580, the Portuguese king died without a direct heir. The closest heir was Philip II of Spain—yuck. He became Philip I of Portugal, ushering in an unhappy 60 years during which three Spanish Philips ruled Portugal.)

Just off the square is Lisbon's oldest hotel (the recommended Hotel Avenida Palace, built to greet those arriving by train, see page 85), the Art Deco facade of the Eden Theater from the 1920s, a TI, a green ABEP kiosk (selling tickets for concerts, movies, bullfights, and sports events) at the southern end, the Elevador da Glória funicular that climbs to the Bairro Alto, and a Metro station. A block to the east is Lisbon's "eating lane" (Rua das Portas de Santo Antão), lined with restaurants.

Greater Lisbon

Avenida da Liberdade—This tree-lined grand boulevard, running north from Rossio, connects the old town near the river (where most of the sightseeing action is) with the newer upper town. Before the great earthquake, this was a royal promenade. After 1755, it was the grand boulevard of Pombal's new Lisbon— originally limited to the aristocracy. The present street, built in the 1880s and inspired by Paris' Champs-Elysées, is lined with banks, airline offices, nondescript office buildings...and eight noisy lanes of traffic. The grand "rotunda"—as the roundabout formally known as Marquês de Pombal is called—tops off the Avenida da Liberdade with a commanding statue of Pombal. Allegorical symbols of his impressive accomplishments decorate the statue. (A single-minded dictator can do a lot in 27 years.) Beyond that lies the fine Edward VII Park. From the Rotunda (Metro: Marquês de Pombal), it's an enjoyable 20-minute downhill walk along the mile-long avenue to the old city (the Baixa). The black-and-white cobbled sidewalks are a Lisbon tradition.

▲▲▲**Gulbenkian Museum**—This is the best of Lisbon's 40 museums. Calouste Gulbenkian (1869–1955), an Armenian oil tycoon, gave Portugal his art collection (or "harem," as he called it). His gift was an act of gratitude for the hospitable asylum granted him during World War II (he lived in Lisbon from 1942 until he died in 1955). The Portuguese consider Gulbenkian— whose billion-dollar estate is still a growing and vital arts foundation promoting culture in Portugal—an inspirational model of how to be thoughtfully wealthy. (He made a habit of "tithing for art," spending 10 percent of his income on things of beauty.) The foundation often hosts classical music concerts in the museum's auditoriums.

Gulbenkian's collection, spanning 5,000 years and housed in a classy modern building, offers the most purely enjoyable museum experience in Iberia—it's both educational and just plain beautiful. The museum is cool, uncrowded, gorgeously lit, and easy to grasp, displaying only a few select and exquisite works from each epoch. Walk through five millennia of human history, appreciating our ancestors by seeing objects they treasured.

Cost, Hours, Location: €3, free Sun, 20 percent discount with LisboaCard, Tue–Sun 10:00–18:00, closed Mon, good €4 90-min audioguide, pleasant gardens, good air-conditioned cafeteria, Berna 45, tel. 217-823-000, www.museu.gulbenkian.pt. To get here from downtown, hop a cab (€4) or take the Metro from Restauradores to São Sebastião, exit the station by El Corte Inglés on Avenida de Aguiar, and walk downhill, past a row of gorgeous, bold 1950s buildings on your left. Before reaching the roundabout, across from the funky, pink Spanish embassy, you'll see a sign pointing right to the *fundação*—walk straight to the museum entrance. From here, Belém is a quick €6 taxi ride away.

➲ **Self-Guided Tour:** From the entrance lobby, there are two wings, covering roughly pre-1500 and post-1500. Following the museum's layout, you'll see...

❶ **Egypt (2,500–500 B.C.):** Ancient Egyptians, believing that life really began after death, carved statues to preserve the memory of the deceased, whether it be a prince (Statue of the Courtier Bes, 664–610 B.C., with an inscription calling him "the king's friend") or a likeness of the family pet. The cat statue nurses her kittens atop a coffin that once held the cat's mummy, preserved for the afterlife. Egyptians honored cats—even giving them gold earrings like the statue's. They believed cats helped the goddess Bastet keep watch over the household. Now, more than 2,500 years later, we remember the Egyptians for these sturdy, dignified statues, built for eternity.

❷ **Greece and Rome (500 B.C.–A.D. 500):** The black-and-red Greek vase (calyx-crater), decorated with scenes of half-human

Gulbenkian Museum

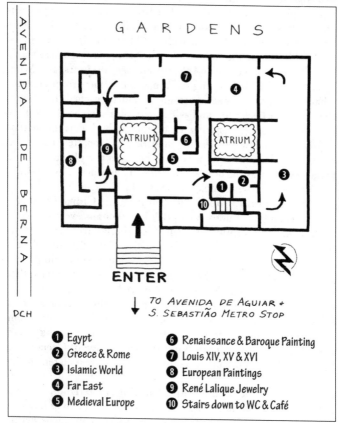

AVENIDA DE BERNA

GARDENS

ATRIUM

ATRIUM

ENTER

↓ TO AVENIDA DE AGUIAR + S. SEBASTIÃO METRO STOP

DCH

❶ Egypt
❷ Greece & Rome
❸ Islamic World
❹ Far East
❺ Medieval Europe
❻ Renaissance & Baroque Painting
❼ Louis XIV, XV & XVI
❽ European Paintings
❾ René Lalique Jewelry
❿ Stairs down to WC & Café

Lisbon

satyrs chasing human women, reminds us of the rational Greeks' struggle to overcome their barbarian, animal-like urges as they invented Western civilization. Alexander the Great (r. 336–323 B.C., seen on a coin) used war to spread Greek culture throughout the Mediterranean, creating a cultural empire that would soon be taken over by Roman emperors (seen on medallions).

Journey even further back in time to the very roots of civilization—Mesopotamia (modern Iraq), where writing was invented. Five thousand years ago, the cylinder seals were used to roll an impression in sealing wax or clay.

❸ **Islamic World (700–1500):** The Muslims who lived in Portugal—as far west of Mecca as you could get back then—might have decorated their homes with furnishings from all over the Islamic world. Imagine a Moorish sultan, dressed in a shirt from Syria, sitting on a carpet from Persia in a courtyard with Moroccan tiles. By a bubbling fountain, he puffs on a hookah.

The culture of Moorish Iberia (711–1492) was among Europe's most sophisticated after the Fall of Rome. The intricate patterns on the glass lanterns are not only beautiful...they're actually quotes (in Arabic) from the Quran, such as "Allah (God) is the light of the world, shining like a flame in a glass lamp, as bright as a star."

❹ **Far East (1368–1644):** For almost 300 years, the Ming dynasty ruled China, having reclaimed the country from Genghis Khan and his sons. When Portuguese traders reached the Orient, they brought back blue-and-white ceramics such as these. They became all the rage, inspiring the creation of both Portuguese tiles and Dutch Delftware. Writing utensils fill elaborately decorated boxes from Japan. Another type of box was the ultimate picnic basket—*bento* was the best way to enjoy the Japanese countryside.

In the other wing, look for the art of...

❺ **Medieval Europe (500–1500):** While China was thriving and inventing, Europe was stuck in a thousand-year medieval funk (with the exception of Arab-ruled Iberia). Most Europeans from the "Age of Faith" channeled their spirituality into objects of Christian devotion. A priest on a business trip could pack a portable altarpiece in his backpack, travel to a remote village that had no church, and deliver a sermon carved in ivory. In monasteries, the monks with the best penmanship laboriously copied books (illuminated manuscripts) and decorated them with scenes from the text—and wacky doodles in the margins. These books were virtual time capsules, preserving the knowledge of Greece and Rome until it could emerge again, a thousand years later, in the Renaissance.

❻ **Renaissance and Baroque Painting (1500–1700):** Around 1500, a cultural revolution was taking place—the birth of humanism. Painters saw God in the faces of ordinary people, whether in Domenico Ghirlandaio's fresh-faced maiden, Frans Hals' wrinkled old woman, or Rembrandt's portrait of an old man, whose crease-lined hands tell the story of his life.

❼ **Louis XIV, XV, XVI (1700–1800):** After the Italian-born Renaissance, Europe's focus shifted northward to the luxurious court of France, where a new secular culture was blossoming. In one tapestry, love is in the air (see cupids flying overhead) as Venus frolics in a landscaped garden. Powder-wigged nobles in their palaces enjoyed the luxury of viewing art like this pagan scene, while relaxing in chairs like the kind you see here. This furniture, once actually owned by French kings (and Marie Antoinette and Madame de Pompadour), is a royal home show. Anything heavy, ornate, and gilded (or that includes curved legs and animal-clawed feet) is from the time of Louis XIV. The Louis XV style is lighter and daintier, with Oriental motifs, while furniture from the Louis XVI era is stripped-down, straight-legged, tapered, and more modern. Listen to find out which clocks still work.

❽ European Paintings (1700–2000): Europe ruled the world, and art became increasingly refined. Young British aristocrats (Thomas Gainsborough portrait) traveled Europe on the Grand Tour to see great sights like Venice (Guardi landscape). Follow the progression in styles from stormy Romanticism (J. M. W. Turner's tumultuous shipwreck) to Pre-Raphaelite dreamscapes *(Mirror of Venus)* to Realism's breath-of-fresh-air simplicity (Manet's bubble-blower) to the glinting, shimmering Impressionism of Monet... Renoir...and the Englishman John Singer Sargent.

❾ René Lalique Jewelry: Finish your visit with the stunning, sumptuous Art Nouveau glasswork and jewelry of French designer René Lalique (1860–1945). Fragile beauty like this, from the elegant turn-of-the-century Belle Époque, was about to be shattered by the tumultuous 20th century. Art Nouveau emphasized forms from nature and valued the organic and artisan over cold, calculated mass production. Ordinary dragonflies, orchids, and beetles become breathtaking when transformed into jewelry. The work of Lalique—just another of Gulbenkian's circle of friends—is a fitting finale to a museum that features both history and beauty.

▲▲Museum of Ancient Art (Museu Nacional de Arte Antiga)—This is Portugal's finest museum for paintings from its glory days, the 15th and 16th centuries. (Most of these works were gathered from Lisbon's abbeys and convents after their dissolution in 1834.) You'll also find a rich collection of furniture, as well as art by renowned European masters such as Hieronymus Bosch, Jan van Eyck, and Raphael—all in a grand palace. Pick up the free informative pamphlet at the entrance. Here are some highlights, starting on the top floor.

Third Floor—Portuguese Paintings: The *Adoration of St. Vincent* is a many-paneled altarpiece by the late-15th-century master Nuno Gonçalves. A gang of 60 real people—everyone from royalty to sailors and beggars—surrounds Lisbon's patron saint. In Room 1, if you've visited the sights in Belém, you'll recognize the Jerónimos monastery before it was fully decorated (painting by Felipe Lobo). Room 2 contains a small collection of paintings that depict Lisbon after the horrific 1755 earthquake.

Second Floor—Japanese Screen and Jewels: Find the enchanting Namban screen painting (Namban means "barbarians from the south"). It shows the Portuguese from a 16th-century Japanese perspective—with long noses as well as great skill at climbing rigging, like acrobats. The Portuguese, the first Europeans to make contact with Japan, gave the Japanese guns, Catholicism (Nagasaki was founded by Portuguese Jesuits), and a new deep-frying technique we know as tempura.

On the same floor, have a quick look at the impressive jewelry collection decorated with the red cross of the Order of Christ, responsible for funding Portuguese explorations. Make your way to a free-standing glass case to see the Monstrance of Belém, made for Manuel I from the first gold brought back by Vasco da Gama. Squint at the fine enamel creatures filling a tide pool on the base, the 12 apostles gathered around the glass case for the Communion wafer (the fancy top pops off), and the white dove hanging like a mobile under the all-powerful God bidding us peace on earth. There is another notable monstrance nearby, as well as more jewels and fine porcelain on the rest of this floor.

First Floor—European Paintings: Pass through the gift shop and look for Bosch's *Temptations of St. Anthony* (a three-paneled altarpiece fantasy, c. 1500, in Room 57) and Albrecht Dürer's *St. Jerome* (just opposite). Note the complete collection of the larger-than-life *Twelve Apostles* by the Spanish master Zurburán.

Cost, Hours, Location: €3, free until 14:00 on Sun, free with LisboaCard, Tue 14:00–18:00, Wed–Sun 10:00–18:00, closed Mon. It's located about a mile west of Praça do Comércio (from Praça da Figueira, take trolley #15E to Cais Rocha, cross street and walk up a lot of steps; or take bus #60 to Rua das Janeles Verdes 9). Tel. 213-912-800. The museum has a good cafeteria with seating in a shaded garden overlooking the river.

▲**National Tile Museum (Museu Nacional do Azulejo)**—Filling the Convento da Madre de Deus, the museum features piles of tiles, which, as you've probably noticed, are an art form in Portugal. They've tried to showcase the tiles as they would have originally appeared (note the diamond-shaped staircase tiles). While the pre-

sentation is low-tech, the church is sumptuous, and the tile panorama of pre-earthquake Lisbon (upstairs) is fascinating (€3, free until 14:00 on Sun, free with LisboaCard, Tue 15:00–18:00, Wed–Sun 10:00–18:00, closed Mon, museum is about a mile east of Praça do Comércio, 10 min on bus #794 from Praça do Comércio in front of TI, bus stop at entrance on Rua da Madre de Deus 4, tel. 218-100-340).

Parque das Nações—Lisbon celebrated the 500th anniversary of Vasco da Gama's voyage to India by hosting Expo '98. The theme was "The Ocean and the Seas," emphasizing the global importance of healthy, clean waters. The riverside fairgrounds are east of the Santa Apolónia Station, in an area revitalized with luxury condos, crowd-pleasing terraces, and restaurants. Ride the Metro to the last stop on the red line (Oriente—meaning east end of town), walk to the water, turn right, and join the people strolling along the riverside.

António Salazar

Q: What do you get when you cross a lawyer, an economist, and a dictator?
A: António Salazar, who was all three—a dictator who ruled Portugal through harsh laws and a strict budget that hurt the poor.

Shortly after a 1926 military coup "saved" Portugal's floundering democracy from itself, General Oscar Carmona appointed António de Oliveira Salazar (1889–1970) as finance minister. A former professor of economics and law at the University of Coimbra, Salazar balanced the budget and the interests of the country's often warring factions. His skill and his reputation as a clean-living, fair-minded patriot earned him a promotion. In 1932, he became prime minister, and he set about creating his New State *(Estado Novo)*.

For nearly four decades, Salazar ruled a stable but isolated nation based on harmony between the traditional power blocs of the ruling class—the military, big business, large landowners, and the Catholic Church. This Christian fascism, backed by the military and secret police, was ratified repeatedly in elections by the country's voters—the richest 20 percent of the populace.

As a person, Salazar was respected, but not loved. The son of a farm manager, he originally studied to be a priest before going on to become a scholar and writer. He never married. Quiet, low-key, and unassuming, he attended church regularly and lived a non-materialistic existence. But when faced with opposition, he was ruthless, and his secret police became an object of fear and hatred.

Salazar steered Portugal through the turmoil of Spain's Civil War (1936–1939), remaining officially neutral while secretly supporting Franco's fascists. He detested Nazi Germany's "pagan" leaders, but respected Mussolini for reconciling with the pope. In World War II, Portugal was officially neutral, but was often friendly with longtime ally Britain and used as a base for espionage. After the war, it benefited greatly from the United States' Marshall Plan for economic recovery (which Spain never received during Franco's rule), and the country joined NATO in 1949.

Salazar's regime was undone by two factors: the liberal 1960s and the unpopular, draining wars Portugal fought abroad to try to keep its colonial empire intact. When Salazar died in 1970, the regime that followed became increasingly less credible, leading to the liberating events of the Carnation Revolution in 1974.

The Vasco da Gama mall has a top-floor beer garden with outside decks that let you drink in the Tejo River view. You can rent a bike by the hour or go up the Vasco da Gama tower (€3, daily 10:00–18:00, tel. 218-956-143). Riding the cable car is a quick way to get from the tower to Oceanário, listed next (€3.50 one-way, €5.50 round-trip, discount with LisboaCard, June–Sept Mon–Fri 11:00–20:00, Sat–Sun 10:00–21:00, service ends one hour earlier off-season). The tide pools of the Tejo are visible along the boardwalk, Passeio das Tágides.

Popular café/bars—such as Bar de Palha—line the waterfront just south of the tower. This area is fully open on Monday (when many Lisbon museums are not) and most vibrant on Sunday afternoons.

Oceanário—Europe's largest aquarium simulates four different oceanic underwater and shoreline environments. Built in a modern version of a ship at sea, the aquarium has an enormous centerpiece, a central tank with lots of fish and the occasional hungry shark. Penguins, sea otters, and weekday-morning school groups are all happily on display (€10.50, 40 percent discount with LisboaCard, daily April–Oct 10:00–19:00, off-season until 18:00, last entry 45 min before closing, tel. 218-917-002, www.oceanario.pt).

Vasco da Gama Bridge—Europe's second-longest bridge was opened in 1998 to connect the Expo grounds with the south side of the Tejo, and to alleviate the traffic jams on Lisbon's only other bridge over the river, the 25th of April Bridge. Built low to the water, its towers and cables are meant to suggest the sails of a caravel ship.

▲25th of April Bridge (25 de Abril)—At 1.5 miles (3,280 feet between the towers), this is one of the longest suspension bridges in the world. The foundations are sunk 260 feet into the riverbed, making it the world's deepest bridge. It was built in 1966 by the same company that made its San Francisco cousin (but notice the lower deck for train tracks). Originally named for the dictator Salazar (see sidebar on page 63), the bridge was renamed for the date of Portugal's 1974 revolution and liberation. For a generation, locals have shown their political colors by choosing which name to use. While conservatives still called it the Salazar Bridge, liberals refer to it as the 25th of April Bridge. Imagine that prior to 1966, there was no way across the Tejo except by ferry.

Cristo Rei (Christ of Majesty) —A huge, 330-foot concrete statue of Christ (à la Rio de Janeiro) overlooks Lisbon from across the Tejo River, stretching its arms wide to symbolically bless the city (or dive into the river). Lisbon's cardinal, inspired by a visit to Rio de Janeiro in 1936, wanted a replica built back home. Increased support came after an appeal was made to Our Lady of Fátima in 1940

The Carnation Revolution

On April 25, 1974, several prominent members of the military reluctantly sided with a growing popular movement to oust the government. They withdrew their support from the military-backed regime that had ruled Portugal under António Salazar for five decades. Only five people died that April day in a well-planned, relatively bloodless coup. Citizens spilled into the streets to cheer and put flowers in soldiers' rifle barrels, giving the event its name—the Carnation Revolution. Suddenly, people were free to speak aloud what they formerly could only whisper in private.

In the Revolution's aftermath, the country struggled to get the hang of modern democracy. Their economy suffered as overseas colonies fell to nationalist uprisings, flooding the country with some 800,000 emigrants. In 1976, the Portuguese adopted a constitution that separated church and state. These changes helped to break down the almost medieval class system and establish parliamentary law.

Mario Soares, a former enemy of the Salazar regime, became the new prime minister, ruling through much of the next two decades as a stabilizing presence. Today, Portugal is a strong example of democratic government.

to keep Portugal out of World War II. Portugal survived the war relatively unscathed, and funds were collected to build this statue in appreciation. After 10 years of construction, it opened to the public in 1959. Currently it's a sanctuary and pilgrimage site, and the chapel inside holds regular Sunday Mass. While the statue was designed to be seen from a distance, an elevator takes visitors to the top for a panoramic view (€4, Mon–Fri 9:30–18:00, Sat–Sun 9:30–17:00, tel. 212-751-000). From left to right, see Belém, the 25th of April Bridge, downtown Lisbon (Praça do Comércio and the green Alfama hilltop with the castle), and the long Vasco da Gama Bridge.

To get to Cristo Rei, catch the 10-minute ferry from downtown Lisbon to Cacilhas (€0.74, 4/hr, more during rush hour, from Cais do Sodré Metro/train station follow signs to *Terminal Fluvial*, which serves many destinations). The bus marked *101 Cristo Rei* takes you to the base of the statue in 15 minutes (€1.05, 3/hr, exit ferry dock left into the maze of bus stops to find the #20 stop with the "101 Cristo Rei" schedule under the awning). Because of bridge tolls to enter Lisbon, taxis from the site are expensive. Consider taking a late-morning ferry to Cristo Rei; catch a taxi from the statue to Porto Brandão and have lunch there (see page 79); and ferry direct to Belém and see the sights. Ferries also go direct from

Cacilhas to Belém. For drivers, the most efficient visit is a quick stop on your way to or from the Algarve.

Belém District

Three miles from downtown Lisbon, the Belém District is a stately pincushion of important sights from Portugal's Golden Age, when Vasco da Gama and company turned the country into Europe's richest power. Belém was the send-off point for voyages in the Age of Discovery. Sailors would stay and pray here before embarking. The tower welcomed them home. The grand buildings of Belém survived the great 1755 earthquake, so this is the best place to experience the grandeur of pre-earthquake Lisbon. After the earthquake, safety-conscious (and rattled) royalty chose to live here—in wooden rather than stone buildings. The modern-day president of Portugal calls Belém home (you could, too—the recommended Jerónimos 8 Hotel is listed in "Sleeping," on page 89).

To celebrate the 300th anniversary of independence from Spain, a grand exhibition was held here in 1940, resulting in the fine parks, fountains, and monuments.

Virtually all of Belém's museums are covered by the LisboaCard (except for the Maritime Museum, which offers a discount) and closed on Monday.

Getting to Belém

You'll get here quickest by taxi (€9 from downtown), or slower and cheaper by trolley #15E (30 min, catch at Praça da Figueira or Praça do Comércio) or by bus #28 (just east of Praça do Comércio opposite Terreiro do Paço boat station). In Belém, the first stop is the Coach Museum; the second is the monastery. Even if you miss the first subtle stop (named Belém), you can't miss the second stop at the massive monastery.

Consider doing Belém in this order: the Coach Museum, pastry and coffee break, Monastery of Jerónimos, Maritime Museum (if interested) and/or lunch at its cafeteria (public access, museum entry not required), Monument to the Discoveries, and Belém Tower. If arriving by taxi, start at Belém Tower, the farthest point, and do the recommended lineup in reverse, ending at the Coach Museum. Belém also has a cultural center, a children's museum, and a planetarium—not priorities for a quick visit. For recommended eateries in this area, see page 78.

When you're through, hop on trolley #15E to return to Praça da Figueira or Praça do Comércio. Bus #28 takes you to downtown Lisbon, and continues to Parque das Nações and Oriente Station.

Tourist Information

The little TI kiosk is directly across the street from the

Belém

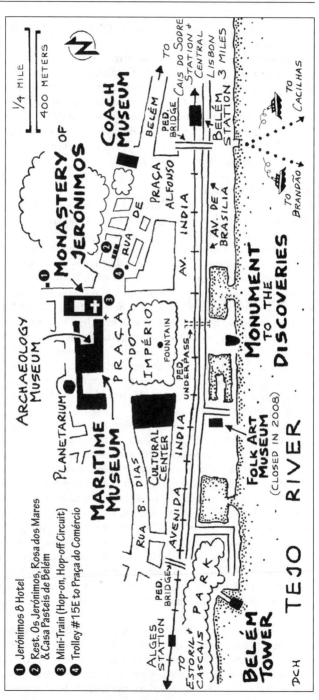

1 Jerónimos 8 Hotel
2 Rest. Os Jerónimos, Rosa dos Mares & Casa Pastéis de Belém
3 Mini-Train (Hop-on, Hop-off Circuit)
4 Trolley #15E to Praça do Comércio

Lisbon

entrance to the monastery (Tue–Sat 10:00–13:00 & 14:00–18:00, closed Sun–Mon, tel. 213-658-455).

A little red-and-white **Carris Mini-Train** does a handy 45-minute hop-on, hop-off circuit of the Belém sights—which can feel far-flung if you're tired—departing nearly every hour from the monastery entrance (€3, discount with LisboaCard, includes audioguide; year-round Tue–Sun hourly from 10:00–17:00 except 13:00, April–Sept extra train at 18:00, July–Aug one more at 19:00, exact pickup times listed at each stop; you can get off to explore a sight and catch the next mini-train).

▲▲Coach Museum

In 1905, the last Queen of Portugal saw that cars would soon obliterate horse-drawn carriages as a form of transportation. She decided to use the palace's riding-school building to preserve her fine collection of royal coaches, which became today's Coach Museum (Museu dos Coches). The collection is impressive, with more than 70 dazzling carriages (described in English) lining the elegant old riding room. Check out the ceiling, which is as remarkable as the carriages, and look for coach #1 (from around 1600). This crude and simple coach was once used by Philip II, King of Spain and Portugal, to shuttle between Madrid and Lisbon. Notice that this coach has no driver's seat—its drivers would actually ride the horses. (You'll have to trust me on this, but if you lift up the cushion, you'll find a potty hole—also handy for road sickness. Imagine how slow and rough the ride would be with bad roads and a crude leather-strap suspension.)

Study the evolution of suspension from the first coach, or "Kotze," made in the 15th century in a Hungarian town of that name. Trace the improvement of coaches through the next century, noticing how the decoration increases, as does the comfort. A Portuguese coat of arms indicates that a carriage was part of the royal fleet. Ornamentation often includes a folk festival of exotic faces from Portugal's distant colonies. Examples of period riding costumes are displayed in cases between many of the coaches.

At the far end of the first room, the lumbering Ocean Coach, as ornate as it is long, stands shining. At the stern, gold figures symbolize the Atlantic and Indian Oceans holding hands, reminding all who view it of Portugal's mastery of the sea. It is flanked by two more equally stunning coaches with similar ocean-exploring symbols.

The second room shows sedan chairs and traces the development of carriages as a common means of transportation. They got lighter and faster, culminating in a sporty, horse-drawn Lisbon taxi.

Wander upstairs to get a glimpse of velvet-covered saddles and special riding gear designed for the royal kids. A spectacular view of the entire building interior is picture-perfect (no flash). The portrait gallery of most Portuguese royalty is handy for putting a face to all the movers and shakers you've read about so far.

Cost, Hours, Location: €3, free Sun until 14:00, free with LisboaCard, Tue–Sun 10:00–18:00, last entry 30 minutes before closing, closed Mon, tel. 213-610-850. A taxi stand is across the street. The Coach Museum is on Rua de Belém, along with the monastery, the guarded entry to Portugal's presidential palace, some fine pre-earthquake buildings, and a famous pastry shop—an obligatory stop for those with a sweet tooth (see page 79).

▲▲▲Monastery of Jerónimos

King Manuel (who ruled from 1495) erected this giant, white limestone church and monastery—that stretches 300 yards along

the Lisbon waterfront—as a "thank you" for the discoveries made by early Portuguese explorers. It was financed in part with "pepper money," a 5 percent tax on spices brought back from India. Manuel built it on the site of a humble sailors' chapel where they spent their last night in prayer before embarking on their frightening voyages. What is the style of Manuel's church? Manueline.

Cost and Hours: The church is free, but the cloisters cost €4.50 (both free Sun until 14:00, free with LisboaCard, no need to stop at ticket counter—just show card to guard, hours for both: May–Sept Tue–Sun 10:00–18:00, off-season until 17:00, last entry 30 minutes before closing, closed Mon and during Sun Mass.

↦ Self-Guided Tour: Here's a tour, starting outside the monastery:

❶ South Portal: The fancy south portal, facing the street, is textbook Manueline. Henry the Navigator stands between the doors with the king's patron saint, St. Jerome (above on the left, with the lion). Henry (Manuel's uncle) built the original sailors' chapel on this site. This door is only used when Mass lets out or for Saturday weddings.

❷ Church Entrance: As you approach the main entrance, the church is on your right and the cloisters are straight ahead. Flanking the church door are kneeling statues of King Manuel I, the Fortunate (left of door), and his wife, Maria (right).

❸ Church Interior: The Manueline style is on the cusp of the Renaissance. Unlike earlier medieval churches, the space is more open. Slender, palm tree–like columns don't break the interior space (as Gothic columns do), and the ceiling is all one height.

Monastery of Jerónimos

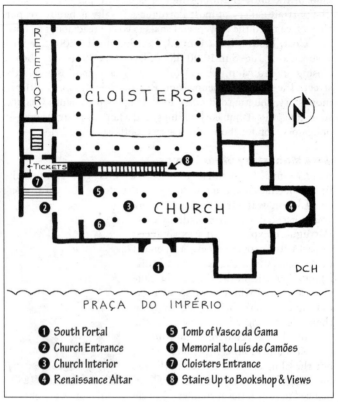

REFECTORY

CLOISTERS

←TICKETS

CHURCH

⑧ Stairs Up to Bookshop & Views

PRAÇA DO IMPÉRIO

DCH

① South Portal
② Church Entrance
③ Church Interior
④ Renaissance Altar
⑤ Tomb of Vasco da Gama
⑥ Memorial to Luís de Camões
⑦ Cloisters Entrance
⑧ Stairs Up to Bookshop & Views

Motifs from the sea hide in the decor. You'll see rope-like arches, ships, and monsters that evoke the mystery of undiscovered lands. Artichokes—eaten for their vitamin C, to fight scurvy—remind us of the hardships sailors faced at sea. After all, the sea brought Portugal 16th-century wealth and power, making this art possible.

❹ Renaissance Altar: Nearly everything here survived the 1755 earthquake, except for the stained glass (replacement glass is from 1940). In the main altar, elephants—who dethroned lions as the most powerful and kingly beasts—support two kings and two queens (King Manuel I is front-left). Many Portuguese churches (such as the cathedrals in downtown Lisbon and Évora) were renovated in Renaissance and Baroque times, resulting in an odd mix of dark, older naves and pretty pastel altars. Walk back on the side with the seven wooden confessional doors (on your right). Notice the ornamental carving around the second one: a festival of faces from newly discovered corners of the world. Ahead of you (near the entry, under a ceiling which is a veritable *Boy Scout's Handbook*

Manueline Architecture
(c. 1480–1580)

Portugal's unique style (from its peak of power under King Manuel I, the Fortunate, r. 1495–1521) reflects the wealth of the times and the many cultural influences of the Age of Discovery. The purpose is decorative, not structural. Whether the building uses pointed Gothic or round Renaissance arches, it can be embellished with elaborate Manueline carved stonework, particularly around windows and doors.

Manueline aesthetic is ornate, elaborate, and intertwined, often featuring symbols from a family's coat of arms (shields with castles, crosses, lions, banners, and crowns) or motifs from the sea (rope-like columns or borders, knots, shells, coral, anchors, and nets). Manuel's personal symbol, the armillary sphere, was a globe of the earth surrounded by movable rings. (Sailors used it to calculate their location on earth in relation to the heavens.)

Architecture students will recognize elements from Gothic's elaborate tracery, the abstract designs of Moorish culture, similarities to Spain's intricate Plateresque style (which dates from the same time), and the elongated excesses of Italian Mannerism.

of rope and knots) is the tomb of Vasco da Gama.

❺ Tomb of Vasco da Gama: The night of July 7, 1497, Vasco da Gama (1460–1524) prayed for a safe voyage in the small chapel that stood here before the current church was built. The next day, he set sail from Belém with four ships (see the caravel carved in the middle of the tomb's side) and 150 men. He was armed with state-of-the-art maps and sailing technology, such as the carved armillary sphere, a globe surrounded by movable rings designed to determine the positions of the sun or other stars to help sailors track their location on Earth. (Some say its diagonal slash is symbolic of the unwritten pact and ambition of Spain and Portugal to split the world evenly, but it actually represents the path of the planets as they move across the heavens.)

Da Gama's mission? To confirm what earlier navigators had hypothesized—that the ocean recently discovered when Bartolomeu Dias rounded Africa was the same one seen by overland travelers to India. Hopefully, he'd find a direct sea route to the vast, untapped wealth of Asia. The three symbols on the tomb show the source of the money (the cross symbolizing the Knights Templar, the soldier monks who funded these voyages), the method (the caravel ship), and the result (Portugal's domination of the globe).

By Christmas, da Gama rounded the Cape of Good Hope. After battling hostile Arabs in Mozambique, he hired an Arab guide to pilot the ships to India, arriving on the southwest coast in Calicut (from which we get the word "calico") in May 1498. He traded for spices, networked with the locals for future outposts, battled belligerent chiefs, and then headed back home. Da Gama and his crew arrived home to Lisbon in September 1499 (after two years and two months on the seas), and were greeted with all-out Vasco-mania. The few spices he'd returned with (many were lost in transit) were worth a staggering fortune. Portugal's Golden Age was launched.

King Manuel dubbed da Gama "Admiral of the Sea of India" and sent him out again, this time to subdue the Indian locals with his sword, establish more trade outposts, and again return home to wealth and honor. Da Gama died on Christmas Eve 1524, in India. His memory lives on due to the adoration of two men: Manuel, who built this large church, and Luís de Camões (honored opposite Vasco), who turned da Gama's history-making voyage into an epic poem.

❻ **Memorial to Luís de Camões:** Camões (kah-MOISH, 1524–1580) is Portugal's Shakespeare and Casanova rolled into one, an adventurer and writer whose heroic poems glorifying the nation's sailing exploits live on today. It was Camões who described Portugal as the place "where land ends and the sea begins."

After college at Coimbra, Camões was banished from the court (1546) for flirting with the noble lady Dona Caterina. He lost an eye soldiering in Morocco (he's always portrayed squinting), served jail time for brawling with a bureaucrat, and then caught a ship to India and China, surviving a shipwreck on the way. While serving as a colonial administrator in India, he plugged away at the epic poem that would become his masterpiece. Returning to Portugal, he published *The Lusiads* (*Os Lusíadas*, 1572), winning minor recognition and a small pension.

The long poem describes Vasco da Gama's first voyage to India in heroic terms, on the scale of Homer's *Odyssey*. *The Lusiads* begins:

Arms and the heroes, from Lisbon's shore,
sailed through seas never dared before,
with awesome courage, forging their way
to the glorious kingdoms of the rising day.

The poem goes on to recite many events in Portuguese history, from the time of the Lusiads (the original pre-Roman natives) onward. Even today, Camões' words are quoted by modern Portuguese politicians in search of a heroic sound bite. And

Portugal's national holiday, June 10, is known as Camões Day, remembering the day in 1580 when the great poet died. The stone monument here—with literary rather than maritime motifs—is a cenotaph (his actual burial spot is unknown).

❼ Cloisters: Leave the church (turn right), purchase your ticket, and enter the cloisters. These restored cloisters are the

architectural highlight of Belém. The lacy arcade is Manueline; the simpler diamond and decorative rose frieze above the top floor is Renaissance. Study the carvings, especially the gargoyles—find a monkey, a kitten, and a cricket. The small basin in the corner (where the monks washed up before meals) marks the entrance to the refectory, or dining hall—today an occasional concert venue lined with fine old tiles.

To the left of the refectory is the burial spot of Portugal's most revered modern poet, Fernando Pessoa (see sidebar on page 45). Continuing around, a large room contains an exhibit of the lengthy restoration process, as well as the tomb of Alexandre Herculano, a Romantic 19th-century poet. Quotes from Herculano adorn his tomb: "Sleep? Only the cold cadaver that doesn't feel sleeps. The soul flies and wraps itself around the feet of the All-Powerful."

If there are rows of flags outside the monastery, a VIP is in town. Heads of state are received in the cloisters with a warm welcome. Fittingly, this is also the site of many important treaty signings, such as Portugal's admittance to the European Union in 1986.

Upstairs (❽), you'll find a bookshop and better views of the church and the cloisters along with exhibits about the monastery's history (women's WC upstairs, men's downstairs—guys, watch your head).

The sheer size of this religious complex is a testament to the religious motivation that—along with money—propelled the Age of Discovery. Monks often accompanied the sailor-pirates on their trading/pillaging trips, hoping to convert the heathen locals to Christianity. Many expeditions were financed by the Knights Templar, a brotherhood of soldier monks from the time of the crusades. (The monks who inhabited these cloisters were Hieronymites—followers of St. Jerome, hence the monastery name of Jerónimos.)

It was a time of extreme Christian faith. King Manuel, who did so much to promote exploration, was also the man who expelled all Jews from the country. (In 1497, the Church agreed to allow him to marry a Spanish princess on the condition that he

Caravels

These easily maneuverable trading ships were fast, small (80 feet), and light (100 tons), with few guns and three triangular-shaped sails (called lateen-rigged sails) that could pivot quickly to catch the wind. They were ideal for sailing along coastlines. Many ocean going caravels were also rigged with a square foresail to make them more stable. (This photo shows the model held by Prince Henry on Belém's Monument to the Discoveries.) Columbus' *Niña* and *Pinta* were re-rigged caravels.

deport the Jews.) Francis Xavier, a Spanish Jesuit, did much of his missionary work traveling in Asia in the service of Portugal.

Age of Discovery Sights and Nearby

Maritime Museum (Museu de Marinha)—If you're interested in the ships and navigational tools of Portugal's Age of Discovery, this museum, which fills the west wing of the Monastery of Jerónimos (listed previously), has good English descriptions and is worth a look. Sailors love it (€3, free Sun 10:00–13:00, 25 percent discount with LisboaCard, April–Sept Tue–Sun 10:00–18:00, off-season until 17:00, closed Mon; facing the planetarium from the square, a decent cafeteria—open to the public—is to your left and the museum entrance is to your right).

▲Monument to the Discoveries (Padrão dos Descobrimentos)—In 1960, the city honored the 500th anniversary of the death of Prince Henry the Navigator by rebuilding this giant riverside monument originally constructed for the 1940 Expo (see photo on page 77; reached from the monastery via a pedestrian tunnel under the busy boulevard). The elevator inside takes you up to a tingly view.

Cost, Hours, Information: €2.50, 30 percent discount with LisboaCard, €5 combo-ticket includes elevator, downstairs exhibits, and the Lisbon Experience video; May–Sept Tue–Sun 10:00–19:00, off-season until 18:00, last entry 30 minutes before closing, closed Mon; tel. 213-031-950.

Movie: Inside the monument, a basement exhibit waxes poetic about the 1940 Expo, praising Portugal's worldly influence, but the highlight is the **Lisbon Experience,** a 30-minute video shown in a comfortable theater at the top of each hour. This relaxing, well-done sweep through the story of the city is a fun

Portugal Explores the Sea

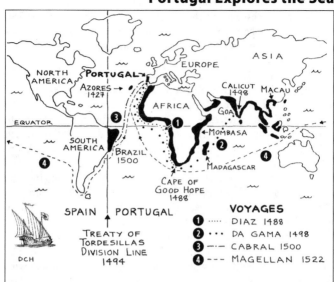

review, and leaves you feeling good about Lisbon (€4, discount with LisboaCard, Tue–Sun 10:00–16:00, closed Mon, in English, a shorter €2 15-min version plays at :40 past the hour).

◐ Self-Guided Tour: Walk around the huge monument. The 170-foot concrete structure shows that exploring the world was a team effort. The men who braved the unknown stand on the pointed, raised prow of a caravel about to be launched into the Tejo River.

Leading the charge is Prince Henry the Navigator (for more about him, see page 126), holding a model of a caravel and a map, followed by kneeling kings and soldiers who Christianized foreign lands with the sword. Behind Henry (on the west side, away from bridge), find the men who financed the voyages (King Manuel I, holding an armillary sphere, his personal symbol), those who glorified it in poems and paintings (like Luís de Camões, holding a poem), and, at the very end, the only woman, Philippa of Lancaster, Henry's British mother.

On the east side (closest to bridge), Vasco da Gama stands with his eyes on the horizon and his hand on his sword. Magellan holds a circle, representing the round earth his ship circumnavigated, while in front of him, Pedro Cabral puts his hand to his heart, thankful to have (perhaps accidentally) discovered Brazil. Various monks, navigators with maps, and crusaders with flags complete the crew. Check out the pillory, decorated with the Portuguese coat of arms and a cross, erected in each place discovered by the

Portuguese—leaving no doubt as to who was in charge.

In the **marble map in the pavement** (a gift from South Africa) in front of the Monument to the Discoveries, follow Portugal's explorers as they inched out into monster-infested waters at the edge of the world.

From their tiny, isolated nation in Europe, the Portuguese first headed south to the coast of Morocco, conquering the Muslims of Ceuta in God's name (1415), and gaining strategic control of the mouth of the Mediterranean. They braved the open Atlantic to the west and southwest, stumbling on the Madeiras (1420), which Prince Henry planted with vineyards, and to the remote Azore Islands (1427).

Meanwhile, they slowly moved southward, hugging the African coast, each voyage building on the knowledge from previous expeditions. They cleared the biggest psychological hump when Gil Eanes sailed around Cape Bojador (Western Sahara, 1434)—the border of the known world—and into the equatorial seas where sea monsters lurked, no winds blew, and ships would be incinerated in the hot sun. Eanes survived, returning home with 200 Africans in chains, the first of what would become a lucrative, if abhorrent, commodity. Two generations later, Bartolomeu Dias rounded the southern tip of Africa (1488), discovering the sea route to Asia that Vasco da Gama (1498) and others would exploit to colonize India, Indonesia, Japan, and China (Macao in 1557, on the south coast).

In 1500, Pedro Cabral (along with Dias and 1,200 men) took a wi-i-i-ide right turn on the way down the African coast, hoping to avoid windless seas, and landed on the tip of Brazil. Brazil proved to be an agricultural goldmine of sugar plantations worked by African slaves. Three hundred years later, gold and gemstones were discovered in Brazil, jumpstarting the Portuguese economy again.

In 1520, Portuguese Ferdinand Magellan, employed by Spain, sailed west with five ships and 270 men, broke for R&R in Rio, continued through the Straits of Magellan (tip of South America), named the Pacific Ocean, and suffered through mutinies, scurvy, and dinners of sawdust and ship rats before touching land in Guam. Magellan was killed in battle in the Philippines, but one remaining ship continued west and arrived back in Europe, having circumnavigated the globe after 30 months at sea.

By 1560, Portugal's global empire had peaked. Tiny-but-filthy-rich Portugal claimed (though they didn't actually occupy) the entire coastline of Africa, Arabia, India, the Philippines, and south China—a continuous stretch from Lisbon to Macao—plus Brazil. The Treaty of Tordesillas (1494) with Spain divvied up the colonial world between the two nations, split at 45 degrees west longitude (bisecting South America—and explaining why Brazil

Lisbon

The Age of Discovery

In 1560, you could sail from Lisbon to China without ever losing sight of land explored by Portugal. The riches of the world poured into the tiny nation—spices from India and  Java (black pepper, cinnamon, and curry powder); ivory, diamonds, and slaves from Africa (sold to New World plantations); sugarcane, gold, and (later) diamonds from Brazil; and, from everywhere, knowledge of new plants, animals, and customs. How did tiny Portugal pull this off?

First, its people were motivated by greed, hoping to break the Arab and Venetian monopoly on Eastern luxury goods (the price of pepper was jacked up 1,000 percent by the time it reached European dinner tables). They were also driven by a crusading Christian spirit, a love of science, and a spirit of adventure. An entire 15th-century generation was obsessed with finding the legendary kingdom of the fabulously wealthy Christian named "Prester John," supposedly located in either India or Africa. (The legend may be based on a historical figure from around 1120 who visited the pope in Rome as "patriarch of India.")

Portugal also had certain natural advantages. Its Atlantic location led to a strong maritime tradition. A unified nation-state (one of Europe's first) financed and coordinated expeditions. And a core of technology-savvy men used and developed their expansive knowledge of navigational devices, astronomy, maps, shipbuilding, and languages.

speaks Portuguese and the rest of the continent speaks Spanish) and 135 degrees east longitude (bisecting the Philippines and Australia).

But all of the wealth was wasted on Portugal's ruling class, who neglected to reinvest it in the future. Easy money ruined the traditional economy and stunted industry, hurting the poor. Over the next four centuries, one by one, Portugal's colonies were lost to other European nations or to local revolutions. Today, only the (largely autonomous) islands of the Azores and Madeiras remain from the once-global empire.

Folk Art Museum (Museu de Arte Popular)—This museum, closed indefinitely for remodeling, takes you through Portugal's folk art one province at a time, providing a sneak preview of what you'll see throughout the country (€1.50, free Sun until 14:00, free with LisboaCard, Tue–Sun 10:00–12:30 & 14:00–17:00, closed Mon, between the Monument and the Tower on Avenida de Brasília—but it's not the white restaurant in the middle of the pond).

Belém Tower

▲**Belém Tower**—Perhaps the purest Manueline building in Portugal (built 1515–1520), this white tower protected Lisbon's

harbor. Today, it symbolizes the voyages that made Lisbon powerful, with carved stone representing ropes, Manuel's coat of arms, armillary spheres, and shields with the cross of Manuel's military, called the Order

of the Cross. This was the last sight sailors saw as they left, and the first as they returned, loaded with gold, spices, and social diseases. When the tower was built, the river went nearly to the walls of the monastery, and the tower was mid-river. Its interior is pretty bare, but the views of the bridge, river, and Cristo Rei statue are worth the 120 steps.

The floatplane on the grassy lawn is a monument to the first flight across the South Atlantic (Portugal to Brazil) in 1922. The original plane (which beat Charles Lindbergh's *Spirit of Saint Louis* across the North Atlantic by five years) is in Belém's Maritime Museum.

If you're choosing between towers, the Monument to the Discoveries is probably the better choice, because it offers a better view of the monastery. Both towers are interesting to see from the outside, whether or not you go up.

Cost, Hours, Information: €3, free Sun until 14:00, free with LisboaCard, May–Sept Tue–Sun 10:00–18:30, off-season until 17:00, last entry 30 minutes before closing, closed Mon, exhibitions sometimes held here, tel. 213-620-034.

Eating in Belém

You'll find snack bars at Belém Tower, a cafeteria at the Maritime Museum, and fun little restaurants along Rua de Belém, between the Coach Museum and the monastery. I like the busy little **Restaurante Os Jerónimos,** where hardworking Carlos treats his customers well and serves fine €9 meals (Sun–Fri 12:00–22:30, closed Sat, Rua de Belém 74, tel. 213-638-423, next to pastry place described later in this chapter).

Another local favorite for over 25 years is **Rosa dos Mares.** Most tourists miss the upstairs dining area, which has a separate entrance to the right of the café of the same name (Tue–Sun 12:00–15:30 & 19:00–22:30, closed Mon, Rua de Belém 110, left of the pastry place, tel. 213-621-801). Attentive service, excellent grilled fish, and reasonable prices (main dishes for about €10) make this an oasis of calm in an otherwise bustling area. Many more fine places with outdoor seating are in the restaurant row behind the McDonald's that faces the park.

The **Casa Pasteis de Belém** café is the birthplace of the wonderful custard tart that's called *pastel de nata* throughout Portugal, but here is dubbed *pastel de Belém*. Since 1837, locals have come to this café to get them warm out of the oven (daily 8:00–24:00, Rua de Belém 84–92). This place's popularity stems mainly from the fact that their recipe is a closely guarded secret—supposedly only three people know the exact proportions of ingredients. Let's hope they never have a group accident. Sit down and enjoy one with a *café com leite*. Sprinkle on as much cinnamon and powdered sugar as you like. If the café is packed, you'll save time and money by ordering at the bar.

For a delightfully untouristy little adventure, consider having lunch across the river in **Porto Brandão.** The ferry terminal is immediately in front of the Coach Museum, across a busy road and train tracks (€0.77 each way, 8-min cruise, ferries depart on the hour and half hour except 1/hr from 13:30–16:30, last ferry departs 23:00 weekdays and 22:00 weekends; for a memorable Tejo experience, tall men can use the urinal while sticking their head out the porthole). Boats continue to Trafaria before returning to Belém via Porto Brandão. Upon arrival, confirm return times carefully.

Porto Brandão is a tiny (and dead) three-street town whose harborfront square has several good fish restaurants. I like cozy, blue-and-white-tiled **Restaurante Porto Brandão** (€10 fish meals, Mon–Fri 12:00–15:00 & 18:00–23:00, Sat–Sun 12:00–23:00, Rua Bento Jesus Caraça 25, tel. 212-959-145). Their *bacalhau à lagareiro* is for garlic lovers. The *cataplana* (a traditional fish-and-veggie stew) and seafood fondue meals are made for two but stuff three (€15–20/person).

SHOPPING

Lisbon—Portugal's capital city—has shopping opportunities that run the gamut from flea markets to the country's biggest shopping mall.

Produce Market—The market closest to downtown is Mercado da Ribeira (Mon–Sat 6:00–14:00, closed for produce on Sun but open for a coin collectors' market, Metro: Cais do Sodré). If you can't make it to the market, any local grocery store should have a large variety of fresh produce and picnic fare.

Pingo Doce is the largest supermarket chain in Portugal, with a handy location just off Rossio (see listing on page 94).

Flea Markets—On Tuesdays and Saturdays, the Feira da Ladra flea market attracts bargain hunters to Campo de Santa Clara in the Alfama (8:00–15:00, best in morning). A Sunday market—with coins, books, antiques, and more—is at Parque das Nações (10:00–18:00, in garden Garcia da Horta, Metro: Oriente), and another coin market jingles at Mercado da Ribeira, listed earlier in this chapter, on Cais do Sodré (Sun 9:00–13:00).

Colombo Shopping Mall—While downtown Lisbon offers decaying but still elegant department stores, a shopping center in Chiado (described next), classy specialty shops, and a teeming flea market, nothing is as impressive as the enormous Centro Colombo, the largest shopping center in Spain or Portugal. More than 400 shops—including FNAC's biggest department store, 10 cinemas, 60 restaurants, and a health club—sit atop Europe's biggest underground parking lot and under a vast, entertaining play center. There's plenty to amuse children here, and the place offers a fine look at workaday Lisbon (daily 10:00–22:00 for shops, but food court and cinemas remain open until 24:00, pick up a map at info desk, Metro: Colégio Militar/Luz takes you right there, tel. 217-113-636).

Armazéns do Chiado—This grand six-floor shopping center connects Lisbon's lower and upper towns with a world of ways to spend money (part of the Chiado walk described earlier in this chapter, lively food court on sixth floor—see page 93). The FNAC department store hides behind an old facade and is known for its helpful English-speaking staff. Here's how to find the mall: If you approach from Chiado, take Rua Garrett, which dead-ends at the main entrance. If coming from the Baixa, head up Rua Assunção toward the mall, where you'll find three subtle entrances on Rua do Crucifixo—through the Sports Zone store (take their escalators up into the mall), at #113, or at #89 (where small, simple, unmarked doorways lead to elevators). The mall is open daily 10:00–22:00 (eateries 10:00–23:00).

El Corte Inglés—The Spanish mega-department store has arrived in Lisbon with a huge store at the top of Edward VII Park. Inside, there's an enormous supermarket with great picnic supplies, a food court, and a cinema (Mon–Sat 10:00–22:00, closed Sun, Avenida António Augusto de Aguiar 31, Metro: São Sebastião, near Gulbenkian Museum, tel. 213-711-700).

NIGHTLIFE

Nightlife in the Baixa seems to be little more than loitering prostitutes and litter stirred by the wind. Head up instead to the Bairro Alto for fado halls, bars, and the Miradouro de São Pedro de Alcântara (view terrace), a pleasant place to hang out. Nearby Rua Diario de Noticias is lined with busy bars and fun crowds spilling onto the street.

The trendy hot spot for young locals is the dock district under the 25th of April Bridge. The Docas (DOH-kash) is a 400-yard-long strip of warehouses turned into pricey restaurants and discos (particularly Doca de Alcântara and Doca de Santo Amaro). Popular places include Hawaii, Salsa Latina, Havana, and Friday's (catch a taxi or trolley #15E from Praça da Figueira to the stop Avenida Infante Santo, take overpass, then a 10-min walk toward bridge; or bus #714 from Praça da Figueira, ask driver for *"Paragem Docas"*). If you're returning late, night bus #201 starts at 1:00 in the morning, and runs every 30 minutes to Cais do Sodré, where you can walk 15 minutes or connect with night bus #205 or #207 to Rossio.

You can hear classical music by national and city companies at the Gulbenkian Museum and the Cultural Center of Belém. Traditional Portuguese theater plays in the National Theater on Rossio and in theaters along Rua das Portas de Santo Antão (the "eating lane," see page 92) stretching north from Rossio. Buy tickets to all arts and sports events at the green ABEP kiosk on Praça dos Restauradores or at the venue itself.

For popular music, these days you're more likely to find rock, jazz, Brazilian, and African music than traditional fado. The monthly *Agenda Cultural* (free at TI, €0.50 at newsstands) provides the most up-to-date listing of world music, arts, and entertainment (in Portuguese only).

▲▲**Fado**—Fado is the folk music of Lisbon's back streets. Since the mid-1800s, it's been the Lisbon blues—mournfully beautiful and haunting ballads about lost sailors, broken hearts, and bittersweet romance. While generally sad, fado can also be jaunty... but in a nostalgic way.

Fado has become one of Lisbon's favorite late-night tourist traps, but it's easy to find a funky bar—without the high prices and tour groups—that still feels very local. Both the Bairro Alto and the Alfama have small, informal fado restaurants. In the Bairro Alto, wander around Rua Diario de Noticias and neighboring streets. In the Alfama, head uphill from the House of Fado museum. Go either for a late dinner (after 21:00) or an even later evening of drinks and music. Homemade "fado tonight" *(fado esta noite)* signs in Portuguese are good news, but even a restaurant

Lisbon

Fado

Fado songs reflect Portugal's bittersweet relationship with the sea. Fado means "fate"—how fate deals with Portugal's

adventurers...and the women they leave behind. These are songs of both sadness and hope, a bittersweet emotion called *saudade* (meaning yearning or nostalgia). The lyrics reflect the pining for a loved one across the water, hopes for a future reunion, remembrances of a rosy past or dreams of a better future, and the yearning for what might have been if fate had not intervened. (Fado can also be bright and happy when the song is about the virtues of cities such as Lisbon or Coimbra, or of the warmth of a typical *casa portuguesa.*)

The songs are often in a minor key. The singer *(fadista)* is accompanied by a 12-string Portuguese *guitarra* (with a round body like a mandolin) or other stringed instruments unique to Portugal. Many singers crescendo into the first word of the verse, like a moan emerging from deep inside. Though the songs are often sad, the singers rarely overact—they plant themselves firmly and sing stoically in the face of fate.

A verse from a typical fado song goes:

> *O waves of the salty sea,*
> *where do you get your salt?*
> *From the tears shed by the women in black*
> *on the beaches of Portugal.*

filled with tourists can come with good food and fine fado. Prices for a fado performance vary greatly. Many have a steep cover charge, while others just bring out a late-night menu (with prices double those at lunch) and expect you to buy a meal. Any place recommended by a hotel has a bloated price for the kickback.

Fado in Bairro Alto: Run by friendly, English-speaking Gabriel, **Canto do Camões** is easy to reserve and a fine value, with good music, tasty food, and an honest business style. If you reserve a few days in advance, Gabriel can prepare a special regional Portuguese meal for you (open at 20:00, music from 21:00 until around 1:00 in the morning, €23-or-more meal required, after 22:00 €11 minimum for two drinks—if seats are available, call ahead to reserve; from Rua da Misericordia, go 2.5 blocks uphill on Travessa da Espera to #38, see map on page 42; tel. 213-465-464, www.cantodocamoes.com, reservas@cantodocamoes.com). When it's busy, the room feels like a stage show, with 25 or 30 tables, mostly tourists, enjoying classic fado (a series of singers accompanied by two guitarists). Relax, spend some time, and close your eyes, or make eye contact with the singer. Let the music and wine collaborate.

Restaurante Adega do Ribatejo is a dark, homey place crowded with locals who enjoy open-mike fado *(fado vadio)* nightly (except Sun) from around 20:30. This is just around the corner from Gabriel's Canto do Camões, less touristy (almost anti-touristy), but really an adventure, which offers a fado dinner with the lights off (€15 meals, Mon–Sat from 19:00, closed Sun, Rua Diario de Noticias 23, see map on page 42, tel. 213-468-343).

Fado in the Alfama: A tiny, fun-loving restaurant, **A Baiuca** serves up spirited fado with traditional home-cooking. The menu and wine list are straightforward, but the pre-dinner munchies are costly—turn them away. The English-speaking manager, Henrique, welcomes fado enthusiasts who just want a drink (€30 meal and fado, best singing Thu–Mon 20:00–24:00; reservations smart, in the heart of the Alfama, just off Rua São Pedro up the hill from House of Fado, at Rua de São Miguel 20, see map on page 91, tel. 218-867-284). This intimate place is a neighborhood affair, as grandma dances with a bottle on her head, and the cooks gaze out of their steamy hole in the wall to catch the musical action. It's surround sound, as everyone seems to get into the music.

Clube de Fado, a big, bustling, touristy place, has good food and fado nightly (€22 entrées, meal service starts at 20:30, music at 21:30, reservations necessary, around corner from cathedral, Rua São João da Praça 94, see map on page 91, tel. 218-882-604).

▲▲▲**Portuguese Bullfight**—If you always felt sorry for the bull, this is Toro's Revenge—in a Portuguese bullfight, the matador is brutalized along with the bull.

In Act I, the horseman *(cavaleiro)* skillfully plants four beribboned barbs in the bull's back while trying to avoid the leather-padded horns. The horses are the short, stocky Lusitano breed, with excellent balance. In Act II, a colorfully clad eight-man suicide squad (called *forçados*) enters the ring and lines up single file facing the bull. With testosterone sloshing everywhere, the leader taunts the bull—slapping his knees and yelling, *touro!*—then braces himself for a collision that can be heard all the way up in the cheap seats. As he hangs onto the bull's head, his buddies pile on, trying to wrestle the bull to a standstill. Finally, one guy hangs on to *o touro*'s tail and "water-skis" behind him. (In Act III, the *ambulância* arrives.)

Unlike the Spanish *corrida de toros*, the bull is not killed in front of the crowd at the Portuguese *tourada*...but it is killed later. (Some brave bulls with only superficial wounds are spared to fight another day.) Spanish aficionados insist that Portuguese fights are actually more cruel, since they humiliate the bull, rather than fight him as a fellow warrior.

Fights are generally held on Thursday at 20:00 and on Sunday afternoons from mid-June through September (tickets €20–50). The ring is small, so there are no bad seats. To sit nearly at ringside, try the cheapest *bancada* seats, on the generally half-empty and unmonitored main floor (Metro: Campo Pequeno). The ring is a spectacular, Moorish-domed brick structure that bears a resemblance to Madrid's bullring. After five years of remodeling, it reopened with a shopping mall underneath and a variety of restaurants inside, oddly including an Argentine steak restaurant. Maybe the beef served was in the ring earlier?

Important note: Half the fights are simply Spanish-type *corridas* without the killing. For the real slam-bam Portuguese-style fight, confirm that there will be *grupo de forçados* (literally, "bull grabbers"). Tickets are always available at the door (no surcharge, tel. 217-932-143 to confirm). For a 10 percent surcharge, you can buy them at the green ABEP kiosk (also sells concert and movie tickets) at the southern end of Praça dos Restauradores.

Movies—In Lisbon, unlike in Spain, most films are in the original language with subtitles. (That's one reason the Portuguese speak better English than the Spanish.) Many of Lisbon's theaters are classy, complete with assigned seats, ushers, and intermissions. Check the newspaper to see what's playing, or drop by the ABEP kiosk at Praça dos Restauradores, where a list of all the movies playing in town is taped to a side window (on the left). São Jorge Theater (midway up Avenida de Liberdade) is a grand old Art Deco movie palace showing choice cinema selected by the same cultural organization that runs the Castelo de São Jorge and the Monument to the Discoveries. More modern options are in malls or at the Monumental complex in the ritzy Saldanha neighborhood (Metro: Saldanha). During the second half of April, an independent film festival draws movie die-hards.

SLEEPING

With a few exceptions, cheaper hotels downtown feel tired and well-worn. Singles cost nearly the same as doubles. Addresses such as 26–3 stand for building #26, third floor (which is the fourth floor in American terms). For hotel locations, see the map on page 86.

Be sure to book in advance if you'll be in Lisbon during its festival—Festas de Lisboa—the last three weeks of June, when parades, street parties, concerts, and fireworks draw crowds to the city. Conventions can clog Lisbon at any time.

In the Center

Central as can be, the Baixa district bustles with lots of shops, traffic, people, street musicians, pedestrian areas, and urban intensity.

On Rossio

$$$ The elegant, central **Hotel Métropole** keeps its 1920s style throughout 36 rooms. It's a bit overpriced, but you're paying for the prime location. The quieter back rooms are smaller, but cost the same unless you ask for a break. Don't be shy—ask (Sb-€160, Db-€170, extra bed-€50, buffet breakfast, air-con, elevator, Rossio 30, tel. 213-219-030, fax 213-469-166, www.almeidahotels.com, metropole@almeidahotels.com). These are rack rates—prices drop by a third in slow times (check website for special discounts or ask when you reserve).

On Praça dos Restauradores

$$$ **Hotel Avenida Palace,** the most characteristic five-star splurge in town, was built with the Rossio Station in 1892 to greet big-shot travelers. Back then, trains were new, and Rossio was the

---

Sleep Code

(€1 = about $1.40, country code: 351)
S = Single, **D** = Double/Twin, **T** = Triple, **Q** = Quad, **b** = bathroom, **s** = shower only. Unless otherwise noted, credit cards are accepted, English is spoken, and breakfast is included.

To help you easily sort through these listings, I've divided the rooms into three categories, based on the price for a standard double room with bath during high season:

$$$ **Higher Priced**—Most rooms €115 or more.
$$ **Moderately Priced**—Most rooms between €60–115.
$ **Lower Priced**—Most rooms €60 or less.

Central Lisbon Hotels and Restaurants

❶ Hotel Métropole		⓮ To Rest. Solar dos Presuntos
❷ Hotel Avenida Palace		⓯ Restaurante Gandhi Palace
❸ VIP Executive Suites Eden		⓰ Pastelaria Suíça
❹ Hotel Lisboa Tejo		⓱ Restaurante Pic-Nic
❺ Grande Pensão Alcobia		⓲ Confeitaria Nacional
❻ Pensão Praça da Figueira		⓳ Armazéns do Chiado Mall
❼ Pensão Gerês		⓴ Restaurante Beira-Gare
❽ Residencial Florescente		㉑ Martinho da Arcada
❾ Albergaria Residencial Insulana		㉒ Rua 1 de Dezembro Eateries
❿ To Avenida da Liberdade Hotels, Ibis Hotels & Cervejaria Ribadouro		㉓ Ca das Sandes (2)
		㉔ Pingo Doce Supermarket
⓫ Cervejaria da Trindade		㉕ Internet Café
⓬ Bonjardim, Rei dos Frangos & Restaurante Machado		㉖ Laundry
⓭ Casa do Alentejo		

only station in town. The lounges are sumptuous, dripping with chandeliers, and the 82 rooms mix elegance with 21st-century comforts (Sb-€175, Db-€205, 15 percent less July–Aug, more expensive suites available, reserve on website for substantial discounts, air-con, elevator, laundry service, free parking, hotel's sign is on Praça dos Restauradores but entrance is at Rua 1 de Dezembro 123, tel. 213-218-100, fax 213-422-884, www.hotel-avenida-palace. pt, reservas@hotel-avenida-palace.pt).

$$$ VIP Executive Suites Eden rents 134 slick and contemporary compact apartments (with small kitchens). It has a roof-

top swimming pool and terrace with commanding city, castle, and river views. The building used to be a 1930s cinema, hence the Art Deco architecture and the slightly pie-shaped rooms. Perfectly located at the Rossio end of Avenida da Liberdade, this is a clean, quiet pool of modernity amid the ramshackle charm of Lisbon. It's also an intriguing option for groups or families of four (Db studio-€121, two-bedroom apartment with bed-and-sofa combo that can sleep four people-€176, breakfast-€9, includes taxes, air-con, elevator, Praça dos Restauradores 24, tel. 213-216-600, fax 213-216-666, www.viphotels.com, res.eden@viphotels.com).

Near Praça da Figueira

$$$ Hotel Lisboa Tejo (leezh-BO-ah TAY-zhoo) is an oasis of 58 comfy ocean-blue rooms with hardwood floors (Sb-€105,

Db-€120, includes crowded buffet breakfast, air-con, elevator, Internet access, laundry service; from southeast corner of Praça da Figueira, walk 1 block down Rua dos Condes de Monsanto and turn left, Condes de Monsanto 2; tel. 218-866-182, fax 218-865-163, www.evidenciahoteis.com, hotellisboatejo@evidenciagrupo.com).

$$ Grande Pensão Alcobia opened in 2006 with 44 crisp, new rooms. It offers a comfortable alternative to higher-priced hotels located in the same part of town, and some upper-floor rooms have views of the Castelo São Jorge (Sb-€45–60, Db-€50–70, Tb-€90–105, 25 percent more in Aug, air-con, small elevator, Poço do Borratem 15, tel. 218-844-150, fax 218-864-201, www.pensaoalcobia.com, residencial.alcobia@mail.ptprime.pt).

$ Pensão Praça da Figueira is justifiably in many guidebooks given its central location and affordable prices. Clean, basic rooms share kitchens on every floor, and a little extra street noise is the only trade-off (S-€28–35, Sb-€38–45, D-€40–45, Db-€48–55, 2 flights up with no elevator, entrance is on Travessa Nova de São Domingos 9 behind Praça da Figueira, tel. 213-426-757, fax 213-424-323, www.pensaopracadafigueira.com, pensaofigueira@clix.pt).

Near Rossio

$$ Pensão Gerês rents 20 bright, basic, cozy rooms with older plumbing but without the dingy smokiness that pervades Lisbon's cheaper hotels. Double-paned windows keep out most of the street noise (S-€45–50, Sb-€55–60, Db-€65–75, Tb-€85–100, 10 percent discount Nov–March with cash and this book, no breakfast, Internet access, uphill a block off northeast corner of Rossio, Calçada do Garcia 6, tel. 218-810-497, fax 218-882-006, www.pensaogeres.com). The Nogueira family speaks some English.

$ Residencial Florescente rents 68 rooms on the "eating lane," a thriving pedestrian street a block off Praça dos Restauradores (see page 92). It's an Old World slumber mill with narrow halls and clean rooms (Sb-€40–45, Db-€50–55, Db twin-€60–70, Tb-€70–80, air-con, free Wi-Fi, Rua Portas de Santo Antão 99, tel. 213-426-609, fax 213-427-733, www.residencialflorescente.com).

$ Albergaria Residencial Insulana, on a pedestrian street, has 32 quiet, airy rooms and a professional, friendly staff (big Sb-€52, Db-€62, extra bed-€15, air-con, elevator, Rua da Assunção 52, tel. 213-423-131, fax 213-428-924, www.insulana.cjb.net, info@insulana.net, Fernando).

Along Avenida da Liberdade

These listings are a 10-minute walk or short Metro ride from the center. The following two places, jointly owned, offer a deal in July and August: free entrance to Lisbon's museums for guests who stay at least three nights.

$$$ Hotel Lisboa Plaza, a large, plush four-star gem, mixes traditional style with bright-pastel classiness. With 106 rooms, it offers snappy and polite service, all the amenities, and a free glass of port with this book (Sb-€146–180, Db-€156–195, Tb-€183–225, higher prices apply March–June and Sept–Oct, larger "superior" rooms cost 25 percent more, buffet breakfast-€14, air-con, laundry service, two non-smoking and one non-allergic floor, free Wi-Fi, parking-€9/day, well-located on a quiet street off busy Avenida da Liberdade a block from Metro: Avenida, Travessa do Salitre 7, tel. 213-218-218, fax 213-471-630, www.heritage.pt, plaza.hotels @heritage.pt).

$$$ Hotel Britania maintains its 1940s Art Deco charm throughout its 33 spacious rooms, offering a clean and professional haven on a tranquil street one block off Avenida da Liberdade. Three new top-floor suites are decorated in a luxurious Mod Deco. Run by the Hotel Lisboa Plaza folks (previous listing), it offers the same four-star standards for the same prices (air-con, elevator, laundry service, non-smoking floor, free Wi-Fi, free street parking or €9/day in next-door garage; Rua Rodrigues Sampaio 17, from Metro: Avenida stop, walk uphill on boulevard, turn right on Rua Manuel de Jesus Coelho and take first left; tel. 213-155-016, fax 213-155-021, www.heritage.pt, britania.hotel@heritage.pt).

$$ Residência Roma, a hardworking little place, rents 40 simple but comfy rooms. It's tucked away on a side street, 50 yards off the big Avenida da Liberdade (Sb-€45–60, Db-€50–70, Tb-€90–105, 25 percent more in Aug, air-con, no elevator, Travessa da Glória 22, tel. 213-460-558, fax 213-460-557, www.residenciaroma .com, res.roma@cyclopnet.pt, Cristina).

$ Residencial 13 da Sorte ("Lucky 13"), like Residência Roma, rents 19 basic rooms on a sleepy side street just off Avenida da Liberdade (big Sb-€35–40, Db-€45–60, Tb-€55–65, air-con, elevator, tile floors, Rua do Salitre 13, tel. 213-539-746, tel. & fax 213-531-851, www.trezedasorte.no.sapo.pt, 13_da_sorte@sapo.pt).

Away from the Center

$$$ In Belém: For modern comforts on the edge of town, consider the newly remodeled **Jerónimos 8 Hotel,** which rents 65 rooms next to the monastery (Sb-€160, Db-€180, extra bed-€15–18, includes buffet breakfast, air-con, double-paned windows, elevator, Internet access, laundry service, Rua dos Jerónimos 8, see map on page 67, tel. 213-300-540, mobile 916-172-701, fax 213-525-148, www.maisturismo.pt/htorre, jeronimos8@almeidahotels.com).

$$ Ibis Hotels: Three Ibis hotels offer no-stress, no-character rooms for a good price in soulless areas away from the center—but with handy Metro stations nearby. Each has non-smoking floors, air-conditioning, and €5 breakfasts (www.ibishotel.com). **Ibis**

Liberdade has the best location (70 rooms, Sb or Db-€68, 2 blocks uphill from Avenida da Liberdade's Hotel Tivoli, Metro: Avenida, Barata Salgueiro 53, tel. 213-300-630, fax 213-300-631). The others are **Ibis Saldanha** (116 rooms, Sb/Db-€65, 2-min walk from Metro: Saldanha, Avenida Casal Ribeiro 23, tel. 213-191-690, fax 213-191-699) and **Ibis José Malhoa** (211 rooms, Sb or Db-€57, next to Metro: Praça de Espanha, Avenida José Malhoa, tel. 217-235-700, fax 217-235-701).

EATING

Ideally, one dinner of your stay in Lisbon should be accompanied by a fado performance. Several good options for this musical dinner are listed under "Nightlife," page 81.

Between the Castle and the Alfama Viewpoint

These are listed in order from the castle to the viewpoint.

Arco do Castelo, an eight-table Indo-Portuguese restaurant, dishes up delicious fish and shrimp curries (how spicy is up to you) from Goa, a former Portuguese colony in India. Top off your €10 meal with a shot of the Goan firewater, *feni,* made from cashews (Mon–Sat 12:30–24:00, closed Sun, just across from ramp leading into castle at Rua do Chão da Feira 25, tel. 218-876-598).

The hip **Restô do Chapitô** offers superb views of the river, whether you relax upstairs amid the tasteful and warm decor, in the woody, pub-like downstairs, or on the welcoming, bohemian patio. Dinner from the rotating international menu costs €20 to €25—less for appetizers (Tue–Fri 19:30–24:00, Sat–Sun 12:00–2:00, closed Mon, free jazz after 23:00, cash only; from below the castle—at Arco do Castelo restaurant—go right on Rua do Chaoda Feira 50 yards downhill, take first right to Costa de Castelo 7; tel. 218-867-334).

Largo do Contador Mor—a wispy, cobbled square a block above the Miradouro de Santa Luzia viewpoint and a block below the castle—has two eateries. **A Tasquinha Restaurante,** at the top of the square, is touristy with marginal service, but it has atmospheric outdoor seating. They serve fine €8 plates of grilled sardines, called *sardinhas assadas* (Thu–Tue 12:00–19:00, closed Wed, Largo do Contador Mor 5). Eat healthy at **Comidas de Santiago,** an inexpensive little salad bar with refreshing summer gazpacho—but understand your bill before you pay (daily 12:00–23:00, Largo do Contador Mor 21, tel. 218-875-805).

For a nice seafood feast, consider dining high in the Alfama at the **Farol de Santa Luzia** restaurant (€17 fixed-price *menu turistico* for lunch, Mon–Sat 12:00–23:00, closed Sun, Largo Santa Luzia 5, across from Santa Luzia viewpoint terrace, no sign but a window

Alfama Restaurants

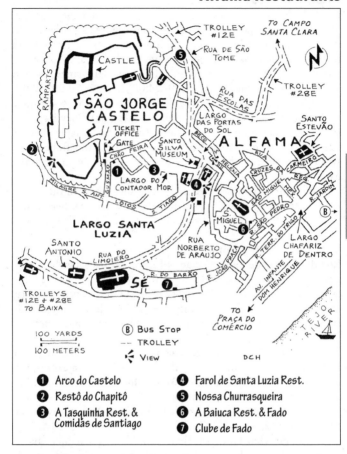

full of decals, tel. 218-863-884). Their service is sometimes slow, but their friendliness makes up for the delay.

To mix in some adventure with your sardines, walk past Portas do Sol and follow the trolley tracks along Rua de São Tomé to a square called Largo Rodrigues Freitas. There you'll find **Nossa Churrasqueira** busy serving chicken, sardines, and cod on rickety tables to finger-lickin' locals with meager budgets (chicken with vegetables-€9, sardines-€5.50, Tue–Sun 12:00–22:00, closed Mon; if riding trolley #12E, it's at the first stop over the big hill). This neighborhood, a gritty chunk of pre-earthquake Lisbon, is full of interesting eateries. Brighten a few dark bars. Have an aperitif; taste the *branco seco* (local dry white wine). Make a friend, pet a chicken, ponder the graffiti, and ponder the humanity ground between the cobbles.

In Bairro Alto

Lisbon's "high town" has plenty of small, fun, and cheap places. The bright **Cervejaria da Trindade,** a Portuguese-style beer hall, is full of historic tiles, seafood, and tourists. It's overpriced and in all the guidebooks, but people enjoy the bright and boisterous atmosphere (€15 meals, confirm prices especially since seafood is charged by weight, daily 12:00–24:00, liveliest 20:00–22:00, closed holidays, air-con, courtyard, a block down from São Roque at Rua Nova da Trindade 20C, tel. 213-423-506). They have five Portuguese beers on tap—Sagres is the standard lager, Sagres Preta is a good dark beer (similar to a porter), and Bohemia is sweet, with more alcohol. Light meals and snacks are served at the bar and in the front.

You'll find many less touristy restaurants deeper in the Bairro Alto on the other (west) side of Rua da Misericordia. See "Fado" under "Nightlife," page 81, for the best option, Canto do Camões.

On the "Eating Lane"

Rua das Portas de Santo Antão is Lisbon's "eating lane"—a galaxy of eateries with excellent seafood (off the northeast corner of Rossio). While the waiters are pushy and it's all very touristy, the lane—lively with happy eaters—is enjoyable to browse. This is a fine spot to down a beer, snack on some snails, and watch the people go by.

The small side street, Travessa de Santo Antão, is famous for three diner-style restaurants popular with locals—**Bonjardim, Rei dos Frangos,** and **Restaurante Machado**—that crank out tasty roasted chicken (paint on some spicy African *piri-piri* sauce) and fries, for eating inside or streetside (daily 11:00–23:00, Travessa de Santo Antão 12, tel. 213-427-424).

Casa do Alentejo, specializing in Alentejo cuisine, fills an old second-floor ballroom. The Moorish-looking building is a cultural and social center for people from the traditionalist southern province of Portugal (see jokes in Évora chapter, page 145) living in Lisbon (two-course special of the day-€11, daily 12:00–15:00 & 19:00–22:00, slip into closed-looking building at Rua das Portas de Santo Antão 58 and climb stairs to the right, tel. 213-469-231). While the food is mainly hearty and simple (like the Alentejanos), the ambience is fabulous. It's a good place to try pork with clams or the eggy almond dessert *encharcada*, both regional specialties. For a full-bodied Alentejo red wine, go with the Borba or simply try the house red.

Restaurante Solar dos Presuntos keeps the theater crowd happily fed with meat and seafood specialties. Its upstairs is subdued, while the downstairs—with a colorful, open kitchen—is touristy and rowdy (€15–20 meals, at the far end of the "eating lane" at Rua das Portas de Santo Antão 150, tel. 213-424-253).

Restaurante Gandhi Palace, a downtown Indian eatery with a friendly staff and nonstop Bollywood movies on the TV, is a local favorite for an inexpensive lunch under €10. Eat in the Pombaline building, or ask for your order to go *(para fora)* and picnic at a viewpoint...with thoughts of Vasco da Gama's India-bound voyage (daily 11:30–15:00 & 18:00–24:00, follow your nose just off Praça da Figueira to Rua dos Douradores 214, tel. 218-873-839).

On and Near Rossio

Pastelaria Suíça (SWEE-sah) is a bright, modern, air-conditioned place popular with locals (in spite of its surly waitstaff) because it's elegant but affordable and free of riff-raff. They serve more than pastry—try the light meals, sandwiches, salads, and fruit cups (daily 7:00–21:00, inexpensive at the bar, reasonable at inside tables, expensive at outside tables overlooking Rossio or Praça da Figueira, located directly between the two squares with entrances and terraces on each). Across the plaza, **Restaurante Pic-Nic** is a slightly lowbrow, bustling diner, good for breakfast or a light meal and people-watching on the sidewalk.

Confeitaria Nacional has been proudly satisfying sweet tooths for over 175 years—they were once praised by Portuguese royalty. Stop in for a tasty pastry downstairs or enjoy Old World sophistication in the dining room upstairs. You'll find the classy setting—with white tablecloths, sparkling chandeliers, and great street-scene views—affordable at lunch, when traditional fixed-price meals are around €10. Salads and the €13 entrées are a good option here (Mon–Sat 8:00–22:00, closed Sun, on Praça da Figueira 18 just opposite Carris ticket booth).

Armazéns do Chiado shopping center has a sixth-floor food court with few tourists in sight, offering a huge selection of fun eateries from traditional Portuguese to Chinese (daily about 12:00–23:00, between the low and high towns, between Rua Garrett and Rua da Assunção; from the low town, find the inconspicuous elevator at Rua do Crucifixo 89 or 113, next to the Baixa-Chiado Metro entrance). Some of the mall's eateries are actual restaurants (that get quiet from about 15:00–18:00); others are smaller fast-food counters that share a common eating area and serve all day. Here are several to consider: **Chimarrão,** a Brazilian place with Brazilian staff (no English spoken), offers an impressive self-serve buffet (€6.50 veggie bar or €9 for carnivores); they also have desserts and tropical juices and fruits (€2.50 or €4.50, separate from buffet). This is where healthy eaters assemble the plate of their dreams—by far the best vegetarian and fruit-filled place I found. Study the exotic juice sheet on the table. Stick with the buffet, since table service doubles the price. (Wait to be seated, raid the meat counter and the salad bar, order drinks at your table, and pay as you leave.) On the same floor at the opposite end, you'll find **Loja das Sopas,** which offers hearty soups with €5 fixed-price meals (find a table in the food court nearby), plus **Caffè di Roma** and a branch of **Café A Brasileira,** with a wide assortment of fancy coffee drinks. A lot of these places have castle views. Opposite Café A Brasileira, **Vitaminas & Companhia** dishes out healthy big-bowl pasta salads topped with tropical fruits.

For cod and vegetables prepared faster than a Big Mac and served with more energy than a soccer team, stand or sit at **Restaurante Beira-Gare,** a greasy-spoon diner with a pork sandwich *(bifana no pão)* house specialty. The soup-and-sandwich deal is only €3 (Mon–Sat 6:00–24:00, closed Sun, in front of Rossio Station at the end of Rua 1 de Dezembro).

Martinho da Arcada, one of poet Fernando Pessoa's old haunts, is a fine option on Praça do Comércio. Founded in 1782, it still enjoys a good reputation, with red-vested waiters serving tasty, traditional cuisine (€20 meals, Mon–Sat 12:00–15:30 & 19:00–22:00, closed Sun, Praça do Comércio 8 at the Rua da Prata corner, tel. 218-879-259).

The street **Rua 1 de Dezembro,** in the Rossio area, is lined with competitive and very cheap restaurants. It's lively for lunch, but dead at dinner. Walk the street and determine the prevailing menu of the day. Most options are self-service, with speed being the priority for the busy office workers who eat here. The chain of little **Ca das Sandes** sandwich shops, found here and scattered about town, offer healthy sandwiches (that you design Subway-style), salads, and occasionally outdoor seating (daily 9:00–20:00). **Pingo Doce** is a fine supermarket one block south of Rossio Station with pre-made fruit and veggie salads (daily 8:30–21:00, you can request a €0.02 plastic bag when checking out, kitty-corner from a Ca das Sandes shop, on Rua 1 de Dezembro and Calçada do Carmo).

Up Avenida da Liberdade: **Cervejaria Ribadouro** is a popular splurge with locals because of its quality meat and shellfish (€15 meals, daily 12:00–24:00, Avenida da Liberdade 155, at intersection with Rua do Salitre, Metro: Avenida, tel. 213-549-411). Note that seafood prices are listed by the kilogram; the waiter will help you determine the cost of a portion. To limit the cost, actually write down the number of grams you want. For a fun, quick meal or snack anytime, order 100 grams (about a quarter of a pound—good for one person) of *percebes*—barnacles—at the bar with a small beer and *pão torrado com manteiga* (toasted bread with butter).

TRANSPORTATION CONNECTIONS

From Lisbon by Train to: Madrid (1/day, "Lusitânia" overnight 22:00–8:49, 10 hrs; first class-€76, second class-€58; ticket and bed: €81 in quad, €102 in double, €147 in single; discount with rail-pass—for example, about €20 for a bed in quad, €40 in double, €78 in single; cash only; train departs from Santa Apolónia Station), **Paris** (1/day, 16:06–13:45, 21.5 hrs, departs Santa Apolónia, arrives at Paris' Gare Montparnasse), **Évora** (2/day, 2 hrs, departs Oriente, may transfer in Casa Branca; bus has more departures daily), **Lagos** (6/day, 3.5–4.5 hrs, departs Oriente, transfer in Tunes), **Tavira** (6/day, 5 hrs, transfer in Faro), **Coimbra** (almost hourly, 2 hrs, departs Santa Apolónia, see page 31 for details), **Nazaré/Valado** (3/day, 3.5–5 hrs, more frequent departures with transfers; bus is better—see below), **Óbidos** (8/day, 2.25 hrs, transfer in Cacém), **Porto** (4–8/day, 3.75–5.5 hrs, departs Santa Apolónia), **Sintra** (4/hr, 35 min, departs Central Rossio Station, €3.20 round trip; for suggested day-trip connections, see page 97). For train info, call tel. 808-208-208. Note: Any train leaving from Santa Apolónia also leaves from the Oriente Station (which has Metro access from downtown) a few minutes later.

To Salema: Both the bus and train take about four to five hours from Lisbon to Lagos (see Lagos connections above and below). Trains from Lisbon to the Algarve leave from the Oriente Station on the Lisboa–Faro line. At Tunes, there is a transfer to a local train that takes you as far as Lagos. From here, it's either a bus or €16 taxi ride to Salema (see page 114 for details).

From Lisbon by Bus to: Coimbra (13/day, 2.5 hrs, €11.50), **Nazaré** (6/day, 2 hrs, €8.30), **Fátima** (hourly, 1.5–2.5 hrs, €9), **Batalha** (4/day, 2 hrs, €9), **Alcobaça** (6/day, 2/day direct, 2 hrs, €8.80), **Óbidos** (8/day, all with transfer in Caldas da Rainha, 1.25 hrs), **Évora** (hourly, 2 hrs, €10.80), **Lagos** (12/day, 4 hrs, some transfer in Albufeira, €17.50, easier than train, must book ahead, get details at TI), **Tavira** (9/day direct, 4.25 hrs, €18), **Madrid** (3/day, 10–16 hrs, €44), **Sevilla** (2/day, 8 hrs, may be less off-season, €40; trains also run to Sevilla, but the bus is your best and fastest option). Bus tickets to Spain are sold by InterCentro Lines in Lisbon, but the service is run by Alsa (www.alsa.es). All buses leave from Lisbon's bus station (Metro: Jardim Zoológico, tel. 707-223-344).

Flying: You can generally buy a plane ticket to Madrid on short notice for as little as €60 or as much as €200, depending on the time of year (usually 5 flights/day). Shop around to get the best deal. Vueling usually has the cheapest flights while specials by Spanair or Iberia may beat their price.

Driving in Lisbon

Driving in Lisbon is big-city crazy. If you're starting your trip in Lisbon, don't rent a car until you're on your way out.

If you enter Lisbon from the north, a series of boulevards takes you into the center. Navigate by following signs to *Centro, Avenida da República, Marquês de Pombal, Avenida da Liberdade, Praça dos Restauradores, Rossio,* and *Praça do Comércio.* If coming from the east over the Vasco da Gama Bridge and heading for the airport, take the first exit after the bridge.

If you're turning in your car upon arrival in Lisbon, consider driving to the airport (rental-car turn-in clearly signposted, no extra expense to drop it here, very helpful TI open late) and riding a sweat-free taxi for €10 to your hotel. Or consider hiring a taxi (cheap) and following it to your hotel.

There are many safe underground pay parking lots (follow the blue *P* signs), but they get more expensive by the hour and can cost €40 per day (at the most central Praça dos Restauradores).

SINTRA

For centuries, Portugal's aristocracy considered Sintra the perfect place to escape from Lisbon. Now tourists do, too. On a day trip to Sintra, you can climb through the Versailles of Portugal, the Pena Palace, and romp along the ruined ramparts of a deserted Moorish castle on a neighboring hilltop.

Sintra is a mix of natural and man-made beauty: fantasy castles set amid exotic tropical plants, lush green valleys, and craggy hilltops with hazy views of the Atlantic and Lisbon. For centuries, Sintra—just 15 miles northwest of Lisbon—was the summer escape of Portugal's kings. Those with money and a desire to be close to royalty built their palaces amid luxuriant gardens in the same neighborhood. Lord Byron called this bundle of royal fancies and aristocratic dreams a "glorious Eden," and even though it's mobbed with tourists today, it's still magnificent. Various music festivals in June and July keep it lively and fun.

With extra time, explore the rugged and picturesque westernmost tip of Portugal at Cabo da Roca. You can also mix and mingle with the jet set (or at least press your nose against their windows) at the resort towns of Cascais or Estoril.

Planning Your Time

By Public Transportation

Sintra Day Trip from Lisbon: Try to arrive in Sintra by 9:45, since most major sights open by 10:00.

Catch the train to Sintra from Lisbon's Central Rossio Station (direct, 4/hr, 35 min). Buy your ticket upstairs in the lobby in front of the tracks, either at the ticket office or from the easy-to-use machines (select English, pop in coins or small bills—€3.20

Near Lisbon

Train Stations
1. Oriente
2. Santa Apolónia
3. Rossio
4. Sete Rios
5. Cais do Sodré

round-trip, free with LisboaCard, TV monitor in lobby lists departure times). Your ticket will eventually be punched by someone on board. During your ride, take in the views of the 18th-century aqueduct (on the left) and the workaday Lisbon suburbs. Sintra is at the end of the line.

If you're staying outside the downtown core, you could depart instead from Lisbon's Sete Rios Station to reach Sintra (in Lisbon, take Metro's blue line to Jardim Zoológico, then follow signs for *comboio* up to ground level). At the green CP ticket vending machine, punch "Sintra" and insert your fare (€3.20 round-trip, free with LisboaCard, 4/hr, 35 min). The train departs from platform Linha 2 upstairs (take escalator to left of ticket machines). Be careful: Many trains use this platform, so make sure your train is marked *Sintra*. On your return, take the Roma-Areeiro train and get off at the Sete Rios Station. (Don't worry if you miss your stop—the last station is on the Metro's red line.)

Loop Trip of the Peninsula from Lisbon: If you're bent on seeing everything west of Lisbon (Sintra, Cabo da Roca, Cascais, and Estoril) in a long day, consider a slam-bam swing around the peninsula by bus on Carris Tours' Sintra Tour from Lisbon (€35, 4.5 hours; see page 39).

It's also possible to make a loop trip using public transportation:

Buy a one-way train ticket to Sintra in Lisbon, and see the sights in Sintra—but instead of buying a €4 ticket on the #434 bus, buy an €8.50 day ticket. This bus pass gets you up the hill to Pena Palace, and also allows you to catch bus #403 (at the Sintra train station) for a trip out to Cabo da Roca. You can hop off at Cabo da Roca, buy a diploma at the TI to prove you were there, then catch bus #403 again for the jaunt to Cascais and a seafood dinner on the waterfront.

Estoril is a short train ride away on the same line to Lisbon, but seeing both Cascais and Estoril is probably redundant, and Cascais is more appealing. (Bullfight fans could enjoy a bullfight—if scheduled—in either city.) From Cascais or Estoril, returning to Lisbon is a snap—just buy a one-way train ticket to Lisbon at the train station. You'll get off at the last stop on the line (Cais de Sodré Station), a five-minute walk from Praça do Comércio in downtown Lisbon.

By Car
Sintra Day Trip from Lisbon: Sintra itself is far easier by train than by car from Lisbon. Consider waiting until after you visit Sintra to pick up your rental car. If you do take a car to Sintra, take the IC-19 freeway out of Lisbon (allow 30 min). When you arrive, follow Sintra *Centro Histórico* signs. Cars are the curse of Sintra—traffic can be terrible and parking difficult. Park your car and use the #434 bus to get around. If you decide (probably regrettably) to drive to the sights, you'll take a one-way winding loop and be encouraged to park as soon as you can or risk having to drive the huge loop again.

Loop Trip: It's possible to make a 70-mile circular trip and drive to all the destinations near Lisbon within a day (Lisbon–Belém–Sintra–Cabo da Roca–Cascais–Lisbon), but traffic congestion around Sintra, especially on weekends and during rush hour, can mess up your schedule.

Continuing to the Algarve: Drivers eager for beach time can leave Lisbon, visit Sintra, and drive directly to the Algarve that evening (4 hours from Lisbon). To get to the Algarve from Sintra/Cascais, get on the freeway heading for Lisbon and exit at the *Sul Ponte A2* sign, which takes you over the 25th of April Bridge and south on A2.

ORIENTATION

Small, hilly Sintra is gravitationally challenged, and its three main sights—the National Palace, Pena Palace, and Moorish Castle—are farther apart than they appear on the tourist maps. The town itself sprawls at the foot of a hill, a 10-minute walk (or shorter bus ride) from the train station. The National Palace, with its unmistakable pair of cone-shaped chimneys, is in the center of the town, a block from the TI. But the other two main sights are a steep, long, uphill walk from town; most prefer to take the local bus. If you're trying to decide, look up from the center of town to see the Moorish Castle wall on top of the hill—that's how far you'll have to hike.

Tourist Information

Sintra has two TIs: a small one in the train station (tel. 219-241-623) and a larger one a block off the main square in the Museu Regional building (both open daily June–Sept 9:00–20:00, Oct–May 9:00–19:00, tel. 219-231-157, both have WCs and sell the LisboaCard, www.cm-sintra.pt). Pick up a free map with information on sights, and a schedule for the #434 shuttle bus. Culture vultures should also pick up a free copy of *Sintra Cultural*, which lists all the current month's events. The TI can arrange *quartos* (rooms in private homes, Db-€25–60) for overnighters.

Arrival in Sintra

By Train: After stopping at the TI in the train station, you can head for the town center on foot (exit station and go left for easy, level 10-min walk) or by bus #434 (exit station to the right, €4, valid all day; for more bus info, see "Getting Around Sintra," page 102). Modern art–lovers can easily visit the Museum of Modern Art before heading into town (exit station to the right).

If you arrive early in Sintra (local bus service starts at 9:35), walk into town. Visit the National Palace, then grab a picnic lunch and catch bus #434 up to the Pena Palace (also has café). Enjoy lunch in the gardens at Pena Palace, and then tour the palace. Walk down to the Moorish Castle ruins and explore. From the castle, take a 30-minute hike down a steep, wooded path into town (get hiking instructions and map at castle entry; fork in path leads down from within the castle grounds). Catch the train back to Lisbon for dinner.

By Car: There's a strip of parking along Volta do Duche, near the town center (€0.50/hr, 2-hour maximum). A small lot is also next to the train station. The most central free parking is on Rio do Porto in the valley just below and northeast of town (after parking, climb the long set of steps to get up to the main square).

Helpful Hints

Closed Days: Note that Pena Palace and the Museum of Modern Art are closed Monday. The National Palace is closed Wednesday.

Sintra

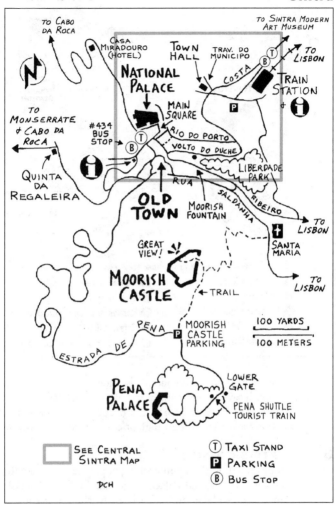

Free Entry: The National Palace, Museum of Modern Art, and the gardens at Pena Palace are free until 14:00 on Sunday.

LisboaCard: This sightseeing pass covers the National Palace (but not the Museum of Modern Art), and gets you a discount on the Pena Palace, Moorish Castle, Toy Museum, and the Monserrate gardens. If you decide to get the pass, buy it at a Lisbon TI before you visit Sintra, because it covers your train ride here (see page 30). It's also sold at Sintra's two TIs (opposite page). Be sure to bring the LisboaCard booklet; some

Central Sintra

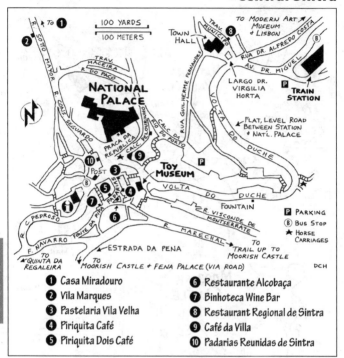

1 Casa Miradouro
2 Vila Marques
3 Pastelaria Vila Velha
4 Piriquita Café
5 Piriquita Dois Café

6 Restaurante Alcobaça
7 Binhoteca Wine Bar
8 Restaurant Regional de Sintra
9 Café da Villa
10 Padarias Reunidas de Sintra

discounts require coupons contained inside.

Bring a Picnic: If saving a few euros is important, consider bringing picnic items purchased in Lisbon. Sintra's reputation as a tourist destination means accordingly high prices for restaurant meals.

Getting Around Sintra

Bus #434 loops together all the important stops: the train station, the town center/TI/National Palace (stop is at TI), the Moorish Castle ruins, Pena Palace, and then back to the train station (June–mid-Sept 4/hr, mid-Sept–May 3/hr, €4 ticket good for 24 hours, buy from driver; first bus starts at 9:35 from train station, last one leaves station at 18:05, 17:05 in winter, entire circuit takes 30 min).

To reach the Pena Palace and Moorish Castle from the town center or the train station, catch bus #434 or take a taxi. Taxis don't use a meter, but have set fares (about €8 from town center or train station to Pena Palace, confirm with driver). On your way to the Pena Palace, you'll pass by the entrance to the Moorish Castle. At the top of the hill, where the bus or taxi drops you off, it's still another 10-minute uphill walk to the Pena Palace entrance (or take green shuttle bus; described later in this chapter).

From the Pena Palace, it's a 15-minute walk backtracking downhill to the Moorish Castle (return to bus-and-taxi stop, then follow signs down road to *Moorish Castle*).

The clip-clop **horse carriages** cost about €30 for 25 minutes (confirm their posted rates). They can take you anywhere; you'll likely see them waiting by the parking lot just in front of the National Palace.

SIGHTS

▲▲National Palace (Palácio Nacional)

While the palace dates back to Moorish times, most of what you'll see is from the 15th-century reign of King John (João) I, with later

Manueline architectural ornamentation from the 16th century. This oldest surviving royal palace in Portugal is still used for official receptions. Having housed royalty for 500 years (until 1910), it's fragrant with history.

Cost, Hours, Location: €4, free with LisboaCard and on Sun until 14:00, Thu–Tue 10:00–17:30, last entry 17:00, closed Wed, no photos. It's the white, Madonna-bra building in the town center, a 10-min walk from the train station (tel. 219-106-840).

⊙ Self-Guided Tour: The palace is a one-way romp with little information provided. As you tour the place, stop in these notable parts of the palace:

Swan Room: This first room is the palace's banquet room. A king's daughter—who loved swans—married into a royal house in Belgium. The king missed the princess so much that he decorated the ceiling with her favorite animal. These aren't the only creatures in the room, though. Check out the ceramic soup tureens designed in the shape of your favorite barnyard animal.

Courtyard: This was a fortified medieval palace, so rather than fancy gardens outside, it has a stay-awhile courtyard within its protective walls. Notice the unique chimneys. Hans Christian Andersen said they looked like two grand bottles of champagne. I disagree. Whatever they look like, they give the kitchen a marvelous open-domed feeling, as you'll see at the end of your tour.

Magpie Room: King John I was caught kissing a lady-in-waiting by his queen. Frustrated by his court—abuzz with gossip—John had this ceiling painted with magpies. But to show what a good-spirited guy he was, around each magpie is the king's slogan—*por bem*, "for good." The 15th-century Moorish tiles are from Spain, brought in before the development of the famous, ubiquitous Portuguese tiles.

King's Bedroom: The king portrayed on the wall where you enter the room is King Sebastian (Dom Sebastião), a gung-ho, medieval-type monarch who went to battle in Africa, following the Moors even after they were chased out of Europe. He disappeared at age 24 (although he was almost certainly killed in Morocco, "Sebastianists" awaited his mythical return into the 19th century). With the king missing, Portugal was left in unstable times with only Sebastian's great uncle (King Henrique) as heir. The new king died within two years, and the throne passed to cousin King Philip II of Spain, leading to 60 years of Spanish rule (1580–1640). Note the ebony, silver, and painted copper headboard of the Italian Renaissance bed. The tiles in this room are considered the first Portuguese tiles—from the time of Manuel I. The corn-on-the-cob motif topping the tilework is a reminder of American discoveries. Wander through more rooms upstairs, and through more quarters to the blue-and-gold...

Stag Room: The most striking room in the palace honors Portugal's loyal nobility. Study the richly decorated ceiling. The king's coat of arms at the top is surrounded by the coats of arms of his children, and below that, the coats of arms of all but one of Portugal's noble families. That family schemed a revolt, so received only a blank niche. The Latin phrase circling the room reads, "Honoring all the noble families who've been loyal to the king." The 18th-century tiles hang from the walls like tapestries. Enjoy the view—a garden-like countryside dotted with mansions of nobility who clamored to be near their king, the hill-capping castle, and the wide-open Atlantic. You're in the westernmost room of the westernmost palace on the European continent.

Kitchen: With all the latest in cooking technology, the palace chef could roast an entire cow on the spit, keep the king's plates warm in the iron dish warmer (with drawers below for the charcoal), and get really dizzy by looking up and spinning around three times. OK, you can go now.

▲▲Pena Palace (Palácio de Pena)

This magical hilltop palace sits high above Sintra, above the Moorish Castle ruins. In the 19th century, Portugal had a very romantic prince, German-born Prince Ferdinand. A contemporary and cousin of Bavaria's "Mad" King Ludwig (of Disneyesque Neuschwanstein Castle fame), Ferdinand was also a cousin of England's Prince Albert (Queen Victoria's husband). Flamboyant Ferdinand hired a German architect to build a fantasy castle, mixing elements of German and Portuguese style. He ended up with a crazy Neo-fortified casserole of Gothic towers, Renaissance

domes, Moorish minarets, Manueline carving, Disney playfulness, and an *azulejo* (tile) toilet for his wife.

Cost, Hours, Location: €8 combo-ticket for palace and gardens, €2.50 with LisboaCard, gardens free on Sun until 14:00, May–mid-Sept Tue–Sun 10:00–19:00, mid-Sept–April Tue–Sun 10:00–17:30, closed Mon, last entry one hour before closing, no photos, view café, tel. 219-105-340, www.parquesdesintra.pt. Purchase your ticket at the small hut opposite the gated entrance. To avoid the 10-minute uphill climb to the palace (and enjoy a lift back down), catch the green shuttle bus just inside the gate at the *paragem* sign (€1.50 round-trip, departures every few minutes in fake vintage Lisbon trolley). If you brought your lunch with you, don't zip up to the palace immediately, but first enjoy the picnic-perfect gardens. Your ticket comes with a map showing a circular, 90-minute walking route. Wander in, find a spot of shade, and enjoy views fit for a king.

◐ Self-Guided Tour: The palace, built in the mid to late 1800s, is so well preserved that it feels as if it's the day after the royal family fled Portugal in 1910 (during a popular revolt that eventually made way for today's modern republic). This gives the place a charming intimacy rarely seen in palaces. English descriptions throughout give meaning to the rooms. Here are the highlights.

Entry: After you hop off the green shuttle bus, walk up through the Moorish archway with alligator decor. Get your ticket

torn, cross the drawbridge that doesn't draw, and join an onion-domed world of tourists frozen in deep knee-bends with their cameras cocked. Bags and cameras must be checked—stow your camera in a pocket prior to entry or surrender it (no photos are allowed inside rooms, but you may want your camera for the spectacular views). At the base of the stairs, you'll see King Ferdinand, who built this castle from 1840 until 1885, when he died. While German, he was a romantic proponent of his adopted culture and did much to preserve Portugal's architectural and artistic heritage.

Courtyard: Note how the palace was built upon the arcaded ruins of a 16th-century monastery. In spite of its plushness, it retains the coziness of several small rooms gathered in two levels around this cloister.

Queen's Bedroom and Dressing Room: Study the melancholy photos of Queen Amelia, King Charles (Carlos I), and their family in this room. The early 1900s were a rocky time for Portugal's royal family. The king and his eldest son were assassinated in 1908. His youngest son, Manuel II, became king until he, his mother the queen, and other members of the royal family fled Portugal during the 1910 revolution. The palm frond on the headboard of the queen's bed was from her last Palm Sunday Mass in Portugal. Poke around. If you lean far enough, you can see Amelia's toilet. And in the next room, how about that padded velvet bidet?

King's Bedroom: The king enjoyed cutting-edge comforts, including the shower/tub imported from England, and even a telephone to listen to the opera when he felt that the Lisbon commute was too much (you'll see the switchboard later). The bedroom is decorated in classic Romantic style—dark, heavy, and busy with knickknacks.

Queen's View Balcony: On the upper floor, enjoy a sweeping view from Lisbon to the mouth of the Tejo River. Find the Cristo Rei statue and the 25th of April Bridge. The statue on the distant ridge honors the palace's architect. Continue your visit to the fantastically furnished Noble's Room, and then wind through the hallways. You'll end at the abundant kitchen; just after, a view café conveniently welcomes us peasants.

▲Moorish Castle (Castelo dos Mouros)

Sintra's thousand-year-old Moorish castle ruins are lost in an enchanted forest and alive with winds of the past. They're a castle-lover's dream come true, and a great place for a picnic with a panoramic Atlantic view. Though built by the Moors, the castle was taken by Christian forces in 1147. What you'll climb on today, while dramatic, was much-restored in the 19th century, but still isn't a level walk—be careful on the irregular, stony steps. To get from Sintra to the ruins, hike up two miles, take a taxi, or ride bus #434—see "Getting Around Sintra," page 102.

Cost and Hours: €4.50, discount with LisboaCard, daily mid-June–mid-Sept 9:00–20:00, May–mid-June and mid-Sept–Oct 9:00–19:00, Nov–April 9:30–18:00, last entry one hour before closing, free flier includes English info and a rough map, tel. 219-237-300, www .parquesdesintra.pt.

More Sights

▲▲Sintra Museum of Modern Art: The Berardo Collection—

Modern art–lovers rave about this private collection, one of Iberia's best. The collection rotates, with 120 of its 800 pieces shown at any given time. The art (along with temporary exhibits) is displayed alongside with thoughtful English descriptions. Previous exhibits have included shows on Nazi war posters, Portuguese Surrealists, and the World Press Cartoon awards (€3, Tue–Sun 10:00–18:00, free on Sun until 14:00, closed Mon; 500 yards from train station, in Sintra's former casino on Avenida Heliodoro Salgado, exit right from train station and go straight for about 8 min through pedestrian mall and past banks into the modern town; tel. 219-248-170, www.berardocollection.com).

Quinta da Regaleira—

This Neo-everything (Manueline/Gothic/Renaissance) 1912 mansion and garden has mystical and Masonic twists. It was designed by an Italian opera-set designer for a wealthy but disgruntled monarchist two years after the royal family was deposed. The two-hour English tour is mostly in the garden (as the palace is quite small) and can be longish unless you're into quirky Masonic esoterica. If you like fantastic caves, bring a flashlight and follow the shaded black lines on the provided maps (€5 self-guided tour, €10 guided tour by reservation only, 8 tours/day in summer, 4/day in winter, maximum 30 people, book by calling 219-106-650, daily 10:00–20:00, closes earlier off-season, last entry one hour before closing, a 10-min walk from downtown Sintra, café, regaleira@mail.telepac.pt). Ask a local to pronounce "Regaleira" for you, and just try to repeat it.

Toy Museum—

Just for fun, you can wander through a collection of several thousand old-time toys, from small soldiers, planes, cars, trucks, and old tricycles to a dolls' attic upstairs. The 20th-century owner João Arbués Moreira started collecting toys when he was 14, and just never quit. He typically hangs around the museum in his wheelchair, and loves to explain to visitors how he acquired each item (€4, discount with LisboaCard, Tue–Sun 10:00–18:00, last entry 30 min before closing, closed Mon, Rua Visconde de Monserrate, 1 block in front of National Palace, tel. 219-242-171, www.museu-do-brinquedo.pt).

Monserrate—

About 2.5 miles outside of Sintra are the wonderful gardens of Monserrate. If you like tropical plants and exotic landscaping, a visit is time well spent (€4.50, discount with LisboaCard, €4.50 extra for guided visit by reservation only, daily mid-June–mid-Sept 9:00–20:00, May–mid-June and mid-Sept–Oct 9:00–19:00, Nov–April 9:30–18:00, last entry one hour before closing, no buses run here—allow about €10 for taxi, tel. 219-237-300, www.parquesdesintra.pt). Some say that the Pena Palace's gardens are just as good as these more famous grounds.

SLEEPING AND EATING

Sleeping

$$$ Casa Miradouro is a beautifully restored mansion from 1893. With six spacious, stylish rooms, an elegant lounge, castle and sea views, and a wonderful garden, it's a worthy splurge. The place is graciously run by Frederic, who speaks English with a Swiss accent (Sb-€83–120, Db-€93–135, priciest April–Oct, buffet breakfast, closed mid-Jan–Feb, non-smoking rooms available, street parking, Rua Sotto Major 55; from National Palace, go past Hotel Tivoli Sintra and 400 yards downhill, note that it's a stiff uphill hike to return to center; tel. 219-107-100 or 219-235-900, fax 219-241-836, www.casa-miradouro.com, mail@casa-miradouro.com).

$ Vila Marques, another elegant old mansion, is much funkier but filled with pride. It has an eccentric grandmotherly flair, hardwood floors, four fine rooms, three suites, and a great garden with birds. Easy to miss, it's 100 yards downhill from Hotel Tivoli and 200 yards down from the National Palace (S-€35, D-€45, D/twin-€50, Db suite-€65, Qb-€80, €5 less Oct–May, one bath per two rooms, no sinks in rooms, suites and quad on garden lack character of cheaper rooms actually in mansion, cash only, Rua Soto Mayor 1, tel. 219-230-027, fax 219-241-155, run by Sra. Maria Marques and her hardworking maids, Maria and Olga).

Eating

On Rua das Padarias

This touristy little cobbled lane is lined with charming shops and eateries. For a light café lunch, try **Pastelaria Vila Velha** (daily, Rua das Padarias 8, tel. 219-230-154).

The venerable **Piriquita** café bills itself as "the" *antiga fabrica de queijadas*—historic maker of tiny, tasty tarts with a cheesy filling

---

Sleep Code

(€1 = about $1.40, country code: 351)
S = Single, **D** = Double/Twin, **T** = Triple, **Q** = Quad, **b** = bathroom, **s** = shower only. Unless otherwise noted, credit cards are accepted, English is spoken, and breakfast is included.

To help you easily sort through these listings, I've divided the rooms into three categories, based on the price for a standard double room with bath during high season:

$$$ **Higher Priced**—Most rooms €115 or more.
  $$ **Moderately Priced**—Most rooms between €60–115.
   $ **Lower Priced**—Most rooms €60 or less.

(daily, at the base of the street). It's a fine place for a sweet and a coffee. Take a seat to avoid groups who rush in to get pastries to go, or do battle and grab a half-dozen for €4. To escape most of the crowds, check out their other shop, **Piriquita Dois,** which has a view terrace (open daily, continue uphill and to the right to Rua das Padarias 2).

Restaurante Alcobaça, located between the two Piriquita cafés mentioned previously, serves typical Portuguese fare. Ignore the bizarre, cave-like decor and the menu options displayed on flat-screen TVs, and concentrate on the excellent food served by helpful waitstaff (entreés-€13, daily, occasionally crowded with groups, Rua das Padarias 7, tel. 219-231-651).

Binhoteca provides wine-lovers with a rest from the palaces, with an astonishing 200 Portuguese wines available by the glass (€2–6 each). Knowledgeable staff provide recommendations and offer samples of local cheeses and sausages. Just wait until after the climb to begin tasting (daily 11:00–22:30, Rua das Padarias 16, tel. 219-240-849).

Other Eateries in Sintra

The industrious, tourist-friendly **Restaurant Regional de Sintra** feeds locals and tourists well (€15 meals, daily 12:00–22:30, ask the waiter to tell you the legend of the rooster on the napkin; 200 yards from train station at Travessa do Municipio 2, exit train station left, go downhill to the first square and to the far right corner; tel. 219-234-444).

Bus drivers and tour guides grab a quiet, cheap lunch in the homey **Café da Villa** (€8 fixed-price meals, daily, generous portions of homemade-style soups and salads, down the road past horse-drawn carriages at Calçada do Pelourinho 2, tel. 219-241-174).

For a take-out bakery sandwich, stop by **Padarias Reunidas de Sintra,** across the square from the National Palace. At the train station, **Pizza Hut**'s salad bar makes an easy stop for a cheap, healthy salad for a picnic in Sintra or on the ride back to Lisbon.

TRANSPORTATION CONNECTIONS

From Sintra to: Lisbon (4 trains/hr, 35 min), **Cascais** (hourly bus #403 also stops at Cabo da Roca, 45–60 min, bus stop at the Sintra train station). For info and advice on day-trip connections from Lisbon, see "Planning Your Time" at the beginning of this chapter.

Near Sintra

Cabo da Roca

Wind-beaten, tourist-infested Cabo da Roca is the westernmost point in Europe, perhaps the inspiration for the Portuguese poet Luís de Camões' line, *"Onde a terra se acaba e o mar começa"* ("Where land ends and the sea begins"). It has a little shop, a café, and a tiny **TI** that sells a "proof of being here" diploma (daily June–Sept 9:00–20:00, until 19:00 off-season). Nearby, on the road to Cascais, you'll pass a good beach for wind, waves, sand, and the chance to be the last person in Europe to see the sun set. For a remote beach, drive to Praia Adraga (north of Cabo da Roca).

Cascais and Estoril

Before the rise of the Algarve, these towns were the haunt of Portugal's rich and beautiful. Today, they are quietly elegant,

with noble old buildings, beachfront promenades, a bullring, a casino, and more fame than they deserve. Cascais (see photo) is the more enjoyable of the two; it's not as rich and stuffy, and has the cozy touch of a fishing village, great seafood, and a younger, less pretentious atmosphere (Cascais **TI** at Visconde de Luz 14, Estoril **TI** at Areada do Parque, shared tel. 214-663-813). Both are a simple day trip from Lisbon (4 trains/hr, 40 min from Lisbon's Cais do Sodré Station).

THE ALGARVE

The Algarve was once known as Europe's last undiscovered tourist frontier. But it's well-discovered now, and if you go to the places featured in tour brochures, you'll find it much like Spain's Costa del Sol—paved, packed, and pretty stressful. Still, there are a few great beach towns left, mostly on the western tip, and this part of the Algarve, the south coast, is part of any sun-worshipper's dream.

Portugal's warm and dry south coast, stretching for some 100 miles, has beach resorts along the water's edge and rolling green hills dotted with orchards farther inland. The coastline varies from lagoon estuaries in the east (Tavira), to sandy beach resorts in the center (from Faro to Lagos), to rugged cliffs in the west (Sagres).

The Moors (Muslims from North Africa who ruled Portugal for five centuries) chose not to live in the rainy north, but rather along the warm, dry south coast, in the land they dubbed Al-Gharb Al-Andalus ("to the west of Andalucía"—the westernmost edge of the huge Islamic world at the time). Today, the Algarve still holds elements introduced by the Muslims—groves of almond and orange trees, and white-domed buildings with pointy chimneys, blue trim, and traditional *azulejos*.

For some rigorous rest and intensive relaxation, make sunny Salema your Algarve hideaway. Here the tourists and fishermen sport the same stubble. It's just you, a beach full of

The Algarve

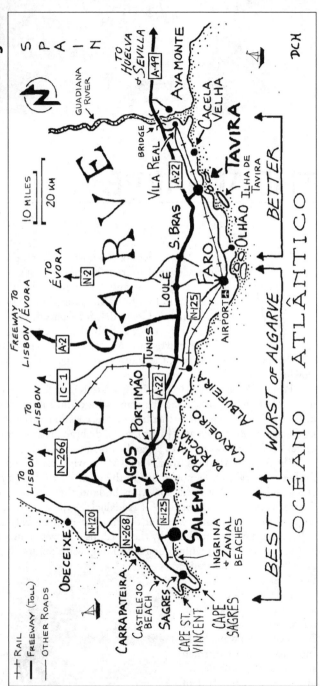

garishly painted boats, your wrinkled landlady, and a few other globetrotting experts in lethargy. Nearby sights include Cape Sagres (Europe's "Land's End" and home of Henry the Navigator's famous navigation school) and the beach-party/jet-ski resort of Lagos. Or you could just work on a tan and see how slow your pulse can get in sleepy Salema. If not now, when? If not you, who?

Planning Your Time

The Algarve is your vacation from your vacation. How much time does it deserve? It depends upon how much time you have, and how much time you need to recharge your solar batteries. On a two-week trip of Portugal, I'd give it three nights and two days. After a full day of sightseeing in Lisbon (or Sevilla, if you're arriving from Spain), I'd push it by driving four hours around dinnertime to gain an entirely free beach day. With two days, I'd spend one enjoying side trips to Cape Sagres and Lagos, and another just lingering in Salema. The only other Algarve stop to consider is Tavira. (If you're visiting in winter, Tavira—which is lively year-round—makes a better stop than tiny Salema, which slows down.)

Getting Around the Algarve

Trains and buses connect the main towns along the south coast (skimpy service on weekends and off-season). Buses take you west from Lagos, where trains don't go. The freeway crossing the Algarve from Lagos to the Spanish border (and on to Sevilla, Spain) makes driving quick and easy. (See "Route Tips for Drivers in the Algarve," at the end of this chapter.)

Salema

One bit of old Algarve magic still glitters quietly in the sun— Salema. It's at the end of a small road just off the main drag between

the big city of Lagos and the rugged southwest tip of Europe, Cape Sagres. Quietly discovered by British and German tourists, this simple fishing village has three beachside streets, many restaurants, a few hotels, time-share condos up the road, a couple of shipwreck bars, English and German menus, a classic beach with a new, paved promenade, and endless sun.

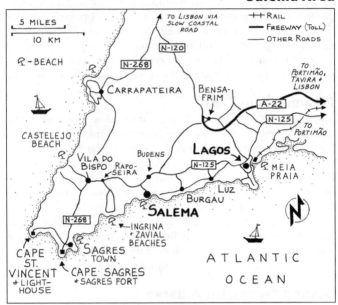

Salema Area

ORIENTATION

Tourist Information

Salema lacks an official TI, but Salema Property and Services (see "Helpful Hints," next page) and people in the bars, restaurants, and pensions have heard all the questions and are happy to provide answers. To study ahead, see www.salema.info.

Arrival in Salema

By Train and Bus: To get to Salema, you'll arrive first at Lagos (with the closest train station), the western Algarve's transportation hub. From there, buses go nearly hourly between Lagos and Sagres (30-min ride, 10 miles, last bus departs Lagos around 20:30, fewer buses on weekends). Catch the bus at either the Lagos bus station (see "Lagos," page 128) or at one of the stops along the waterfront of the historic town. About half the buses go right into the village of Salema. The others (marked *cruzt* in the schedule) drop you at the top of the road (that must be *cruzt*) into Salema (bus continues to Figueira). From here, it's a 20-minute walk downhill into the village.

By Car: If you're coming from Spain on the freeway, exit at the second Lagos exit (marked *Lagos Oeste/Vila do Bispo*) and follow *Sagres/Vila do Bispo* signs. Turn off at the sign for *Salema*. Parking is free and easy on the street (beware of the "no parking" signs—*estacionamento proibido*—near the bus stop). If you want to stop in Lagos before continuing to Salema, take the first exit *(Lagos Este)*. Leave Lagos via the street Avenida dos Descobrimentos, and follow signs to *Sagres/Vila do Bispo.*

By Taxi: A cab from Lagos to Salema takes 20 minutes and costs about €16 (metered, but ask for an estimate first; see "Helpful Hints," below).

Helpful Hints

Money: Salema has an ATM at the entrance of the Atlântico restaurant (see "Eating," page 122), but it wouldn't hurt to bring along a few extra euros just in case. Not all Salema restaurants accept credit cards; most of the accommodations require cash; and there's no backup in case of an ATM malfunction.

Internet Access: You can get online at Salema Property and Services (next) and at A Aventura Bar (see "Nightlife," page 119). Pensión Maré has access, but only for guests (see page 120).

Handy Services: An agency called **Salema Property and Services** posts bus and train schedules, offers three-day to one-week condo rentals in Salema, arranges excursions, offers Internet access, Wi-Fi, and broadband phone service, and has free tourist maps of Lagos and the Algarve. You can also rent a car (€45/day or less), moped, and/or a mountain bike (normally open Mon–Fri 9:30–19:00, Sat 10:00–14:00, some Sun in summer, Oct–May closed at lunch, in tiny strip mall across from Hotel Residencial Salema, tel. 282-695-855, fax 282-695-920, www.salemapropertyandservices.com).

Taxi: Your hotel can arrange a taxi, or you can call Jose direct at mobile 919-385-139 or 919-422-061. Jose and his wife Isabel (a tour guide who speaks fluent English) have two cars and are at your service. It's €16 to the Lagos bus station or €30 for a quick 75-minute scenic tour of Cape Sagres/Cape St. Vincent, with short stops and commentary (can also wait in Sagres for €7/hr). This can be a great value when two couples team up to share the excursion. For €250, you could even taxi to Lisbon, Évora, or Sevilla. You'll see Jose at the taxi stall in the center parking lot.

SELF-GUIDED TOUR

Welcome to Salema

Salema has a split personality: The whitewashed old town is for locals, and the other half was built for tourists—both groups pursue a policy of peaceful coexistence. Tourists laze in the sun, while locals grab the shade.

Town Square Market Action: Salema's flatbed truck market rolls in weekday mornings—one truck each for fish, fruit, and vegetables, and a five-and-dime truck for clothing and other odds and ends. The tooting horn of the fish truck wakes you at 8:00. The bakery trailer sells delightful fresh bread and "store-bought" sweet rolls each morning (about 8:00–11:00). Weekday afternoons around 14:00, the red mobile post office stops by (unless the government cuts its funding).

Fishing Scene: Salema is still a fishing village—but just barely. While the fishermen's hut no longer hosts a fish auction, you'll still see the old-timers enjoying its shade, oblivious to the tourists, while mending their nets and reminiscing about the old days when life was "only fish and hunger." In the calm of the summer, boats are left out on buoys. In the winter, the community-subsidized tractor earns its keep by hauling the boats ashore. (In pre-tractor days, such boat-hauling was a 10-person chore.)

Octopus is the main catch. The pottery jars stacked everywhere are octopus traps. Unwritten tradition allocates different chunks of undersea territory to each Salema family. The traps are tied about 15 feet apart in long lines and dropped offshore. Octopi, thinking these jars would make a cozy place to set an ambush, climb in and get ambushed themselves. When the fishermen hoist them in, they hang on—unaware they've made their final mistake. The fisherman maces them out of their pot with a squirt of bleach. The octopus flops angrily into the boat bound for the market and, who knows...maybe onto your dinner plate.

Beach Scene: Suntanners enjoy the beach May through September. (I once got a sunburn in early May.) Knowing their tourist-based economy sits on a foundation of sand, locals hope and

pray that the sand returns after being washed away each winter (some winters leave the beach just a pile of rocks). At the west end of the beach, look for the dinosaur footprints in a big, flat yellowish rock (www.geology.west-algarve.net).

Beach towns must provide public showers and toilets. You can rent beach items (lounges-€3/day, bamboo sun shades-€2.50) at the Atlântico restaurant and at Salema's Balneario Municipal (daily

Salema

1. Romantik Villa
2. Hotel Residencial Salema
3. Pensión Maré
4. Ribeiro Rooms
5. Acacio Rooms
6. Casa Duarte
7. Boia Bar & Rest.
8. Atlântico Restaurant
9. Mira Mar Restaurant
10. Restaurante O Lourenço & Carioca Bar
11. Carapau Frances
12. Restaurante O Barco
13. Salema Market
14. To Vila Velha Rest. & Castelejo Rest.
15. Alisuper Grocery
16. Salema Property & Services

Within the map image:

OCEANO ATLÂNTICO

BEACH

To BOCA DO RIO
CLIFFS

BARS

MAIN STREET →
LOTS OF QUARTOS

FISHING BOATS
PROM-ENADE

FISHING BOATS

PHONES

BUS STOP

TAXI **TOWN SQUARE** (PARK HERE)

FISH. HUT

To HIGHWAY N 125
LAGOS & SAGRES &

WC + SHOWER

STREAM

DCH

To "CONDO TOWN" & FIGUEIRA BEACH

CLIFFS

To END OF THE EARTH

✳NOTE: MAP NOT TO SCALE
TOWN SQUARE TO CASA DUARTE = 3 MIN. WALK

Salema

14:00–19:00 in summer, showers-€1). The fountain in front of the Balneario Municipal is a reminder of the old days. When water to the village was cut off, this was always open. Locals claim the beach is safe for swimming, but the water is rarely really warm.

A pre-breakfast stroll eastward is a pristine way to greet the new day. On the west end of the beach, at low tide, you can climb over the rocks past tiny tide pools to secluded Figueira Beach. (But be aware of when the tide comes in, or your route back will have to be over land.) While the old days of black-clad widows chasing topless Nordic women off the beach are gone, nudism is still risqué today. If you go topless, do so with discretion. Over the rocks and beyond the view of prying eyes, Germans grin and bare it.

Community Development: The whole peninsula (west of Lagos) has been declared a natural park, and further development close to the beach is forbidden. The village of Salema is becoming less and less ramshackle as it's gradually bought up by northern Europeans for vacation or retirement homes. Salema will live with past mistakes, such as the huge hotel in the town center that pulled some mysterious strings to go two stories over code. Up the street is a sprawling community of Club Med–type vacationers who rarely leave their air-conditioned bars and swimming pools. Across the highway a mile or two inland is an even bigger golfing resort (worth exploring by car) with a spa, pool, and tennis courts.

SIGHTS

Coastal Boat Tours—Local English-speaking guide Sebastián offers a two-hour scenic cruise along the coast. He gives a light commentary on the geology and plant and bird life as he motors halfway to Cape Sagres and back. Trips include nipping into some cool blue natural caves. Morning trips are best for bird-watching (herring gulls, falcons). Kicking back and watching the cliffs glide by, I felt like I was scanning a super-relaxing gallery of natural art. Consider being dropped at (nude) Figueira Beach just before returning to Salema. If you're going for just the boat ride, bring a sweater, camera, and sunscreen; if you're planning to walk back from Figueira Beach—which is a 50-minute hike to Salema—also bring beach shoes, a picnic, and extra water. Remember, some of these beaches only exist when the tide is low (check the tide table in the fishing hut on Salema's beach). Easygoing and gentle Sebastián charges little more than what it costs to run his small boat (€20 per person, mid-June–mid-Sept daily 10:30 and 13:30, 2–5 passengers, tel. 282-695-458, mobile 963-441-753, ask for Sebastián at fishermen's hut or book his tour through Pensión Maré or Salema Property and Services).

NIGHTLIFE

Salema has several late-night bars, each worth a visit. Consider a pub crawl to sample the local drinks. *Armarguinha* (ar-mar-GWEEN-yah) is a sweet, likeable almond liqueur. *Licor beirão* (LIK-kor bay-ROW; row rhymes with cow) is Portuguese amaretto, a "double distillation of diverse plants and aromatic seeds in accordance with a secret old formula." *Caipirinha* (kay-peer-EEN-yah), tasty and powerful, is made of fermented Brazilian sugarcane with lime, sugar, and crushed ice. And *moscatel* is the local sweet dessert wine.

Guillerme Duarte's **A Tabúa Bar** is the liveliest by Salema standards, offering patrons its famous sangria. Just up the street, at **A Aventura Bar,** Bertrand offers a pleasant atmosphere for sipping drinks (the *caipirinha* is good) and sending email. And, up the hill (next to Restaurante O Lourenço), the on-again-off-again **Carioca Bar** is a more bohemian-style hangout. For a late dessert or a sangria on the beach, drop by **Mira Mar.** Or just grab a bench on the promenade and ponder the moon and the waves.

SLEEPING

Salema is crowded July through mid-September (and August is horribly packed). Prices jump up in July and August, and the place is partially closed down in winter.

For maximum comfort, there's no need to look beyond Pensión Maré. There's a basic and utilitarian high-rise hotel in the center of town. But for economy and experience, stay in a *quarto*

Sleep Code

(€1 = about $1.40, country code: 351)
S = Single, **D** = Double/Twin, **T** = Triple, **Q** = Quad, **b** = bathroom, **s** = shower only. When a price range is given, the lowest is the winter rate and the highest is the peak-season summer rate. Credit cards are accepted only at Pensión Maré and Hotel Residencial Salema. English is spoken unless otherwise noted.

To help you easily sort through these listings, I've divided the rooms into three categories, based on the price for a standard double room with bath:

  $$$ **Higher Priced**—Most rooms €80 or more.
   $$ **Moderately Priced**—Most rooms between €45–80.
    $ **Lower Priced**—Most rooms €45 or less.

(room), most of which are along the main road that parallels the waterfront. Fisherfolk happily rent out rooms in their homes, most of which have separate private entrances.

Quartos don't serve breakfast, and breakfast at hotels isn't until 8:30 (after the bread guy arrives at Salema). Early birds can enjoy coffee and pastries from 7:30 on at Solmar Café next to Salema Property and Services, opposite Hotel Residencial Salema.

Pensión and Hotels

$$$ Romantik Villa, run by Lisa from Brazil, is a stylish house on top of the hill with three rooms, an apartment, a garden, and a swimming pool. This mini-resort in a modern residential complex is tastefully decorated and a good spot for people who want quiet—so it's not ideal for children (Db-€80–90, includes breakfast; apartment-€100–120, no breakfast; cash only; Praia de Salema, tel. 282-695-670, mobile 967-059-806, www.romantikvilla.com, romantikvilla @sapo.pt). To get to the villa, head up from the beach past Restaurante O Lourenço, take a right at the phone booth just after the grocery store, into Urbanização Beach Villas, and look for #M5.

$$$ Hotel Residencial Salema, the oversized hotel towering crudely above everything else in town, is a good value if you want a basic, comfortable room handy to the beach. Recently renovated, its 32 red-tiled rooms all have air-conditioning, balconies, and partial views (Sb-€81, Db-€91 mid-July–mid-Sept; Sb-€65, Db-€70 June–mid-July and late Sept; Sb-€53, Db-€58 March–May and Oct–Nov; closed Dec–Feb, 10 percent discount through 2008 with this book, includes breakfast, elevator, rents cars and mopeds, tel. 282-695-328, fax 282-695-329, www.hotelsalema.com, hotel .salema@clix.pt).

$$ Pensión Maré, a blue-and-white building looking over the village above the main road into town, is the best hotel value in Salema. Two easygoing Danes, Jorn and Sigrun, run the place, offering six comfortable rooms (Sb-€38–53, Db-€50–70, Tb-€65–85, includes wonderful breakfast) and three fully equipped apartments (Db-€50–80, extra bed-€10, no breakfast) in a tidy paradise (10 percent discount with this book and cash if arranged discreetly and in advance, free Internet access, Praia de Salema, tel. 282-695-165, fax 282-695-846, excellent website www.the-mare.com has good Salema information). Jorn will hold a room with a phone call and a credit-card number.

Apartments

Renting an apartment is a popular option that falls comfortably between staying in a hotel and spending the night in someone's home (see information on *quartos,* next). Jorn and Sigrun, who run Pensión Maré, also manage two houses and three apartments near the beach (Db-€45–80, Tb/Qb-€65–100, minimum 3–4 nights, cash only, tel. 963-609-205, www.salema4u.com, jorn @salema4u.com).

Quartos and Camping

Quartos abound along the residential street (running left from the village center as you face the beach). Ask one of the locals at

the waterfront, or check at the Boia Bar or Salema Market. Prices vary with the season, plumbing, and view, but if you're only staying one night, you're bad news. Doubles cost about €25–45 (forget breakfast and credit cards). Many places offer beachfront views—it's worth paying extra for rooms *com vista* (with a view). Some apartments are bright and sprawling, while some rooms are dark and musty. *Quarto* landladies generally speak only a little English, but they're used to dealing with visitors. Many will clean your laundry for about €4 or so. If you're settling in for a while or are on a tight budget, park your bags and travel partner at a beachside bar and survey several places. Except for August weekends, there are always rooms available for those dropping in. Especially outside of July and August, prices can be soft.

$ Maria Helena and Jorge Ribeiro, a helpful young couple, rent two small, simple doubles (S or D-€35 all year, one has a tiny view) and a charming treehouse-type suite with a kitchen, a view terrace, and a view toilet for Db-€40–50 (Rua dos Pescadores 83, tel. 282-695-289, mobile 965-825-356).

$ The **Acacio family** rents a humble ground-floor double (D-€25–30) and a fine upstairs apartment with kitchenette, balcony over the beach, and a great ocean view for up to five people (Db-€45, Tb-€50, Qb-€70, on "*quartos* street" at #91, tel. 282-695-473). Silvina doesn't speak English and she pouts if you're staying only one night.

$ Casa Duarte has three pleasant rooms (all with views), a communal kitchenette, and two terraces (D-€35–45, €5 less for two or more nights, tel. 282-695-206 or their English-speaking daughter, Cristina, at tel. 282-695-307; or contact son Romeu, who owns the Salema Market). From "*quartos* street," turn right at Clube Recreativo, then left on the paved path. Duarte's is #7, the first building on the right.

Campers who don't underestimate the high tides sleep free and easy on the **beach** (public showers available in the town center) or at a well-run **campground** with bungalows a half-mile inland, back toward the main road.

EATING

Eat fresh seafood here, eternally. The local specialty is *cataplana*—fish, tomatoes, potatoes, onions, and whatever else is available—big enough for two or three, and cooked a long time in a traditional copper pot (somewhere between a pressure cooker and a steamer). Also look for grilled golden bream *(dourada grelhada)* and giant prawns *(camarões)*.

Salema has six or eight places that all serve fine €10 meals. Happily, those that face the beach (the first three listed here) are the most fun and have the best service, food, and atmosphere. For a memorable last course at any of these places, consider taking your dessert wine *(moscatel)*, Brazilian sugarcane liquor mixed with lime *(caipirinha),* or coffee to the beach for some stardust on the side.

The **Boia Bar and Restaurant,** at the base of the residential street, has a classy beachfront setting, noteworthy service by a friendly gang, and a knack for doing whitefish just right (always with free seconds on good orange and green vegetables). Their vegetarian lasagna and salads are popular, as is their €7 bacon-and-eggs breakfast (daily 9:30–22:00, tel. 282-695-382).

The **Atlântico**—noisy, big, busy, and right on the beach—originated as a temporary beach restaurant and now enjoys a prime spot in a brand-new building. It has long dominated the Salema beach scene and is known for tasty fish, a wonderful beachside terrace, and friendly service (daily 12:00–24:00, serving until 22:00, also rents lounge chairs and bamboo sun shades, ATM outside, tel. 282-695-142).

The intimate **Mira Mar,** farther up the residential street, is a last vestige of old Salema (unlike the Boia and Atlântico, which were both funky beachfront eateries until major renovations in 2004). Florentine and Dieter offer a more creative menu for those venturing away from seafood. Their €6.50 tapas plate—a hearty array of cold meats, veggies, and munchies—can make a meal, and their *caldeirada* is a delightful Portuguese fish-and-vegetables stew, like *cataplana* without the copper pot (Sun–Fri 12:00–24:00, closed Sat, cash only).

Restaurante O Lourenço, a block up the hill, has no ambience or view but offers good-value meals, has a local clientele, and is *the* place for *cataplana* (€20 for 2 people). Paulo serves, while his mother, Aldina, cooks (daily 8:00–24:00, cash only; from Hotel Residencial Salema cross bridge, restaurant is a half-block uphill on your left; tel. 282-698-622).

Salema

Need a break from fish?

At **Carapau Frances,** Spiros and Gabrielle, a Greek/French couple, serve good Greek and Italian food, including salads, vegetarian options, and cheap pizzas (daily 19:00–22:30, cash only, on the town square).

Restaurante O Barco offers more creative cooking, including "the best pepper steak in town" and occasionally has an enormous paella cooking at the entrance. While it has a Greek Isle atmosphere, it's not on the beach (daily 12:00–24:00, indoor/outdoor seating, live music on Saturday evenings, tel. 282-695-149).

Romeu's **Salema Market** has all the fixings for a great picnic (fresh fruits, veggies, bread, sheep's cheese, sausage, and *vinho verde*—new wine, a Portuguese specialty with a refreshing taste) to take with you to a secluded beach or Cape Sagres. Helpful Romeu also changes money and gives travel and *quarto* advice (daily July–Sept 8:00–20:00, Oct–June 8:00–13:00 & 15:00–20:00, on the "*quartos* street"). Another good grocery store, **Alisuper,** is in the tiny strip mall across from Hotel Residencial Salema.

Drivers who want a classy meal outside of town should consider the elegant **Vila Velha Restaurante** in Sagres (page 128) or the more rustic **Castelejo Restaurante** at the surreal Praia do Castelejo (page 127).

Cape Sagres

In the days before Columbus, when the world was presumed to be flat, this rugged southwestern tip of Portugal was the spot closest to the edge of the Earth. Prince Henry the Navigator, determined to broaden Europe's horizons and spread Catholicism, founded his navigators' school here, and sent sailors ever further into the unknown. Shipwrecked and frustrated explorers were carefully debriefed as they washed ashore.

ORIENTATION

Portugal's "end of the road" is two distinct capes. Windy **Cape St. Vincent** is actually the most southwestern tip. It has a desolate lighthouse that marks what was referred to even in prehistoric times as "the end of the world" (open daily 10:00–17:00, closed for restoration during part of 2008). Snoop around, peek over the far

edge, and ask the attendant to spin the light for you. Outside the lighthouse, salt-of-the-earth merchants sell figs, seaworthy sweaters (€25 average), and the *"Letzte Bratwurst vor Amerika"* (last hotdog before America). **Cape Sagres,** with its old fort and Henry the Navigator lore, is the more historic cape of the two. At either cape, look for daredevil windsurfers and fishermen casting off the cliffs.

Lashed tightly to the windswept landscape is the salty **town of Sagres,** above a harbor of fishing boats. Sagres is a popular gathering place for the backpacking crowd, with plenty of private rooms in the center and a barely existent beach and bar scene.

Tourist Information: The TI is on the main street, Avenida Comandante Matoso (Tue–Sat 9:30–13:30 & 14:30–17:30, closed Sun–Mon, tel. 282-624-873).

SIGHTS

Sagres Fort and Navigators' School

The former "end of the world" is a craggy, windswept, wedge-shaped point that juts into the Atlantic (short drive or 15-min walk from Sagres). In 1420, Prince Henry the Navigator used his Order's funds to establish a school here for navigators. Today, little remains of Henry's school, except the site of buildings replaced by later (sometimes new) structures. An 18th-century fortress, built on the school's original battlements, dominates the entrance to the point (€3, May–Sept 10:00–20:30, until 18:30 off-season, tel. 282-620-140).

1. Plaque Inside Entrance: After entering through the 18th-century battlements, find the carved stone plaque that honors Henry. The ship in the plaque is a caravel, one of the small, light craft that was constantly being reinvented by Sagres' shipbuilding grad students. The astrolabe, a compact instrument that uses the stars for navigation, emphasizes Henry's role in the exploration process.

2. Wind-Compass: Sagres' most impressive sight—a circle on the ground, 100 feet across and outlined by round pebbles—is a mystery. Some think it was a large wind-compass *(rosa-dos-*

Cape Sagres

ventos). A flag flying from the center could immediately announce the wind's direction. Others speculate it's a large sundial. A pole in the center pointing toward the North Star (at a 37-degree angle, Sagres' latitude) would cast a shadow on the dial showing the time of day.

3. Remains of the School: The row of buildings beyond the wind-compass is where the school once was. The **tower-cistern** (abutting the end of the modern Exhibition Centre) is part of the original dorms. The small whitewashed 16th-century **Church of Our Lady of Grace** replaced Henry's church. The former Governor's House is now the restaurant/gift shop complex. Attached to the gift shop is a **windbreak wall** that dates from Henry's time, but is largely rebuilt.

The Sagres school taught mapmaking, shipbuilding, sailing, astronomy, and mathematics (for navigating), plus botany, zoology, anthropology, languages, and salesmanship for mingling with the locals. The school welcomed Italians, Scandinavians, and Germans and included Christians, Muslims, and Jews. Captured Africans gave guest lectures. (The next 15 generations of Africans were not so lucky, being sold into slavery by the tens of thousands.)

Besides being a school, Sagres was Mission Control for the explorers. Returning sailors brought spices, gold, diamonds, silk, and ivory, plus new animals, plants, peoples, customs, communicable diseases, and knowledge of the routes that were added to the maps. Henry ordered every sailor to keep a travel journal that could be studied. Ship designs were analyzed and tweaked, resulting in the square-sailed, oceangoing caravels that replaced the earlier coast-hugging versions.

It's said that Ferdinand Magellan (circumnavigator), Vasco da Gama (found sea route to India), Pedro Cabral (discovered Brazil), and Bartolomeu Dias (Africa-rounder) all studied at Sagres (after Henry's time, though). In May 1476, the young Italian Christopher Columbus washed ashore here after being shipwrecked by pirates. He went on to study and sail with the Portuguese (and marry a Portuguese woman) before beginning his American voyage. When Portugal denied Columbus's request to sail west, Spain accepted. The rest is history.

4. The Point: Beyond the buildings, the granite point itself is windswept, eroded, and largely barren, except for hardy, coarse vegetation admired by botanists. Walk on level paths around the edge of the bluff (a 40-min round-trip walk), where locals cast lines and tourists squint into the wind. You'll get great seascape views of Cape St. Vincent, with its modern lighthouse on the site of an old convent. At the far end of the Sagres bluff are a naval radio station, a natural cave, and a promontory called "Prince Henry's Chair."

Sit on the point and gaze across the "Sea of Darkness," where

Cape Sagres

Prince Henry the Navigator
(1394–1460)

No swashbuckling sailor, Henry was a quiet scholar, an organizer, a religious man, and the brains behind Portugal's daring sea voyages. The middle child of King John (João) I of Portugal and Queen Philippa of England, he was one of what was dubbed "The Marvelous Generation" *(Ínclita Geração)* that drove the Age of Discovery. While his brothers and nephews became Portugal's kings, he worked behind the scenes.

At age 21, he planned the logistics for the large-scale ship invasion of the Muslim city of Ceuta (1415) on the north coast of Morocco, taking the city and winning knightly honors. Awed by the wealth of the city—a terminus of the caravan route—and intrigued by the high-quality maps they found there, Henry decided to organize expeditions to explore the Muslim world. He hoped to spread Christianity, contain Islam, tap Muslim wealth, and find Prester John's legendary Christian kingdom, said to exist somewhere in Africa or Asia.

As head of the Order of Christ—a powerful brotherhood of soldier-monks—Grand Master Henry used their money to found a maritime school at Sagres. While Henry stayed home to update maps, debrief returning sailors, order supplies, and sign paychecks, brave seamen traveled off under Henry's strict orders not to return until they'd explored what was known as the "Sea of Darkness."

monsters roam. Long before Henry's time, Romans considered it the edge of the world, dubbing it Promontorium Sacrum—Sacred ("Sagres") Promontory. Pilgrims who came to visit this awe-inducing place were prohibited to spend the night here—it was for the gods alone.

In Portugal's seafaring lore, capes, promontories, and land's ends are metaphors for the edge of the old, and the start of the unknown voyage. Sagres is the greatest of these.

Beaches

Many beaches are tucked away on the drive between Salema and Cape Sagres. Most of them require a short walk after you stop along N-125. In some cases, you leave your car on access roads or cross private property to reach the beaches—be considerate. In

They discovered the Madeira Islands (1420), which Henry planted with vineyards, and the Azores (1427), which Henry colonized with criminals. But the next expeditions returned empty-handed, having run into a barrier—both a psychological and physical one. Cape Bojador (at the southwest corner of modern Morocco), with its reefs and currents, was seen as the end of the world. Beyond that, sea serpents roamed, while the hot equatorial sun melted ships, made the sea boil, and turned white men black.

Henry ordered scared, superstitious sailors to press on. After 14 unsuccessful voyages, Gil Eanes' crew returned (1437), unharmed and still white, with new knowledge that was added to corporate Portugal's map library.

Henry himself gained a reputation as an intelligent, devout, non-materialistic, celibate monk who humbled himself by wearing horsehair underwear. In 1437, Henry faced a personal tragedy. His planned invasion of Tangier failed miserably, and his beloved little brother Fernão was captured. As ransom, the Muslims demanded that Portugal return Ceuta. Henry (and others) refused, Fernão died in captivity, and Henry was devastated.

In later years, he spent less time at court in Lisbon and more in desolate Sagres, where he died in 1460. (He's buried in Batalha; see page 166.) Henry died before finding a sea route to Asia and just before his voyages really started paying off commercially. A generation later, Vasco da Gama would sail to India, capping Henry's explorations and kicking off Portugal's Golden Age.

Salema, ask at Pensión Maré or Salema Property and Services for directions to beaches before you head to Sagres. Furnas beach is fully accessible by car. You can access Ingrina and Zavial beaches by turning south in the village of Raposeira. Many beaches have bars (the one at Ingrina beach is famous for its spicy garlic prawns—*camarão piri-piri*).

The best secluded beach in the region is **Praia do Castelejo,** just north of Cape Sagres (from the town of Vila do Bispo, drive inland and follow the signs for 15 min). If you have a car and didn't grow up in Fiji, this really is worth the drive. Overlooking the deserted beach is **Castelejo Restaurante,** which specializes in octopus dishes and *cataplana,* the hearty local seafood stew (daily 12:00–22:00, 7.5 miles from Salema at Praia do Castelejo, tel. 282-639-777). While beaches between Salema and Sagres offer more of a seaside landscape, beaches north of São Vicente are more rugged and wild because they're exposed to ocean wind and weather. If there's no sand in Castelejo when you visit, blame it on nature and enjoy the rock formations instead.

SLEEPING AND EATING

Sleeping: $$$ Pousada do Infante, lavish and on the waterfront, provides a touch of local elegance in Sagres. This classy *pousada* (historic inn) is a reasonable splurge with a magnificent setting. At breakfast, you can sip coffee and enjoy the buffet while gazing out to sea (Sb/Db-€105–230, tel. 282-620-240, fax 282-624-225, www.pousadas.pt, recepcao.infante@pousadas.pt).

Eating: Vila Velha Restaurante, another splurge, offers wonderfully unforgettable meals, especially their rabbit stew (mid-July–mid-Sept daily 18:30–22:00, closed Mon off-season, reservations smart, Rua Patrão Antonio Faustino, near the *pousada* listed above, tel. 282-624-788).

TRANSPORTATION CONNECTIONS

From Salema, Sagres is a 20-minute drive or hitch, a half-hour bus trip (nearly hourly trips from Salema, check return times), or a taxi ride (€30 for a 75-min round-trip, plus €7/hr for waiting time in Sagres; see Salema's "Helpful Hints," earlier in this chapter, for a taxi recommendation).

Lagos

Lagos, with a beach-party old town and a jet-ski marina, is as enjoyable as a big-city resort can be. This major town on the west end of the Algarve was the region's

capital in the 13th and 14th centuries. The first great Portuguese maritime expeditions embarked from here, and the first African slave market in Europe was held here. Though not advertised by the local TI, the slave market does appear on the TI's town map and currently operates as an art gallery (look for small *Galeria Mercado de Escravos* sign).

ORIENTATION

The old town, defined by its medieval walls, stretches between Praça Gil Eanes and the fort. It's a whitewashed jumble of pedestrian streets, bars, funky craft shops, outdoor restaurants, mod fountains and sculptures, and sunburned tourists. Search out the sea-creature designs laid in the pavement—some of them will

Lagos

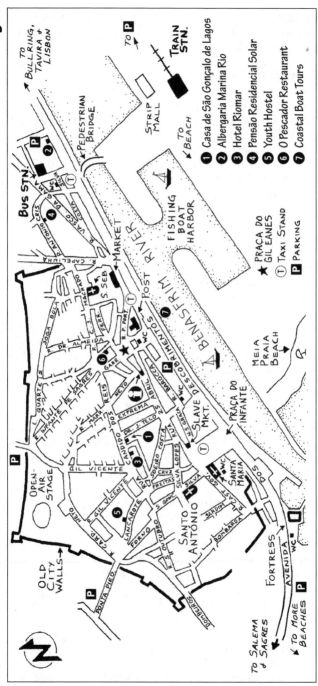

Lagos

1 Casa de São Gonçalo de Lagos
2 Albergaria Marina Rio
3 Hotel Riomar
4 Pensão Residencial Solar
5 Youth Hostel
6 O Pescador Restaurant
7 Coastal Boat Tours

★ Praça Do Gil Eanes
Ⓣ Taxi Stand
Ⓟ Parking

probably be on your plate at dinner. The beaches with the exotic rock formations—of postcard fame—begin just past the fort, with easy access via hiking trails.

Tourist Information

The Câmara Municipal TI is downtown, at Largo Marquês de Pombal (daily July–Aug 10:00–20:00, Sept–June until 18:00). Transportation schedules are handily posted outside. Another TI is a bleak six-minute walk from the bus station, oddly marooned on a traffic roundabout at the entrance to town (May–Sept Tue–Thu 9:30–19:00, Fri–Mon 9:30–13:00 & 14:00–17:30; Oct–April daily 9:30–13:00 & 14:00–17:30, behind bus station, take Rua Vasco da Gama to the right, and continue straight, on roundabout across from boat-shaped fountain en route to Portimão, tel. 282-763-031).

Arrival in Lagos

The train and bus stations are a five-minute walk apart, separated by the marina and pedestrian bridge over a river. Neither station has luggage storage.

If you are coming from Spain on the A22 freeway, exit at Lagos Este and follow signs to *centro*. Parking lots are plentiful. The most convenient are between the largest public squares, Praça do Gil Eanes and Praça do Infante (€1/2.25 hrs, Mon–Fri 8:00–19:00, Sat–Sun 8:00–13:00, otherwise free).

SIGHTS

Coastal Boat Tours—Along the harborfront, you'll be hustled to take a sightseeing cruise. Old fishermen ("who know the nickname of each rock along the coast") sit at anchor on board, while their salespeople on the promenade hawk 45-minute exotic rock and cave tours for €10.

More serious maritime adventures are sold (April–Oct) by a string of established companies with offices just over the marina bridge.

Bom Dia offers two different tours by sailboat: a two-hour €21 grotto tour (with a chance to swim) and a half-day €48 BBQ cruise that's basically a grotto tour with a meal (cash only, in marina at Lagos 10, WC on board, smart to reserve at least a day ahead in Aug, tel. 282-087-587, www.bomdia.info, info@bomdia-boattrips.com).

Bom Dia, with partner **Algarve Dolphins,** is also in the dolphin-spotting game. Speedy boats whisk you through the waves in search of flippered friends. Ninety-five percent of trips have sightings, but if your trip doesn't, you'll be able to ride the next day for free if space and availability allow (€30, 90 min, hourly departures, tel. 282-087-587, www.algarve-dolphins.com).

Dolphin Seafaris, which also has a high rate of dolphin sightings, offers 90-minute dolphin-watching cruises (€30, 5/day in summer, cash only, uses big and sturdy inflatable lifeboat, tel. 282-799-209 or mobile 919-359-359, www.dolphinseafaris.com).

▲**Church of Santo António**—Rebuilt in part after the 1755 earthquake, this is considered one of the best Baroque churches in Portugal and is dedicated to the patron saint of the military, António. The church (free entry, but rarely open) and adjoining regional archaeological and ethnology museum are worth a look (€2, Tue–Sun 9:30–12:30 & 14:00–17:00, closed Mon).

Bullfights—Lagos occasionally has a small, just-for-tourists bullfight in its dinky ring from June through September on most Saturdays at 18:30. Seats are a steep €25, but the 90-minute show is a thriller. Matadors face three bulls with covered horns. While the earlier portion on horseback is elegant, it gets rowdier later in the show, when a gang of guys pile on the bull while someone grabs the beast's tail and "water-skis" along behind. The event is accompanied by a three-person orchestra. Remember that the Portuguese, with few exceptions, have toned down the fights, and do not kill the bull during the show—they do it later (see also "Portuguese Bullfight" on page 83). Signs all along this touristy coastline advertise bullfights *(Stierkampf)* in German to attract tourists. The town hall (Câmara Municipal), not the TI, has the most up-to-date schedule for bullfights.

SLEEPING

(€1.40 = about $1, country code: 351)
When a price range is given, the lowest is the winter rate and the highest is the August rate. Lagos is enjoyable for a resort its size, but remember that Salema, a village paradise, is only a taxi ride (20 min, €16, metered, but ask for estimate first) or bus ride (30 min) away. If you missed the last bus to Salema (leaves Lagos around 20:30), Albergaria Marina Rio and Pensão Residencial Solar are both within 100 yards of the bus station. Everyone speaks English.

$$$ Casa de São Gonçalo de Lagos, a beautifully decorated 18th-century home with a garden, lovely tile work, parquet floors, and elegant furnishings, is a fine value. While the downstairs rooms are relatively plain, upstairs you'll find a plush Old World lounge, a dreamy garden, and 13 classy old rooms with all the comforts (Sb-€40–70, Db-€50–90, Tb-€70–125, depending on room and season, includes breakfast, cash or AmEx card only, closed Nov–March, Rua Candido dos Reis 73, on a pedestrian street

2 blocks off Praça Luís de Camões, a square that's a block behind the main square, tel. 282-762-171, fax 282-763-927).

$$$ The big, slick **Albergaria Marina Rio** faces the marina and the busy main street immediately in front of the bus station. Its 36 modern, air-conditioned rooms come with all the amenities but not-so-smiley service. Pricier marina views come with noise; quieter rooms are in the back. All rooms have twin beds (Sb-€45–101, Db-€48–104, extra bed-€16–31, includes breakfast and tax, small rooftop pool and terrace, elevator, Internet access, laundry service, Avenida dos Descobrimentos-Apartado 388, tel. 282-780-859, fax 282-769-960, www.marinario.com, marinario @net.vodafone.pt).

$$ Hotel Riomar, next door to the Casa de São Gonçalo de Lagos mentioned earlier in this section, is a modern, blocky, tour-friendly place providing 42 rooms and more comfort than character for a decent price (Db–€45–60, Tb–€65–85, Qb–€85–100, includes breakfast, air-con, elevator, back rooms lack street noise, Rua Candido dos Reis 83, tel. 282-770-130, fax 282-763-927).

$$ Pensão Residencial Solar rents 29 very basic rooms (Sb-€27–47, Db-€38–73, includes breakfast and a fan, cheaper D-€20–40 rooms in annex up the hill and in *quartos* in the center, elevator, Rua António Crisogno dos Santos 60, tel. 282-762-477, fax 282-761-784).

$ The Club Med–like **youth hostel** is a lively, social, cushy hammocks-in-the-courtyard experience (dorm bed in quad-€11–16, one D-€26–35, five Db-€32–43, includes breakfast, kitchen facilities, Internet access, priority given to hostel members, non-members of any age welcome, Rua Lançarote de Freitas 50, tel. 282-761-970, fax 282-769-684, lagos@movijovem.pt).

EATING

You'll find a variety of lively choices for dinner branching out in all directions from Praça Gil Eanes. Most of them offer a similar sampling of grilled fish with plenty of vegetables, but other options range from Italian to Indian. Home-style cooking is better closer to the market. One good choice is **O Pescador,** popular with both locals and tourists. In a simple, bright, paper-napkin atmosphere, they serve good *picanha* (Brazilian flank steak) and grilled fish (daily 12:00–22:00, Rua Gil Eanes 6–10, tel. 282-767-028).

TRANSPORTATION CONNECTIONS

From Lagos by Train and Bus to: Lisbon (6 trains/day, 4–5 hrs, transfer in Tunes; 13 buses/day, 4 hrs, some transfer in Albufeira; €18 for either bus or train), **Évora** (1 bus, at 8:30, 6 hrs, transfer in

Albufeira; 2 trains, at 8:20 and 17:15, 6–7 hrs, transfers at Tunes and Funcheira), **Tavira** (9 trains/day, 3 hrs; 6 buses/day, 3 hrs, both usually transfer in Faro). Confirm times locally. Train info: tel. 808-208-208, bus info: tel. 289-899-700.

Connecting Lagos and Sevilla, Spain, by Bus: There are two buses per day in each direction during summer (€19, about 5.5 hrs from Lagos bus station to Sevilla's Plaza de Armas bus station, buy ticket a day or two in advance May–Oct). In winter, two buses run Monday through Friday only (no weekend service). Ask the TI or a local travel agency for the latest bus schedule. This is the usual schedule, but confirm it locally: Lagos 6:30 to Sevilla 13:00; Lagos 13:45 to Sevilla 20:15; Sevilla 7:30 to Lagos 12:00; Sevilla 16:30 to Lagos 21:00. Note that Spanish time is one hour later than Portuguese time.

From Lagos to Salema: Take a bus (nearly hourly, fewer on weekends, 30 min) or a taxi (€16, 20 min); see "Helpful Hints" on page 115 for details. In Lagos, to get to the bus station from the train station (ignore the "*quartos* women" who tell you Salema is 40 miles away), walk left out of the train station, go through the pink strip mall, cross the arched pedestrian bridge and then the main boulevard, and angle right over to the white-and-yellow EVA bus station (tel. 282-762-944, www.eva-bus.com). Before heading to Salema, pick up return bus schedules and train schedules for your next destination (though as a fallback, Salema Property and Services in Salema has posted schedules).

Tavira

Straddling a river with a lively park, chatty locals, and boats that share its waterfront center, Tavira is a low-rise, easygoing alterna-

tive to the other more aggressive Algarve resorts. It's your best eastern Algarve stop. Because Tavira has good connections by bus and train (it's on the trans-Algarve train line, with nearly hourly departures both east and west), many travelers find the town more accessible than Salema. And, if you're driving from Sevilla to Salema, it's the perfect midway stop on the four-hour trip (just two miles off the freeway).

You'll see many churches and fine bits of Renaissance architecture sprinkled throughout the town. These clues are evidence that 500 years ago Tavira was the largest town on the Algarve (with

1,500 dwellings according to a 1530 census) and an important base for Portuguese adventurers in Africa. The silting up of its harbor, a plague, the 1755 earthquake, and the shifting away of its once-lucrative tuna industry left Tavira in a long decline. Today, the town has a wistful charm and lives off its tourists.

ORIENTATION

Tavira straddles the Rio Gilão two miles from the Atlantic. Everything of sightseeing and transportation importance is on the south bank. A clump of historic sights—the ruined castle and main church—fills its tiny fortified hill and tangled Moorish lanes. But today, the action is outside the old fortifications along the riverside Praça da República square and the adjacent shady fountain- and bench-filled park. The old market hall is beyond the park. And beyond that is the boat to the beach island. The old pedestrian-only "Roman Bridge" leads from Praça da República to the north bank (with two recommended hotels and most of the evening and restaurant action).

Tourist Information

The TI is up the cobbled steps from the inland end of Praça da República (Tue–Thu 9:30–19:00, Fri–Mon until 17:30, closed during lunch and on weekends off-season, Rua Galeria 9, tel. 281-322-511). The TI's free leaflet describes a dozen churches with enthusiasm. But for most tourists, the town's sights can all be seen quickly (see "Welcome to Tavira" walk, next page).

Arrival in Tavira

The train station is a 10-minute walk from the town center *(centro)*. To get to the center, leave the station in the direction of the blue *Turismo* sign, and follow this road downhill to the river and Praça da República. The riverside bus station is three blocks from the town center; simply follow the river into town. Drivers can park on the street, along Rua da Liberdade (*zona pago*, €0.40/hr), for up to four hours.

Helpful Hints

Internet Access: Café Anazu has a gang of computers available (Mon–Sat 10:30–16:00 & 18:00–24:00, Sun 10:30–15:00, just over the bridge at Rua Pessoa 11). There are a few free terminals at the City Hall.

Bike Rental: You can rent bikes at **Sport Nautica** (just down from Café Anazu, Rua Pessoa 26, tel. 281-324-943).

Tavira

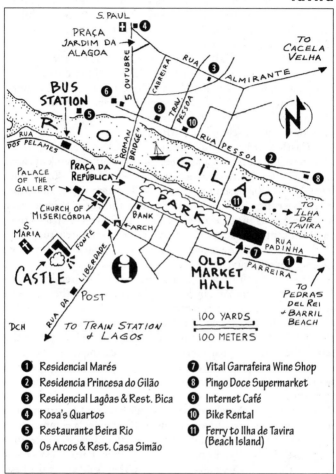

① Residencial Marés
② Residencia Princesa do Gilão
③ Residencial Lagôas & Rest. Bica
④ Rosa's Quartos
⑤ Restaurante Beira Rio
⑥ Os Arcos & Rest. Casa Simão
⑦ Vital Garrafeira Wine Shop
⑧ Pingo Doce Supermarket
⑨ Internet Café
⑩ Bike Rental
⑪ Ferry to Ilha de Tavira (Beach Island)

SELF-GUIDED WALK

Welcome to Tavira

This quick walk starts just before the TI (uphill from the town square) and covers everything of importance.

Old Town Gate: Only this unimpressive gate (just below the TI) survives from Tavira's 16th-century walls. Check out the crown and spheres—meant to remind visitors that they are in the kingdom of Portugal—and the holes for bars that once locked the door.

Church of Misericórdia: At the top of the lane (above the TI), the Church of Misericórdia faced the city gate. Its facade, dating from 1541, is considered the best Renaissance facade in the

Algarve. Inside, you'll see a multitude of blue-and-white tile panels that show you how to lead a good Christian life. Meanwhile, a zealous attendant will make sure you don't take any photos inside (Mon–Fri 9:30–12:30, closed Sat–Sun).

Palace of the Gallery: From the church, hike left up the stepped lane to the Palace of the Gallery. This 17th-century Baroque palace, nearly the town's highest point, is nicknamed "Tavira's Acropolis." It's the biggest private mansion in town, but it also houses a smaller exhibition center on contemporary art that's open to the public (closed Sun–Mon).

Castle Garden: Climb left to the big Church of Santa Maria (which we'll return to in a minute). On your left is a hunk of castle with a door leading to a garden (free, Mon–Fri 8:00–17:00, Sat–Sun 9:00–17:00). The base of the castle wall is supposedly Neolithic, while later inhabitants—the Phoenicians in the eighth century B.C., the Moors in the eighth century A.D., and the Portuguese in the 13th century—added their own layers to the structure. The castle grounds are now a fragrant garden, offering a fine city view. Overlooking the city, notice Tavira's unique "treasury" rooftops—a little roof for each room of a building, likely inspired by visions brought home from Asia by local explorers. Gaze to the right and see tower-wall remnants sprouting up between houses.

Church of Santa Maria: Once a mosque, this church was transformed in the 13th century. Inside, the second chapel on the left is the only part that survived the 1755 earthquake. The third chapel has fine pink columns. The "marble" is actually painted wood, since there was no marble in the Algarve and no money to import it.

Entry to the church's museum (crude but beautiful art in three rooms) and bell tower (peer past the bells to enjoy a commanding city view, with surviving bits of town wall and coastline nearby) each cost €1. Japanese-inspired paintings show Portuguese sailors braving the stormy seas offshore Tavira. There's a WC at the base of the bell tower.

Roman Bridge: Leave the church, walk straight through a small garden down to the street, turn left, and make another left on Rua da Liberdade. Reach the riverfront, and find the pedestrian bridge on your left. The "Roman Bridge" may not be Roman, but it was here when the Moors came. The current structure is from 1657, with parts rebuilt after a 1989 flood. The more functional bridge on your right was designed to be temporary, until the Roman Bridge was fixed. But they decided it (rather than the Roman Bridge) was better for car traffic, and since 1989, the old bridge has been pedestrian-only. Don't cross yet, but continue to the...

Riverside Park and Old Market Hall: This is where old folks gossip and children play. Walk past the bandstand and more "treasury" roofs (on the right) to the old market hall. A few black-and-white photos show how, in the 1990s, this was a noisy, colorful fish and produce market. Today, it's for cafés and shops.

Beyond the market hall are a few fishing boats. Local fishermen are weathering tough times as the "natural park" classification of the coastal areas makes aggressive netting illegal, and Spanish fishermen are selling their catch for far less.

SIGHTS

▲**Ilha de Tavira**—Tavira's great beach island is a hit with travelers. Ilha de Tavira is a long, almost treeless sandbar with a campground, several restaurants, and a sprawling beach. A summer-only boat takes bathers painlessly from downtown Tavira to the island (€1 round-trip, July–mid-Sept about hourly 8:00–20:00, timetable at TI, departs from dock next to old market hall). It's an enjoyable ride even if you just go round-trip without getting out. Or you can bus, taxi, ride a rental bike, or bake during a shadeless 1.25-mile walk out of town to Quatro Aguas, where the five-minute ferry shuttles sunbathers to Ilha de Tavira (€1.50, ferry runs constantly with demand all year, last trip near midnight in high season to accommodate diners).

Near Tavira
▲**Barril Beach**—This fine beach resort is 2.5 miles from Tavira. Walk, rent a bike, or take a city bus to Pedras del Rei, and then catch the little train (usually runs year-round) or walk 10 minutes through Ria Formosa National Park to the resort. Get details at the TI.

Cacela Velha—Just a couple miles east of Tavira (half-mile off the main road), this tiny village sits happily ignored on a hill with its fort, church, one restaurant, a few *quartos,* and a beach with the open sea just over the sandbar, a short row across its lagoon. The restaurant serves a sausage-and-cheese specialty fried at your table. If you're driving, swing by, if only to enjoy the coastal view and to imagine how nice the Algarve would be if people like you and me had never discovered it.

SLEEPING

(€1 = about $1.40, country code: 351)
Everyone speaks English unless otherwise noted. Prices usually shoot up in August. For the best value, head to Rosa's, below.

$$ Residencial Marés, on the busy side of the river amid all the strolling and café ambience, has 25 good rooms, a restaurant, and a rooftop terrace. Some rooms on the second floor have balconies overlooking the river (Sb-€30–50, no singles in Aug; Db-€85 in Aug, €70 in July and Sept, otherwise €55; extra bed-€10, includes breakfast, air-con; Rua José Pires Padinha, on the TI side of the river just beyond old market hall; tel. 281-325-815, fax 281-325-819, maresresidencial@mail.telepac.pt).

$$ Residencia Princesa do Gilão, modern and hotelesque, offers 22 bright rooms. Choose between riverfront or quiet rooms on the back with a terrace (prices vary with the month, Sb-€40–60, Db-€50–70, Tb-€60–80, Qb-€65–85, includes breakfast, cash only, grumpy management, Rua Borda de Agua de Aguiar 10, cross Roman bridge and turn right along river, tel. & fax 281-325-171).

$ Residencial Lagôas is spotless, homey, and a block off the river. Friendly Maria offers a communal refrigerator, laundry wash-board privileges, and a rooftop patio with a view made for wine and candles (S-€20, D-€30, Db-€40, Tb-€50, no gouging in July and Aug, cheaper off-season, no breakfast, cash only, Rua Almirante Candido dos Reis 24, tel. 281-322-252, easy phone reservations). Cross the Roman Bridge from Praça da República, follow the middle fork on the other side, and turn right where it ends.

$ For a quiet, spacious, comfortable stay, **Rosa's Quartos** is worth the communication struggles. Rosa rents 12 big, gleaming, marble-paved rooms on a quiet alley behind her front-door entrance. These bright rooms are comfier and larger than most hotels in town (D-€30, Db-€35, T-€45, Tb-€50, €5 more in Aug, cash only, tel. 281-321-547, ring bell, friendly Rosa doesn't speak English). To get to Rosa's, go over the bridge and through Jardim da Alagoa square to Rua da Porta Nova 4, which is immediately across from St. Paul's church with an unmarked door.

EATING

Tavira is filled with reasonable restaurants. Lively, top-end places face the riverbank just beyond the old market hall. A few blocks inland, hole-in-the-wall places offer more fish per dollar. After dinner, take a stroll along the fish-filled river, with a pause on the Roman Bridge or in the park (if there's any action in the bandstand).

To find three good riverside eateries, cross the Roman Bridge, turn left, go upstream through the tunnel, and you'll see the rickety tables. **Restaurante Beira Rio** has great fish and an extensive menu (€10 meals, nightly 18:00–22:30, tel. 281-323-165). The neighboring **Os Arcos** and **Restaurante Casa Simão** are simpler, with cheap and tasty grilled fish.

For seafood, I enjoyed the inexpensive and relaxed **Restaurante Bica,** below the recommended Residencial Lagôas (see "Sleeping").

Vital Garrafeira offers picnic supplies, but it's mainly about port. It has an excellent, well-priced selection of port, plus higher-end Portuguese wines that are difficult to find elsewhere (daily 8:00–13:00 & 14:30–19:00, Rua José Padinha 66, tel. 281-322-482).

Picnics: Forage at the popular **Pingo Doce** supermarket chain, just across the river (daily 8:00–20:30).

TRANSPORTATION CONNECTIONS

From Tavira to: Lisbon (train or bus works fine: 6 trains/day, 5 hrs, transfer in Faro, arrive at Oriente; 9 direct buses/day, 4.25 hrs), **Lagos** (9 trains/day, some change in Faro, 3 hrs; 6 buses/day, 3 hrs). No official luggage storage is available at either station, but if you're making a quick stop, the ticket seller at the bus station can store small bags. Train info: tel. 808-208-208, bus info: tel. 281-322-546.

Route Tips for Drivers in the Algarve
Lisbon to Salema (185 miles, 3.5 hrs): Following the blue *Sul Ponte* signs, drive south over Lisbon's 25th of April Bridge. A short detour just over the bridge takes you to the giant concrete statue of Cristo Rei (Christ in Majesty). Continue south by freeway until you hit the coast, and follow signs west to Lagos. Take the Lagos Oeste/Vila do Bispo exit and follow signs to *Vila do Bispo* and *Sagres*. If you pay attention, you'll see the turnoff for Salema before Vila do Bispo. A modern freeway, less traffic, and the glory of waking up on the Algarve make doing this drive in the evening after a full day in Lisbon a reasonable option.

Algarve to Sevilla (175 miles, 3 hrs): Drive east along the Algarve. It's a 1.5-hour drive from Salema to Tavira. Some hills are crowned by rotting windmills and others by mobile-phone towers. To visit Lagos, park along the waterfront by the fort and the Mobil gas station. From Lagos, hit the freeway (A22, direction: Lisboa/Faro, then Espanha) to Tavira. Leaving Tavira, follow the signs to *Espanha*. You'll cross over the bridge into Spain (where it's one hour later) and glide effortlessly (90 min by freeway) into Sevilla.

Tavira

ÉVORA

Deep in the heart of Portugal, in the sizzling, arid plains of the southern province of Alentejo, historic Évora (EH-voh-rah) has been a cultural oasis for 2,000 years. With an untouched provincial atmosphere, a fascinating whitewashed old town, museums, a cathedral, a chapel of bones, and even a Roman temple, Évora (pop. 50,000) stands proudly amid groves of cork and olive trees.

Évora—a traditional, conservative city with a small-town feel—added a university about 25 years ago. You'll see plenty of college-age students here, along with lots of retirees—but comparatively few 30- to 40-year olds. There's not much to keep graduates around, and this generation gap—spurred by the clash between old versus new—has lead to two types of *eborenses:* those who treat you with kindness, and those who look at you a little suspiciously. As a result, Évora is the right place to test out your new Portuguese phrasebook (and maybe make a new friend by doing so).

Planning Your Time

With frequent bus connections to Lisbon (hourly, 2 hours), Évora makes a decent day trip from Portugal's capital city. You can stop by for an overnight stay en route to or from the Algarve, which is five hours away (one bus or two trains a day). Drivers can sandwich Évora between Lisbon and the Algarve, exploring dusty droves of olive groves and scruffy seas of peeled cork trees along the way. Take the freeway from the Algarve to Beja, and the nearly-as-fast highway from Beja to Évora. A super freeway zips you from Évora to Lisbon in 90 minutes.

With a day in Évora, take the "Welcome to Évora" walk

Évora

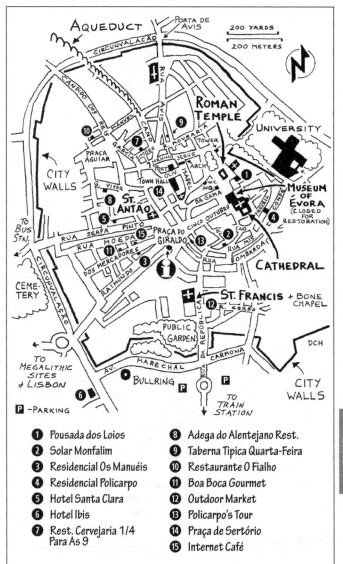

P –PARKING

1. Pousada dos Loios
2. Solar Monfalim
3. Residencial Os Manuéis
4. Residencial Policarpo
5. Hotel Santa Clara
6. Hotel Ibis
7. Rest. Cervejaria 1/4 Para Ás 9
8. Adega do Alentejano Rest.
9. Taberna Tipica Quarta-Feira
10. Restaurante O Fialho
11. Boa Boca Gourmet
12. Outdoor Market
13. Policarpo's Tour
14. Praça de Sertório
15. Internet Café

outlined on the next page, have a quick lunch, see the remaining sights, and enjoy a leisurely, top-notch dinner. After dinner, stroll the back streets and ponder life, like the retired men of Évora do.

ORIENTATION

Évora's old town, contained within a medieval wall, is surrounded by the sprawling newer part of town. The major sights—the Roman Temple and early Gothic cathedral—crowd close together at the old town's highest point. A subtle yet still-powerful charm is contained within the medieval walls. Find it by losing yourself in the quiet lanes of Évora's far corners.

Tourist Information

Pick up a free map at the TI on the main square at Praça do Giraldo 73 (April–Oct daily 9:00–19:00, Nov–March daily 9:00–18:00, tel. 266-730-032). The TI offers an excellent 90-minute **city walk** every morning at 10:00 (€12, minimum of two people, no reservation required, tel. 963-702-392). The tour hits the sights already described in this chapter, but it's a great opportunity to connect with a local and enliven your visit. Policarpo Tours also offers guided city walks, as well as bus tours to Megalithic sights nearby (see page 152).

Arrival in Évora

The bus station is on Avenida São Sebastião. To reach the town center from the station, it's either a short taxi ride (€4) or a 10-minute walk (exit station right, and continue straight all the way into town, passing through the city walls at the halfway point). The train station is on Avenida Dr. Barahona. From the train station to the center, it's a taxi ride (€5) or a long 25-minute walk up Avenida Dr. Barahona, continuing straight—on Rua da República—after you enter the city walls.

Drivers will find Évora's old town frustrating because of its tiny one-way streets. Use one of many free parking lots encircling the town just outside the walls; most hotels are only a short walk away.

Helpful Hints

Internet Access: The big place in town is **Cybercenter,** with 20 computers and lots of local kids playing games (just downhill from main square at Rua dos Mercadores 42). The town hall, on Praça de Sertório, has six free computers, though there's usually a wait.

Taxis: Cabs can be helpful in this small but confusing town. They're parked on the main square (€3.25 minimum for 4 kilometers—likely the farthest you'd go in compact Évora).

Shuttle Bus: The blue line on the streets marks the route of the Linha Azul (Blue Line), a shuttle bus that circles through the town, offering tired locals a convenient ride and tourists easy transport to and from the parking lots outside the walls. Hop on for a city joyride (€0.50, they stop for anyone who waves).

SELF-GUIDED WALK

Welcome to Évora

Évora's walled city is compact, and these sights are all within a five-minute walk of the main square, Praça do Giraldo (PRA-suh doo zhee-RAHL-doo). The

walk takes about an hour, plus time visiting sights. If it's a hot day, go early in the morning or late in the afternoon (last entry to the cathedral at 16:30).

Background: Since becoming a World Heritage Site in 1986, the city has strictly preserved the old center. It works hard to be people-friendly and inviting. The charming colors you see are traditional in Alentejo: Yellow trim is believed to repel evil spirits, and blue actually does keep away flies. Monster garbage cans hide under elegant smaller ones; at night, trucks lift entire hunks of sidewalk to empty them. Jacaranda trees—imported from Brazil 200 years ago—provide shade through the summer and purple flowers in the spring.

From Romans to Moors to Portuguese kings, this little town has a big history. Évora was once a Roman town (second century

B.C. to fourth century A.D.), important because of its wealth of wheat and silver, as well as its location on a trade route to Rome. We'll see Roman sights, though most of Évora's Roman past is buried under the houses and hotels of today (often uncovered by accident when plumbing work needs to be done in basements).

The Moors ruled Évora from the 8th to the 12th centuries. Around the year 1000, Muslim nobles divided up the caliphate into small city-states (like Lisbon), with Évora as this region's capital. And during its glory years (15th–16th centuries), Évora was favored by Portuguese kings, even serving as the home of King John III (1502–1557, Manuel I's son who presided over Portugal's peak of power...and its first decline).

Welcome to Évora Walk

PRAÇA DO GIRALDO — WALK BEGINS & ENDS HERE

• *Start at Évora's main square...*

Praça do Giraldo: This square was named for Giraldo the Fearless, the Christian knight who led a surprise attack and retook Évora from the Moors in 1165. As thanks, Giraldo was made governor of the town and the symbol of the city. (Évora's coat of arms is a knight on a horse; see it crowning the lampposts.) On this square, all that's left of several centuries of Moorish rule is their artistry, evidenced by the wrought-iron balconies of the buildings that ring the square (and the occasional, distinctive Mudejar "keyhole" window found throughout the town).

Until the 16th century, the area behind the *Turismo* (TI) was the Jewish Quarter. At the time, Christians believed that the Bible prohibited them from charging interest for loans. Jews did the moneylending in Évora instead, and the streets in the Jewish Quarter still bear names related to finance, such as Rua da Moeda (Money Street) and Rua dos Mercadores (Merchants' Street).

During the 16th century, the Roman triumphal arch that used to stand on Praça do Giraldo was demolished to make way for the Church of Santo Antão (at the end of the square). In front of the church is a 16th-century fountain—once an important water source for the town (fed by the end of the aqueduct) and now a popular hangout for young and old.

Alentejo Region

Southeastern Portugal is very sunny and very dry. The rolling, empty plains of the Alentejo (ah-len-TAY-zhoo) are dotted with large orchards and estates, Stone Age monoliths, Roman aqueducts, Moorish-looking whitewashed villages, and thick-walled, medieval Christian castles.

During the Christian reconquest of the country, Alentejo was the war zone. When Christian conquerors were victorious over the Muslims, they turned over huge tracts of recaptured land to the care of soldier-monks. These recipients came from various religious-military orders, including the Knights Templar and the Order of Christ (which Prince Henry the Navigator once headed—see the Prince Henry sidebar on page 126). Évora was governed by the House of Avis, which produced the kings of Portugal's Age of Discovery.

Despite its royal past, the Alentejo (the land "beyond the River Tejo," from the Latin *alem Tejo*) is an unpretentious land of farmers. Having been irrigated since Roman and Moorish times, the region is a major producer of wheat, cattle, wine... and trees. You'll see cork trees (green leaves, knotted trunks, red underbark of recently harvested trunks), oak (native to the country, once used to build explorers' caravels), olives (dusty green-silver leaves, major export crop), and eucalyptus (tall, coughdrop-smelling trees imported from Australia, grown for pulp).

Today, the Alentejo region is known for being extraordinarily traditional, even considered backward by snooty Lisboans. The people of Alentejo are the butt of jokes. It's said you'll see them riding motorcycles in pajamas...so they can better lay into the corners. Many Portuguese call porno flicks "Alentejo karate." When I met a sad old guy from Alentejo, I asked him what was wrong; he explained that he was on the verge of teaching his burro how to live without food...but it died. In traditional Alentejo homes, there's always a chair next to the bed, so they can sit down to rest after they get up.

In the 16th century, King John III (mentioned previously) lived in Évora for 30 years. The TI is inside the palace where the king's guests used to stay, but others weren't treated as royally. A fervent proponent of the Inquisition, King John sanctioned the deaths of hundreds of people burned as heretics on this square.

On Tuesday mornings, the square is a traditional cattle-and-produce market. Ranchers and farmers gather without their goods to make deals. It's a medieval stock exchange based on trust. Notice the C.M.E. board (opposite the TI, near the start of Rua 5 de Outubro), where people gather to see who has died recently. You'll see the initials "C.M.E." all over town, from lampposts to manhole covers, but don't think it's only about death. It's an abbreviation for "Câmara Municipal de Évora"—Évora's town hall.

• *Leave the square on Rua 5 de Outubro (opposite the TI office). Take the first left (at Mr. Pickwick's Restaurante) on Alcárcova de Cima, which means "the place with water" in Arabic. A few steps farther on, you'll see a portion of a Roman wall built into the buildings on your right.*

Roman Remnants: A series of modern windows show more of the Roman wall, which used to surround what is now the inner core of the town. Below the last window, you can actually see the red paint of a Roman villa built over by the wall. The wall that currently encircles Évora is from the 14th century, having been fortified in the 17th century during Portugal's fight for independence from Spain.

• *Walk straight, sniffing the wonderful scent of pastries coming from the kitchen of Café Arcada (we'll visit the café at the end of this walk), and cross the intersection to find the...*

Aqueduct: This blunt granite columned end is a relic from the 16th century. The Portuguese have such a fondness for their aqueduct reservoirs that they give them a special name—*Mãe d'Agua* (Mother of Water). As you walk, notice the abnormally high sidewalk to your left. It's the aqueduct channel, supported by stone pillars on the outskirts of town. (Here, it's at street level.)

• *Continue straight on Travessa de Sertório. Within a block, you'll reach a square.*

Praça de Sertório and the Town Hall: The tallest white building on the square is the town hall. Any up-and-coming project for Évora is displayed inside here, including aerial views and scale models that visualize what the future city will look like. Go inside (Mon–Fri 9:00–17:30, closed Sat–Sun, six computers with free Internet access).

Inside the town hall, in the dark corner on the right, is a view of a Roman bath that was uncovered during some building repair. An adjacent painting depicts Romans enjoying the steam. To the right of this overlook is more of the ongoing excavation.

• *Exit the town hall to the right, and take an immediate right around the building. Look up to see a church built into a Roman tower (once part of the Roman wall you saw earlier) and, farther on, the arcaded post office (correios). Walk under the arcades and take the first left, on Rua de Dona Isabel. You'll immediately see a...*

Roman Arch: This arch, the Porta de Dona Isabel, was once a main gate in the Roman wall. Below are some of the original Roman pavement stones, which are large and irregular in size and placement.

When you pass under the Roman wall, you're entering a neighborhood called Mouraria (for the Moors). After Giraldo the

Fearless retook Évora, the Moors were still allowed to live in the area, but on the other side of this gate, beyond the city walls. They were safe here for centuries...until the Inquisition expelled them in the 16th century.

• *Turn right, walking along the road to a patch of grass showing Évora's coat of arms: Giraldo on horseback again. Turn right at the tower, called the Five Corners (Cinco Esquinas) for its five sides, and walk a block up Rua A. F. Simões to...*

Évora's Sight-Packed Square: Here, at the town's high point (1,000 feet above sea level), you'll see the Roman Temple, a public garden, and the dressy Jardim do Paço restaurant, known for its beautiful garden setting, pricey food, and summer evening concerts. Also on the square is the fancy Pousada dos Loios (listed in "Sleeping"), once a 15th-century monastery but now a luxurious hotel with small rooms (blame the monks).

• *To the left of the* pousada, *stairs lead down to a church.*

Igreja dos Loios dos Duques de Cadaval: Stop in to see the church's impressive gold altarpiece. This is the lavish mausoleum chapel of the noble Cadavals (still a big-time family, which is why they charge a fee to enter). You'll walk upon Cadaval tombstones throughout your visit; taped Gregorian chants add to the ambience. Look for the two small trapdoors in the floor that flank the aisle, midway up the church. One opens up to a well (imagine the thoughts going through a bad boy's mind while sitting on this pew during a long service); the other reveals an ossuary stacked with bones. The tilework around the altar is from the 17th century—mere decoration with traditional yellow patterns. Along the nave, the tiles are 18th-century, with scenes illuminating Bible stories. The popularity of these tiles coincided with the flourishing of tapestries in France and Belgium that had the same teaching purpose. The grilled windows you see allowed cloistered monks to attend Mass. The room to the right of the altar contains rare Muslim tilework, ancient weaponry, and religious art, including a cleverly painted Crucifixion (€3, skip the €5 combo-ticket that includes the palace, Tue–Sun 10:00–12:30 & 14:00–18:00, closed Mon, no photos—strictly enforced).

• *Located across the square is the...*

Roman Temple: With 14 Corinthian columns, this temple was part of the Roman forum and the main square in the first century A.D. Today, the town's open-air concerts and events are staged here against an evocative temple backdrop. It's beautifully floodlit at night. While previously known as the Temple of Diana, it was more likely dedicated to the emperor.

Museum of Évora: This museum stands where the Roman forum once sprawled. While the museum is closed indefinitely for restoration, part of the collection may be on display at Santa Clara Church, near recommended Hotel Santa Clara. An excavated section of the forum is in the courtyard of the museum, surrounded by a delightful mix of Roman finds, medieval statuary, and 16th-century Portuguese and Flemish paintings.

• *Across the square from the museum is a white building with the top windows trimmed in yellow. This is the...*

Tribunal of the Inquisition: While there's no need to enter this building, which is now used by the university, it stands as a reminder of Évora's notorious past. Here, thousands of innocent people, many of them Moors and Jews, were tried and found guilty. After being condemned, the prisoners were taken in procession through the streets to be burned on the main square. In front of this building is a granite sculpture of a coffin with a body inside—a memorial to those who were killed.

• *Go to the left of the Inquisition headquarters to find a little street called...*

Rua de Vasco da Gama: Globetrotting da Gama lived on this street after he discovered the water route to India in 1498. His house, not open to the public, is 30 yards down the street at the smudged #15 on your right.

• *Backtrack and turn right for the...*

Cathedral: Located behind the museum, this cathedral was built after Giraldo's conquest—on the site of the mosque. (For more on the cathedral, see "Sights," next page.) The first cardinal of this church was Dom Henrique, who founded the town's university in 1559. Later, Dom Henrique became King Henrique after his great-nephew, the young King Sebastian, presumably died in North Africa in a disastrous attempt to chase the Moors out of Africa. (Not the brightest plan.) Henrique ruled only two years before he died. Because he was a cardinal—and therefore supposedly chaste—he left no direct descendants. The throne of Portugal passed to his cousin, King Philip II of Spain, beginning a bleak 60-year period of Spanish rule (1580–1640)—the start of Évora's decline.

• *Head downhill on the little street opposite the cathedral's entrance. You're walking on...*

Rua 5 de Outubro: This shopping street, which has served this same purpose since Roman times, connects Évora's main sights with its main square. The name of the road celebrates October 5, 1910, when Portugal shook off royal rule and became a republic. The street is lined with products of the Alentejo region: cork (even used as postcards), tile, leather, ironwork, and Arraiolos rugs (handmade, with a distinctive weave, in the nearby town of the same name).

On the shopping street, after you pass the intersection with Rua de Burgos, look left to see a blue **shrine** protruding from the wall of a building. The town built it as thanks to God for sparing it from the 1755 earthquake that devastated much of Lisbon. Ahead of you is the main square. The Chapel of Bones and town market are just a few blocks away on your left. But first, stop by Café Arcada, under the arcade across from the church. Considered the best pastry shop in town (with the surliest staff), it serves good coffee and the local specialty: fresh, sweet cheese tarts (*queijada,* kay-ZHAH-duh, pre-pay at the bar).

SIGHTS

In Évora

▲▲**Cathedral**—Portugal has three archbishops, and one resides here in Évora. This important cathedral of Santa Maria de Évora,

built in the late 12th century, is a transitional mix of Romanesque and Gothic. The tower to the right is Romanesque (more stocky and fortress-like), and the tower to the left is Gothic (lighter, more windows). As usual, this was built upon a mosque after the *Reconquista* succeeded here. That mosque was built upon a Christian Visigothic chapel, proving that religious and military tit for tat is nothing new.

Inside the cathedral, midway down the nave on the left, is a 15th-century painted marble statue of a pregnant Mary. It's thought that the first priests, hoping to make converts out of Celtic pagans who worshipped mother goddesses, felt they'd have more success if they kept the focus on fertility. Throughout Alentejo, there's a deeply felt affinity for this ready-to-produce-a-savior Mary. Loved ones pray here for blessings during difficult deliveries. Across the aisle, a more realistic Renaissance Gabriel, added a century later, comes to tell Mary her baby won't be just any child. The 16th-century pipe organ still works, and the 18th-century high altar is Neoclassical. The muscular Jesus—though carved in wood—matches the marble all around.

Each corner of the **cloister** bears a carving of one of the four evangelists. In the corner, a spiral stairway leads to the "roof," providing a close-up view of the cathedral's fine lantern tower, fortress-like crenellations, and grand views of the Alentejo plains. This "fortress of God" design was typical of the Portuguese

Romanesque style. Back on ground level, a simple chapel niche (on opposite corner from cloister entry) has a child-sized statue of another pregnant Virgin Mary (midway up wall on right) and the sarcophagi of four recent archbishops.

The **museum** is worth visiting. Center-stage in the first room is an intricate 14th-century, French-made, puzzle-like ivory statue of Mary *(Virgem do Paraiso)*. Her "insides" open up to reveal the major events in her life. A photo below shows Mary folded up and ready to travel. Next, a long room lined with crude 15th-century Alentejo paintings has an extremely dramatic Rococo crucifix and the sacred treasures of this church, the richest in Alentejo. In the last room, a glass case displays a sparkling reliquary, containing pieces of the supposed True Cross (in a cross shape), heavily laden with more than a thousand true gems, rotating and brightly spot-lighted to show off every facet.

The sunlit **choir,** which dates from the late 15th to early 16th century, overlooks the cathedral. Its oak stalls are carved with scenes of daily life (hunting boars, harvesting, and rounding up farm animals). The huge contraption in the middle is a music stand. Notice the wide edge on the ends of the seats. Even the older clerics were expected to stand up for much of the service. But when the seat is flipped up, the edge becomes a ledge, making it possible for clerics to sit while they respectfully "stood."

Cost, Hours, Location: Entry to the church is €1; the church and cloister together cost €1.50; and the church, cloister, and museum combo price is €3. The cathedral is open daily July–Aug 9:00–17:00 and Sept–June 9:00–12:30 & 14:00–17:00 (last entry 30 min before closing, audioguide not very useful, photos OK except in museum, WC under cloister entry).

▲▲▲**Church of St. Francis and the Chapel of Bones**—To get to the church from the main square, take the road to the left of the

imposing Bank of Portugal. At the end of the arcade, turn right on Rua da República. You'll see the church to your left just ahead.

Imagine the church in its original, pure style—simple, as St. Francis would have wanted it. It's wide, with just a single nave lined by chapels. In the 18th century, it became popular for wealthy families to buy fancy chapels, resulting in today's gold-leaf hodgepodge. The huge Baroque chapel to the left of the altar is over-the-top, with St. Francis and Claire, his part-ner in Christ-like simplicity, surrounded by anything but poverty. It's slathered in gold leaf from Brazil. The fine 18th-century tiles tell stories of St. Francis' life.

The entrance to the **bone chapel** (Capela dos Ossos) is outside, to the right of the church entrance. The intentionally thought-provoking message above the chapel reads: "We bones in here wait for yours to join us" (€1, additional €0.25 to take photos, June–Aug Mon–Sat 9:00–12:45 & 14:30–17:45, Sept–May Mon–Sat until 17:15, opens at 10:00 Sun and holidays). Inside the macabre chapel, bones line the walls, and 5,000 skulls stare blankly at you from walls and arches. They were unearthed from various Évora churchyards. This was the work of three monks who were concerned about society's values at the time. They thought this would provide Évora, a town noted for its wealth in the early 1600s, with a helpful place to meditate on the transience of material things in the undeniable presence of death. The bones of the three Franciscan monks who founded the church in the 13th century are in the small white coffin by the altar.

When you've finished reflecting on mortality, pop into the **market** (on Rua da República behind the church), busiest in the morning and on Saturday (closed Mon). Wander around. It's a

great slice-of-life look at this community. People are proud of their produce. *"Posso provar?"* (POH-soo proo-VAHR) means "Can I try a little?" *Provar* some cheese and stock up for a picnic.

Now take a refreshing break in the **public gardens** (Jardim Publico, main entrance across from market, at the bottom of Praça 1 de Maio). Just inside the gate, Vasco da Gama looks on with excitement as he discovers a little kiosk café nearby selling sandwiches, freshly baked goodies, and drinks. For a fine little lunch, try an *empada de galinha* (tiny chicken pastry) and possibly another *queijada* (sweet cheese tart). The gardens, bigger than they look, contain an overly restored hunk of the 16th-century Royal Palace (right of entry gate). Behind the palace, look over the stone balustrade to see a kids' playground and playfields. Life goes on—make no bones about it.

▲**University**—First known as the College of the Holy Spirit, this institution was established as a Jesuit university in 1559 by Dom Henrique, the cathedral's first archbishop (1512–1580). He was John III's brother and later became a cardinal, grand inquisitor, and Portugal's king. Two hundred years later, Marquês de Pombal (see sidebar, page 52), the powerful minister of King José I, decided that the Jesuits had become too rich, too political, and—as the sole teachers of society—too closed to modern thinking. He abolished the Jesuit society in 1759 and confiscated their wealth.

The university was closed until 1979, when it reopened as a secular school. Injecting 8,000 students into this town of 50,000 people (with 14,000 inside the walls) brought Évora a new vitality...and discos. Unlike an American-style campus, the colleges are scattered throughout the town.

The main entrance of the university is the old courtyard on the ground level (downhill from the original Jesuit chapel). Enter the inner courtyard (free Mon–Sat mornings, €1.50 Sat 15:00–18:00 and Sun 10:00–14:00 & 15:00–18:00, tel. 266-740-800). While it's fun to visit when classes are in session, on Sunday all the rooms—though empty—are wide open for visitors. Attractive blue-and-white tiles (the biggest and best-preserved collection south of Lisbon) ring the walls and the classrooms (which line the courtyard arcades), with the theme of the original class portrayed in the tiles. Poke or peek into a classroom to see the now-ignored pulpit. (Originally, Jesuit priests were the teachers, and information coming from a pulpit was not to be questioned.)

On Sundays, you can enter the room directly across the courtyard from the entrance. Major university events are held here under the watchful eyes of Cardinal Henrique (the painting to the left) and young King Sebastian (to the right).

The university shop to the right of this room gives you a great look at the tiles. In the 16th century, this was a classroom for students of astronomy—note the spheres and navigational instruments mingled with cupids and pastoral scenes. Imagine the class back then. Having few books, if any, the students (males only) took notes as the professor taught in Latin from the lectern in the back.

The cafeteria (off the second smaller courtyard behind the main one) thrives with students and offers super-cheap meals (Mon–Fri 8:30–18:00, closed Sat–Sun, WC).

Near Évora
Megalithic Sights—Near Évora, you'll find stony sights, including menhirs (solitary standing stones, near Guadalupe and elsewhere); dolmens (rock tombs at Anta do Zambujeiro and Anta Capela de São Brissos); cromlechs (rocks in formation à la Stonehenge, at Cromeleque dos Almendres; see next page); and a cave with prehistoric paintings (Gruta do Escoural, closed Mon). Depending on how much you want to see, you can do a 15- to 45-mile loop from Évora by **bus** or by **car** (list of rental-car agencies available at Évora's TI).

Policarpo's Tour offers bus tours of the megaliths (€20, two-person minimum, cash only, no guide, 3.5 hours, runs daily depending on demand, book two days in advance in summer, Rua 5 de Outubro 63, tel. 266-746-970, www.incoming-alentejo.com, info@incoming-alentejo.com). Policarpo also offers an €18 two-hour walking tour of Évora (if a minimum of four people sign up) and a €20 four-hour visit to the hilltop fortress town of Monsaraz (two-person minimum, stops at local winery).

Cromeleque dos Almendres—This 4,000-year-old Portuguese Stonehenge stands in the midst of cork trees down a dirt road that's a five-mile (20 min) drive west of Évora (take main highway to Lisbon in the direction of Guadalupe, follow clear signposts to stones). Those in a hurry should skip the first signposted site (a lone 10-foot menhir) and continue to the second—95 rounded granite stones erected in the shape of an oval that likely served as a ritual gathering spot for Stone Age sun-worshippers. A posted description (in English) at the site tells more. Stop and pet the sheep if they happen to be grazing nearby.

Bullfighting—Bullfights are rare in Évora, but nearby towns advertise fights on Saturday and Sunday through the season (just outside southern city wall, roughly Easter–Sept, details from TI). Notice that women are on the program now (perhaps to give a tired sport a little kick).

SLEEPING

$$$ Pousada dos Loios, formerly a 15th-century monastery, is now a classy hotel renting 30 well-appointed cells. While the rooms are tiny, this luxury hotel sprawls with many fine public spaces, courtyards, and a small swimming pool. Unfortunately, the staff is less than accommodating (Db-€250, less Nov–March, air-con, free parking, Convento dos Loios, across from Roman Temple, tel. 266-730-070, fax 266-707-248, www.pousadas.pt, recepcao.loios @pousadas.pt).

$$ Solar Monfalim, a 16th-century noble house, seems unchanged from when it received its first hotel guests in 1892. This elegant hacienda-type accommodation, with homey lounges and a Valium ambience, rents 26 rooms in a central and quiet location (Sb-€50–60, Db-€60–85, extra bed-€20–25, air-con, pleasant breakfast room with balcony, parking-€4, Largo da Misericordia 1, tel. 266-750-000, fax 266-742-367, www.monfalimtur.pt, reservas@monfalimtur.pt).

$$ At stately **Residencial Os Manuéis,** 14 cozy rooms surround an airy central patio. Breakfast can be served on the terrace with views of the sweeping Alentejo plains, while the Church of St. Francis looms in the distance. Eduardo makes you feel at home

Sleep Code

(€1 = about $1.40, country code: 351)
S = Single, **D** = Double/Twin, **T** = Triple, **Q** = Quad, **b** = bathroom,
s = shower only. Unless otherwise noted, credit cards are
accepted, English is spoken, and breakfast is included.
    To help you easily sort through these listings, I've divided
the rooms into three categories, based on the price for a standard double room with bath:

  $$$ Higher Priced—Most rooms €100 or more.
   $$ Moderately Priced—Most rooms between €50–100.
    $ Lower Priced—Most rooms €50 or less.

and loves to share his knowledge of Portugal (Sb-€35–60, Db-
€40–65, suite-€60–80, extra bed-€15, air-con, no elevator, free
parking, Rua do Raimundo 35, tel. 266-769-160, fax 266-769-161,
www.residencialosmanueis.com, res.osmanueis@sapo.pt).

$$ Residencial Policarpo, filling another 16th-century
nobleman's mansion, also has a homey feel, with 20 simple
rooms—each one unique—tucked around a courtyard. Joaquim,
Michele, and David Policarpo carry on the family tradition of
good hospitality (S-€30, Sb-€52, D-€40, Db-€57, Tb-€70, about
€10 less in low season, cash only, double-paned windows, air-con
in rooms with bathroom, no elevator, terrace, fireplace, easy park-
ing, two entrances: Rua da Freiria de Baixo 16 and Rua Conde
da Serra, near university, tel. 266-702-424, fax 266-703-474,
www.pensaopolicarpo.com, mail@pensaopolicarpo.com).

$$ Hotel Santa Clara, renting 41 comfortable rooms on a
quiet side street, is solid, professional, and tour-friendly. Part of the
Best Western chain, it lacks character, but comes with a good location and price (Sb-€68, Db-€79, air-con, Travessa do Milheira 19;
from Praça do Giraldo, take Rua Pinta Serpa downhill, then right
on Milheira; coming from the bus station, turn left on Milheira
after you enter city wall; tel. 266-704-141, fax 266-706-544, www
.hotelsantaclara.pt, hotelsantaclara@mail.telepac.pt).

$$ Hotel Ibis, a cheap chain hotel, has 87 identical Motel
6–type rooms located a 15-minute walk from the center, just out-
side the city walls. Simple to find and offering easy parking, it's a
cinch for drivers—but staying here is like eating at McDonald's in
Paris (Sb/Db-€59, €49 Oct–July, breakfast-€5.50, one child under
12 sleeps free, air-con, elevator, parking, Quinta da Tapada, tel.
266-760-700, fax 266-760-799, www.ibishotel.com).

Versatile Cork

The cork extracted from the bottle of wine you're having with dinner is probably more local than the wine. The Alentejo region is known for producing cork. From the center of a baseball to a gasket on the space shuttle, from bulletin boards

to coasters, cork is a remarkable substance, spongy and pliable, but resistant to water.

Cork—used mainly for bottle stoppers—comes from the bark of the cork oak *(Quercus suber)*, a 30-foot tree with a sprawling canopy and knotty trunk that grows well in dry heat and sandy soil. After 25 years, a tree is mature enough for harvest. The outer bark is stripped from the trunk, leaving a "wound" of red-colored "blushing" inner bark. It takes nine years for the bark to grow back, and then it can be harvested again—a cork tree keeps producing for more than 100 years. After harvesting, the bark is boiled to soften it up, then flattened. Machines cut the cork into the desired shape, or punch out bottle stoppers. These are then polished, producing tasteless, odorless seals for wine bottles.

Portugal produces more than half the world's supply of cork (with Spain making much of the rest). These days, many wine stoppers are made from plastic, which could become a threat to cork production. So far the business remains strong, thanks to cork's insulating and acoustical applications, but some fear that if cork eventually loses its economic value, the survival of the forests—and the special ecosystem they support—will be at risk.

EATING

Restaurante Cervejaria 1/4 Para As 9 (Quarter to Nine) steams up with local families and tourists chowing down on favorites such as *arroz de tamboril* (a rice and seafood stew) and *açorda de marisco* (a spicy soup with clams, shrimp, and bread spiced with Alentejano herbs like cilantro). They have an excellent wine list, but I like to let the waiter recommend something good (€15 meals, daily 12:00–16:00 & 19:00–23:00, some outdoor seating, Rua Pedro Simões 9, near exposed kink in aqueduct off Rua do Menino Jesus, tel. 266-706-774).

Adega do Alentejano is like an above-ground wine cellar. Locals choose from cheap (€9/plate) traditional dishes, including tasty pork options. The menu is scrawled on chalkboards at the entrance and throughout the restaurant. Go early, as the place can fill up. Ask to watch them pour your *jarra* of house wine from the large earthenware vats at the back. If you didn't try *ginjinha* in Lisbon or Óbidos, finish your meal with a glass of this house-made cherry liqueur (Mon–Sat 12:00–15:00 & 19:00–22:00, closed Sun, cash only, Rua Gabriel Victor do Monte Pereira 21-A; from main square go alongside church on Rua João de Deus, then take third left and keep walking; tel. 266-744-447).

Taberna Tipica Quarta-Feira is a rustic eight-table tavern, festooned with patriotic Portuguese decor, where Zé Dias and his family proudly and expertly serve country cooking, including rabbit and partridge in season. Don't expect to be able to order from a menu here—they usually serve just the food that they felt like cooking that day, making this a truly unique experience (€20 fixed-price meal comes with a fine wine, Mon–Sat 12:00–15:00 & 19:30–22:00, closed Sun, hidden on a narrow street just north off Rua da Mouraria at Rua do Inverno 16, tel. 266-707-530).

Restaurante O Fialho is a famous place where white-coated waiters feed Alentejo cuisine to Bogart-like locals. With €25 meals, it's expensive, but arguably offers the best food in town (Tue–Sun 12:00–24:00, closed Mon, arrive before 20:00 or make a reservation, air-con, Travessa das Mascarenhas 14; from main square go right alongside church—Rua João de Deus—for a 5-min walk, take first left after public square with theater; tel. 266-703-079).

Boa Boca Gourmet is just the spot for a good bottle of wine and some snacks. While it's not a restaurant, it offers enough tasty treats for a light meal—including wonderful cheeses, preserves, sausages, and even foie gras. Visit on Saturday to try a wide variety of their products (daily 10:30–19:00, Rua dos Mercadores 54, tel. 266-704-632).

TRANSPORTATION CONNECTIONS

From Évora to: Lisbon (by bus: almost hourly, 2 hrs; by train: 2/day, 2–3.5 hrs, change in Casa Branca, stops at Lisbon's Oriente Station), **Lagos** (by bus: 2/day, 6 hrs, transfer in Albufeira; by train: 2/day, 6–7 hrs with transfers at Funcheira and Tunes), **Coimbra** (4 buses/weekday, erratic scheduling on weekends, more options with transfer in Lisbon, 4.5 hrs), **Madrid** (2 buses/day, 7.5–10 hrs, book Spain tickets at Anibal Tours in Hotel da Cartuxa or at Eurolines/Intersul office on second floor of bus station; the 7.5-hour bus is overnight). Portugal bus info (no English spoken): tel. 266-769-410.

NAZARÉ
AND NEARBY

Nazaré • Batalha • Fátima • Alcobaça • Óbidos

Nazaré, an Atlantic-coast fishing town turned resort, is both black-shawl traditional and beach-friendly. Several other worthy sights are within easy day-trip distance of Nazaré. You can drop by Batalha to see its monastery, the patriotic pride and architectural joy of Portugal. If the spirit moves you, the pilgrimage site at Fátima is nearby. Alcobaça has Portugal's largest church (and saddest romance). And Portugal's incredibly cute walled town of Óbidos is just down the road.

Planning Your Time

While the far north of Portugal has considerable charm, those with limited time can enjoy maximum travel thrills here. This area is an ideal stop if you're interested in a small-town side-trip north from Lisbon, or if you're coming in from Salamanca or Madrid, Spain.

On a two-week trip through Portugal, Nazaré merits a day. There's another day's worth of sightseeing in Alcobaça, Batalha, and Fátima (I'd prioritize in that order). See Óbidos on the way to or from Nazaré.

Nazaré

I got hooked on Nazaré back when colorful fishing boats littered its long, sandy beach. Now the boats motor comfortably into a new harbor 30 minutes' walk south of town, the beach is littered with frolicking families, and it seems that most of Nazaré's 10,000 inhabitants are in the tourist trade. But I still like the place.

Nazaré Fashions:
Seven Petticoats and Black Widows

Nazaré is famous for its women who wear skirts with seven petticoats. While this is partially just a creation for the tourists, there is some element of truth to the tradition. In the old days, women would sit on the beach waiting for their fishermen to sail home. To keep warm in the face of a cold sea wind while staying modestly covered, they'd wear several petticoats in order to fold layers over their heads, backs, and legs. Even today, older and more traditional women wear short skirts made bulky by several—but not seven—petticoats. The ensemble is completed with a head scarf, chunky gold earrings, and house slippers.

You'll see some women wearing black, a sign of mourning. Traditionally, if your spouse died, you wore black for the rest of your life. This tradition is still observed, although in the last generation, widows did begin remarrying.

You'll be greeted by the energetic applause of the surf, widows with rooms to rent, and big plates of steamed shrimp. Relax in the Portuguese sun in a land of cork groves, eucalyptus trees, ladies in petticoats, and men who stow cigarettes and fishhooks in their stocking caps.

Even with its summer crowds, Nazaré is a fun stop that offers a surprisingly good look at old Portugal. Somehow the traditions survive, and the locals are able to go about their black-shawl ways. Wander the back streets for a fine look at Portuguese family-in-the-street life. Laundry flaps in the wind, kids play soccer, and fish sizzle over tiny curbside hibachis. Squadrons of sun-dried and salted fish are crucified on nets pulled tightly around wooden frames

and left under the midday sun. (Locals claim they are delightful... but I don't know.) Off-season Nazaré is almost empty of tourists—inexpensive, colorful, and relaxed, with enough salty fishing-village atmosphere to make you pucker.

Nazaré doesn't have any blockbuster sights. The beach, tasty seafood, and the funicular ride up to Sítio for a great coastal view are the bright lights of my lazy Nazaré memories.

Plan some beach time here. Sharing a bottle of chilled *vinho verde* (young white wine, a specialty of Portugal) on the beach at sundown is a good way to wrap up the day.

Nazaré

❶	Albergaria Mar Bravo	❻	Restaurante A Tasquinha
❷	Hotel Maré	❼	Casa Oficina Restaurant
❸	Residencial A Cubata	❽	A Barca Restaurant
❹	Ribamar Hotel-Restaurant	❾	To Restaurante O Luis
❺	Julia Pereira Rooms & Casa dos Frangos Rest.	❿	Laundry
		⓫	To Internet Access

ORIENTATION

Nazaré faces its long beach, stretching north from the new harbor to Sítio, the hill-capping old part of town. Survey the town from Avenida da República, which lines the waterfront (leaving the bus station, turn right and walk a block to the waterfront). Scan the cliffs. The funicular climbs to Sítio. Also to your right, look at the road kinking toward the sea. The building (on the kink) with the yellow balconies is the Ribamar Hotel (also listed on page 162), next to the TI. Just beyond the Ribamar, you'll find the main square (Praça Sousa Oliveira, with banks and ATMs) and most of my hotel listings.

Sitting quietly atop its cliff, Sítio feels like a totally separate village. Its people don't fish; they farm. Take the funicular (see details later in this chapter) up to the top for a spectacular view.

Tourist Information: The TI faces the beach south of the main square (daily July–Aug 9:00–21:00, April–June and Sept 9:00–13:00 & 14:30–19:00, Oct–March 9:30–13:00 & 14:30–18:00, tel. 262-561-194). Ask about summer activities and bullfights in Sítio.

Helpful Hints

Markets: A **flea market** pops up near Nazaré's town hall every Friday (9:00–13:00, at the inland end of the street the bus station is on) and the colorful **town market** bustles with fresh fish, produce, and caged rabbits in the morning (daily 8:00–13:00, Oct–May closed Mon, green building kitty-corner from bus station just behind taxi stand).

Internet Access: Café.com offers the fastest connection in town (daily 9:30–24:00, six terminals, in Edificio Atlântico on Avenida da República toward the new port), but the **Cultural Center Library** offers 30 minutes for free (Mon–Fri 9:30–13:00 & 14:00–19:00, Sat 15:00–19:00, closed Sun, on main road along beach to harbor).

Laundry: At Lavanderia Nazaré, close to the bus station, Fátima will wash, dry, and fold your laundry for pickup the next day (€3.20/kg—about 2 lbs, Mon–Sat 9:00–13:00 & 15:00–19:00, closed Sun, Rua Branco Martins 17, tel. 262-552-761).

SIGHTS AND ACTIVITIES

The Beach—It's the domain of the summertime beach tents, a tradition in Portugal. In Nazaré, the tents are run as a coopera-tive by the old women you'll see sitting in the shade ready to col-lect €6 or more a day. The beach is groomed and guarded, and in the evening, piped music is played. Flags indicate danger level: red (no one allowed in the water), yellow (wading is safe), and green (no problem).

If you see a mass of children parading through town down to the beach, they're likely from a huge dorm in town, where poorer kids from this part of the country are put up for a summer break.

Boats used to line the beach in summer and fill the squares

in winter, but when the harbor was built in 1986, that's where the boats ended up. Today, only re-creations occur (on most Sundays in May), when boats line the main square to show the hands-on fishing process of the past (confirm exact days with the TI).

Funicular to Sítio—Nazaré's funicular was originally built in 1889—the same year as the Eiffel Tower—by the same disciple of Eiffel who built the much-loved elevator in Lisbon. The equipment and stations, however, have been modernized. Ride up the lift (follow signs to *ascensor*); it goes every 15 minutes (€0.80 each way, first run at 7:00, July–Aug every 5 min until 22:30, then every half-hour until 2:00 in the morning; Sept–June on the quarter-hour until 21:30, then every half-hour until midnight; WCs at each station). Walk to the staggering Nazaré viewpoint behind the station at the top, then to the main viewpoint past the many vendors at the promontory (wave to America).

N? SENHORA DA NAZARÉ

Visit the small chapel dedicated to Our Lady of Nazaré. The story is depicted on tiles throughout the town. Dom Fuas, a local noble, was hunting deer and became so absorbed in the chase that he didn't realize he was about to go over the cliff. The Virgin Mary appeared suddenly and stopped him, saving his life. (The unfortunate deer didn't see Mary in time.)

Activities at Sítio—Sítio stages Portuguese-style bullfights on Saturday nights in summer (July–mid-Aug, tickets from €10 at kiosk in Praça Sousa Oliveira). Sítio's NorParque is a family-friendly water park with a pool, slides, and Jacuzzi (€10 for adults, €8 for kids ages 6–11, cheaper after 14:00, June–mid-Sept 10:30–19:00, closed mid-Sept–May, opening may be delayed until July depending on weather, confirm hours at TI, watch for free shuttle bus parked on the main drag, tel. 262-562-282).

For panoramic views over the north beach *(praia norte)*, stroll

toward the Farol lighthouse (10-min walk from Sítio's main square); Restaurante Arimar, on the left along the way, is a good place to take in the sunset with drinks or dinner (avoid windy days). Restaurante O Luis, also in Sítio, is worth finding (see "Eating," later in the Nazaré section).

Nazaré

SLEEPING

You should have no problem finding a room, except in August, when the crowds, temperatures, and prices are all at their highest. You'll find plenty of hustlers meeting each bus and Valado train, waiting along the promenade. Even the normal hotels get into the act during the off-season. I've never arrived in town without a welcoming committee inviting me to sleep in their *quartos* (rooms in private homes).

I list a price range for each hotel: The lowest is for winter (roughly Jan–March), the highest for mid-July through August. The rest of the year (approximately April–mid-July and Sept–Dec), expect to pay about midrange. You will save serious money if you arrive with no reservations and try your hand at bargaining, even at hotels.

Hotels

$$$ Albergaria Mar Bravo is on the main square and the water-front. Its 16 comfy rooms are great—modern, bright, fresh—and they come with balconies, eight of them with views (Sb-€50–90, Db-€50–120, prices vary depending on view and month, view breakfast room, free parking, air-con, elevator, attached restaurant serves seafood, Praça Sousa Oliveira 71-A, tel. 262-569-160, fax 262-569-169, www.marbravo.com, info@marbravo.com).

$$$ Hotel Maré, just off the Praça Sousa Oliveira, is a big, modern American-style hotel with 36 rooms, some tour groups, and a rooftop terrace (Sb-€40–80, Db-€53–103, Tb-€57–118, all with air-con and balconies, double-paned windows, elevator, free parking lot, Rua Mouzinho de Albuquerque 8, tel. 262-561-122, fax 262-561-750, www.marehotel.com, hotel.mare@mail.telepac.pt).

$$$ Residencial A Cubata, a friendly place on the water-front on the north end, has 22 small, comfortable rooms and older bathrooms (Sb-€50–90, Db-€60–130, depends on view and season, noisy bar below, though they've added soundproofing, Avenida da República 6, tel. 262-561-706, fax 262-561-700). For a peaceful night, forgo the private balcony, take a back room (saving some money), and enjoy the communal beachfront balcony.

$$ Ribamar Hotel-Restaurant has a prime location on the waterfront, with an Old World, hotelesque atmosphere, including 25 rooms with dark wood and four-poster beds (Sb-€25–55, Db-€30–89, prices flexible, four rooms with balconies, good attached restaurant downstairs; parking-€5/day, €10 in Aug; Rua Gomes Freire 9, tel. 262-551-158, fax 262-562-224, ribamar.nazare@mail.telepac.pt but fax is preferred). Look for the yellow awnings and balconies.

Sleep Code

(€1 = about $1.40, country code: 351)
S = Single, **D** = Double/Twin, **T** = Triple, **Q** = Quad, **b** = bathroom,
s = shower only. Unless otherwise noted, you can assume
credit cards are accepted; breakfast is included at hotels, but
not *quartos;* and English is spoken.

To help you easily sort through these listings, I've divided
the rooms into three categories, based on the price for a standard double room with bath in summer. The rest of the year,
it's 10–20 percent less:

  $$$ Higher Priced—Most rooms €80 or more.
   $$ Moderately Priced—Most rooms between €50–80.
    $ Lower Priced—Most rooms €50 or less.

Quartos

I list no dumpy hotels or cheap pensions, because the best budget
option is *quartos*. Like nowhere else in Iberia, locals renting spare
rooms clamor for your business here. Except perhaps for weekends
in August, you can stumble into town any day and find countless
women hanging out on the street (especially around the bus station) with fine modern rooms to rent. I promise. The TI's partial
list of *quartos* totals 200. If you need a cheap room, they've got it.
Their rooms are generally better than hotel rooms—for half the
cost. Your room is likely to be large and homey, with old-time-
elegant furnishings (with no plumbing, but plenty of facilities
down the hall). Many *quartos* are located in a quiet neighborhood, six short blocks off the beachfront action. I'd come into
town and have fun looking at several places. Hem and haw, and
the price goes down.

$ Nazaré Amada rents seven fine rooms (average price for
Db–€45, €35 Oct–June, Rua Adrião Batalha, garage, tel. 262-552-
206, mobile 962-579-371).

$ Julia Pereira, who used to live in Canada, rents five nice
rooms with private baths in a central location. Ask for an ocean
view (average price for Db–€30–50, slightly more in Aug, on Praça
Dr. Manuel Arriaga next to Casa dos Frangos and above café, tel.
262-553-516, mobile 967-468-011, eduardacorreia@gmail.com).

EATING

Nazaré is a fishing town, so don't order *hamburguesas*. Fresh
seafood is tasty all over town, more expensive (but affordable)
along the waterfront, and cheaper further inland. Waiters will

usually bring you food (such as olives or bread) that you didn't order. Don't touch it, or you'll pay for it. Double-check your bill to make sure you're not being charged for something you didn't eat.

In this fishing village, even the snacks come from the sea. *Percebes* are local boiled barnacles, sold as munchies in bars and on the street. Merchants are happy to demonstrate how to eat them and let you sample one for free (say *"Posso provar?"*). They're great with beer in the bars.

Try Portugal's light, young wine, *vinho verde;* with its champagne-like taste, it's perfect with shellfish. *Amêndoa amarga* is the local amaretto. For a tasty pastry, try a *pastel de feijão* (fay-ZHOW) from any café. This small tart with a puff-pastry shell has a filling similar to pecan pie, but it's actually made of white beans.

Popular **Restaurante A Tasquinha** dishes up authentic Portuguese cuisine with a cozy blue-and-white picnic-bench ambience. Friendly, hardworking Carlos and his family serve their fish with a special sauce. He'll come to your table to personally check on your meal (Tue–Sun 12:00–15:00 & 19:00–22:30, closed Mon, Rua Adrião Batalha 54, tel. 262-551-945).

The family-run **Casa Oficina** serves home-style seafood dishes, not fancy but hearty, in a friendly setting that makes you feel like you're eating at someone's kitchen table. You are. Sit with the locals, talk about what's on TV, and draw your home state on the paper tablecloth (daily 12:00–15:00 & 19:00–22:00, if it's quiet at night, it may be closed, Rua das Flores 33, off Praça Dr. Manuel Arriaga; facing the restaurant Casa dos Frangos, take street immediately left; tel. 262-083-703).

Mom-and-daughter **A Barca** bursts with yellow decor, televised soap operas, and tasty *sardinhas grelhadas* (grilled sardines). It's these kind of cozy, local spots—good for budget-conscious travelers—that take the touristy edge off Nazaré (daily 10:00–24:00, Rua Adrião Batalha 75).

Chicken addicts can get roasted chicken to go at **Casa dos Frangos** (€6 chicken, daily 9:30–13:00 & 15:30–20:30, Praça Dr. Manuel Arriaga 20), while picnic-gatherers can head for the covered *mercado* across from the bus station (daily 8:00–12:00, closed Mon Oct–May). Other to-go and picnic options can be found in any number of mini-markets along Rua Sub-Vila.

Restaurante O Luis in Sítio serves excellent seafood and local cuisine to an enthusiastic crowd in a cheery atmosphere. While few tourists go here, the friendly white-coated waiters make you feel welcome (€10 dinners, Fri–Wed 12:00–24:00, closed Thu, air-con, Rua Dos Tanques 7, tel. 262-551-826). This place is worth the trouble if you want to eat well: Ride the funic-

Nazaré and Nearby

ular up to Sítio and exit right; take the steps down to the main drag; turn right on the main drag and walk to the bullring; take the street downhill left of the bullring; then walk three minutes to Praça de Touros.

TRANSPORTATION CONNECTIONS

Nazaré's bus station is in the center, on Avenida Vieira Guimarães, one block inland from the waterfront. The nearest train station is at Valado (three miles toward Alcobaça, connected by semi-regular €1.25 buses and reasonable, easy-to-share €8 taxis). To avoid this train-station headache, consider using intercity buses instead of trains. If you're heading to Lisbon, trains and buses work equally well. While the train station is three miles from Nazaré and a trip to Lisbon requires a transfer in Cacém, you'll arrive at Lisbon's very Central Rossio Station (near recommended hotels). Lisbon's bus station is a metro (or taxi) ride away from the center.

From Nazaré/Valado by Train to: **Coimbra** (6/day, 2.5 hrs, change at Bifurcação de Lares; bus is faster—see below), **Lisbon** (3/day, 3.5–5 hrs, more frequent departures with transfers). Train info: tel. 808-208-208.

Nazaré by Bus to: Alcobaça (stopping at Valado, 11/day, 15 min), **Batalha** (7/day, 1 hr, some change at São Jorge), **Óbidos** (12/day, 1 hr; bus is better than train, most transfer in Caldas da Rainha), **Fátima** (2/day, 1.5 hrs), **Coimbra** (5/day, 2 hrs, some transfer in Leiria), **Lisbon** (7/day, 2 hrs). Buses are scarce on Sunday. Bus info: tel. 707-223-344.

Day-Tripping from Nazaré to Alcobaça, Batalha, Fátima, or Óbidos: Traveling by bus, you can see both Alcobaça and Batalha in one day (but not on Sun, when bus service is sparse). Alcobaça is easy to visit on the way to or from Batalha (and both are connected by bus with Óbidos). Ask at the bus station or TI for schedule information, and be flexible. Fátima has the fewest connections and is farthest away. Without a car, Fátima is not worth the trouble for most, but if you're heading by bus to Coimbra, you can go via Fátima. A taxi from Nazaré to Alcobaça costs about €15; agree on the price before leaving town.

Batalha

On August 14, 1385, two armies faced off on the rolling plains of Batalha to decide Portugal's future—independence or rule by Spanish kings? The Portuguese King John (João) I ordered his 7,000 men to block the road to Lisbon. The Spanish Castilian king, with 32,000 soldiers and 16 modern cannons, ordered his men to hold their fire. But when the Portuguese knights dismounted from their horses to form a defensive line, some hotheaded Spaniards—enraged by such a display of unsportsmanlike conduct by supposedly chivalrous knights—attacked.

Shoop! From the side came 400 arrows from English archers fighting for Portugal. The confused Castilians sounded the retreat, and the Portuguese chased them, literally, all the way back to Castile. A mere half-hour (and several hundred deaths) after it began, the Battle ("Batalha") of Aljubarrota was won. (Spaniards say they were defeated by the plague.) King John I claimed the Portuguese crown, and thanked the Virgin Mary with a new church and monastery.

The only reason to stop in the town of Batalha is to see its great monastery, considered Portugal's finest architectural achievement and a symbol of its national pride. Unfortunately, the highway runs directly in front of the monastery, but at least there's no missing it from the road.

Tourist Information

The TI, behind the monastery, has free maps and information on buses (daily May–Sept 10:00–13:00 & 15:00–19:00, Oct–April 10:00–13:00 & 14:00–18:00, Praça Mouzinho de Albuquerque, tel. 244-765-180). Batalha's market day is Monday morning (market is 200 yards behind monastery).

Arrival in Batalha

If you take the bus to Batalha, you'll be dropped off a block behind the monastery and TI. If you have any difficulty locating the monastery, ask anyone to point you toward the *mosteiro*. There's no official luggage storage, but you can leave luggage at the TI if you ask nicely, or at the monastery's ticket desk while you tour the cloisters. If you're driving, follow the signs to *Batalha* and park free alongside the church.

SIGHTS

▲▲▲Monastery of Santa María

Here's a self-guided tour of the town's most important sight.

Exterior (1388–1533): The Church of Our Lady of Victory (c. 1388–1550) is a fancy late Gothic (pointed-arch) structure decorated with lacy Gothic tracery—stained-glass windows, gargoyles, railings, and Flamboyant pinnacles representing the flickering flames of the Holy Spirit. (Inside, we'll see even more elaborate Manueline-style ornamentation, added towards the end of its construction.) The church's limestone has mellowed over time into a warm, rosy, golden color.

The equestrian statue outside the church is of Nuno Alvares Pereira, who commanded the Portuguese in the battle and masterminded the victory over Spain. Before entering the church, study the carvings on the main entrance. Notice the two ranks of figures in the archway over the entrance: first rank—angels with their modesty wings; second rank—the angel band with different instruments, including a hillbilly washboard. At the top of the pointed arch are two small coats of arms: Portugal's on the right and the House of Lancaster's on the left (a reminder of the marriage of John I and Philippa that cemented centuries of friendship between Portugal and England).

Cost and Hours: The church is free, and the Royal Cloisters cost €4.50 (daily April–Sept 9:00–18:30, Oct–March 9:00–17:30, last entry 30 min before closing, free on Sun until 14:00, tel.

244-765-497). On your way in, buy a ticket for the cloisters (at the ticket counter on your immediate left); the staff at the Founder's Chapel (listed below) will check for it.

Church Interior: The tall pillars leading your eye up to the "praying hands" of pointed arches, the warm light from stained-

glass windows, the air of sober simplicity—this is classic Gothic, from Europe's Age of Faith. The church's lack of ornamentation reflects the vision of the project's first architect, Afonso Domingues (worked 1388–1402). Compared to Alcobaça's monastery (see page 176), this interior is dimmer and feels more somber, though the stained glass more dramatically colors the floors and columns. The first chapel on the right is the...

Founders' Chapel (Capela do Fundador): Center-stage is the double sarcophagus (that's English style) of King John I and his English queen, Philippa. The tomb statues lie together on their backs, holding hands for eternity. This husband-and-wife team ushered in Portugal's two centuries of greatness.

John I (born 1357, ruled 1385–1433), the bastard son of Dom Pedro I (King Peter I, see sidebar on page 178), repelled the Spanish invaders, claimed the throne, consolidated his power by confiscating enemies' land to reward his friends, gave Lisbon's craftsmen a voice in government, and launched Portugal's expansion overseas. His five-decade reign greatly benefited Portugal. John's motto, *"Por bem"* ("For good"), is carved on his tomb. He established the House of Avis (see the coat of arms carved in the tomb) that would rule Portugal through the Golden Age. John's descendants (through both the Avis and Bragança lines) would rule Portugal until the last king, in 1910.

John, indebted to English soldiers for their help in the battle, signed the friendship Treaty of Windsor with England (1386). To seal the deal, he was requested to marry Philippa of Lancaster, the granddaughter of England's king. You can see their respective coats of arms carved at the head of the tomb.

Philippa (c. 1360–1415)—intelligent, educated, and moral— had already been rejected in marriage by two kings. John was also reluctant, reminding the English of his vow of celibacy as Grand Master of the Order of the Cross. He retreated to a monastery (with his mistress) before finally agreeing to marry Philippa (1387).

Philippa won John's admiration by overseeing domestic policy,

Batalha

Batalha's Monastery of Santa María

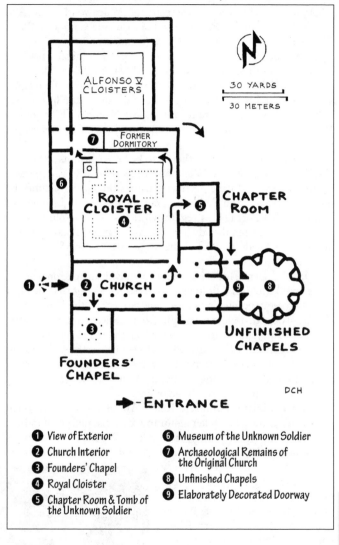

1 View of Exterior

2 Church Interior

3 Founders' Chapel

4 Royal Cloister

5 Chapter Room & Tomb of the Unknown Soldier

6 Museum of the Unknown Soldier

7 Archaeological Remains of the Original Church

8 Unfinished Chapels

9 Elaborately Decorated Doorway

boosting trade with England, reconciling Christians and Jews, and spearheading the invasion of Ceuta (1415) that launched the Age of Discovery.

At home, she used her wide knowledge (she was trained personally by Geoffrey Chaucer and John Wycliffe) to inspire her children to greatness. She banished John's mistress to a distant convent, but raised their children almost as her own, thus sparking the rise of the Bragança line that would compete for the throne.

John and Philippa produced a slew of talented sons, some of whom rest in tombs nearby. These are the golden youth of the Age of Discovery that the Portuguese poet Luís de Camões dubbed "The Marvelous Generation" *(Ínclita Geração)*.

Henrique (wearing a church for a hat and a metal wreath in front) is Prince Henry the Navigator (1394–1460, see sidebar on page 126). When Philippa was on her deathbed with the plague, she summoned her son Henry to her side and made him swear he would dedicate his life to finding the legendary kingdom of Prester John—sending Henry on his own journey to explore the unknown.

Fernão, Henry's kid brother, attacked the Muslims at Tangier (1437) and was captured. When his family refused to pay the ransom (which would have meant returning the city of Ceuta), he died in captivity. Son Pedro, a voracious traveler and student of history, ruled Portugal as regent while his six-year-old nephew Afonso grew to manhood (heir Afonso's father, Duarte—John and Philippa's eldest—died of the plague after ruling for only five years; see "Unfinished Chapels," page 172).

The Founders Chapel is a square room with an octagonal dome. Gaze up (like John and Philippa) at the ceiling, an eight-pointed star of crisscrossing pointed arches—a masterpiece of the Flamboyant Gothic style—that glow with light from stained glass. The central keystone (with John's coat of arms) holds all the arches-within-arches in place. Remember this finished chapel—a lantern roof atop tombs in an octagonal space—when you visit the Unfinished Chapels later. Don't miss out on the original paint job of red-and-green arches. From the church, you enter the adjoining...

Royal Cloister (Claustro Real): Architecturally, this open courtyard (show your ticket again to enter) exemplifies Batalha's essence: Gothic construction from circa 1400 (the pointed arches surrounding the courtyard) filled in with Manueline decoration from circa 1500. The tracery in the arches features the cross of the Order of Christ (headed at one time by Prince Henry the Navigator) and armillary spheres—skeletal "globes" that showed what was then considered the center of the universe: planet Earth. The tracery is supported by delicate columns with shells,

pearls, and coils of rope, plus artichokes and lotus flowers from the recently explored Orient.

Stop here and picture Dominican monks in white robes, blue capes, and tonsured haircuts (shaved crown) meditating as they

Portugal's House of Avis and Its Coat of Arms

Seen on monuments at Belém, Batalha, Sagres, and even on the modern Portuguese flag, the Avis coat of arms is a symbol of the glorious Age of Discovery, when Portugal was ruled by kings of the Avis family.

In the center of the shield are five smaller shields arranged in the form of a cross. (One theory says that, after several generations of battle, the family shield—passed down from father to son—got beaten up, and the cross ripped apart into five pieces, held there by nails—the dots on the coat of arms.) Around the border are castles, representing Muslim cities conquered by Portugal's Christian kings. (Some versions have fleur-de-lis and personal emblems of successive kings.)

Some Important House of Avis Kings

Pedro I (Peter I, r. 1357–1367)—Buried with his beloved Inês de Castro at Alcobaça (see sidebar on page 178).

John I (r. 1385–1433)—Pedro's bastard son, who protected Portugal from a Spanish takeover and launched overseas expansion.

Manuel I (r. 1495–1521)—Ruler when all the overseas expansion began to pay off financially. He built the Monastery of Jerónimos at Belém, decorated in the ornamental style that bears his name (see architecture sidebar on page 71).

John III (r. 1521–1557)—Ruler during Portugal's peak of power... and at the beginning of its decline.

Sebastian (r. 1557–1578)—Because he was lost in battle, the nation lost its way, leading to takeover by Spain.

slowly circled this garden courtyard. They'd stop to wash their hands at the washbasin (*lavabo*, in the northwest corner, with a great view back at the church) before stepping into the adjoining refectory (dining hall) for a meal. Continue to the...

Chapter Room: The self-supporting star-vaulted ceiling spans 60 feet, an engineering tour-de-force by Master Huguet, a foreigner who became chief architect in 1402. Huguet brought Flamboyant Gothic decoration to the church's sober style. The ceiling was considered so dangerous to build (it collapsed twice) that only prisoners condemned to death were allowed to work on it. (Today, unknowing tourists are allowed to wander under it.) Huguet supposedly silenced skeptics by personally spending the night in this room. (It even survived the 1755 earthquake.) Besides this ceiling, Huguet designed the Founder's Chapel and the Unfinished Chapels.

Portugal's **Tomb of the Unknown Soldier** sits under a mutilated crucifix called *Christ of the Trenches*—which accompanied Portuguese soldiers into battle on the western front of World War I. The three small soldiers under the flame—which burns Portuguese olive oil—are dressed to represent the three most valiant chapters in Portuguese military history: fighting Moors in the 12th century, Spaniards in the 14th century, and Germans in the 20th century.

Follow the signs to the gift shop *(loja),* and if you like military history, stop in briefly to see all the offerings from various countries to the Portuguese unknown soldier. Of particular interest is a photograph of the WWI crucifix taken in the trenches (the actual crucifix is the one displayed in the Chapter Room you just visited). Walk past the ho-hum **archaeological remains** of the original church construction and into the next cloister. It's not nearly as interesting after seeing the Royal Cloister, so follow the exit signs to a square outside the church. Head right, to the...

Unfinished Chapels (Capelas Imperfeitas): The Unfinished Chapels are called by that name because, well, that's not a Gothic sunroof overhead. This chapel behind the main altar was intended as an octagonal room with seven niches for tombs, topped with a rotunda ceiling (similar to the Founders' Chapel). But only the walls, support pillars for the ceiling, and a double tomb were completed.

King Duarte and his wife, Leonor, lie hand in hand on their backs, watching the clouds pass by, blissfully unaware of the work left undone. Duarte (1391–1438), the oldest of John and Philippa's sons, was the golden boy of the charmed family. He wrote a how-to book on courtly manners. When, at age 42, he became king (1433), he called a *cortes* (parliament) to enact much-needed legal reforms. He financed and encouraged his brother Prince Henry's initial overseas explorations. And he began work on these chapels, hoping to make a glorious family burial place. But Duarte died young of the plague, leaving behind an unfinished chapel, a stunned nation, and his six-year-old son, Afonso, as the new king.

Leonor became the regent while Afonso grew up, but she proved unpopular as a ruler, being both Spanish and female. Duarte's brother Pedro then ruled as regent before being banished by rivals.

In 1509, Duarte's grandson, King Manuel I, added the elaborately decorated **doorway** (by Mateus Fernandes), a masterpiece of the Manueline style. The series of ever larger arches that frame the door are carved in stone so detailed that they look like stucco. See carved coils of rope with knots, some snails along the bottom, artichokes (used to fend off scurvy), corn (from American discoveries), and Indian-inspired motifs (from the land of pepper). Contrast the doorway's Manueline ornamentation with the Renaissance simplicity of the upper-floor balcony, done in 1533.

Manuel abandoned the chapel after Vasco da Gama's triumphant return from India, channeling Portugal's money and energy instead to building a monument to the Age of Discovery launched by the Avis family—the Jerónimos Monastery in Belém (where he's buried).

TRANSPORTATION CONNECTIONS

From Batalha by Bus to: Nazaré (7/day, 1 hr, some change at São Jorge), **Alcobaça** (8/day, 30 min), **Fátima** (3/day, 1 hr), and **Lisbon** (4/day, 2 hrs). Expect fewer buses on weekends.

By Car: Batalha is an easy 10-mile drive from Fátima. You'll see signs from each site to the other.

Fátima

On May 13, 1917, three children were tending sheep when the sky lit up and a woman—Mary, the mother of Christ, "a lady brighter than the sun"—appeared standing in an oak tree. (It's the tree to the left of the large basilica.) In the midst of bloody World War I, she brought a message that peace was coming. The war raged on, so on the 13th day of each of the next five months, Mary dropped in again to call for peace and to repeat three messages. Word spread, bringing many curious pilgrims. The three kids—Lucia, Francisco, and Jacinta—were grilled mercilessly by authorities trying to debunk their preposterous visions, but the children remained convinced of what they'd seen. (In 1930, the Vatican recognized the Virgin of Fátima as legit.)

Finally, on October 13, 70,000 people assembled near the oak tree. They were drenched in a rainstorm when suddenly, the sun came out, grew blindingly bright, danced around the sky (writing "God's fiery signature"), then plunged to the earth. When the crowd came to its senses, the sun was shining and the rain had dried.

Today, tens of thousands of believers come to rejoice in this modern miracle, most of them during the months of May to October. Many walk from as far away as Lisbon. Depending on the time of year you visit, you may see scores of pilgrims with reflective vests walking along the smaller highways. Fátima, Lourdes (in France), and Međugorje (in Bosnia-Herzegovina) are the three big Mary sights in Europe.

Mary's Three Messages

1. Peace is coming. (World War I is ending. Later, during World War II, Salazar justified keeping Portugal neutral by saying it was in accordance with Mary's wishes for peace.)
2. Russia will reject God and communism will rise, bringing a second great war.
3. Someone will try to kill the pope. (This third message was kept a secret for decades, supposedly lying in a sealed envelope in the Vatican. In 1981, Pope John Paul II was shot. He visited Fátima in 2000, meeting the surviving visionary, beatifying the two who had died, and publicly revealing this long-hidden third secret.)

ORIENTATION

Fátima welcomes guests. Surrounding the square are a variety of hotels, restaurants, and tacky souvenir stands. Except on the 12th and 13th of most months, cheap hotel rooms abound.

Tourist Information: The TI is near the basilica (daily April–Sept 10:00–13:00 & 15:00–19:00, Oct–March 10:00–13:00 & 14:00–18:00, Avenida José Alves Correia da Silva, tel. 249-531-139).

SIGHTS

Church of the Holy Trinity (Igreja da Santíssima Trindade)— Opened in the fall of 2007, this gigantic modern church has a capacity of 9,000 devotees (daily 11:00–18:00, services Sat at 11:00 and Sun at 11:00, 15:00, and 16:30, www.santuario-fatima.pt). It makes room for the large number of pilgrims who can't all fit inside the 900-seat basilica (described below).

Chapel of Apparitions—This marks the spot where Mary appeared to the three children (located outside the church, beneath a canopy). Services take place daily 7:30–21:30 in a variety of languages; check the posted schedule for English.

Basilica—The huge Neoclassical basilica (1928–1953) has a 200-foot tower with a golden crown and crystal cross-shaped beacon on top. (Dress modestly to enter the church). Inside you'll find a painting depicting the vision,

chapels dedicated to the Stations of the Cross, and the tombs of the children who saw the vision. Two died shortly after the visions in the worldwide flu epidemic. The third, Lucia (the only one with whom Mary actually conversed), passed away at the age of 97 in 2005. She lived as a Carmelite nun near Coimbra for most of her life.

Pilgrimage—On the 13th of each month from May through October, and on August 19, up to 100,000 pilgrims come to Fátima. Some shuffle on their knees, traversing the mega-huge, park-lined esplanade (which is more than 160,000 square feet) leading to the church. Torch-lit processions occur on two nights (usually the 12th and 13th). In 1967, on the 50th anniversary of the miracle, 1.5 million pilgrims—including the pope—gathered here.

Museums—Visitors may want to check out two "museums" in town. The **Museu de Cera de Fátima** is a series of rooms telling the story of Fátima's visitation one scene at a time, using wax figures (€4.50, daily April–Oct 9:30–18:30, Nov–March 10:00–17:00, English leaflet describes each vignette, www.mucefa.pt). The **Museu 1917 Aparições** tells the same story with a low-tech sound-and-light show (€2.50, daily April–Oct 9:00–19:00, Nov–March 9:00–18:00, in building complex near enormous Hotel de Fátima, worthless without English soundtrack playing—ask). While the  wax museum is better, both exhibits are pretty cheesy for those not inclined to take Fátima too seriously.

TRANSPORTATION CONNECTIONS

From Fátima by Bus to: Batalha (3/day, 1 hr), **Coimbra** (7/day, 1 hr), **Nazaré** (2/day, 1.5 hrs), and **Lisbon** (hourly, 1.5–2.5 hrs, depending on route); service drops on Sunday. Note that the stop closest to the basilica is listed on bus schedules as Cova de Iria, *not* Fátima.

Alcobaça

This pleasant little town is famous for its church, one of the most interesting in Portugal. I find Alcobaça a better stop than Batalha.

Tourist Information: The English-speaking TI is across the square from the church (May–Sept daily 10:00–13:00 &

15:00–19:00, Oct–April closes at 18:00, Praça 25 de Abril, tel. 262-582-377).

Arrival in Alcobaça: If you arrive by bus, it's a five-minute walk to the town center and monastery. Exit right from the station (on Avenida Manuel da Silva Carolino), walk a half-block uphill (car parking lot visible in distance), take the first right, and continue straight (on Rua Dom Pedro V). Hang a left just after passing a small plaza, and you are in the main square.

If you're arriving by car, follow the *Mosteiro* or *estação rodoviário* (bus station) signs at the roundabout. A parking lot just uphill from the bus station is currently free, but locals say that the town hall will soon be charging (expect a max of €0.50/hr).

SIGHTS

▲▲**Cistercian Monastery of Santa Maria**—This abbey church, despite its fully Baroque facade, represents the best Gothic build-

ing in Portugal. It's also the country's largest church, and a clean and bright break from the heavier Iberian norm. Afonso Henriques began construction in 1178 after taking the nearby town of Santarém from the Moors. It became one of the most powerful abbeys of the Cistercian Order and a cultural center of 13th-century Portugal. This simple abbey is designed to be filled with hard work, prayer, and total silence.

Cost and Hours: €4.50, daily April–Sept 9:00–19:00, Oct–March 9:00–17:00, tel. 262-505-128.

Nave and Tombs of Dom Pedro and Inês: A long, narrow nave leads to a pair of finely carved Gothic tombs (from 1360). These are of Portugal's most tragic romantic couple, Dom Pedro (King Peter I, 1320–1367, on the right) and Dona Inês de Castro (c. 1323–1355, on the left). They rest feet-to-feet in each transept,

so that on Judgment Day they'll rise and immediately see each other again. Pedro, heir to the Portuguese throne, was hopelessly in love with the Spanish aristocrat Inês (see sidebar, page 178).

Notice the carvings on the tombs. Like religious alarm clocks, the attending angels are poised to wake the couple on

Judgment Day. Pedro will lie here (as inscribed on the tomb) *"Até ao fim do mundo"*—until the end of the world, when he and Inês are reunited. The "Wheel of Life" below the finely combed head of Pedro shows scenes from his life with Inês.

Elsewhere on the coffin are scenes from the life of St. Bartholomew—being skinned alive. Pedro's tomb is supported by lions, a symbol of royalty. Opposite, Inês' tomb is supported by the lowly scum who murdered her...one holding a monkey, a symbol of evil. Study the relief at the feet of Inês: Heaven, the dragon mouth of Hell, and jack-in-the-box coffins on Judgment Day. Although Napoleon's troops vandalized the tombs, the story of Pedro and Inês endures *até ao fim do mundo.* Look at the reliquary next to the tomb of Inês to see a lock of her hair, her crown, and even the knife used for her murder.

More Tombs and Relics in the Sacristy: To the right of the king's tomb, step into the neo-Gothic Hall of Tombs for more deceased royalty. Behind the High Altar is the sacristy. The room is indefinitely closed for maintenance, but look at the fine Manueline door. In the rear of the nave (where you entered), find the...

Hall of Kings: This hall—where you pay to enter the monastery—features statues of most of Portugal's kings, along with 18th-century tiled walls telling the story of the 12th-century conquest of the Moors and the building of the monastery. The sculpture facing the entrance features Afonso Henriques, first king of Portugal and founder of this monastery, being crowned by Pope Innocent III and St. Bernard.

Cloisters: Cistercian monks built the abbey in 40 years, starting in 1178. They inhabited it until 1834 (when the Portuguese king disbanded all monasteries).

The monks spent most of their lives in silence, and were allowed to speak only when given permission by the abbot. To enjoy this cloister like the monks did: Meditate, pray, exercise, and connect with nature. As you multitask, circle counterclockwise until you reach the fountain—where the monks washed up before eating. In the cloisters, the fountain marks the entry to the...

Refectory (Dining Hall): Imagine the hall filled with monks eating in silence as one reads from the Bible atop the "Readers' Pulpit." Food was prepared next door.

Kitchen: The 18th-century kitchen's giant three-part oven could roast seven oxen simultaneously. The industrious monks

Alcobaça

Pedro and Inês

Twenty-year-old Prince Pedro met 17-year-old Inês at his wedding to Inês' cousin Constance. The politically motivated marriage was arranged by Pedro's father, the king. Pedro dutifully fathered his son, the future king Fernando, with Constance in Lisbon, while seeing Inês on the side in Coimbra. When Constance died, Pedro settled in with Inês. Concerned about Spanish influence, Pedro's father, Afonso IV, forbade their marriage. You guessed it—they were married secretly, and the couple had four children. When King Afonso, fearing rivals to his ("legitimate") grandson's kingship, had Inês murdered, Prince Pedro went ballistic. He staged an armed uprising (1355) against his father, only settled after much bloodshed.

Once he was crowned King Pedro I the Just (1357), the much-embellished legend begins. He summoned his enemies, exhumed Inês' body, dressed it in a bridal gown, and put it on the throne, making the murderers kneel and kiss its putrid rotting hand. (The legend continues...) Pedro then executed her two murderers—personally—by ripping out their hearts, eating them, and washing them down, it is said, with a fine *vinho verde*. Now that's *amore*.

rerouted part of the River Alcoa to bring in running water.

Dormitory: Take the stairs up to the bare dormitory, from which you can see the transept of the church where Inês is buried. Pedro is in the distance, too. On this floor, there is also a terrace onto the adjacent cloister and a stairway to the upper cloister with views to the abbey.

▲**Mercado Municipal**—An Old World version of Safeway is housed happily here under huge steel-and-fiberglass arches. Inside the covered market, black-clad dried apple–faced women choose fish, uncaged and feisty chickens, ducks, and rabbits from their respective death rows. Wander among figs, melons, bushels of grain, and nuts (Mon–Sat 9:00–13:00, closed Sun, best on Mon). It's a five-minute walk  from the TI or just down the block from the bus station; ask a local, *"Mercado municipal?"* There's also a flea market in town on Mondays by the Alcoa River.

▲▲**National Museum of Wine (Museu Nacional do Vinho)**—This museum, a half-mile outside Alcobaça (on the road to Batalha and Leiria, right-hand side), offers a fascinating look at the wine of Portugal (€2, Mon–Fri 9:00–12:30 & 14:00–17:30, closed Sat–Sun, tel. 262-582-222, www.ivv.min-agricultura.pt; your car is safer parked inside the gate). Run by a local cooperative winery, the museum teaches you more than you need to know about Portuguese wine in a series of rooms that used to house fermenting vats. With some luck, you can get a tour—much more hands-on than French winery tours—through the actual winery.

TRANSPORTATION CONNECTIONS

From Alcobaça by Bus to: Lisbon (7/day, 2/day direct, 2 hrs, some transfer in Caldas da Rainha), **Nazaré** (11/day, 15 min, stops at Valado), **Batalha** (8/day, 30 min), **Fátima** (3/day, 1 hr, more frequent with transfer in Batalha). Bus frequency drops on Sunday. A taxi to the Nazaré/Valado train station costs about €7; to Nazaré, up to €10. Bus info: tel. 808-200-370.

Óbidos

Postcard-perfect Óbidos (OH-bee-doosh) sits atop a hill, its 14th-century wall (45 feet tall) corralling a bouquet of narrow lanes and

flower-bedecked whitewashed houses. Óbidos is ideal for photographers who want to make Portugal look as pretty as it can be.

Founded by Celts (c. 300 B.C.), then ruled by Romans, Visigoths, and Moors, Óbidos was unique as Portugal's "wedding city." In 1282, when King Dinis brought his new bride Isabel here, she liked the town so much he gave it to her (whatta guy). Later kings carried on the tradition—the perfect gift for a king to give to a queen who has everything. (Beats a toaster.) Today, this medieval walled town is popular for lowly commoners' weddings. Preserved in its entirety as a national monument, it survives on tourism. Every summer morning at 9:30, the tour groups flush into town. Óbidos is especially crowded in August, but it's worth a quick visit anyway. Ideally, arrive late one day and leave early the next, enjoying the town as you would a beautiful painted tile. Or arrive midday and encounter the crush of tour groups.

Tourist Information: The TI is at Óbidos' main pay parking lot (€0.50/hour, TI open daily May–Sept 9:30–19:30, shorter hours off-season, detailed audioguide-€5/2 hrs, tel. 262-959-231). Another TI is on the main drag, Rua Direita.

Arrival in Óbidos: Ideally, take a bus to Óbidos and leave by either bus or train. If you arrive at the train station, you're faced with a 20-minute uphill hike into town. The bus drops you off and leaves from a stop that's much closer (upon arrival, go up the steps and through the archway on the right). Because there's no bus station and the train station is unstaffed, there's no official place to store luggage in town.

If you arrive by car, don't drive into tiny, cobbled Óbidos. Ample tourist parking is provided outside of town; another lot is by the castle/*pousada* (free, follow Pousada/Estalagem road, clean public WC as you walk into town). If you are staying inside the city walls, you need to walk to your hotel to get a magnetic card that will allow you in with your car.

SELF-GUIDED WALK

Welcome to Óbidos

Main Gate: Enter through the main gate in Óbidos' 14th-century wall. Stop to gaze up at the scenes related to the town's history—depicting centuries of battles and religion in blue-and-white tiles.

Like Dorothy entering a medieval Oz, you're confronted by two wonderful cobbled lanes. The top lane is the town's main drag, littered with tourists shopping and leading straight through Óbidos to its castle (ahead, you can see its square tower, where this walk finishes).

Walk the Wall: After entering the old town through the main gate, notice the steep stairs (to your left) accessing the scenic if treacherous sentry path along the wall (other access points are near the castle/*pousada,* and uphill from the main church). You'll get views of the city and surrounding countryside from the 40-foot-high walls. The west (uphill) wall is best, letting you look over the town's white buildings with red roofs and blue or yellow trim. You can almost gaze at the Atlantic, six miles away. Until the 1100s, when the bay silted up, the ocean was half as far away, making this a hilltop citadel guarding a natural port. The aqueduct is from the 16th century.

• *Bypass the wall walk for now and head into town. Follow...*

Rua Josefa d'Óbidos: Continue straight along this less-traveled, lower brick lane and notice the whitewash that keeps things cool; the bright blue-and-yellow trims, traditionally designed to define property lines; and the potted geraniums, which bloom most of the year, survive the summer sun well, and keep mosquitoes away. The Church of St. Peter has a fine, newly restored Baroque altar covered with Brazilian gold leaf, which contrasts with the otherwise Gothic interior built prior to the 1755 earthquake (daily April–Sept 9:30–12:30 & 14:30–19:00, Oct–March 9:30–12:30 &

Óbidos

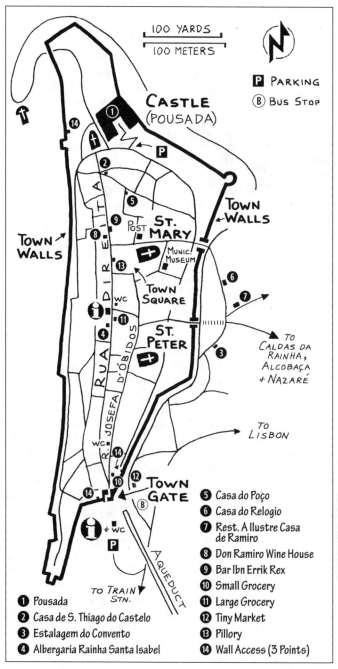

100 YARDS
100 METERS

Ⓟ PARKING
Ⓑ BUS STOP

CASTLE
(POUSADA)

Ⓟ

TOWN WALLS

TOWN WALLS

POST

ST. MARY

MUNIC! MUSEUM

WC

TOWN SQUARE

ST. PETER

WC

TO CALDAS DA RAINHA, ALCOBAÇA & NAZARÉ

TO LISBON

RUA DIREITA

JOSEFA D'ÓBIDOS

TOWN GATE

Ⓑ

TO TRAIN STN.

AQUEDUCT

Ⓟ

WC

① Pousada
② Casa de S. Thiago do Castelo
③ Estalagem do Convento
④ Albergaria Rainha Santa Isabel
⑤ Casa do Poço
⑥ Casa do Relogio
⑦ Rest. A llustre Casa de Ramiro
⑧ Don Ramiro Wine House
⑨ Bar Ibn Errik Rex
⑩ Small Grocery
⑪ Large Grocery
⑫ Tiny Market
⑬ Pillory
⑭ Wall Access (3 Points)

Óbidos

14:30–17:00). After peeking in, exit the church and climb uphill to the main tourist drag.

• *Then turn right on...*

Rua Direita: Walking toward the castle on this main shop-

ping drag, you'll pass typical shops and a public WC before reaching the...

Town Square: The lone column at the side of the road is the 16th-century **pillory.** Local bad boys were tied to this to endure whatever punishment was deemed appropriate. Studying it closely, you will notice Queen Leonor's crown circling the entire pillory. Now look even closer on the side facing the castle. The carved hanging shrimp net represents how fishermen found the body of 16-year-old Afonso, son of Manuel I and Leonor, in the Tejo River after a tragic and mysterious death. The net eventually became part of the queen's coat of arms. The huge pots you see underneath the awning were once in the central market and held olive oil instead of flowers. The small Municipal Museum, opposite the flower pots, is not worth the €1.50 unless you enjoy stairs, religious art, and Portuguese inscriptions. But at the bottom of the square, do enter the...

Church of St. Mary of Óbidos: Grab a seat on a front pew, surrounded by classic 17th-century tiles (church open daily). Notice the fine painted-wood ceiling over each of the three naves. To the left of the altar is a niche with a delicate Portuguese Renaissance tomb, featuring a pietà carved out of local limestone. On the right are three paintings, including *The Mystical Marriage of St. Catherine,* by Óbidos' most famous artist, the nun Josefa d'Óbidos (1634–1684). Return to the main shopping drag and turn right for the...

Final Stretch to the Castle: On the left, pop into the **Don Ramiro Wine House.** This welcoming showcase for regional products—wine, cheese, and meat—serves your choice of wine by the half-bottle, and, if you'd like a light meal, a sampler plate of meats and cheese. Its atmospheric setting is dominated by a big, old grape press (open daily 8:30–20:00, on the main drag). Across the street, **Bar Ibn Errik Rex** is the most characteristic (and touristy) of several Óbidos *ginjinha* bars. Óbidos is famous for this much-loved Portuguese cherry liqueur, but you'll pay €2.50 a glass here and only €1 a shot in Lisbon (see description on page 56).

• *The main drag dead-ends at the top of town and the...*

Pousada: This former castle is now a fancy hotel with nine rooms (Db-€180–220, tel. 262-955-080, fax 262-959-148, recepcao .castelo@pousadas.pt).

On January 11, 1148, Afonso Henriques (Portugal's first king) led a two-pronged attack to liberate the town from the Moors. Afonso attacked the main gate at the other end of town (where tourists enter), while the Moorish ruler huddled here in his castle. Meanwhile, a band of Afonso's men snuck up the steep hillside behind the castle disguised as cherry trees. The doomed Moor ignored his daughter when she turned from the window and asked him, "Daddy, do trees walk?"

A lane to the left leads to the stairs accessing the town wall. But go uphill to the right, following the *pousada* signs to the terrace with the telescope for a look at the city. After savoring the view, go back to the bottom of the *pousada* and enter the archway to your right. Walk for one minute until you see the city wall. Turn around for a spectacular view of the castle—it's yours for the taking.

• *You can return to your starting point three ways: hiking along the upper town wall, exploring photogenic side lanes, or shopping and drinking your way back down the main drag.*

SIGHTS

Near Óbidos
Caldas da Rainha—A 10-minute drive or taxi ride from Óbidos, Caldas da Rainha is famous for its therapeutic springs, which have attracted royalty looking for rheumatism cures and aristocrats wanting to make the scene. A venerable hospital now sits on the source of those curative waters. The charming old center is more workaday than Óbidos, as mono-block development has swamped the outskirts. But the town is still filled with unexpected surprises. Stroll the lovely public gardens near the hospital, uncover the hidden meanings of the various stenciled graffiti, and gaze at a multitude of Art Deco buildings. Caldas da Rainha provides a good glimpse of everyday Portugal, with the charm punched up just a notch. Ideally, drop by any morning (except Mon), when its farmers market fills Praça da República with fruits, veggies, nuts, flowers, and lots of busy locals.

SLEEPING

(€1 = about $1.40, country code: 351)
To enjoy Óbidos without tourists, spend the night. Here are reasonable values in this overpriced toy of a town.

$$$ Casa de S. Thiago do Castelo, a fancy and characteristic little guesthouse at the base of the *pousada*/castle, rents eight elegantly appointed rooms around a chirpy *Better Homes and Tiles* patio. Lower levels offer three different salons to relax in, including one with a classy billiards table (Sb-€65, Db-€80 April–Oct, free parking, Largo de S. Thiago, tel. & fax 262-959-587, Paula and Alice).

$$$ Estalagem do Convento was built to house monks— but they never showed up. Now it welcomes guests with solemn charm. The restaurant is somewhat pricey, but worth the splurge for the ambience. Consider eating here, even if you don't stay the night (Sb-€82, Db-€100, suites-€116–137, extra bed-€18, air-con, outside wall with easy parking, Rua D. João de Ornelas, tel. 262-959-216, fax 262-959-159, www.estalagemdoconvento.com, estconventhotel@mail.telepac.pt).

$$ Albergaria Rainha Santa Isabel is a hotelesque place marked by flags on the main drag in the center of the old town. If you're driving and feeling bold, call first to let them know you're approaching, stop long enough to drop your bags and get a parking permit, and drive on to the town square to park (Sb-€55–67, Db-€62–85, depending on room, higher in Aug, third person-€20, air-con, elevator, on the main one-lane drag, Rua Direita, tel. 262-959-323, fax 262-959-115, www.arsio.com).

$$ Casa do Poço, with four dim, basic rooms around a bright, folksy courtyard, is just one of many homes renting rooms in the old center (Sb-€40–45, Db-€50–60, Travessa da Mouraria, follow main street to Casa de S. Thiago do Castelo then go downhill to the right, tel. 262-959-358, fax 262-959-282).

$ Casa do Relogio is a rustic eight-room place at the downhill end of town, just outside the wall. It's friendly and easygoing, providing no-stress parking and great comfort for the price (Sb-€40–45, Db-€45–58, Tb-€80 in peak of summer, Rua da Graça 12, tel. & fax 262-959-282, casa.relogio@clix.pt, Sarah).

EATING

Óbidos is tough on the average tourist's budget. Consider a picnic or one of the many cafés that offer cheap, basic meals.

Restaurante A Ilustre Casa de Ramiro is a big place 50 yards downhill from (and outside of) one of the town's east gates. It's dressy and characteristic but touristy, with a four-language menu (€20 dinners, Fri–Wed 12:30–15:00 & 19:30–22:30, closed all day Thu and Fri lunch, Rua Porta do Vale, tel. 262-959-194).

Picnics: Pick up your picnic at the small grocery store just inside the main gate (on the lower brick road), the larger grocery in the center on Rua Direita, or the tiny market just outside the town wall.

TRANSPORTATION CONNECTIONS

From Óbidos to: Nazaré (12 buses/day, 1 hr, most transfer in Caldas da Rainha), **Lisbon** (8 buses/day, 1.25 hrs, all transfer in Caldas da Rainha; 8 trains/day, 2.25 hrs, transfer in Cacém), **Alcobaça** (3 buses/day, 1.5 hrs). Far fewer buses run on weekends.

By Car to Lisbon: From Óbidos, the tollway zips you directly into Lisbon (€7).

COIMBRA

The college town of Coimbra—just two to three hours north of Lisbon by train, bus, or car—is Portugal's Oxford, and the country's easiest-to-enjoy city.

Don't be fooled by the drab suburbs. Portugal's center for 200 years, Coimbra (koh-EEM-brah) remains second only to Lisbon culturally and historically. It served as Portugal's leading city while the Moors controlled Lisbon. The ports of Lisbon and Porto only surpassed landlocked Coimbra when Portugal's maritime fortunes rose. Today, Coimbra is Portugal's third-largest city (pop. 168,000) and home to its oldest and most prestigious university (founded 1290). When school is in session, Coimbra bustles. During school holidays, it's sleepy. But any time of year, you can explore the great Arab-flavored old town—a maze of people, narrow streets, and tiny *tascas* (restaurants with just a few tables).

Planning Your Time

On a two-week swing through Portugal, give Coimbra a day. Browse through its historic university, fortress-like cathedral, and lively old town. If you're driving from central Spain, Coimbra makes a good first stop in Portugal.

ORIENTATION

Coimbra is a mini-Lisbon, with everything good about urban Portugal without the intensity of a big metropolis. I couldn't design a more delightful city for a visit. Skip Coimbra's modern center (with the shopping malls) and stick to the charming old town.

Coimbra

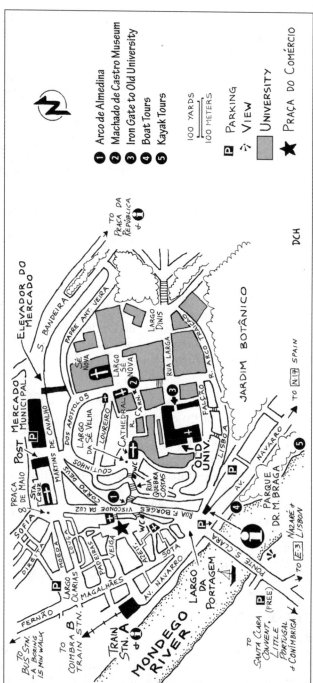

1 Arco de Almedina
2 Machado de Castro Museum
3 Iron Gate to Old University
4 Boat Tours
5 Kayak Tours

100 YARDS
100 METERS

P PARKING
VIEW
UNIVERSITY
★ PRAÇA DO COMÉRCIO

Coimbra

From Largo da Portagem, the main square by the river, everything is within an easy walk. The TI and plenty of good budget rooms are within several blocks of the train station. The best views are from its low and high points: looking up from the far end of Santa Clara Bridge (Ponte Santa Clara) and looking down from the observation deck of the old university.

Coimbra's old town—a maze of timeworn shops, houses, and stairways—has two parts: the lower (Baixa) and the upper (Alta). The dividing line between these two sections is the main pedestrian street, which is named Visconde da Luz at one end and Rua de Ferreira Borges at the other. It runs from the Praça 8 de Maio to the Mondego River.

To get to the university from this main pedestrian thoroughfare, follow the streets that wind their way up the side of the hill. These little lanes, which give the area a village-like feel, meander like a Moroccan medina up to the city's highest point, the old university. To save yourself some uphill climbing, use Coimbra's elevator (Elevador do Mercado, see page 194) and/or little electric minibus (see "Getting Around Coimbra," page 190).

Tourist Information

Pick up a free info-packed map and the monthly cultural calendar at the helpful English-speaking TI at Largo da Portagem (June–Sept Mon–Fri 9:00–19:00, Sat–Sun 10:00–13:00 & 14:30–17:30; Oct–May Mon–Fri 9:30–13:00 & 14:00–17:30, Sat–Sun 10:00–13:00 & 14:30–17:30; entrance on Avenida Emídio Navarro, tel. 239-488-120, www.turismo-centro.pt, rtc-coimbra@turismo-centro.pt). You can get bus schedules printed out for you here, and find information on sights in central Portugal.

Two more TIs are near the university: on Largo Dinis (Mon–Fri 9:00–18:00, Sat–Sun 9:00–12:30 & 14:00–17:30, tel. 239-832-591) and on Praça da República (Mon–Fri 10:00–18:30, closed Sat–Sun, tel. 239-833-202). Yet another TI is at the town market hall, Mercado Municipal (Mon–Sat 9:00–18:00, closed Sun, tel. 239-834-038).

Arrival in Coimbra

By Train

There are two main Coimbra train stations, Station B and Station A (neither has luggage storage). Major trains (e.g., from Lisbon and Salamanca) stop only at B (think Big). From there, you can take a five-minute shuttle train to the very central Station A (free with the ticket that got you to Station B). To find out exactly which train to take to get from B to A, ask any station employee, *"Para Coimbra A (ah)?"* Some local trains (e.g., to Nazaré and occasionally to Porto) stop at both stations.

Station B, which is more of a train platform than a full train station, has an ATM in one of its outside walls, opposite the *informações* office. Taxis wait across the tracks (figure about €3 to Station A or your hotel). Station B also has a ticket office, but with limited hours (the reservation desk at Station A, is far better).

Station A has a helpful English-speaking *informações* office tucked away in a waiting room to the left of the main entrance, where you can get train schedules (daily 9:00–12:00 & 13:00–18:00 with occasional weekend closures, tel. 808-208-208). The ticket office next to the tracks is the best and most central place in town to buy train tickets and make train reservations (including for trips to Spain).

By Bus

The bus station, on Avenida Fernão de Magalhães (tel. 239-855-270), has two ATMs (one inside, one outside). A baggage check that looks like a mailroom is across from the *informações* office and to the right (€1 per bag, Mon–Fri 8:00–18:30, closed Sat–Sun). The station is an easy 15-minute walk from the center; exit the bus station to the right, and follow the busy street into town. You can also catch bus #29 or take a taxi (€4).

There's no need to make a special trip to the bus station just to get bus schedules (the TIs print timetables upon request) or to buy tickets (travel agencies sell them; see "Helpful Hints," next page). If you're walking to the bus station to catch a bus to leave Coimbra, take Avenida Fernão de Magalhães almost to its intersection with Cabral, and look to the left—the Neptuno café is by the station's subtle entrance.

By Car

From Lisbon, it's an easy two-hour straight shot on the slick Auto-Estrada A1 (€11 toll). You'll pass convenient exits for Fátima and the Roman ruins of Conímbriga along the way. Leave the freeway on the easy-to-miss first Coimbra exit, then follow the *Centro* signs. Two and a half miles after leaving the freeway, you'll cross the Mondego River. Take Avenida Fernão de Magalhães directly into town. Most hotels are near Station A and the Santa Clara Bridge. If you arrive from north Portugal or central Spain, follow signs for *Centro/Largo da Portagem*.

The large lot immediately across the river is your best bet for free parking (you may need to wait for a spot to open up). You can also look for free parking along the streets over the river, but these aren't as safe as a lot. In town, you'll find big, convenient, clearly marked pay garages. The largest in-town parking lot is centrally located under the government office, called Loja da Cidadão (on Avenida Fernão de Magalhães, 800 spots, €1/hr 7:00–20:00, €0.70/hr overnight). Most hotels can provide up-to-date information on the best parking options.

Helpful Hints

Money: ATMs and banks (Mon–Fri 8:30–15:00, closed Sat–Sun) are plentiful.

Internet Access: Internet Coimbra Câmara Municipal has eight computers and offers free access for a half-hour. Because it's city-funded and free, you need to reserve a time slot in advance—drop by and show your passport to sign up (Mon–Fri 9:00–20:00, Sat–Sun 10:00–22:00; coming from the pedestrian street, it's past Praça 8 de Maio on your left at #38). For a standard Internet café, hike 10 minutes out of the old town from Praça 8 de Maio up Rua Olímpio Nicolau to the slick, modern **Spacenet** (€1/30 min, Mon–Sat 10:00–24:00, Sun 14:00–24:00, Avenida Sá da Bandeira 67, tel. 239-836-844); they can also connect your laptop to broadband. If you have a laptop and want free Wi-Fi, the riverfront park (Parque Dr. Manuel Braga) is a hotspot that occasionally works.

Car Rental: Avis has a tiny office in Station A (Mon–Fri 8:30–12:30 & 15:00–19:00, closed Sat–Sun, tel. & fax 239-834-786, toll-free tel. 800-201-002), and **Hertz** is near the bus station at Rua Padre Estevão Cabral (tel. 239-834-750).

Bus Tickets: The **Abreu travel agency** sells domestic bus tickets, as well as Intercentro company international tickets to Salamanca, Spain (€28), and beyond. They charge a small commission, but it's worth it (Mon–Fri 9:00–12:30 & 14:30–18:30, plus May–Sept Sat 9:00–12:30, closed Sun, Rua da Sota 2; leaving Station A, it's 100 yards to your left; tel. 239-855-520).

Local Guides: While the city doesn't offer walking tours, the TI has a list of private guides, such as **Maria Jose Fernandes** (mobile 934-093-542, mariajf@portugalmail.pt) and **Cristina Bessa** (tel. 239-835-428, ffbessa@mail.telepac.pt). Local guides charge €85 for a half-day tour.

Getting Around Coimbra

If you're arriving by train at Station B, you'll need to take the free shuttle train to Station A (see "Arrival in Coimbra," page 188), which is within about a 10-minute walk of everything I've listed.

While most visitors do the entire city on foot, taxis are cheap (around €3–4 for a short ride) and a good option if you've been up and down too many hills.

The cute little electric minibus (nicknamed *pantufinhas,* or "grandma's slipper") is silent and easy; it's designed to get grandmas—and anyone else—up and down the steep hills of the old town. It makes a continuous 20-minute loop through the lower old town (Baixa) and around the upper old town (Alta), passing through Largo da Portagem, down the pedestrian shopping lane to Praça 8 de Maio, and by the old cathedral. There are no regular stops—you just wave it down and tell the driver when you want off (€1.50, or use a multiple-ride pass—described next. Bus #34 goes from the old town to the university.

Local buses are expensive (€1.50, better value three-ride pass-€1.80, 11-ride pass-€6, no time limit, sharable, also valid for Coimbra's Elevador do Mercado to top of town).

SELF-GUIDED WALK

Welcome to Coimbra's Old Town

Coimbra is fun on foot, especially along its straight (formerly Roman) pedestrian-only main drag. This tour takes about two hours, including a visit to the university.

• *Start your walk at the...*

Santa Clara Bridge: This bridge, Ponte Santa Clara, has been an important link across the Mondego River since Roman times. For centuries, it had a tollgate *(portagem).* The non-Coimbra end of the bridge offers a fine Coimbra view.

• *At the end of the bridge on the Coimbra side is...*

Largo da Portagem: This square is a great place for coffee or a pastry. Try Pastelaria Briosa (best pastries) or Café Montanha (with a big brass palm tree inside). The town's two special treats are *pastel de Santa Clara* (pastry made with almonds and marmalade) and *pastel de Tentúgal* (rolls of puff pastry stuffed with eggs and cream, and dusted with powdered sugar, €0.90 each). In the center of the square is a statue of the prime minister who, in 1834, shut down the city's convents and monasteries, and earned the nickname "friar killer."

• *Stroll down the pedestrian street (Rua de Ferreira Borges). After a 200-yard-long gauntlet of clothing stores, take the stairs (to your left) leading to a terrace overlooking the square below (pay public WC, sanitários, in the stairwell).*

Coimbra in History

1064 Coimbra is liberated from the Moors.

1139 Portugal's first king, Afonso Henriques, makes Coimbra his capital.

1211 Portugal's first parliament of nobles *(cortes)* convenes at Coimbra.

1256 Lisbon replaces Coimbra as Portugal's capital.

1290 The university is founded under "the poet king," Dinis (r. 1279–1325). Originally in Lisbon, it moved to Coimbra in 1308.

1537 The university, after moving back to Lisbon, finally settles permanently in Coimbra under Jesuit administration.

1810 Napoleon's French troops sack Coimbra, then England's Duke of Wellington drives them out.

1928 António Salazar, a professor of political economy at Coimbra, becomes Minister of Finance and eventually dictator of Portugal.

Praça do Comércio: This pleasant square is shaped like a Roman chariot racecourse—and likely was one 2,000 years ago. In the Middle Ages, they used this place for bullfights. Beyond Praça do Comércio stretches the heart of the old town. Look at your map. The circular street pattern outlines the wall used by Romans, Visigoths, Moors, and Christians to protect Coimbra. Historically, the rich could afford to live within the protective city walls (the Alta, or high town). Even today, the Baixa, or low town, remains a poorer section, with haggard women rolling wheeled shopping bags, children running barefoot, and men lounging on the square like it's their life's calling. But it's a fine area for wandering around during the day to explore small shops and eateries, and to get thoroughly disoriented.

• *Return to the pedestrian street.*

At the top of the stairs, you'll see the Edifício Chiado (part of the Museu Municipal, with free local art exhibits). At the corner (on your right), steps lead up through an ancient arched gateway—Arco de Almedina—into the old city and to the old cathedral and university. Later, after visiting the university, we'll finish this walk by going downhill through this arch.

Farther along the pedestrian drag, stop at the picturesque corner just beyond the cafés (where the building comes to a triangular corner). The steep road climbs into Coimbra's historic ghetto (no Jewish community remains) and the wonderful **À Capella** fado nightclub (see "Fado," page 202).

As you stroll along, you'll know it's graduation time if students' photos are displayed in photographers' windows. Check out the graduates decked out in their traditional university capes (displaying rips on the hem—left side for family, right side for friends, backside for girlfriends) and color-coded sashes (yellow for medicine, red for law, and so on).

• *The pedestrian street ends at Praça 8 de Maio with the...*

Church of Santa Cruz: Soak in this church's impressive facade. Notice the low-key white wires on the statuary—they're

electrified to keep pigeons from dumping their corrosive loads on the tender limestone. Go inside; it's the most active religious spot in town. The musty church is lavishly decorated with 18th-century tiles that tell the stories of the discovery of the Holy Cross (on left) and the life of St. Augustine (on right; the church is of the Augustinian order). The pulpit is considered one of the finest pieces of Renaissance work in Portugal.

Step behind the altar for a close-up look at two fine 16th-century tombs. On the left lies the first Portuguese king, Afonso Henriques (1095–1185). Afonso "The Conqueror" reclaimed most of Portugal from the Moors, declared himself king, got the pope to approve the title, and settled down in his chosen capital—Coimbra. There, his wife gave birth to young Sancho, who later became king. Sancho I (1154–1211, tomb on right) was known as "The Populator." He saw the destruction that war had brought to the country, and set about rebuilding and repopulating, inviting northern-European Crusaders (such as the Knights Templar) to occupy southern Portugal.

In the 16th century, while on a pilgrimage to Santiago de Compostela, the great King Manuel I dropped by this church and was underwhelmed by the two kings' original tombs. He commissioned these beautifully carved replacements—much more fit for kings. Study the intimate faces. Notice how the kings seem only to be resting. (To make themselves more comfortable, they've "hung" their helmets and arm-guards just behind them.) For €2.50, you can explore the sacristy (entrance to right of main altar) and see the treasures of the church, pass through the impressive chapter room into a fine Manueline "cloister of silence," and check out the slick new art gallery filling the monks' former dining hall (Mon–Sat 9:00–12:00 & 14:00–17:30, Sun 16:00–17:30).

People (and pigeons) survey the Praça 8 de Maio scene from the terrace of the recommended **Café Santa Cruz** (to the right of church, see "Eating," page 208). Built as a church, but abandoned with the dissolution of the monasteries in 1834, this was the 19th-century haunt of local intellectuals. The altar is now used for lectures, poetry readings, small concerts, and art exhibits (the women's room is in a confessional).

• *Continue past the church and the city hall (Câmara Municipal, pop in quickly for a glance at a hilly 3-D model of Coimbra, or make an appointment across the street for free Internet access—see "Helpful Hints," earlier in this chapter) to the noisy street. Turn right, and go a block to find a park with a fountain (once a monastery cloister and Renaissance garden) and the cheap, handy Self-Service Restaurant Jardim da Manga (see "Eating," page 208). Keep going uphill along the busy Rua Olímpio Nicolau di Fernandes past the big post office to the...*

Mercado Municipal: This modern covered market is fun to explore and great for gathering picnic supplies (Mon–Sat 8:00–14:00 but some stalls open later, closed Sun). It's clean and hygienic, but maintains the colorful appeal of an old farmers market. See the "salt of the earth" in the faces of the women selling produce (their men are off in the fields...or the bars). These ladies aren't shy about trying to sell their goods, even to tourists. For

a sandwich and glass of wine for less than €2, head to the Bar do Mercado Requinte at the end of the ground floor. Check out the photos of the old market on the wall, and then go upstairs for bread, more meat, and veggies. Follow your nose to the glass doors at the far end, with all the fresh fish and dried cod. The Portuguese are the world's biggest cod eaters, but because cod is no longer found in nearby waters, the local favorite is imported from Norway. To the Portuguese, cod *(bacalhau)* tastes much better dried and salted than fresh. This section housed the original market—you can recognize the wrought-iron work from the photos you've just seen on the ground floor at the bar.

• *From the fish hall, swim outside and find the sleek city elevator.*

Elevador do Mercado: Take the elevator to the top of the hill (€1.50/trip if you pay elevator operator, €1.80/3 trips or €6/11 trips if you buy tickets in store next door—marked *loja*—or at most kiosks; no time limit, sharable, also valid for buses; elevator runs Mon–Sat 7:30–22:00, Sun 10:00–22:00). Don't insert your ticket in the machine until the elevator operator is there.

The lift whisks you up the long, steep hill (stop midway to

transfer to funicular, no need to validate ticket again), offering commanding views of Coimbra en route. At the top, exit to the right and head uphill, following signs to *Universidade*. Fifty yards up the cobbled lane, at the first intersection and crest of the hill, you'll find a local fraternity house called Real República Corsários das Ilhas (literally "Royal Commune of the Island Pirates"). Notice the prominent graffiti on the wall that links McDonald's and the G8 (group of the eight most powerful countries) with the skull and crossbones. These small university frat houses, called *repúblicas*, are communes that traditionally house about a dozen students from the same region or provincial town. While some are highly cultured, the rowdier ones are often decorated with plunder from their pranks—stolen traffic signs and so on—giving rise to the local saying, "At night, many things happen in Coimbra."

• *Walk on past the Machado de Castro Museum (on right, closed for restoration until sometime in 2008, described on page 201) to the big, fascist-designed university square (Praça da Porta Férrea). The Iron Gate entry to the old university is on your right.*

University: Explore the university (described in "Sights and Activities" on page 196), then continue this town walk.

• *Leave the university—facing the Iron Gate, turn right, backtrack one block, and take the steps down into the old town (following the steep lanes toward the old cathedral).*

As you wander, notice the white-paper diamonds in the windows—they mean "student room available for rent." Continuing on, you'll come to the old cathedral (Sé Velha, described on page 201). Facing the cathedral is the recommended **Restaurante Trovador,** offering fado performances nearly every night (see "Eating," page 208; reservations essential for fado). The colorful little **Café Sé Velha,** on the corner immediately below the cathedral, is tiled with fine, traditional scenes from Coimbra. From there, a blue line on the cobbles marks the route of the electric minibus service (see "Getting Around Coimbra," page 190). Take the steep stairway leading down to the Rua Quebra Costas, the "Street of Broken Ribs." At one time, this lane had no steps, and literally *was* the street of broken ribs. During a strong rain, this becomes a river. On your left at #50, find the photo shop that depicts traditional student life. The lane's many shops show off the fine local blue-and-white ceramic work called *faiança*. If you can't make it to Morocco, this dense jungle of shops and markets may be your next best bet.

• *Rua Quebra Costas ends at...*

Arco de Almedina: This is the double set of arches (named "Gate to the Medina") we saw earlier from the pedestrian street Rua de Ferreira Borges. Part of the old town wall, the arches act as a double gate with a 90-degree kink in the middle for easier defense. Looking back and up, notice the two square holes in the ceiling, through which soldiers would pour boiling oil, turning attacking Moors into fritters. The holes are rudely nicknamed *mata-cães*—dog killers. The second arch was added later (likely for *Reconquista* defense). Pass through and you'll end up unscathed on the pedestrian street.

SIGHTS AND ACTIVITIES

▲▲▲Coimbra's Old University

This venerable 700-year-old university, founded in 1290, was modeled after Bologna's university (Europe's first, A.D. 1139). It's a stately three-winged former royal palace (from when Coimbra was the capital), beautifully situated overlooking the city. At first, law, medicine, grammar, and logic were taught. Then, with the rise of seafaring in Portugal, astronomy and geometry were added. While Lisbon's university is much larger, Coimbra's university (with 25,000 students) is still the country's most respected. For visitors, the university marks the top of the old town. While most of it is fascist-era sprawl, the old core of the university (the palace section, with its iron gate, courtyard, fancy ceremonial halls, chapel, and library) makes for an interesting visit.

Cost and Hours: A combo-ticket for the two university sights that charge admission—the Grand Hall and King John's Library—is €6 (otherwise €3.50 each, April–Oct daily 9:00–19:20, Nov–March daily 10:00–16:40, ticket office closes 20 min before sights, www.uc.pt/en/informacaopara). You'll get an entry time for the library (see "King John's Library," page 200). Buy your ticket at the counter located inside the Biblioteca Geral (large building to the left and outside of the Iron Gate).

Getting There: To get to the university, consider taking the "Welcome to Coimbra" walk, page 191, using the elevator from the Mercado Municipal to get to the top of the hill. Or take a taxi to the Iron Gate, then sightsee Coimbra downhill.

Iron Gate—Find the gate to the old university (on Praça da Porta Férrea). Before entering, stand with your back to the gate (and the old university) and look across the stark, modern square at the fascist architecture of the new university. In what's considered one of the worst cultural crimes in Portuguese history, the dictator António Salazar tore down half of Coimbra's old town to build these university halls. Salazar, proud that Portugal was the last European power to hang onto its global empire, wanted a fittingly monumental university here. After all, Salazar—along with virtually everyone of political influence in Portugal—had been educated at Coimbra, where he studied law and then became an economics professor. If these bold buildings are reminiscent of Mussolini's E.U.R. in Rome, perhaps it's because they were built in part by Italian architects for Portugal's little Mussolini.

OK, now turn and walk through the Iron Gate. Traditionally, freshmen—proudly wearing their black capes for the first time—pass through the Iron Gate to enroll. Also traditionally, they had to pass through an Iron Gate gauntlet of butt kicks from upperclassmen to get out.

Walk into the...

Old University Courtyard—The university's most important sights all face this square: the Grand Hall (up the grand stairway on the right between you and the clock tower), St. Michael's Chapel (straight ahead, through the door, then to the left), and King John's Library (across the square, furthest door on left, flanked by columns).

The statue in the square is of King John III. While the university was established in 1290, it went back and forth between Lisbon and Coimbra (back then, university students were adults, privileged, and a pain to have in your town). In 1537, John III finally established the school permanently in Coimbra (away from Lisbon). Standing like a good humanist (posing much like his contemporary, England's King Henry VIII), John modernized Portugal's education system in the Renaissance style. But he also made the university the center of Portugal's Inquisition.

Coimbra's Old University

Survey the square with your back to the gate. The dreaded sound of the clock tower's bell—named the "baby goat" for its nagging—calls students to class. On several occasions, the clapper has been stolen. (No bell... no class. No class...big party.) A larger bell (the "big goat") rings only on grand and formal occasions.

The arcaded passageway (upstairs) between the Iron Gate and the clock tower is called Via Latina, from the days when only Latin was allowed in this part of the university.

See the following sights in any order you like. If you want to visit the Grand Hall and/or King John's Library, remember that you need to purchase your ticket at the Biblioteca Geral (to the left and outside of the Iron Gate). Note that regardless of the admission time you're given to see the library, they may let you in early.

The Grand Hall (Sala dos Capelos)—Enter from the middle of Via Latina, climb the tiled stairway, and show your ticket. The Grand Hall is the site of the university's major academic ceremonies, such as exams and graduations. Tourists look down from balconies above the room. It was originally the throne room of the royal palace. Today, the rector's light-green chair sits like a throne in front. During ceremonies, students in their formal attire fill the

benches, and teachers sit along the perimeter as gloomy portraits of Portuguese kings watch from above. Since there is no clapping during these formal rituals, a brass band (on the wooden platform in the back) punctuates the ceremonies with solemn music.

View Catwalk (Varanda): Continue around the Grand Hall, past an ornately decorated former royal stateroom (now a place where oral exams are taken) and out onto the narrow observation deck for the best possible views of Coimbra. The viewpoint will usually be open, but may be closed if the weather's bad. The "only 10 people on the balcony at a time" rule is enforced by an on-duty guard who has the door key.

From the viewpoint, scan the old town from right to left. Remember, before Salazar's extension of the university, this old town surrounded the university. The Baroque facade breaking the horizon is the "new" cathedral—from the 16th century. Below that, with the fine arcade, is the Machado de Castro Museum, housed in the former bishop's palace and located atop a Roman site (see page 201). And below that, like an armadillo, sits the old cathedral.

If you see any gaily painted yellow-and-blue windows, they mark a *república* frat house. Travelers during November and May might see parades of rowdy students in funny costumes, draped in signs, dragging tin cans—all part of the traditional initiation rites marking the beginning and end of the school year. This is when new students receive—and graduating students burn—the small colored ribbons of their chosen major (see sidebar). Look beyond the houses to the Mondego River, the lengthiest entirely Portuguese river. Over the bridge is the 17th-century Santa Clara Convent—at 590 feet, the longest building in Coimbra.

Coimbra

The Burning of Ribbons

Europe's third-oldest university has longstanding traditions to match. If you're lucky enough to be in Coimbra at the end of the academic year (sometime in May, depending on the academic calendar), you'll witness a big party that's not to be missed.

The "Burning of Ribbons" *(Queima das Fitas)* began in the 1850s, when a group of students who passed their final fourth-year exams gathered outside the Iron Gate and marched together to the lower town. They burned their ribbons (which were used to bind and carry their books) in a small fire, representing their passage from student to professional. Fifty years later, that simple event had become enormously popular and was added to the other academic celebrations. Floats and parades came later, and the ribbon-burning was done at night. The following day was made an academic holiday—the official time when all students move up one level.

Students who will enter their last year of studies and recent graduates *(finalistas)* participate in the party these days, but of course the graduates get the most attention. Women wear simple white shirts with black skirts and black stockings. Men dress up more formally in black suits—some with tails—as well as their university cape, a wide sash with various badges, a top hat, and a cane. Different accent colors, proudly displayed on the top hats and canes, represent the different departments and indicate which degree the student earned (yellow is for medicine, red is for law, light blue is for computer science, etc.). For good luck after graduation, men take their canes and tap other students' top hats three times. (Of course, the taps get out of control, and lots of students end up losing the tops of their hats.)

Much drinking accompanies this rite of passage, but it's the one time of year when folks in Coimbra don't seem to mind. Ribbon-burning parties are also celebrated in Porto, and to a lesser extent in Lisbon. Join the fun, and offer an appropriately colored flower to a new graduate. You may be invited to the party.

St. Michael's Chapel—This chapel is behind the 16th-century facade (enter through door to the right of facade—once inside, push the door on the left marked *capela*, free admission). The architecture of the church interior is Manueline—notice the golden "rope" trimming the arch before the altar. The decor is from a later time. The altar is 17th-century Mannerist, with steps unique to Portugal (and her South American colonies), symbolizing the steps the faithful take on their journey to heaven. The 2,100-pipe,

18th-century German-built organ is notable for its horizontal "trumpet" pipes. Found only in Iberia, these help the organist perform the allegorical fight between good and evil—with the horizontal pipes trumpeting the arrival of the good guys. The box seats for the royal family are above the loft in the rear. Students and alums enjoy the privilege of having their weddings here.

The **Museum of Sacred Art,** further down the corridor, may still be closed for renovation in 2008. When it reopens, a painting of John the Baptist will again point the way to art that nuns and priests find fascinating. The museum was created in 1910 to keep the art in Coimbra when the new republic wanted to move it all to Lisbon. (Also in the corridor, you'll find WCs and a cheap student-filled café with a lovely view of the river from the terrace.)

▲King John's Library—One of Europe's best surviving Baroque libraries, this grand building displays 30,000 books in 18th-

century splendor. The zealous doorkeeper locks the door at every opportunity to keep out humidity. Buzz (on left) to get into this temple of thought. While ticket-sellers are quick to issue entry times requiring a long wait, you're likely to get in early if you humbly ask the attendant if you can enter now. Once you've received permission to enter, you might still have to wait outside a while, as other groups finish their 10-minute visits (followed by a 10-min closure to control humidity level). Inside, at the "high altar," stands the library's founder, the absolute monarch King John V (1689–1750), who considered France's King Louis XIV an inspiration.

The reading tables, inlaid with exotic South American woods (and ornamented with silver ink wells), and the precious wood shelves (with clever hideaway staircases) are reminders that Portugal's wealth was great—and imported. Built Baroque, the interior is all wood. Even the "marble" on the arches of triumph that divide the library into rooms is just painted wood. (Real marble would add to the humidity.) The resident bats—which live in the building, but not the library itself—are well cared for and appreciated. They eat insects, providing a chemical-free way of protecting the books, and alert the guard to changing weather with their "eee-eee" cry. Look for the trompe l'oeil Baroque tricks on the painted ceiling. Gold leaf (from Brazil) is everywhere, and the Chinese themes are pleasantly reminiscent of Portugal's once vast empire. The books, all dating from before 1755, are in Latin, Greek, and Hebrew. Imagine being a student in Coimbra centuries ago, when this temple of learning stored the world's knowledge like a vast filing cabinet. As you leave, watch how the doorman uses the giant key as a hefty doorknob.

In Coimbra

Machado de Castro Museum—The museum is closed for restoration until sometime in 2008, but check at the TI or the sight to be sure. Housed in the old bishop's palace, it contains ceramics, 14th- to 16th-century religious sculpture (mostly taken from the dissolved monasteries), and a Roman excavation site. Upstairs, look for the impressive 14th-century *Cristo Negro* carved in wood. Until a decade ago, when this statue was cleaned (and the black—from candle soot—came off), it was considered to be a portrait of a black Christ. Before you return downstairs, enjoy the views from the top-floor arcade.

The Roman building, with a basement crisscrossed with empty tunnels, provided a level foundation for an ancient Roman forum that stood where the museum does today. At the entrance, read the Latin-inscribed Roman stone: bottom line—"Aeminiens," referring to the people who lived in Roman Coimbra, then called Aeminium; fifth line—the fourth-century emperor of the day, "Constantio"; and the second line—a reference perhaps to an early alliance of barbarian tribes from the North Atlantic. Notice the few economical "plug-on" Roman busts—from the days when they'd keep the bodies, but change the heads each time a new emperor took power. The museum sometimes houses art exhibitions here in the Roman tunnels or on the ground floor (if not closed for renovation, then likely open Tue–Sun 9:30–12:30 & 14:00–17:30, closed Mon, www.ipmuseus.pt). Visit this before or after the old university, since both are at roughly the same altitude.

Old Cathedral (Sé Velha)—Same old story: Christians push out the Moors (1064), tear down their mosque, and build a church. The Arabic script on a few of the stones indicates that rubble from the mosque was used in the construction. Notice the crenellations along the roof of this fortress-like Romanesque church; the Moors, though booted out, were still considered a risk. If this reminds you of Lisbon's cathedral, it should...it was designed by the same French architect.

The giant holy-water font shells are a 19th-century gift from Ceylon (now Sri Lanka), and the walls are lined with 16th-century tiles from Sevilla, Spain. The three front altars are each worth a look. The main altar is a fine example of Gothic styling. The 16th-century chapel to the right contains one of the best Renaissance altars in the country. The apostles all look to Jesus as he talks, while musical angels flank the holy host. To the left of the High Altar, the Chapel of St. Peter shows Peter being crucified upside down. The fine points of the carving were destroyed by Napoleon's soldiers.

On the right just before the transept is a murky painting of Queen Isabel (St. Elizabeth) with a skirt full of roses. This 13th-century Hungarian princess—with family ties to Portugal—is a local favorite with a sweet legend. Against the wishes of the king, she always gave bread to the poor. One day, when he came home early from a trip, she was busy doling out bread from her skirt. She pulled the material up to hide the bread. When the king asked her what was inside (suspecting bread for the poor), the queen—unable to lie—lowered the material and, miraculously, the bread had turned to roses. For this astonishing act, she was canonized as a saint in 1625.

The peaceful cloister (entrance near back of church) is the oldest Gothic cloister in Portugal. Well maintained, though its walls are decaying, the courtyard offers a fine framed view of the cathedral's dome. A tomb from 1064 in the cloister belongs to Coimbra's first Christian, post-*Reconquista* governor (church is free, no-photos policy—but rarely enforced, cloisters cost €1; church open Mon–Thu 10:00–18:00, Fri 10:00–12:00, Sat 10:00–15:00, cloister closes 13:00–14:00, closed Sun; the public is welcome to come to Mass, ask TI for schedule, WCs on your right inside cloister).

▲**Fado**—Portugal's unique, mournful traditional music, fado, is generally performed by women. But in Coimbra, men sing the fado. Roving bands of male students—similar to the tuna bands in Spain's Salamanca—serenade around town for tips and the hearts of women. During the tourist season, you'll find sit-down fado nightly at **Restaurante Trovador** and **Fado Diligencia** (see "Eating," page 208), the **À Capella** piano bar (described in next paragraph), and in the streets—the mayor organizes Thursday street concerts through the summer. The **Galeria Almedina**, under the Arco de Almedina, also puts on free authentic fado shows (Sat in June–Aug, ask at TI for details).

À Capella, on the hill above the Church of Santa Cruz, is a tiny chapel that's been turned into a piano bar. While they often play jazz in the winter, it's all fado in the summer (nightly after 22:00). Come for the fado, the very cool scene, and the snacks and drinks (no cover but €5 minimum, reservations smart, at the triangular corner midway down the main drag, climb the steep Rua do Corpo de Deus 300 yards until you see the old chapel on your left, tel. 914-657-717).

Parque Dr. Manuel Braga—Coimbra's inviting riverside park sprawls upstream from the Santa Clara Bridge. You'll find boat tours, the recommended Italian restaurant Restaurante Itália and the Mondego Irish Pub (page 209), a strip of trendy evening spots, and the Portuguese Pavilion from the Hannover Expo (2000 World's Fair in Hannover, Germany).

Little Portugal (Portugal dos Pequenitos)—This is a children's (or tourist's) look at the great buildings and monuments of Portugal and its former empire in miniature, scattered through a park a couple of blocks south of town, straight across the Santa Clara Bridge. Wanting to boost national pride, Salazar commissioned architect Cassiano Branco to build these mini-replicas in 1940. If you've been through some of Portugal already, it's fun to try and identify the buildings you've already seen and look at what's to come (€6–7 depending on their schedule, daily March–May 10:00–19:00, June–mid-Sept 9:00–20:00, mid-Sept–Feb 10:00–17:00, last entry 30 min before closing).

Kayaks, Cruises, and Adventure Sports—To enjoy the region's natural beauty, consider these activities.

Kayaking: The company called **O Pioneiro do Mondego** buses you from Coimbra to Penacova (15 miles away), from where you can kayak down the Mondego River for about four hours back into Coimbra (€20, 10 percent discount with this book, daily June–Sept, one- and two-person kayaks available, book by phone, meet at park near TI, tel. 239-478-385 to reserve, www.opioneirodomondego.com, Derek speaks English). Most people stop to swim or picnic on the way back, so it often turns into an all-day journey. For the first 12.5 miles, you'll go easily with the flow, but you'll get your exercise paddling the remaining stretch. To avoid the workout (and the more boring part of the Mondego River), ask to be picked up 2.5 miles before Coimbra, at Portela do Mondego, where the river's current slows down.

Cruises: If you'd rather let someone else do the work, **Basófias** boats float up and down the river on a 55-minute trip that runs daily except Monday (€8; departures from dock across from TI at 15:00, 16:00, and 17:00; two more in summer at 18:00 and 19:00, schedule posted at dock, tel. 239-912-444, www.basofias.com).

Adventure Sports: Located in the nearby town Foz da Figueira, **Capitão Dureza** specializes in at-your-own-risk activities: rappelling, rafting, and canyoning (pickup and drop-off in Coimbra, book by tel. & fax 233-427-772, www.capitaodureza.com).

Near Coimbra

▲Conímbriga Roman Ruins—Portugal's best Roman site is impressive...unless you've been to Rome. What remains of the city is divided in two, in part because its inhabitants tore down buildings to erect a quick defensive wall against an expected barbarian attack. Today, this wall cuts crudely through the site.

Getting There: The ruins are nine miles southwest of Coimbra, on the road to Lisbon. Two different **bus** companies serve the route: Joalto and AVIC. On weekdays, two buses leave for the ruins each morning across from Coimbra's Station A (€1.60, Mon–Fri 9:05 and 9:35, Sat–Sun 9:35 only, AVIC bus stop is on the riverside opposite the station, 30-min trip). The return bus leaves from Conímbriga's parking lot (Mon–Sat 13:00 and 18:00, Sun 18:00 only). Confirm the destination by asking, *"Vai para Conímbriga?"* Otherwise, you could end up on one of the frequent buses to Condeixa (runs twice hourly) that stops a mile short of the ruins.

Drivers should cross the Santa Clara Bridge and go uphill, following signs to *Condeixa*. Continue straight through town, and you will see brown signs guiding you to the ruins. Consider driving to Conímbriga on your way to or from Coimbra on Auto-Estrada A1; the freeway exit is clearly marked.

◯ Self-Guided Tour: Purchase your tickets inside the main building, then enter the ruins before visiting the museum (€3, open daily June–Sept 9:00–20:00, Oct–May 10:00–18:00, museum closed Mon but site accessible, www.conimbriga.pt). Helpful arrows guide you through the site. Explore the remnants of the old town first, and save the mansion—under the protective modern roofing—for the grand finale. You'll first see remains of different houses and shopping arcades, most with wonderful mosaics intact. Note how the columns are made of preformed wedges. After you see the public baths, walk around the wall.

The Wall: Locals hastily built this immense structure for their own protection, and it shows. Once the Roman Empire retreated from this area, invaders from the north went on the offensive (beginning around A.D. 465). A Christian Germanic tribe conquered the city and built a basilica at the end of this wall.

Continuing along the wall, you'll see parts of a house belonging to a local landowner. Walk through the fields to the rest of the site. Other houses and public baths are out there, even though they're poorly signposted. As you explore the site, you'll see the sparse ruins of the old forum. Backtrack to pass under the aqueduct and go around it. Look for the fallen stones, which once supported the structure, until you reach the site's most important find (under a protective roof). The **House of the Fountains** is an entire dwelling, with most of its rooms and mosaics intact. Don't spend €0.50 on the lazy fountain show (wait for one of the school groups to do it for you), but enjoy the stories told in the mosaics. Simple portraits, horses, and numerous hunting scenes illustrate the daily routine in this town during Roman times.

The Museum: Return to the delightful museum that shows the discoveries from decades of excavation. The room to the right of the ticket counter describes daily life in Conímbriga. You'll see coins, dinnerware, and even grooming utensils (find the spoon-shaped ear cleaners)—all with good English descriptions. The opposite room contains a miniature replica of the forum, along with fine mosaics and a few tombstones. The best mosaic is of the mythological, bull-headed Minotaur—follow the maze from the center until you are safely out. The museum's café is an excellent spot to have lunch before catching the return bus to Coimbra (€7 meals, same hours as museum). Or bring a picnic lunch, and eat in the gardens.

SLEEPING

These listings are an easy walk from the central Station A and Santa Clara Bridge. For the cheapest rooms, simply walk a block from Station A into the old town, and choose one of countless *dormidas* (cheap pensions). River views come with traffic noise.

$$$ Hotel Astória gives you the thrill of staying in the city's finest old hotel. Their 62 rooms have been rated among the most characteristic in Portugal (Sb-€86–108, Db-€103–121, extra bed-€33, includes breakfast, 10 percent discount with this book—show it at check-in, air-con, elevator—Coimbra's first, fine Art Deco lounges, ask hotel about parking or try public parking opposite hotel-€0.50/hr, central as can be at Avenida Emídio Navarro 21, tel. 239-853-020, fax 239-822-057, www.almeidahotels.com, gm.astoria@almeidahotels.com). Rooms with river views don't cost extra, but come with some street noise. I prefer the quieter city-view rooms on the back.

$$ Hotel Bragança's dark lobby leads to 83 clean and comfortable but sometimes smoky rooms with modern bathrooms. The wood paneling and furniture transport you back to Portugal in the 1950s (Sb with shower-€35, Sb with tub-€48, smaller Db with

---

Sleep Code

(€1 = about $1.40, country code: 351)
S = Single, **D** = Double/Twin, **T** = Triple, **Q** = Quad, **b** = bathroom, **s** = shower only. Unless indicated otherwise, you can assume credit cards are accepted and English is spoken.

To help you easily sort through these listings, I've divided the rooms into three categories, based on the price for a standard double room with bath during high season (April–Sept). The rest of the year, it's 10 to 20 percent less.

  $$$ Higher Priced—Most rooms €80 or more.
  $$ Moderately Priced—Most rooms between €50–80.
  $ Lower Priced—Most rooms €50 or less.

Coimbra Hotels and Restaurants

1. Hotel Astória
2. Hotel Bragança
3. Residência Coimbra
4. Residência Domus
5. Ibis Hotel
6. Pensão Santa Cruz
7. Residencial Larbelo
8. To Pousada de Juventude
9. Restaurante Trovador
10. Fado Diligência
11. Adega Paço do Conde
12. Self-Service Rest. Jardim da Manga
13. Café Santa Cruz
14. Restaurante O Serenata
15. Restaurante Zé Manel
16. O Bizarro
17. "Eating Lane" (Rua das Azeiteiras)
18. Restaurante Itália
19. To Mondego Irish Pub & Other Eateries
20. Covered Market
21. À Capella Fado Bar
22. Internet Coimbra Câmara Municipal
23. Spacenet Internet Café

shower-€55, larger Db with tub-€60, Tb with tub-€75, Qb-€85, 10 percent discount with this book, breakfast included, air-con, elevator, free parking in small lot at entrance if space available, Largo das Ameias 10 next to Station A, tel. 239-822-171, fax 239-836-135, www.hotel-braganca.com, geral@hotel-braganca.com).

$ Residência Coimbra provides top hotel quality in a 10-year-old building for pension prices. Its 15 fine air-conditioned rooms are buried in the old town on a quiet pedestrian lane, yet it's only 250 yards from Station A (Db-€40–50, 5 percent discount with this book, includes breakfast, all rooms have double beds, Rua das Azeiteiras 55, tel. 239-837-996, coimbra@gmail.com, Maria and Jose).

$ Residência Domus, tucked away in a corner, rents 20 decent rooms in a cozy atmosphere (Sb-€25–28; Db-€25–30, Db with air-con-€35–40, double beds cheaper than twins; Tb-€45, 10 percent discount with this book, includes breakfast, Rua Adelino Veiga 62, tel. 239-828-584, fax 239-838-818, www.residencialdomus.com, residencialdomus@sapo.pt, Sr. Santos).

$ Ibis Hotel, a modern high-rise, has 110 orderly little rooms that come with all the comforts. Well located on a riverside park, this impersonal though reliable chain hotel is three blocks past the Santa Clara Bridge and the old town (Sb/Db-€43–52, breakfast-€5.50, two smoke-free floors, elevator, easy €3.50/day parking in basement, Avenida Emídio Navarro 70, tel. 239-852-130, fax 239-852-140, www.ibishotel.com, h1672@accor.com).

$ Pensão Santa Cruz overlooks the charming and traffic-free square called Praça 8 de Maio at the end of the pedestrian mall. It's a bright, homey place with 14 simple rooms that Vincent van Gogh would have enjoyed painting. You'll find lots of stairs, dim lights, and rickety balconies worth requesting (D-€15–25, Db-€25–30, most expensive June–Aug, prices are soft—ask for a discount, cash only, in-room modem access, Praça 8 de Maio 21, third floor, tel. & fax 239-826-197, www.pensaosantacruz.com, mail@pensaosantacruz.com, friendly Walter, Anna, and Oswald run the show).

$ Residencial Larbelo, with Old World character, mixes frumpiness and former elegance in its 17 rooms. The old-fashioned staircase, classic breakfast room, and gentle non-English-speaking management takes you to another age (Sb-€25, Db-€45, Tb-€50, cheaper Oct–March, breakfast-€2.50, air-con, in front of the Santa Clara Bridge at Largo da Portagem 33, tel. 239-829-092, fax 239-829-094, residenciallarbelo@sapo.pt).

$ Pousada de Juventude, the youth hostel, offers 71 rooms on the other side of town in the student area past Praça da República. It's friendly, clean, and well run, but is no cheaper than a simple *pensão* (€11 in four- to six-bed rooms, S-€26, Db-€28, Rua António Henriques Seco 14, tel. 239-822-955, coimbra@movijovem.pt).

Coimbra

EATING

Specialities of this hilly Beira region include *leitão* (suckling pig), *cabrito* (baby male goat), *chanfana* (goat cooked in wine), *Serra* cheese, and rich, red *Bairrada* and *Dão* wines. The local pastries are *pastel de Santa Clara* (made with almonds and marmalade) and *pastel de Tentúgal* (flaky puff pastry with a sweet eggy filling and a dusting of powdered sugar). Be aware that most of these restaurants—as well as most of Coimbra—shut down on Sunday.

Eating with Fado

Restaurante Trovador, while a bit touristy, serves good food in a classic and comfortable setting, with entertaining dinner fado performances nearly nightly in summer from 21:30 (Fri-Sat only off-season). It's *the* place for an old-town splurge (daily fixed-price meal-€15–20, Mon–Sat 12:30–15:00 & 19:30–22:30, closed Sun, facing the old cathedral on Largo de Sé Velha 15, reservations essential to eat with the music—ask for a seat with a music view, tel. 239-825-475).

Fado Diligencia is a good spot for a fado sing-along in a warm, relaxed atmosphere, with or without dinner. They even know a few Beatles tunes, so request your favorite and take center stage if you're feeling bold. Food and drinks are reasonable, with a €5 minimum (€15 dinners, shows daily 22:30–2:00 in the morning, Rua Nova 30; from Praça 8 de Maio, take Rua Sofia to your second left, Diligencia is 2 blocks up on your right; tel. 239-827-667).

Eating Without Fado

Adega Paço do Conde knows how to grill. Choose your seafood or meat selection from the display case as you enter. They'll pop it on the grill, serve it up, and then you can grab your table. Students, solo travelers, families, and pigeons like this homey place (€6 meals, Mon–Sat 11:00–22:00, closed Sun, Rua Paço do Conde 1; from Praça do Comércio, take the last left—Rua Adelino Veiga, opposite the church, and walk 2 blocks to small square—Largo Paço do Conde; tel. 239-825-605, Alfredo).

Self-Service Restaurant Jardim da Manga is handy for a quick, easy, and cheap meal with locals. Sit indoors or outdoors next to a cool and peaceful fountain. Just slide a tray down the counter and pick what you like (€7 meals, Sun–Fri 12:00–14:30 & 19:00–22:00, closed Sat, in Jardim da Manga, behind Church of Santa Cruz, tel. 239-829-156).

Café Santa Cruz, next to the Church of Santa Cruz, is Old World elegant, with great coffee, simple toasted sandwiches, and outdoor tables offering great people-watching over Praça 8 de Maio (daily 8:00–22:30).

Coimbra

Restaurante O Serenata is country-kitchen cozy and fun, serving simple €8 meals (Mon–Sat 12:00–15:00 & 19:00–23:00, closed Sun, between Station A and Largo da Portagem at Largo da Sota 6, tel. 239-826-729).

Restaurante Zé Manel is tiny, rustic, and authentically local. Judging from the walls—caked with notes from happy eaters—and the line of people waiting for a table, this place is a popular favorite. They serve about 20 local dishes (€8 for one person, €14 for two, Mon–Sat 12:00–15:00 & 19:30–22:00, closed Sun, no reservations, arrive early or wait; sign is high above on lamppost, 20 yards directly behind Hotel Astória at Beco do Forno 12, tel. 239-823-790).

O Bizarro is a small white-tablecloth hole-in-the-wall that serves up tasty Portuguese food at a good price (Sun–Fri 12:00–15:00 & 18:00–22:00, 30 yards behind Hotel Astória at Rua Sargento Mor 44).

"Eating Lane": Coimbra's Baixa (lower town) has its own mini-version of Lisbon's "eating lane." **Rua das Azeiteiras** is chock-full of homey local eateries serving Portuguese standards to both locals and tourists. Options range from fancy to crowded eat-with-the-neighbors dining (generally open 12:00–15:00 & 18:00–23:00). I liked tiny **Restaurante Viela** at #33, but poke around this short street and check out the handwritten menus for what's fresh.

Trendy Eating on the Riverside: Literally hanging over the river, modern **Restaurante Itália**—at Parque Dr. Manuel Braga, opposite the TI—serves good Italian food (€8 pizza and pastas, €10–12 meals, daily 12:00–24:00, dinner reservations smart, riverside tables limited to parties of four when busy, tel. 239-838-863). Farther down toward the Portuguese pavilion is a small strip of hip restaurants, all with modern indoor or breezy riverside seating. The **Mondego Irish Pub** serves hamburgers, steaks, and Irish beer with live music—generally Irish—most nights (daily from noon until after midnight, tel. 239-837-092).

Picnics: Shop at the colorful covered market Mercado Municipal, behind the Church of Santa Cruz (see "Mercado Municipal," page 194; Mon–Sat 8:00–14:00, closed Sun) or at tiny *mini-mercados* in the side streets. The well-maintained gardens along the river across from the TI are picnic-pleasant.

TRANSPORTATION CONNECTIONS

From Coimbra by Bus to: Alcobaça (2/day, 1.5 hrs), **Batalha** (3/day with transfer in Leiria, 1.25 hrs), **Fátima** (7/day, 1 hr), **Nazaré** (5/day, 2 hrs), **Lisbon** (22/day, 2.5 hrs), **Évora** (3/day direct, 4.5 hrs, more options with transfer in Lisbon), **Porto** (almost hourly, 1.5 hrs). Bus info: tel. 239-855-270. Frequency drops on weekends, especially Sunday.

By Train to: Nazaré/Valado (6/day, 2.5 hours, transfer in Bifurcação de Lares; the bus is a better option—see above—because Nazaré/Valado train station is 3 miles away from Nazaré), **Porto** (nearly hourly, 1.25 hrs on Alfa Pendular line or 2.25 hrs on slow Regional line—confirm before buying); most long-distance trains end at Porto's non-central Campanhã Station), **Lisbon** (almost hourly on Alfa Pendular service, 2 hrs; regional service equally frequent but takes 4 hrs; for Lisbon center, get off at Santa Apolónia Station; for Lisbon airport, hop off at Oriente Station and take the bus to airport; all Coimbra/Porto trains stop at both stations 9 min apart). Train info: tel. 808-208-208, www.cp.pt.

To Salamanca, Spain: The best option is the direct **bus** (€28, departs daily at 12:00, arrives at 17:15 in Salamanca, then continues on to Madrid, arriving at 20:00); to guarantee a place, book a couple of days in advance. You can confirm schedules and buy your bus ticket by phone or in person at the friendly Abreu travel agency in Coimbra (see "Helpful Hints," page 190) more easily than at Coimbra's bus station (Intercentro office, tel. 239-827-588, no English spoken).

I'd avoid taking the **train** to Salamanca because of its inconvenient arrival time: One train per day on the Sud-Expresso line departs Coimbra at 18:15 and drops you in Salamanca at 24:00 (4.75 hrs, note that Spanish time is 1 hour later). The Salamanca train station is not centrally located, so it's best to reserve your accommodations in advance, as you won't be tucking into bed until two in the morning, Portuguese time.

PORTO

To get a complete picture of Portugal, visit Porto—the capital of the north and the country's second city (with 265,000 residents and a metropolitan area sprawling to include over a million). Porto, proud of the things that make it different, fiercely clings to its longstanding rivalry with Lisbon...especially where soccer is concerned.

Porto (locals call it POR-too) is less polished than Lisbon, but it's also full of Old World charm. Houses with red-tiled roofs tumble down the hills to the riverbank, prickly church towers dot the skyline, mosaic-patterned stones line streets, and flat-bottomed boats called *rabelos* ply the lazy river.

The city's name comes from the Romans, who dubbed the port town Portus Cale. When Porto's Christians conquered the southern Moors in the Middle Ages, the city's name became the name of the whole country. The many British people who have shaped Porto have also dubbed it "Oporto" ("the port"), a corruption of the town's true name. While various guidebooks and postcards call it this, locals never do.

Porto's tourism slogan, "Authenti**city**," captures its gritty warts-and-all character. The people of Porto claim they're working too hard to worry about being pretty. As an oft-repeated saying goes, "Coimbra studies, Braga prays, Lisbon parties...and Porto works."

Straight-laced, nose-to-the-grindstone Porto has enjoyed something of a cultural renaissance in recent years. In 2001, it was designated as a European Capital of Culture. Two exciting showpieces of contemporary architecture have been built in the last several years: the Serralves Museum and the House of Music.

Porto

Porto Overview

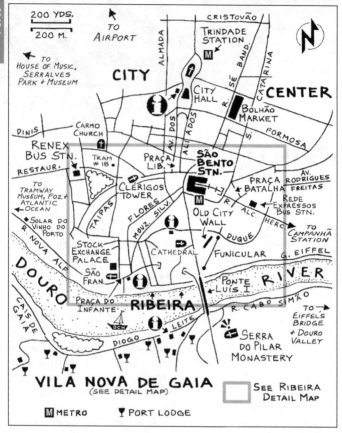

European Union money has been pouring in, funding a revamping of the public transportation system and more. With this ongoing construction, Porto is ever-changing, often chaotic, and still well worth a visit. At a minimum, use it as a gateway to the stunning Douro Valley.

For visitors, Porto itself is interesting, offering two high-impact sightseeing thrills: the postcard-perfect ambience of the riverfront Ribeira district, and the opportunity to learn more about (and taste) the port wine that ages here. Porto also features other unexpected treats, including sumptuous Baroque churches and civic buildings, a bustling real-world market hall, and quirky but worthwhile museums.

Though the weather is always changing, it's usually marginal. You're likely to get sun and rain at the same time—causing the locals to exclaim, "The widow's going to remarry."

Planning Your Time

Porto offers one very busy day's worth of sightseeing (or better yet, two relaxed days). Begin your day by exploring the urban city center above the town (poke around the market hall and climb Clérigos Tower for a visual orientation). Wander past the cathedral and clamber down one of the steep lanes to the Ribeira district for lunch. Spend 30 minutes each touring the breathtaking interiors of the Stock Exchange Palace and São Francisco Church. Then head across the river to tour a couple of port-wine lodges before returning to Ribeira for dinner. With a second day, slow down, taste more port, cruise the river, and add a visit to the Serralves Museum and Park.

Ideally, combine your visit to Porto with a trip up the Douro Valley (about two hours away—see next chapter).

ORIENTATION

Porto sprawls on the hilly north bank of the Douro River, near where the river meets the Atlantic Ocean. The tourist's Porto is compact, but confusing and steep—making distances seem longer. Get a good map and wear comfortable walking shoes (or just grab a taxi whenever you need a quick connection).

It helps to think of the tourist's Porto in three parts: The first is the **Ribeira** (ree-BAY-rah), right on the river, with a twisty street plan and oodles of atmosphere. Praça Infante Dom Henrique (Henry the Navigator Square), near the top of the Ribeira, has several intriguing sights, including the Stock Exchange Palace and São Francisco Church.

From here, ramshackle old homes scramble steeply uphill toward the second part of town, the modern **city center,** which hovers above the Ribeira and surrounds the broad boulevard called Avenue of the Allies (Avenida dos Aliados). This area is the urban business center of Porto, packed with office buildings and shoppers, and peppered with hotels. You'll also find a smattering of squares, monuments, and sights (including the market hall and cathedral). At the bottom of the city center, Clérigos Tower stands as the city's most recognizable landmark.

Across the river shine the neon signs of Porto's main tourist attraction, the port-wine cellars *(caves do vinho do porto)* in **Vila Nova de Gaia,** the third part of Porto, although it's technically another town.

The Douro is spanned by six bridges (two steel, four concrete). The only one you're likely to cross is the monstrous steel **Ponte Dom Luís I** (cars and pedestrians use lower level; upper level for Metro trains only).

Visitors venturing farther out find Porto to be a city of contrasts. Its outskirts boast bright, spacious, prim residential neighborhoods, like those around Serralves Museum and Park.

Tourist Information

Porto has three TIs: in the **city center** across from City Hall (at the top of Avenida dos Aliados, Rua Clube dos Fenianos 25, tel. 223-393-472 or 223-293-470); at the top of the **Ribeira,** a block above the river, kitty-corner from the Stock Exchange Palace (Rua Infante Dom Henrique 63, tel. 222-060-412); and on the **cathedral square** (closed weekends Sept–May, no telephone consultations). These three TIs have the same schedule (June–mid-Sept Mon–Fri 9:00–18:30, Sat–Sun 10:00–18:00; mid-Sept–May Mon–Fri 9:00–17:30, Sat–Sun 9:30–16:30; www.portoturismo .pt). A fourth TI is in Vila Nova de Gaia, officially outside the city limits (see page 230).

Pick up the free one-page city map (with sights and hotels) and the useful information pamphlet. They also sell reasonably priced museum booklets and city-walk guides (€1–2), none of which are essential. The Porto Tour Pass (€7.50/one day), covering public transport plus minor discounts at sights, isn't a good value for most visitors (consider the AndanteTour card, listed later, instead). The free quarterly *Agenda Cultural* guide lists cultural events in the city in Portuguese and English; it's especially handy for events at the House of Music (www.casadamusica.com). If you'll be visiting the Foz district (listed on page 222), pick up the *Rede de Transportes* map.

In the main TI on Avenida dos Aliados, you'll also find the helpful **transport office** (called Loja da Mobilidade). They can answer your questions about transportation to, within, or out of Porto; they can especially help you understand the bus-station mess (see "Arrival in Porto," next) and get a handle on the ever-changing local transit picture (toll-free tel. 808-200-166, www .stcp.pt).

Arrival in Porto

By Train: Porto has two train stations. Regional trains, including those serving the Douro Valley, use the very central **São Bento Station** (for a description of this beautifully decorated station, see page 225). Facing the exit in the left corner is a Loja da Mobilidade office (generally open daily 7:30–20:00). You can purchase train tickets here as well as the hassle-free AndanteTour card (see "Getting Around Porto").

Trains coming from farther away, including Lisbon and Coimbra, arrive at the similarly manageable **Campanhã Station,** on the east edge of town. If your train stops at both stations, get off at São Bento (it's closer to central hotels). If you have to get off at Campanhã, you have three options for getting into the center: Take a taxi to your hotel (figure €7 with luggage to most city-center accommodations); catch another train to the São Bento Station (6/hr, free on any ticket to Porto); or use the new Metro across the street (take it to the Trindade stop, then transfer to the yellow line for either Aliados or São Bento stations; note that the Metro is not practical for those staying near the Ribeira).

By Bus: Confusingly, each of Porto's many bus companies operates its own garage, meaning there's no central bus station. The transport office in the main TI can clear up the chaos (see "Tourist Information," opposite page). All of the bus garages are more or less in the city center. Here are a few of the more useful companies, with their addresses and telephone numbers: **Rede Expressos** (to Lisbon and Coimbra; Rua Alexandre Herculano, tel. 222-006-954, www.rede-expressos.pt); **RENEX** (to Lisbon; Campo Mártires da Pátria 37, tel. 222-003-395, www.renex.pt); **Rodonorte** (to Lisbon and Coimbra; Rua Ateneu Comercial do Porto, tel. 222-004-398, www.rodonorte.pt); and **Internorte** (to Spain, including Santiago de Compostela and Madrid; Praça da Galiza 96, tel. 226-052-420, www.internorte.pt).

By Car: Central Porto is a headache by car. Stow it at your hotel or a nearby parking garage. Approaching from Lisbon and Coimbra on the A1 expressway, pay a toll and then follow signs for *Ponte da Arrábida*. After crossing the bridge, take the first right and follow *centro* signs (or the little bull's-eyes) into downtown.

By Plane: Porto's airport is 11 miles north of the city center. Since it's international (with connections beyond Iberia), it's used by people throughout northern Portugal and Spain. The new Metro connects the airport to the center (Trindade stop). You can also take the STCP Aerobus (€5 for a one-day AndanteTour card transport pass, every 30 min from 7:30–20:00, drops you right downtown at Avenida dos Aliados) or a taxi (figure €20). Airport info: tel. 229-432-400.

Helpful Hints

Closed Day: Virtually all Porto museums are closed on Monday.

Festivals: Porto's big holiday is St. João Day (for St. John, the city's patron saint) on June 24. Festivities start the night of June 23 with partying and fireworks, and continue on the 24th with a *rabelo* regatta.

Internet Access: OnWeb Cyber Bar is a handy Internet café with fast access and great ambience (Mon–Sat 10:00–2:00 in the morning, Sun 15:00–2:00 in the morning, a block below TI at Avenida dos Aliados 291). Another quick and easy option is **PT Comunicações** at the base of the same street (Mon–Fri 8:00–20:00, Sat–Sun 10:00–20:00, Avenida dos Aliados 62).

Laundry: A convenient full-service laundry hides almost underground at the west end of the Ribeira district (between São Francisco Church and the river on Rua da Reboleira). Look for the silver *Câmara Municipal* sign. Drop off your laundry, pay €6 for the load, wander the Ribeira, and pick it up two hours later (Mon 8:30–14:00, Tue–Fri 8:30–19:30, Sat 8:30–19:00, closed Sun).

Best Views: There are fine views all along the Ribeira riverfront embankment, but they're even better from across the river in Vila Nova de Gaia (looking back toward Porto). You'll enjoy the views from the top of Clérigos Tower, from the terrace next to the cathedral, or from Mosteiro da Serra do Pilar (the monastery across the river, just above the big steel Ponte Dom Luís I bridge). But the best vantage point of all is from a boat in the river itself (see "Cruising the Douro," page 220).

Getting Around Porto

By Bus, Tram, and Metro

The city is currently engaged in what is supposedly Europe's biggest construction project—extending its tramlines and gradually building a new, mostly aboveground Metro. (Smug Lisboners love to tease that only Porto would build an aboveground "underground.")

Porto's public transportation system can be confusing. It's often changing, but here's what the picture currently looks like: The network includes buses, trams, the new Metro, and a funicular (see next page).

Buses are not very useful for tourists, except for the routes that go to the port-wine lodges in Vila Nova de Gaia across the river (#901 and #906). Another route runs from the beach in Foz to the Serralves Museum (#203). Service is generally speedy, but avoid buses during rush hour, when traffic slows to a crawl due to construction congestion.

Three interconnecting **tram** lines of interest to a tourist are the #1, #18, and #22. The #1 line (Infante/Passeio Alegre) uses a historic car that shudders along the river from the Ribeira, past several museums, to the Foz district and the Atlantic Ocean (see "Tram to Foz" on page 222). The #18 (Restauração/Cordoaria) begins at Carmo Church and wobbles to the recommended Tramway Museum. The newest line, #22, runs through the city center from shopping street Rua de Santa Catarina, past recommended hotels on Rua Passos Manuel, cutting through Avenida dos Aliados and ending near Carmo Church.

Metro lines include blue, red, and green (all connecting Campanhã Station to the center); yellow (includes São Bento Station and Vila Nova de Gaia, across the river); and purple (connecting the airport to the center and Campanhã Station). All Metro lines converge at the Trindade stop, two blocks behind the city hall and Avenida dos Aliados (www.metrodoporto.pt).

Prices are confusing, since the bus and Metro systems don't entirely cooperate. Your fare depends on your mode of transportation and which "zones" you travel in. It's simplest to buy an AndanteTour Card.

AndanteTour Card: This €5 card takes the confusion out of the overly complicated public transport system. It covers all mass-transit options (Metro, trams, buses, funicular, and trains) for 24 hours after its first use (a 72-hour, €11 version is also available). The cards are sold at Loja da Mobilidade centers (São Bento Station and the TI at Avenida dos Aliados), Andante stores (one at the airport), and some bus and train ticket offices. A confusing 24-hour AndanteTour card that covers five major sights is available for €10, but the few euros saved doesn't compensate for the headache (www.metrodoporto.pt).

By Funicular
A handy funicular (Elevador dos Guindais) connects the Ribeira district (at the base of the Ponte Dom Luís I bridge) to the top of the steep hill above (at the remains of the city wall, down the Rua de Augusto Rosa from Praça da Batalha). If you're dining in the Ribeira, note that the funicular stops running at 20:00 (€1.35, covered by AndanteTour card, every 10 min, daily 8:00–20:00).

By Taxi
Taxis are a good option in this hilly city. Most rides are fairly short and cost only around €3. For rides within the city limits, the meter should be on T1 during the day (€2 drop charge) and T2 at night (21:00–6:00 in the morning, €2.35 drop charge). Each kilometer costs about €0.40. A luggage surcharge of €1.60 is legit. It's easy to find taxi stands, and you'll pay €0.75 more to call one (try Invicta, tel. 225-076-400).

TOURS

The city of Porto operates an ingenious, extremely useful agency called **Porto Tours** in an old medieval watchtower next to the cathedral (April–Oct Mon–Fri 10:00–19:00, Sat–Sun 10:00–18:00; Nov–March Mon–Fri 10:00–17:00, Sat 10:00–14:00, closed Sun; Calçada Dom Pedro Pitões 15, tel. 222-000-073, www.portotours .com, reservas.portotours@mail.telepac.pt). This organization,

Porto at a Glance

▲▲**Strolling the Ribeira Embankment** Porto's picturesque riverfront, with its arcades and colorful traditional homes. **Hours:** Always open.

▲▲**Port-Wine Lodges at Vila Nova de Gaia** Porto's most popular tourist activity: touring the cellars where its most famous product ages...and tasting some, too. **Hours:** Varies, but generally daily, last tours at 18:00, some lodges closed Sat–Sun.

▲**Solar do Vinho do Porto** Classy one-stop spot for port tastings. **Hours:** Mon–Sat 14:00–24:00, closed Sun.

▲**Cruising the Douro** Lazy one-hour cruises up and down the river, offering the city's top views. **Hours:** Generally daily 10:00–20:00 in summer (until 17:00 off-season).

▲**São Francisco Church** Gothic church dripping with Baroque gold. **Hours:** daily March–June 9:00–19:00, July–Sept 9:00–20:00, Oct–Feb 9:00–17:30.

▲**Stock Exchange Palace** Astonishing monument to civic pride, with room after sumptuous room. **Hours:** By tour only, daily April–Oct 9:00–19:00, Nov–March 9:00–13:00 & 14:00–18:00.

▲**Clérigos Church and Tower** Porto's towering landmark, with a 225-step climb to sweeping views over the urban sprawl. **Hours:** Daily 9:30–13:00 & 14:30–19:00.

▲**São Bento Train Station** Entry hall decorated with huge and impressive *azulejo* (tile) murals. **Hours:** Always open.

which takes no commission and is not biased toward any particular company, will help you sort through all of the walking, bus, boat, and even helicopter tour options in Porto and up the Douro. They'll also confirm times, answer questions, and sell tickets for the tours. Walking tours on different topics can be reserved online through their website (€32 per person).

Porto Tours can help you arrange for a private **local guide** (around €100/half-day, higher rates on weekends). Maria Jose Aleixo is good; you can contact her directly (€85/half-day, tel. 962-700-156, aleixo19@sapo.pt).

In this steep, tiring city, a **bus tour** is worth considering. You

▲**Rua Santa Catarina** The main shopping drag, with Art Nouveau and Art Deco landmarks. **Hours:** Traffic-free during the day; quiet at night.

▲**Market** Lively old-fashioned produce and meat market...with old-fashioned sanitary conditions. **Hours:** Mon–Fri 8:30–17:00, Sat 8:30–13:00, closed Sun.

▲**Serralves Foundation Contemporary Art Museum and Park** Sprawling park with impressive museum, Art Deco mansion, and relaxing grounds. **Hours:** Museum open April–Sept Tue–Thu 10:00–19:00, Fri–Sat 10:00–22:00, Sun 10:00–20:00; Oct–March Tue–Sun 10:00–19:00; closed Mon; park and house open April–Sept Tue–Sun 10:00–20:00, Oct–March Sat–Sun until 19:00, closed Mon.

Tramway Museum Collection tracing the history of electrical transport. **Hours:** Tue–Fri 9:30–12:30 & 14:30–18:00, Sat–Sun 15:00–19:00, closed Mon.

House of Henry the Navigator Birthplace of the explorer, with history exhibits. **Hours:** Tue–Sat 10:00–12:30 & 14:00–17:30, Sun 14:00–17:30, closed Mon.

Cathedral (Sé) Monstrous church overlooking the town, with fine *azulejo*-decorated cloister and otherwise dull interior. **Hours:** Church open daily in summer 9:00–12:30 & 14:30–19:00, until 18:00 in winter; cloister and sacristy open daily in summer 9:00–12:15 & 14:30–18:00, until 17:15 in winter, closed Sun morning.

House of Music New Modernist concert hall with performances of jazz, fado, and more. **Hours:** Tours daily 10:30–18:00, concerts almost daily.

have two options: a typical stay-mainly-on-the-bus tour (€30, 3.5 hours, live guide in four languages) and a Historical Porto hop-on, hop-off version (€10, 2-hour circuit with nine stops, can hop off and catch a later bus, 10 buses/day, daily 9:30–18:00).

A silly **tourist train** includes a stop at a port-wine lodge across the river (€6, 75 min, 2/hr, leaves from in front of cathedral daily on the hour, 10:00–17:00 in high season, less frequently off-season, tel. 800-203-983).

For **taxi tours** of the town and side-trips to the Douro Valley and even Santiago, consider Rent A Cab tour company (details at Porto Tours, www.rentacab.pt).

Porto

SIGHTS

Along the Riverfront

The riverfront Ribeira (ree-BAY-rah, meaning "riverbank") district is where it's at in Porto. It's the city's most scenic and touristy quarter, with the highest concentration of good restaurants (and postcard racks). I've listed these sights beginning in the Ribeira, then stretching west (toward the Foz district).

▲▲Strolling the Cais da Ribeira (Embankment) and Praça da Ribeira (Square)—This is Porto's best lazy-afternoon activity. As you stroll, imagine the busy port scene before the promenade was reclaimed from the river—riverboats laden with cargo lashed to the embankment, off-loading their wine and produce into 14th-century cellars (still visible). The old arcades lining the Ribeira promenade are jammed with hole-in-the-wall restaurants (most not as "local" as they seem) and souvenir shops. Behind the arcades are skinny, colorful houses draped with drying laundry fluttering like flags, while the locals who fly them stand on their little balconies, gossiping. Riverfront property taxes were based on frontage—promoting the construction  of these narrow, deep, and undeniably picturesque buildings.

The Ribeira neighborhood looks up at the Ponte Dom Luís I bridge, rising 150 feet above the river. In the 1880s, Teofilo Seyfrig, a protégé of Gustave Eiffel, stretched this Eiffel Tower–sized wrought-iron contraption across the 500-foot-wide Douro. Eiffel himself built a bridge in Porto, the Ponte Dona Maria Pia, a bit upstream.

While it offers few individual sights, the Ribeira is Porto's most enjoyable neighborhood for killing time and basking in Old World atmosphere. Shoppers eventually find **O Cântaro,** run by the English-speaking Oliveira family (Mon–Sat 9:00–19:00, closed Sun, a block back from embankment near the east end—toward the bridge—at Rua da Lada 50–56, tel. 223-320-670). Among the trinkets for sale are ceramics, hand-painted tiles, embroidery, and filigree. Ask them for a filigree-making demonstration to see tiny gold and silver wires twisted and soldered into intricate patterns.

▲Cruising the Douro—"Six Bridges" cruises, operated by several different companies, leave continually from the Ribeira riverfront. These relaxing 50-minute excursions float up and down the river, offering a fine orientation and glimpses of all of Porto's bridges (including the majestic steel Ponte Dona Maria Pia, right next to the new concrete Ponte de São João). The boats, which generally

run daily 10:00–20:00 in summer (until 17:00 off-season), come in two types: smaller traditional *rabelos* (€7.50, boats described below) and bigger modern cruise boats (€8–10). Each tour is essentially the same. To avoid being overcharged, shop around a bit before committing to a boat.

Moored in Porto and all along the Douro River are the old-fashioned boats called *rabelos*. These were once the only way to transport the wine downriver to Porto. These boats, which look Asian, have flat bottoms, a big square sail, and a very large rudder to help them navigate the rough, twisty course of the river (for more info, see page 253). The region's famous port wine is produced about 60 miles up the river and aged in lodges here.

▲Solar do Vinho do Porto—This port wine–tasting facility, operated by the Port and Douro Wines Institute (which runs a similar place in Lisbon—see page 43), is Porto's finest spot for sampling a stunning array of ports. The price per taste or per bottle depends on the quality of the port, from €1 to a small fortune (light food, but no meals). If they call it "port," you'll find it here, in plush tasting rooms inhabiting an elegant old villa and riverview tables in the garden—delightful at sunset. While it's more fun to tour the cellars across the river, this is a handy one-stop opportunity to try several ports. And after 18:00, when all the lodges close, this stays open (Mon–Sat 14:00–24:00, closed Sun, Rua de Entre Quintas 220, tel. 226-094-749, www.ivp.pt). The villa shares a lush park with a domed sports hall, just up from the river beyond the Ribeira in the direction of Foz (see next page). Take tram #1 from Ribeira, then hike uphill; or, from the city center, take tram #18 from Carmo Church, tell the driver where you want to stop, and walk across the street. But your quickest option is to taxi to and from here, as this place is fairly far from anything else I've described in this chapter.

Tramway Museum (Museu do Carro Eléctrico)—Porto is proud of its tram tradition and is committed to bringing them back as an integral part of the public transit system. In 1872 (40 years after being invented in the US), the first trams in Iberia began operating in Porto, pulled by horses and oxen. Dubbed *"americanos"* based on their origin, the tram network was electrified in 1904. Essential for connecting suburbs with the city center, there were more than 100 tram lines still in use by the 1970s. However, buses and byproducts of economic prosperity (cars) almost eliminated this important part of the city's heritage. This clever museum-in-a-warehouse displays beautifully restored examples of trams from different eras, including 1950s buses and a brand-new hydrogen-powered city bus. You can climb aboard many for a fun Rice-A-Roni–style experience...just ding the bell. The most atmospheric way to arrive at the museum is via tram #18. Sit on restored wicker seats and see a little of workaday Porto, plus some river views from up above (€3.50, Tue–Fri 9:30–12:30 & 14:30–18:00, Sat–Sun 15:00–19:00, closed Mon, Alameda Basílio Teles 51, tram #18 from Carmo Church behind Clérigos Tower ends at museum, tram #1 stops here as well, trams covered by AndanteTour card, tel. 226-158-185, http://museu-carro-electrico.stcp.pt).

Tram to Foz—An antique tram car (line #1) scenically rattles its way from the Ribeira district (in front of São Francisco Church, later in this chapter), along the Douro, to the Foz district (buy €1.35 two-zone ticket from driver, good for one hour, free with AndanteTour card, trip takes about 20 min, departures generally at top and bottom of each hour from 9:00 until around 19:00).

Foz do Douro (or simply "Foz") is one of Porto's trendiest, greenest, wealthiest, and most relaxing quarters, situated where the river meets the Atlantic. There's no real destination in Foz; simply wander through the park (Jardim do Passeio Alegre, with miniature golf, fancy old WC pavilion, and a nondescript café), hike up to the lighthouse, ponder the sea, watch fishermen mending their nets, smell the seaweed, and tram back. If you have the time and good weather, take a boardwalk stroll to the beach, Praia dos Ingleses. It's a relaxing break from the busy downtown area. You can combine a trip here with a visit to the Serralves Museum. (Either catch bus #203 from the beach to the museum, or take a taxi; it's easy to hail a cab or find a taxi stop—*praça de taxis*.)

Near Praça Infante Dom Henrique

These sights are on or near Praça Infante Dom Henrique (Henry the Navigator Square), a long block uphill from the Ribeira district.

▲**São Francisco Church**—This is Porto's only church in the Gothic style—complete with a rose window, stair-step buttresses, and a statue of St. Francis of Assisi on the front. Today, it's a museum with three parts: a so-so collection of items from the church and monastery; the strange but boring catacombs *(ossário)* under the church, tightly packed with the bones of former parishioners (the bodies are left under the wooden floor boards to rot and then transferred to the neat little niches in the walls); and, the unquestionable highlight, the extravagant Baroque church interior, from the 17th and 18th centuries.

While the church was ravaged by Napoleon and by the Portuguese during their 19th-century civil war, the interior remains stunning, with lavish wood carvings slathered in 900 pounds of gold. Wander down the main aisle like a bewildered 18th-century peasant. On the right, find the monks being beheaded by Moors. On the left, find the over-the-top Jesse's Tree (1718), a very literal interpretation of the family tree of Jesus, resting upon Mary—here, St. Mary of good voyages, the patron saint of navigators (€3 gets you into all three sections, daily March–June 9:00–19:00, July–Sept 9:00–20:00, Oct–Feb 9:00–17:30, no photos in church, Rua Infante Dom Henrique, tel. 222-062-100).

▲**Stock Exchange Palace (Palácio da Bolsa)**—This unassuming building is neither a stock exchange nor a palace, but a breathtaking monument to civic and commercial pride, with some of the most lavishly decorated rooms in Portugal.

The people of Porto have always taken pride in being hard workers. Commerce came to define Porto, as royalty or religion would define other cities (like Lisbon and Braga, respectively). The Commercial Association of Porto (Associação Comercial do Porto) even had its own system of courts and a representative to the king. In 1832, the monastery of the São Francisco Church burned down, and the queen offered the property to the Commercial Association. They seized the opportunity to show off, crafting a building that would demonstrate the considerable skill of Porto's tradesmen.

You'll tour a dozen rooms. The place is rife with symbolism and intricate, time-consuming craftsmanship intended only to impress: the complex patterned floors, carefully pieced together with Brazilian and African wood (Portugal's colonies); an incredibly detailed inlaid table, created over three years using wood scraps from those same floors; and a room that looks like it's made of finely carved woodwork and bronze—until you realize it's all painted plaster and gold leaf. Almost everything is original, and little refurbishment has been needed.

The knock-your-socks-off finale is the sumptuous Arabian Room. This grand hall—inspired by Granada's Alhambra—was painstakingly decorated in the Moorish style over 18 years with wood, plaster, and gold leaf.

The "Palace" can only be visited on a guided tour. (The building still houses the offices of the Chamber of Commerce, and is often rented out for events.) Tours leave every 30 minutes in whatever language is necessary (often English plus another language). You may have to wait up to 30 minutes for an English tour; it's easy to call ahead to set up an appointment (€5, daily

April–Oct 9:00–19:00, Nov–March 9:00–13:00 & 14:00–18:00, last visit 30 min before closing, no photos inside, in big building marked *Associação Comercial do Porto* on Rua Ferreira Borges, tel. 223-399-013, www.palaciodabolsa.com).

House of Henry the Navigator (Casa do Infante)—Porto's favorite son was supposedly born in this mansion 600 years ago (which later became the main customs house). This museum is currently a work-in-progress, which explains its haphazard state. But fans of ancient history will enjoy the Roman mosaics found on-site and the reconstruction of the building when it was the customs house (€2, free on weekends, Tue–Sat 10:00–12:30 & 14:00–17:30, Sun 14:00–17:30, closed Mon, last entry 30 min before closing, Rua da Alfândega 10, tel. 222-060-400). For more on Hank, see page 126.

In the City Center

The modern urban sector of Porto has few museums, but there are a handful of interesting squares, churches, and monuments here. I've listed these sights in walking order—roughly from top to bottom, beginning at City Hall (near the TI) and working downhill toward the cathedral and then back around through the shopping district.

Avenue of the Allies (Avenida dos Aliados)—This is the main urban drag of Porto—named for the alliance created in 1387 when the Portuguese King John (João) I married the English princess Philippa, establishing a long and happy trading partnership between the two nations. Lined with elaborate examples of various architectural eras (mostly Art Nouveau and Art Deco), it reminds me of Prague's Wenceslas Square. This strip is  where the city goes to work, watched over by the huge city hall (Câmara Municipal, at the top). Behind that is the Trindade Church, and nearby you'll find the station (also called Trindade) where all of Porto's Metro lines converge.

The bottom of the avenue is known as **Praça da Liberdade** (Liberty Square). A few steps in front of you is an equestrian statue of Dom Pedro—a hero in the 1832 Civil War who advocated for a limited constitutional monarchy. Dom Pedro won...and he's holding the constitution to prove it.

Orient yourself using an imaginary clock for a compass. Start by facing the horse. The city hall is at the top of the square. At about 2 o'clock (behind the trees) is the "Imperial McDonald's," perhaps the fanciest in Europe (formerly the Imperial Café).

Check it out, and ponder the battle of cultural elegance against global economic efficiency. At 3 o'clock is the way to the blue-tiled church of St. Ildefonso (up the hill, in the shopping district). At 4 o'clock (50 yards away) is the corner of the São Bento Station. And at 9 o'clock is Clérigos Church, with its famous view tower.

▲**Clérigos Church and Tower (Igreja e Torre dos Clérigos)**— This oval-shaped church with a disproportionately tall tower is the masterwork of Nicolau Nasoni, a man who chose to go for Baroque (see sidebar, next page).

The real attraction is climbing the tower—one of Porto's icons. Two hundred twenty-five steps take you 250 feet up to the top, where you'll be greeted by a jumble of tightly packed red roofs and commanding views over the city. Nasoni built the tower in six sections, each one more elaborate than the last, topped with a round dome and spiked with pinnacles. Imagine trying to climb this tower from the outside, then consider that a father-son duo did just that in 1917 (€2, daily 9:30–13:00 & 14:30–19:00, Rua São Filipe de Nery, tel. 222-001-729).

The little frilly white building across the covered parking-lot square is worth a peek. **Lello & Irmão bookstore,** built in 1906, boasts a lacy exterior and a fancy Art Nouveau interior. It looks like wood, but it's mostly made of painted plaster with gold leaf. Follow the quaint tracks to the book trolley. Climb the sagging staircase to a cute tearoom (Mon–Fri 10:00–19:30, Sat–Sun 10:00–19:00, Rua das Carmelitas 144).

Backtrack, crossing Avenida dos Aliados, and continue on to the...

▲**São Bento Train Station (Estação São Bento)**—The main entry hall of this otherwise dull station features some of Portugal's finest *azulejos*. These vivid, decorative hand-painted tiles show historical and folk scenes from the Douro region. Upper tiles on the

left (when facing the tracks) show local forces preparing to reconquer the south of Portugal and add it to the kingdom. Tiles on the opposite wall (far right when looking at the tracks) show the 1387 wedding of Portugal's King John I and the English princess Philippa, which established the Portuguese-English alliance. (Notice the fine portrait of

Nicolau Nasoni
(1661–1773)

In the 1720s—a boom time in Porto—the Italian Nasoni found work as a painter in Porto. His swirling, colorful paintings wowed Porto, and Nasoni got plenty of work. He married a Portuguese woman, had five kids, and made Porto his home. Soon, he was employed as an architect, hiring skilled local artisans to turn his trademark cherubs, garlands, and cumulus clouds into granite, wood, and poured plaster. Even stark medieval churches had their facades topped with Baroque towers and their interiors paneled and spackled in billowy gilded designs. Prolific to the max, Nasoni redid Porto in the Baroque style (much as Bernini did in Rome), creating palaces and churches throughout the area.

The Clérigos Church, which consumed three decades of his life (1731–1763), shows his flair for theatrics. He fit the structure into its hilltop location, putting the tower at the back on the highest ground, dramatically reinforcing its height. Nasoni worked in stages: first the church, then the Chapter House (residence for priests and monks), and topped it all off with the tower.

The church facade displays Nasoni's characteristic frills, garlands, and zigzags. Inside is an oval-shaped nave built out of granite and marble, but covered with ornate carvings. See the high altar—a wedding-cake structure with Mary on top—and the tomb of Nasoni, who asked to be buried here.

Philippa and the depiction of the cathedral as it looked in the 14th century.) Below is the immediate result of the marriage—their son, Prince Henry the Navigator, shown conquering Ceuta for Portugal in 1415. While humble Ceuta was just a small chip of Morocco (across from Gibraltar), it marked an important first step in the creation of a soon-to-be vast Portuguese empire. The trackside tiles celebrate the traditional economy, such as the transport of port wine. The multicolored tiles near the top show different modes of transportation, including Roman chariots (left above *Saída* exit sign), and progressing to the arrival of the first train (left corner above Philippa). Notice the words Douro and Minho near the ceiling. These are the major rivers in this part of Portugal, and the key regions linked by these trains. Porto's favorite meeting point is right here, "under the clock."

To orient yourself from the station, stand outside with your back to the main entrance. Over your right shoulder (two blocks up the hill) is Praça da Batalha (Battle Square), the gateway to Porto's shopping district and old-fashioned market hall (see "Porto's

Shopping Neighborhood," next page). At 2 o'clock is the bottom of Avenida dos Aliados. On the hill to your left is the cathedral. And the streets in front of you lead down to the left to the Ribeira.

Cathedral (Sé) This hulking, fortress-like 12th-century Romanesque cathedral graced with an 18th-century Baroque

remodel job is gloomy and stark inside. While big and important, it's actually pretty dull. But the adjacent cloister and the main altarpiece make a visit worthwhile. The altarpiece sums up the exuberance of Porto in the 1720s, when the city was booming, the local bishop was temporarily away in Lisbon, and Italian Baroque was sweeping through town. On the side walls flanking the altar are faded faux-architecture paintings by Nicolau Nasoni (see sidebar, opposite page), the Italian who came to Porto to paint the cathedral's sacristy and soon became the city's most influential architect. See his grand staircase out in the cloister (and also his Clérigos Church, page 225).

The cloister's walls are decorated with elaborate *azulejo* tiles illustrating the amorous poetry of the Bible's "Song of Songs." The €0.50 pamphlet is pretty skimpy, but the well-produced €5 English guidebook explains it all, including the text that inspired the *azulejos* (cathedral entry free, open daily in summer 9:00–12:30 & 14:30–19:00, until 18:00 in winter; cloister and sacristy cost €2 to enter, daily in summer 9:00–12:15 & 14:30–18:00, until 17:15 in winter, closed Sun morning; Terreiro da Sé, tel. 222-059-028).

In the cathedral's small square, you'll find a fine view of the old town, the Baroque spiral pillory where harsh justice was once doled out, and the massive **Bishop's Palace,** still the home of the bishop and his offices. The immensity of this 18th-century building reflects the bishop's power in that era. It dominates the skyline of Porto. A surviving gate from Porto's two-mile-long wall, which protected the city in the 14th century, currently houses the **Porto Tours** office (an excellent resource for information on all kinds of activities in the city—see page 217).

Facing the cathedral, walk around to the left to the statue of Vímara Peres, a Christian warrior who reconquered this region from the Moors in 868 (it was lost again within two generations, and remained under Muslim control until the final reconquest in about 1100). From here, survey the city and find the church with the blue facade in the distance. The São Bento Station is just to its right, and the tarnished copper dome of the city hall breaks the skyline above it. Below you spreads the seedy district called

"Sé" (meaning "cathedral" and referring to the *Se*at of the Catholic church). This neighborhood, the oldest in town, is run-down and depopulating; the government is encouraging people to move in by luring them with economic incentives. The streets—filled with drug users and prostitutes beyond the medieval gate—twist their way down into the Ribeira district.

A 300-yard walk up the street behind the cathedral (to the bottom of Rua da Augusto Rosa) takes you to the impressive last remains of the town wall (access from the leafy square for fine river views), and the top of the Funicular dos Guindais (which zips down to the Ribeira riverfront). Hike two blocks up Rua da Augusto Rosa to Praça da Batalha (described next) and the start of the shopping district.

Porto's Shopping Neighborhood

Porto's bustling, local-feeling shopping district is a wonderful place to people-watch. Most of the action is along Rua Santa Catarina, which runs roughly parallel to Avenida dos Aliados a few blocks east. Begin at Praça da Batalha (just up Rua 31 de Janeiro from São Bento Station), and follow this route to the Old World market hall.

Praça da Batalha (Battle Square)—This square has a fine tiled church, the Igreja de Santo Ildefonso (its tiles reminiscent of Ming dynasty blue-and-white ceramics were all the rage in Baroque Portugal, depicting scenes from the life of the church's patron saint), the 19th-century National Theater (originally the Opera House), and the impressive Art Deco Cinema Batalha. While no longer showing movies, the main cinema has been converted into a concert venue. Around the swoopy overhang by the trolley tracks is the entrance to the recommended Restaurante Batalha (see "Eating" later in this chapter). This

square, with its inviting benches, is where the old guys hang out. At the north end of the square, branching off to the left of the blue-tiled church, is...

▲**Rua Santa Catarina**—Porto's main shopping street is busy and (mostly) traffic-free by day, quiet by night. A stroll along here gives you a sense for today's Porto—as well as yesterday's, including the venerable Art Nouveau Café Majestic, the circa-1900 hangout for the local intelligentsia. Step in. Porto's pet name for a little coffee is *cimbalino*—named for the traditional Italian espresso-making machines. Outside Café Majestic (on the nearby corner), the FNAC department store has an Art Deco glockenspiel performance (daily

at 9:00, 12:00, 15:00, and 18:00) in which Henry the Navigator, St. John the Baptist—Porto's patron saint—and two poets (who look like Lincoln and Einstein) parade around.

The Rua Santa Catarina sidewalk is a good example of *calçada á portuguesa,* Portugal's unique limestone and basalt mosaic work. It's handmade and high-maintenance...but apparently worth the effort and expense to locals. Notice all of the shoe stores. Along with wine, northern Portugal's industry is powered by textile and shoe factories.

If you head up the street two blocks and turn left on Rua Formosa (note the Pearl of the Market shop at #279, filled with traditional and edible souvenirs), you'll run into the...

▲**Market (Bolhão)**—Porto's vibrant traditional market still thrives, despite competition from newer shopping malls. This is a great place to wander—especially in the morning—and take in the sights, sounds, and smells of real-world Porto (Mon–Fri 8:30–17:00, Sat 8:30–13:00, closed Sun).

As you enter, the butchers are to the left, the fishermen to the right, and produce and flowers dead ahead. Check out the butcher section, with half-pigs hanging from the ceiling, and display cases full of unusual specialties...such as *sangue cozido* (coagulated cow blood). Then wander through the seafood section. If it's springtime, you may see a favorite local delicacy pulled from the river: *lampreia* (eel). They say eels are so tasty because they dine on the flavorful garbage in the Douro. The market's old-fashioned sanitary conditions aren't quite up to European Union snuff, but the EU seems to look the other way.

Around the market are lively shops. At one corner is Casa Horticula, with a wide variety of seeds. In bakery windows, the big, round, dark *broa* breads, made with corn and rye, are moist inside and hard outside. The breads with bits of sausage baked in are called *folar.* The cheeses on display are either *ovelha* (sheep) or *cabra* (goat). *Bom-apetite!*

Port-Wine Lodges in Vila Nova de Gaia

Just across the river from Porto, the town of Vila Nova de Gaia is where much of the world's port wine comes to mature. Port-wine grapes are grown, and a young port is produced, about 60 miles upstream in the Douro Valley. Then, after sitting for a winter in silos, the wine is shipped here, to age for years in lodges on this cool, north-facing bank of the Douro. Eighteen companies run

Vila Nova de Gaia

100 YARDS
100 METERS

TO PORTO CENTER

RIBEIRA DISTRICT

DOURO RIVER

PONTE LUIS I
UPPER LEVEL
LOWER LEVEL

LARGO MIGUEL BOMBARDA

SERRA DO PILAR MONASTERY

BOAT TRIPS

LARGO CRUZ

R. PIEDADE

AVENIDA DA REPUBLICA

Jardim do Morro

EATERIES

AV. RAMOS

R. GOMES

R. BARÃO

R. LEO. DE FREITAS

LUIS CAMÕES

Gen. Torres

❶ Calém
❷ Sandeman
❸ Taylor & Restaurante Barão de Fladgate

❹ Croft
❺ Graham's
❻ Ferreira's
❼ Kopke Shop

Ⓜ METRO STATION
↘ VIEW

these lodges, holding down the port fort and offering tours and tastings. For wine connoisseurs, touring a port-wine lodge *(cave do vinho do porto)* and sampling the product is a ▲▲ attraction. Like so many miniature "Hollywood" signs climbing the riverbank, you'll see the 18 different com-

pany names proudly marking their lodges in Vila Nova de Gaia.

Venturing into Vila Nova de Gaia is well worth the trip. But to taste port from all the lodges under one roof without leaving Porto, visit the Solar do Vinho do Porto (see page 221).

Orientation: Vila Nova de Gaia (or just "Gaia") is technically a separate town from Porto, even though it's just across the river and feels like part of the city. The town operates its own handy **TI** with information about the lodges (mid-June–mid-Sept daily 10:00–18:00, closed Sun off-season, on the riverbank near Sandeman lodge at Avenida Diogo Leite 242, tel. 223-703-735, www.cm-gaia.pt). A string of fine eateries lines the main drag, Rua

Guilherme Gomes Fernandes, just past the Ramos Pinto lodge. Drinks-with-a-view options are available all along the waterfront.

Getting to Vila Nova de Gaia: Simply walk (or catch a cab) from the Ribeira district across the big steel Ponte Dom Luís I bridge. From the city center, take bus #901 or #906 (every 30 min, stop across from São Bento Station). After crossing the bridge, the bus stops first at the Calém lodge, then near Sandeman and the TI, then climbs the curves to the Graham's lodge.

Tours and Tastings: Port tasting is a subjective business, and no single lodge is necessarily the best. If you're a port enthusiast, you probably already have a favorite (or can quickly decide on one, with a little enjoyable research). Though more serious European visitors choose one lodge to visit, American tourists are known to hop between three or four in a single day...before stumbling back to their hotels. Allow 30 minutes per visit.

At any lodge, the procedure is about the same. Individual travelers simply show up and ask for a tour. Pass any wait time by learning about the port (via posted information or a video) or simply get started on the tasting. Sometimes the tours and tastings are free; other times, there's a modest entry fee (which is refunded if you buy a bottle). Before you go (or while you're waiting for your tour), read the "Port-Wine Crash Course" sidebar on the next page, "Brits on the Douro" (page 250) and "Growing—and Stomping—Grapes in the Douro Valley" on page 252.

The highest-profile company, **Sandeman,** is sort of the Budweiser of port—a good first stop for novices. They were the first port producer to create a logo for their product, which you'll see everywhere: a mysterious man wearing a black cloak (representing a Portuguese student's cape) and a rakish *Shadow* hat (worn by Spanish horse-riders, symbolizing the sherry that Sandeman makes in Jerez). Sandeman provides the most corporate, mainstream, accessible experience for first-timers—with a short walk, a 10-minute video, and two tastes (€3, daily March–Oct 10:00–12:30 & 14:00–18:00, Nov–Feb 9:30–12:30 & 14:00–17:30, right on the riverfront at Largo Miguel Bombarda 3, tel. 223-740-533, www.sandeman.com). But if you're serious about port—or want to pretend to be—go elsewhere. Note that because Sandeman and Ferreira (described later in this chapter) are part of the same conglomerate, if you take one tour you get a half-price discount for the other.

Port-Wine Crash Course

Port is a medium-sweet wine (20 percent alcohol), usually taken as a *digestif* after dinner, sometimes with strong cheese to balance its powerful flavor. The wine is fortified with *aguardente* (grape brandy, more like grappa, sometimes called "grape essence") at a ratio of about 4:1. This brandy is also distilled from wine, so it blends nicely with the port. The introduction of brandy halts fermentation early, killing the yeast and leaving more sugar in the port (standard wines ferment for 10–12 days; port for only 2–3 days). Vintners constantly monitor sugar levels to attain the precise sweetness they want. After the brandy is added, the wine ages in wood or in bottles, anywhere from two years to (for big spenders) longer than a century.

For most people, "port" means a tawny port aged 10 to 20 years—the most common type. But there are actually multiple varieties of port; the two general categories are wood ports (aged in wooden vats or barrels) and vintage ports (aged in bottles). Over 40 varieties of grapes, both red and white, can be used for port production.

The basics: Inexpensive **ruby** is young (aged three years), red, and has a strong, fiery taste of grape and pepper. Note that some ports are **white**—young and robust, but with white grapes (some white "ports" sold today are an attempt to approximate Spain's dry *fino* sherries, but sweet versions exist—look for *lágrima* on the label for these).

Tawny, the wood port with a leathery color, is the most typical version—the one most Americans imagine when they think of port. It's older, lighter, mellower, and more complex than L.B.V. (described later in this chapter). It's aged in smaller barrels, maximizing exposure to wood (and, therefore, oxygen)—which gives it a nuttier flavor than the more fruity, younger ports. Tawny port is aged 10, 20, 30, or 40 years, but it's not all the same vintage; to enhance the complexity of the flavor, any tawny is a combination

For more discriminating tastes, try Taylor and Croft (now affiliated with each other). I toured the classy **Taylor** lodge—near the top of the hill, with stunning views back on Porto—and enjoyed it. After watching an informative video, I learned a little about the history of the company (which, like many port producers, began in the sheep business) and about the Douro Valley's unique microclimates (see next chapter). Then I saw the various sizes of several different ages. So a "30-year-old tawny" is predominantly 30 years old, but also has minor components that are 10 or 20 years old. Once blended, it takes about eight months for the various ports to "marry," though no producer would release an immature tawny. It's ready to consume when you buy it.

Vintage port (if you can afford it) is a ruby. Rather than being a blend from many different years, it comes from a single harvest. Only wine from the very best years is selected by lodges to become vintage. After port ages for two years in wooden casks, it's tasted by the Port Wine Institute to determine whether it's worthy of the vintage label. (If not, it may be kept in wooden casks longer to become L.B.V.) There are usually only two or three vintage years per decade, and the year 2000 was deemed as one of the best ever. If the port is good enough to be classified as vintage, it's bottled and aged another 10 to 30 years or more—using glass, rather than wood, makes the difference in the aging process. Sediment is common in the bottles, so it must be decanted. And if it's really old, the cork may deteriorate—so the top of the bottle is heated up with a pair of red-hot tongs, then cold water is poured over it to break it off cleanly. Bottles of port can be stored upright, rather than on their side like regular wines.

Late Bottle Vintage (L.B.V.) was invented after World War II, when British wine-lovers couldn't afford true vintage port. L.B.V. is a blend of wines from a single year, which age together in huge wooden vats for four to six years. The size of the vats means less exposure to wood, which makes it age more quickly, but without losing its fruitiness and color. After five years, it's bottled and sold (later than an actual vintage port—hence the name). This affordable alternative saved the port-wine industry.

Port's stodgy image makes it unpopular among young Portuguese. Lodges have not escaped the multinational conglomerate game, but new owners often retain the brand name to keep loyal customers and invent marketing techniques to attract new ones. Many Americans consider port an acquired taste; for this reason, many port producers along the Douro also make a more straightforward red wine. But as I always say, "Any port in a storm...."

of wooden vats in which different kinds of ports are aged (free, Mon–Fri 10:00–18:00, also Sat in July–Aug, always closed Sun, high up but worth the hike at Rua do Choupelo 250, tel. 223-742-800, www.taylor.pt). Their restaurant, **Barão de Fladgate,** offers fancy lunchtime views along with an opportunity to recharge for more tastings. Many consider it the best dining in Porto (daily 12:30–15:00 & 19:30–22:30, no dinner served Sun).

The **Croft** tour is similar, but you also get to see vintage port being aged in bottles, as well as a fun "library" of dusty old ports (the oldest is from 1834). While the views are not as good as the lodges described earlier in this chapter, you'll learn how to properly open and present an old bottle of port (free, daily 10:00–18:00, Largo Joaquim de Magalhães 23, tel. 223-742-800, www.croftport.com).

Other popular lodges include Scottish-owned **Graham's,** with expansive views of the city similar to those from Taylor's. Their tour emphasizes traditional methods still employed by the company, including the invention of a stainless-steel treader to mimic the grape-stomping process. Tastings and tours are free, but they also offer a €30 port-wine sampling that includes a taste of their highly praised 2000 vintage port—currently selling for €150 a bottle. Their 10-year tawny is also excellent (May–Sept daily 9:30–18:00; Oct–April Mon–Fri 9:30–13:00 & 14:00–17:30, closed Sat–Sun; Rua Rei Ramiro, Quinta do Agro 514, climb the hill or buses #901 and #906 drop you near the entrance, tel. 223-776-330, www.grahams-port.com). **Ferreira's** lodge comes with classical music "to help age the wine" (interesting tour, some fine museum artifacts, €2.50 includes two port tastings, daily 10:30–12:30 & 14:00–18:00, look for big sign at the end of the riverfront promenade at Avenida Ramos Pinto 70, tel. 223-746-107).

Kopke is recognized as one of the best in the business because they were the first. Unfortunately, their lodge doesn't receive visitors, but they've opened a shop along the waterfront to allow people to experience what they've been doing well since 1638. The staff offers concise explanations and some fine ports by the glass (average price-€2.50). For true luxury on the palate, nothing beats a 30-year Kopke tawny (daily June–Oct 10:00–20:00, Nov–May 10:30–19:30, Avenida Ramos Pinto 280, tel. 220-126-431).

For more ideas, ask the TIs in Porto or Nova Vila de Gaia for a handy map of all the wine cellars, or just follow the signs.

Away from the Center

▲Serralves Foundation Contemporary Art Museum and Park (Fundação de Serralves)—Porto's contemporary art museum, surrounding park, and unique Art Deco mansion are a ▲▲▲ half-day excursion for art-lovers...and worthwhile for anyone looking for a lush green space to relax in (€2.50 for park only, €5 for museum and park; museum open April–Sept Tue–Thu 10:00–19:00, Fri–Sat 10:00–22:00, Sun 10:00–20:00; Oct–March Tue–Sun 10:00–19:00; closed Mon; park and house open April–Sept Tue–Sun 10:00–20:00, Oct–March Sat–Sun until 19:00, closed Mon; café, tel. 808-200-543, www.serralves.pt). The complex is about 1.5 miles west of the center in a wealthy residential neighborhood at Rua Dom João de Castro 210, just south of the

busy Avenida da Boavista. From the center, you can reach it most easily via taxi; the bus service isn't great, but you can take bus #203 to the Serralves stop (less convenient from downtown—the most central place to catch it is at the big Boavista Rotunda near Casa da Música).

The complex—which claims to be the most visited museum in all of Portugal—is managed by the Serralves Foundation. The Foundation was formed in 1989 with two goals: the advancement of contemporary art, and the appreciation of landscape and environment as an artistic concept. These goals, symbolized by the giant red hand shovel near the front gate, drive the layout of the complex: a gigantic contemporary art facility on the edge of a carefully planned park. The whole thing is based around the Art Deco mansion of a count who lived here in the 1930s. When the Foundation was formed, the government bought the house and surrounding land for them to encourage them to pursue their goals. A decade later, in 1999, the museum opened.

The **museum** presents temporary exhibits by Portuguese and global artists. The enormous, blocky U-shaped building was designed by prominent Portuguese architect Álvaro Siza, who was greatly inspired by the existing mansion. As in most important contemporary-art museums, its vast white exhibition spaces are modified to suit the art displayed (windows and walls continually disappear and reappear). The museum also contains an auditorium and a library. If you're making a day of it, consider the museum's **restaurant,** which serves cheap, good cafeteria-style food for lunch, then goes upscale—with a stylish makeover in the late afternoon—to become a fancy, expensive dinner spot.

The **park** around the museum has been designed very carefully to compartmentalize each section; when you're in one part of the grounds, you can't see the rest. This is a very peaceful place to wander. Hiding in here somewhere are a pleasant rose garden, a tea house overlooking a former tennis court, a lake, a small farm with animals, a gardening school, and Casa de Serralves itself.

The **house (Casa de Serralves)** is, for many, the most interesting part of the whole experience: a huge pink Art Deco mansion that looks like the home of a 1950s Hollywood celebrity. On two sides, long manicured hedges and fountains stretch to the horizon. Look for the private chapel in back—also pink Art Deco. You can usually go inside the house to check out the cavernous interior. As you step through the fancy gate inside the living room, remember that in the last century, someone actually lived here. Ponder how the design of this place is reflected in the museum. The best part is upstairs: the mirrored, pink-marbled bathroom, dramatically overlooking the grounds. (Casa de Serralves is included in park admission, same hours as park.)

House of Music (Casa da Música)—This landmark concert hall finally opened in 2005 after years of construction postponements. It was designed by the firm of Dutch architect Rem Koolhaas, called OMA, which also built Seattle's Central Library. Contemporary-architecture fans will find it at the big Boavista Rotunda northwest of the center. Guided tours take you through the interior, or you can attend a concert of anything from world music to classical to jazz to fado (tours-€2, April–Sept 7/day 10:30–18:00, fewer tours off-season, tickets for tours sold until 10 minutes before start time, concert tickets run €5–20—generally about €15, info/reservation tel. 220-120-214, www.casadamusica.com). For a schedule of upcoming, nearly daily events, pick up the free quarterly, *Agenda Cultural*, at any TI.

SLEEPING

There are lots of cheap sleeps in Porto—but none in the desirable Ribeira district (where prices are higher). I've listed the only two options in Ribeira, along with several fine places up above, in the city center. The cheaper the place, the greater the chance that English isn't spoken (and the grottier the bathroom). You'll almost always have to climb a few stairs to get to the elevator, if they have one.

In the City Center

There are several cheap pensions lining the big Avenida dos Aliados, but they're generally a bad value (with old furnishings and lots of street noise). I've found better options nearby, generally within a few blocks of this main drag.

$$$ Quality Inn Praça da Batalha offers 113 predictable business-class rooms near the São Bento Station. It shares a square with a beautiful *azulejo* church and the beginning of Porto's pedestrian shopping drag (rates fluctuate wildly: Sb-€50–75, Db-€65–85, but generally rates are more like Sb-€65, Db-€70–80; non-smoking rooms, air-con, elevator, Internet access and Wi-Fi, Praça da Batalha 127, tel. 223-392-300, fax 222-006-009, www.choicehotelseurope.com, quality.batalha@grupo-continental.com).

$$$ Hotel Internacional fits 35 super-modern rooms into the heavy granite-and-tile shell of an old monastery just two blocks off the Avenida dos Aliados. It offers hotel formality, typical amenities, and a good location at a reasonable price (Sb-€60–70, Db-€70–90, prices depend on day and season, air-con, elevator, Rua Do Almada 131, tel. 222-005-032, fax 222-009-063, www.hi-porto.com, info@hi-porto.com).

$$ Grande Hotel de Paris Residencial brags it was the first hotel in Porto with water in the rooms. Its 45 faded but fine rooms—all with antique furniture—are spread out over three interconnected buildings, each with a grand atrium and sloping floors. This proudly

Sleep Code

(€1 = about $1.40, country code: 351)
S = Single, **D** = Double/Twin, **T** = Triple, **Q** = Quad, **b** = bathroom,
s = shower only. Unless otherwise noted, breakfast and taxes
are included, credit cards are accepted, and English is spoken.

To help you easily sort through these listings, I've divided
the rooms into three categories, based on the price for a standard double room with bath during high season:

$$$ **Higher Priced**—Most rooms €75 or more.
$$ **Moderately Priced**—Most rooms between €40–75.
$ **Lower Priced**—Most rooms €40 or less.

run place has big, classy public spaces (Sb-€48–58, standard Db-
€54–64, highest prices are for Aug, extra bed-€20–25, 10 percent
discount with this book off-season, cash only, non-smoking rooms,
elevator, Internet access, relaxing garden, Rua da Fábrica 27–29, 1
block up from Avenida dos Aliados, tel. 222-073-140, fax 222-073-
149, www.ghparis.pt, reservas@ghparis.pt, David).

$$ Residencial São Marino is a lesser-value pension with
14 simple rooms and a beautiful tiled entryway overlooking a
charming, peaceful square (Sb-€38, Db-€45–50, Tb-€55–60,
higher prices are for July–Aug, Praça Carlos Alberto 59, tel. 223-
325-499, fax 222-054-380, www.residencialsmarino.com, info
@residencialsmarino.com, no English spoken).

$$ Residencial O Escondidinho rents 23 smallish and spar-
tan but solid rooms with modern bathrooms at reasonable rates
(Sb-€35, Db-€45–50, includes breakfast, elevator, across from
Pensão Residencial Belo Sonho at Rua Passos Manuel 135, tel. 222-
004-079, fax 222-026-075, residencialescondidinho@aeiou.pt).

$ Pensão Duas Nações is a well-run place—as comfy as such
a cheap place can be—with 20 colorful rooms and we-try-harder
management. It overlooks a square straight up Rua Fábrica, a few
blocks from Avenida dos Aliados. The "two nations" are Portugal
and Brazil, still friends after all these years (S-€14, Sb-€23, D-€23,
Db-€30, T-€36, Tb-€40, Q-€46, Qb-€48, cash only, no breakfast
but adjacent to handy café, Internet in lobby, Praça Guilherme
Gomes Fernandes 59, tel. 222-081-616, www.duasnacoes.com.pt,
duasnacoes@mail.telepac.pt).

$ Pensão Residencial Belo Sonho is well maintained and fam-
ily-run (no English spoken), just up the street from Café Majestic
and the main shopping drag, Rua Santa Catarina. Its 15 rooms are a
good value (Sb-€18–30, Db-€25–40, Tb-€35–60, higher prices for
June–Sept, cash only, Rua Passos Manuel 186, tel. 222-003-389).

Central Porto Hotels and Restaurants

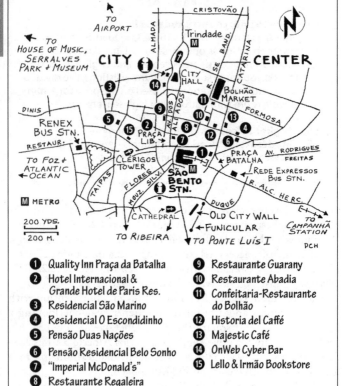

1. Quality Inn Praça da Batalha
2. Hotel Internacional & Grande Hotel de Paris Res.
3. Residencial São Marino
4. Residencial O Escondidinho
5. Pensão Duas Nações
6. Pensão Residencial Belo Sonho
7. "Imperial McDonald's"
8. Restaurante Regaleira
9. Restaurante Guarany
10. Restaurante Abadia
11. Confeitaria-Restaurante do Bolhão
12. Historia del Caffé
13. Majestic Café
14. OnWeb Cyber Bar
15. Lello & Irmão Bookstore

In the Ribeira

There are only a couple of hotels convenient to the Ribeira scene, and neither is a particularly good value. But...location, location, location.

$$$ Pestana Porto Hotel is a worthwhile splurge, with Porto's best location, right on the Douro in the heart of the Ribeira action. Its 48 rooms occupy two old Ribeira buildings, now converted to plush accommodations and connected by glass walkways (standard Sb-€150, riverview Sb-€176, standard Db-€167, riverview Db-€193, extra bed-€54, Internet discounts often available, air-con, elevator, Praça de Ribeira 1, tel. 223-402-300, fax 223-402-400, www.pestana.com, pestana.porto@pestana.com).

$$$ Hotel da Bolsa, a few blocks above the Ribeira scene, is plush and modern, with more comfort than character. It has a great location and 36 decent rooms (Sb-€60–72, Db-€74–87, Sb/Db with view-€100, extra bed-€18–21, higher rates are for April–Oct, air-con, elevator, Rua Ferreira Borges 101, tel. 222-026-768, fax 222-058-888, www.hoteldabolsa.com, reservas@hoteldabolsa.com).

EATING

Porto is famous for its tripe. Legend has it that when Porto's favorite son, Prince Henry the Navigator, set out for his explorations, the city slaughtered all of its mature livestock to send along with his crew—keeping only the guts for themselves. While waiting for the next generation of animals to grow up, Porto's cooks devised many ingenious ways of preparing innards. The tradition stuck, and to this day, people from Porto are known as *tripeiros*. These days, it plays a more subtle role. You'll most typically see it Porto-style *(tripas a moda do Porto)*: barely present in a thick stew, with beans, sausage, chicken, and scant vegetables. The tripe itself doesn't have much taste—though I couldn't keep myself from thinking about digestive processes while I ate it.

For something easier to stomach, try *caldo verde*—a tasty soup made with potatoes and thinly chopped cabbage. For a quick meal, locals like a *Francesinha* ("little French girl")—a sandwich with various meats, dripping with a seafood-based gravy.

Many restaurants save their patrons money by portioning their dishes for two people. Generally, if the menu has two price columns, the cheaper list is for smaller portions *(meia dose,* or "1/2," plenty for one person) and the higher-priced list is for dishes that will easily feed two (listed as *dose,* or "1").

In the Ribeira

There's a wide range of dining options in the Ribeira, and they're all touristy. Strolling along the waterfront and following your nose is a

good option. You can also try wandering the back lanes to find a spot that feels right—you'll be trading river views for lower prices and local color. If you're looking for specific guidance, here are some possibilities. The seafood's fresh, except on Mondays (since fishermen don't go out on Sundays).

Dom Tonho, atop the arcade near the bridge, is every local's top recommendation for a Ribeira splurge. The place is white-tablecloth classy, at once Old World and mod. The food—traditional Portuguese cuisine, with an emphasis on fresh fish—is only slightly more expensive than nearby tour-group alternatives (most main meat and fish dishes €16 plus seafood splurges, daily 12:30–15:00 & 19:30–23:00, nice wine list,

Hotels and Restaurants in Porto's Ribiera District

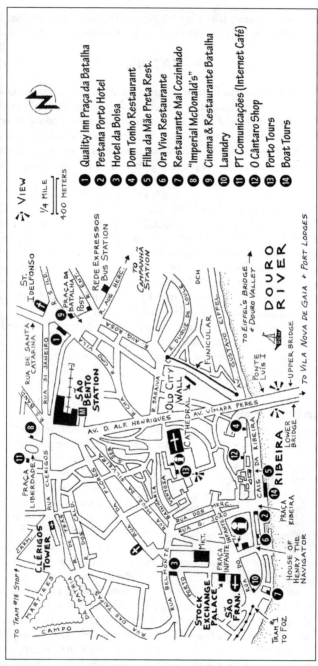

1 Quality Inn Praça da Batalha
2 Pestana Porto Hotel
3 Hotel da Bolsa
4 Dom Tonho Restaurant
5 Filha da Mãe Preta Rest.
6 Ora Viva Restaurante
7 Restaurante Mal Cozinhado
8 "Imperial McDonald's"
9 Cinema & Restaurante Batalha
10 Laundry
11 PT Comunicações (Internet Café)
12 O Cântaro Shop
13 Porto Tours
14 Boat Tours

VIEW

¼ MILE
400 METERS

indoor and outdoor seating, fancy dining area upstairs, Cais da Ribeira 13–15, tel. 222-004-307). Its pricey but tempting appetizers are explained well on the menu. They also have a mod portable location set up directly across the river in Vila Nova de Gaia with wonderful outdoor seating (daily 12:30–15:30 & 19:30–23:00).

Filha da Mãe Preta is a cut above the several interchangeable midrange places along the embankment. Sit outside with Douro views or in the tiled interior (most dishes €9–14, full courses splittable for two people, Mon–Sat 12:00–22:30, closed Sun, check out gigantic mural of Porto upstairs, Cais da Ribeira 40, tel. 222-055-515).

Ora Viva Restaurante is a humble but exuberantly decorated long-and-skinny dining hall a block off the waterfront. The hardworking Pinto family specializes in traditional grilled meat and fish dishes. It's a little less touristy than the Ribeira norm, with locals, decent food, and good prices (€7 meals, Rua Fonte Taurina 83, tel. 222-052-033). Antonio promises a free glass of port wine (before or after your dinner) if you show him this book.

If you need to satisfy your fado fix, there are a few options in Porto. **Restaurante Mal Cozinhado** ("Poorly Cooked") features professional fado performers, expensive dishes (€15–20), and fancy drinks (€5–15). The food and drinks are overpriced, but consider them the entrance fee for the fado (open for dinner nightly at 20:30; if not dining, there's a €4 cover fee and a €25 drink minimum; music starts at 21:30 and ends at 1:00 in the morning; a couple of blocks up from the Douro at Rua do Outeirinho 11, tel. 222-081-319).

In the City Center

Restaurants are scattered all around the city center, but since this is a business district, many of them are lunch-only. The food is surprisingly good and very affordable. Menus are often handwritten (posted on paper tablecloths outside) with €1 soups and €5 plates. Remember that most coffee and pastry shops do double-duty as lunch spots, so wander around and see what people are having. Good locations abound on the pedestrian Rua do Sampaio Bruno and on the side streets of Rua do Almada (one block west of Avenida dos Aliados). The dining's more atmospheric in Ribeira, but these are convenient if you're staying in the center.

The famous "Imperial McDonald's," inhabiting the former Imperial Café at the bottom of Avenida dos Aliados, is actually the most elegant fast-food spot you'll ever find. From here, there are plenty of eateries nearby—walk around the block to the local bistro **Restaurante Regaleira** (open daily, Rua do Bonjardim 87, tel. 220-006-465) and several cheap and venerable diners. Across the boulevard and uphill a block is the classy **Restaurante Guarany** (open daily, Avenida dos Aliados 85, tel. 223-321-272).

Restaurante Abadia gives customers a warm welcome and has two floors of happy eaters—locals and tourists—dining on large portions of straightforward Portuguese cuisine. This place is a no-brainer for a fine, central meal. Split a huge half-portion of their Porto-style tripe with your travel partner, balanced with something a little more predictable, such as a sizzling mini-hibachi of roasted chicken and potatoes (€10 half-portions and tasty omelets, €15 splittable full-portion main dishes, Mon–Sat 11:30–15:30 & 18:30–23:00, closed Sun, head one block east of Sá da Badeira near Bolhão market to side street Rua do Ateneu Comercial do Porto 22–24, tel. 222-008-757).

Confeitaria-Restaurante do Bolhão, which faces the market-hall entrance, has been pleasing local shoppers since 1896. This bustling bakery/brasserie offers enticing takeout items in front and an inviting old-time dining hall in the rear (the more elegant basement is less lively and soulful). You'll find fresh baked goods, omelets, and fish, along with €4 soup and sandwich specials (daily 6:00–21:00, Rua Formosa 339, tel. 223-395-220).

Historia del Caffè has American-style coffee drinks, ice-cream concoctions, good soups, and €3 toasted sandwiches. Hip, modern, and popular with young people, it's convenient for a caffeine jolt or a quick meal in the center (Mon–Sat 7:30–20:00, closed Sun, 50 yards down from Café Majestic at Rua de Passos Manuel 63).

The **Majestic Café** isn't just a coffee house—it's an institution. This elegant Art Nouveau café has been Porto's neighborhood living room for over a century. Today, it's a fine place for a coffee or a light—and expensive—lunch (Mon–Sat 9:30–24:00, closed Sun, Rua Santa Catarina 112, tel. 222-003-887).

You can sneak a peek inside the streamlined Cinema Batalha (see page 228) by grabbing a cheap buffet meal at **Restaurante Batalha,** located on the top floor. The food presentation is simple but the atmosphere is Art Deco–elegant (daily 12:00–15:00 & 19:00–22:00, Praça de Batalha, entrance on side by trolley tracks).

TRANSPORTATION CONNECTIONS

Trains

Regional trains use the more central São Bento Station; long-distance trains use the Campanhã Station on the east edge of town. The two stations are connected by frequent trains (see "Arrival in Porto," page 214). All trains leaving São Bento also stop at Campanhã (the next station).

From Porto's São Bento Train Station to: Peso da Régua (12/day, 2–2.5 hrs), **Pinhão** (5/day, 2.5–3 hrs, all transfer in Peso da Régua).

From Campanhã Train Station: Fast Alfa Pendular and Intercity trains (both require reservation, buy at station) go to **Coimbra** (almost hourly, 1.25 hrs on Alfa Pendular line or 2.25 hrs on slower Regional line—confirm before buying) and **Lisbon** (6/day, 3.5–4 hrs).

To reach **Santiago de Compostela, Spain,** you'll take a train bound for the Spanish port city of Vigo (€13, 1/day, 7:55 departure, 5.5 hrs, ticket only purchased as far as Vigo, must buy another ticket in Spain to continue to Santiago; en route to Vigo, you may change at the border town of Valença). Once in Spain, you can change to the Santiago-bound train in Vigo, but most conductors will encourage you instead to change trains before that, in the town of Redondela. This works fine, since Vigo is on a dead-end track, so that any train going to Vigo also goes through Redondela on the way. (In other words, if you change in Vigo instead of Redondela, you'll simply spend more time on the train and less time at the station.) Frustratingly, rail-information people in Porto generally can't tell you much about parts of the journey beyond the Spanish border. Consider instead a bus tour if you have extra cash and less time (next).

Buses

Remember, each bus company has its own mini-station; there's no central bus terminus (for addresses and telephone numbers, see "Arrival in Porto," page 214). Various companies compete on the same route (for example, four companies go to Lisbon). Ask the transport office at the TI about the handiest bus for your itinerary (see "Tourist Information," page 214; toll-free tel. 800-220-905). Don't bother trying to get to the Douro Valley (Peso da Régua or Pinhão) by bus; it takes twice as long as the train.

From Porto by Bus to: Coimbra (operated by Rede Expressos, Rodonorte, and others; best is Rede Expressos—11/day, 1.5 hrs, more frequent early and late, sparse mid-afternoon), **Lisbon** (best via RENEX or Rede Expressos, at least hourly, 3 hrs), **Santiago de Compostela, Spain** (run by Internorte; 4/week in winter, 6/week in summer, 5.25 hrs, €21).

Santiago Note: To get to Santiago de Compostela, Spain, consider taking an expensive but convenient all-day guided bus tour from Porto. It leaves daily at 8:00 and takes two to three hours via the expressway. (You can skip out on the return to Porto.) But this is a pricey alternative—the cheapest fares are €120. For information on these tours, ask at the Porto Tours office (see page 217; www.portotours.com).

DOURO VALLEY

Vale do Douro

The best single activity in northern Portugal is exploring the scenic Douro (DOH-roo) Valley—the birthplace of port wine—with its otherworldly, ever-changing terrain sculpted by centuries of hardy farmers. The river's steep, craggy, twisting canyons have been laboriously terraced to make a horizontal home for grape vines and olive and almond trees. Unlike the Rhine, the Loire, and other great European rivers, the Douro was never a strategic military location. So, rather than fortresses and palaces, you'll see farms, villages...and endless tidy rows of rock terraces, which took no less work—and are no less impressive—than those castles and châteaux. Locals brag, "God made the earth, but man made the Douro."

The Douro River begins as a trickle in Spain (where it's called Duero), runs west for 550 miles (350 miles of which are in Portugal), and spills into the Atlantic at Porto. The name likely means "river of gold" (though some trace it to a Celtic word for water), perhaps because of the way the sun shines on the water, or the golden-brown silt it carries after a heavy rain.

In the 17th century, British traders developed a taste for the wines from the Douro region. "Op-port-unity" knocked in 1756, when the Marquês de Pombal demarcated the region—establishing it as the only place that port wine could be produced. To this day, port remains the top industry—and tourist draw—of the Douro Valley. The 50-mile stretch on either side of Pinhão is home to some 4,000 vintners and scores of *quintas*—vineyards that produce port (and often table wine and olive oil). While many *quintas* are private, others offer tours and tastings, and some have accommodations as well.

The Douro hillsides change colors throughout the year—dusty

brown in winter, scrubby green in summer, and glowing gold in fall. The 5,000-foot-high Serra do Marão mountain range guards the region, protecting it from the ocean air and creating a microclimate perfect for growing grapes. The temperature varies from snowy in the winter to arid and 100°F degrees in the summer. Much of the Douro's dramatic ambience was changed in the 1970s, when a series of dams were built for hydroelectric power, taming the formerly raging river into the meandering stream seen today.

But while the scenery and the port are sublime, the towns along the Douro (Peso da Régua and Pinhão) are fairly dull. If you've got wheels, consider staying at one of the many *quintas* that offer accommodations—ranging from simple rooms on family farms to one of the most breathtaking *pousadas* in Portugal. To many, the Douro Valley will feel low-energy and underwhelming (especially outside of September's harvest time), but it does have the world's best port and a unique—if subtle—charm.

Planning Your Time

This area merits two days (including travel time to and from Porto, with an overnight along the river). Port-wine enthusiasts may well want more time. If you want only a glimpse, you can see the Douro as a day trip from Porto, either on your own (about 2 hours by car or 2–3 hours by train each way) or with a package tour (see page 249). I find the city of Porto more interesting and would favor it over the Douro Valley when allocating limited vacation time.

Note that since Porto is a business-oriented city, its hotels are often cheaper on weekends. In contrast, the Douro Valley—since it's primarily a tourist zone—is more crowded (and often more expensive) on weekends. Ideally, visit Porto on the weekend and the Douro during the week.

Drivers should make a beeline for this best part of the Douro Valley (see next section), and explore at will. Without a car, you're limited as to where you can stay and which *quintas* you can tour—but you still have enough options to make the trip worthwhile. To maximize sightseeing thrills, take the slow boat cruise from Porto to Peso da Régua. Visit the sights in Régua, then settle in for the night (or, if you're staying in Pinhão, take the train or boat there). In the morning, hike to Quinta de la Rosa (near Pinhão) for the 11:00 tour and tasting. When you've had enough of the wine and rugged scenery, head back to Porto via train.

Douro Valley

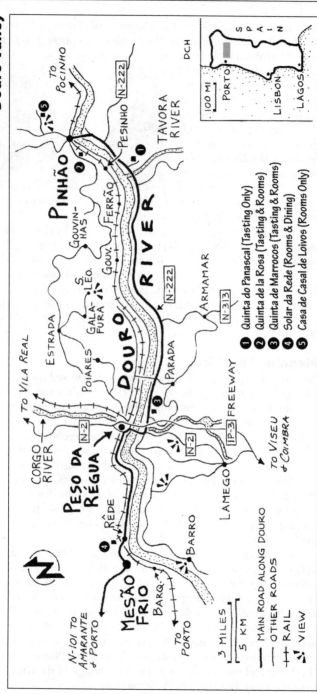

1 Quinta do Panascal (Tasting Only)
2 Quinta de la Rosa (Tasting & Rooms)
3 Quinta de Marrocos (Tasting & Rooms)
4 Solar da Rede (Rooms & Dining)
5 Casa de Casal de Loivos (Rooms Only)

— MAIN ROAD ALONG DOURO
— OTHER ROADS
↟ RAIL
↘ VIEW

3 MILES
5 KM

ORIENTATION

The Douro runs for 350 miles through the northern Portuguese heartland. The most interesting segment—and the heart of the port-wine–growing region—is easily the 17-mile stretch between Peso da Régua and Pinhão.

Coming from Porto, you'll see that the first 55 miles of the Douro are pretty and lush. When you reach the town of **Mesão Frio,** the terrain becomes far more arid and dramatic. The prized demarcated port wine–growing region of the Douro technically begins here, and stretches all the way to the Spanish border.

Peso da Régua, about seven miles beyond Mesão Frio, is the biggest town of the region and a handy home base. Seventeen miles beyond Peso da Régua is smaller **Pinhão.** Each town has a big, fancy hotel and one or two cheap *residencials*, with a *quinta* nearby. Peso da Régua benefits from more striking scenery, but feels urban and functional; Pinhão enjoys more of a small-town ambience and has better accommodations. Neither is worth going out of your way to visit.

The Douro Azul company has something of a monopoly in the region, operating the biggest tour boats and running several of the accommodations (including Vintage House Hotel in Pinhão and the Solar da Rede *pousada* near Peso da Régua).

I've described the most enjoyable and accessible stretch of the Douro, but there's much more—vineyards stretch all the way to Spain. The train goes as far as Pocinho. Just south of Pocinho, Vila Nova de Foz Côa sits between the Douro and a fine "archaeological park" with cave paintings.

A big part of your Douro experience will be determined by where you choose to sleep. The only memorable place is the classic Vintage House Hotel in Pinhão. Both the Quinta de la Rosa and Quinta de Marrocos offer you a homey farm experience. And the Solar da Rede *pousada* is a royal countryside retreat. All are described later in this chapter.

Getting Around the Douro Valley

By Boat: Lazy cruise boats float up and down the Douro between Porto, Peso da Régua, and Pinhão. (The feisty Douro was tamed in the 1970s by a series of five dams with locks, including the highest one in Europe, the Barragem do Carrapatelo—which inches boats up and down, like a giant elevator, over 140 feet.)

The boat trip takes about seven hours from Porto to the

heart of the Douro, and it comes with lunch and passage through two locks (longer trips include a third lock between Peso da Régua and Pinhão). If you've got the time and don't have a car, this is a slow but scenic way to enjoy the Douro Valley.

Various companies do the trip; generally, several different boats run daily April through November (only Sat–Sun in March, no boats Dec–Feb). Figure €70–90 to Régua or Pinhão; seniors should ask about discounts, especially on weekdays. Most travelers take a train or bus back to Porto from Régua on the same day as part of a package deal. But if you want to spend the night on the Douro, it's easy to catch a train back on your own (or buy a two-day package, which includes lodging).

The largest company, **Douro Azul,** has big boats that are popular with tour groups. It's often a bit more expensive, but the service is professional and the food is good. They also offer various package itineraries that include overnights at fancy hotels and *pousadas* (tel. 223-402-500, www.douroazul.com).

Some travelers prefer smaller companies, which can cost a little less and offer a more personal experience. Your best bet is to comparison-shop the options for the day you want to cruise with the excellent **Porto Tours** office in Porto. Since it's run by the city, this agency offers unbiased advice and charges no commission (April–Oct Mon–Fri 10:00–19:00, Sat–Sun 10:00–18:00; Nov–March Mon–Fri 10:00–17:00, Sat 10:00–14:00, closed  Sun; in old medieval watchtower next to cathedral at Calçada Dom Pedro Pitões 15, tel. 222-000-073 daily 9:00-19:00, www .portotours.com, portotours@mail.telepac.pt).

By Train: A regional train connects Porto's São Bento Station with Peso da Régua (13/day, 2–2.5 hours); some of these trains continue another 30 minutes to Pinhão (5/day). There's also a historic steam train that choo-choos you between Douro towns on Saturdays (April–Oct, Régua to Pinhão costs €7, 40 min, other towns also possible; run by Douro Azul, see contact info above).

By Car: The region is easy by car. From Porto, zip on the A4 expressway to Amarante, then N101 through the mountains to Mesão Frio (total trip to Régua around two hours). Once in the heart of the Douro, the riverside road follows the north bank from Mesão Frio to Régua. From there, you'll cross to the south bank (on the middle of the three bridges) to continue on N222 into the valley to Pinhão (where you'll cross back to reach the town). The 17-mile stretch of river covered in this chapter is about a 30-minute drive—everything I've mentioned is no more than a few minutes' side-trip from the river.

When passing through Amarante, it's an easy and logical pit-stop to detour into the town center to check out the old Roman bridge and impressive church and convent of São Gonçalo.

If you're driving from Coimbra to the Douro Valley, you'll save time and mileage by coming directly through the mountains (via Viseu and Lamego), rather than taking the expressway up the coast to Porto and then over.

TOURS

Quintas Tours and Tastings

The main attraction of the Douro Valley is touring the *quintas*, the farms that produce port and table wines. It's an informal scene and easy for drivers; simply pull into any *quinta* listed here (or any marked *rota do vinho do Porto*), and ask for a quick tour and a taste. Even if they have a specific time for tours (listed below where applicable), you can often get a shorter, less formal tour at other times. Ideally, call ahead and ask when you should show up.

Each *quinta* (KEEN-tah) works differently; most tours and tastings are free. The tours of big companies' *quintas* are slick, but feel like stripped-down versions of the tours you'll do in the port-wine lodges back in Porto (with the happy exception of Quinta do Panascal—next). The smaller, independent *quintas* are more intimate, and offer a chance to meet the people who have devoted their lives to making the best wine they can.

At *quintas* operated by big companies, it's fine not to buy. But if a family-run place gives you an in-depth tour, it's polite to buy at least a token bottle.

These are the best *quinta* experiences on this stretch of the Douro. I've noted the best options for non-drivers.

▲▲**Quinta do Panascal**—This wonderful *quinta* produces Fonseca—a name familiar to port-lovers for its high quality. The affordable, tasty Bin No. 27 is their best-known ruby. It's the only *quinta* that allows you to roam on your own through the terraced vineyards. From the riverside road you'll side-trip up the valley of the Távora River. Venturing up the rough gravel road, you'll feel like you are discovering a special, hidden gem. Yet upon arrival, you'll enjoy the slick efficiency of a corporate producer (Fonseca also

Brits on the Douro: The History of Port

Port is actually a British phenomenon. Because Britain isn't suitable for growing grapes, its citizens traditionally imported wine from France. But during wars with France (17th and 18th centuries), Britain boycotted French wine and looked elsewhere. They considered Portugal—but since it was farther away, wine often didn't survive the long sea journey to England.

The port-making process was supposedly invented accidentally by a pair of brothers who fortified the wine with grape brandy to maintain its quality during the long trip to England. The wine picked up the flavor of the oak, and the English grew to like the fortified taste and oaky flavor. Port production was perfected by the British in the succeeding centuries, hence many ports carry British-sounding names (Taylor, Croft, Graham).

In 1703, the Methuen Treaty reduced taxation on Portuguese wines—making port even more popular. In 1756, Portugal's Marquês de Pombal demarcated the Douro region—the first such designation in Europe. From that point on, only true "port wine" came from this region, following specific regulations of

owns Taylor, and is a port-wine giant). Because of its delightfully remote location, and because it gets you out among the grapes, it's the best *quinta* tour on the Douro.

The tour is self-guided, so there's no wait once you arrive. You'll be given a 30-minute audioguide and set free to wander through the vineyards and take in the sweeping views (while listening to dry, humorless commentary about the history of port and of the company). Then you'll return to the lodge to watch a 10-minute video (which brings the otherwise still fields to life) while tasting two ports (free, daily 10:00–18:00 in summer, Sat–Sun Nov–March by reservation only, tel. 254-732-321, www.fonseca.pt).

Getting There: This place is only accessible by car; it's well-marked off the Régua–Pinhão road (N222), up a thrilling little side road that follows the Távora River as it branches off from the Douro (closer to Pinhão).

▲**Quinta de la Rosa**—This family-run *quinta* is serious about its wine and eager to show it off on an in-depth, friendly one-hour tour of the facility with a generous finale of four tastings (€2.50; tours April–Oct Mon–Fri at 11:00, call to arrange weekends and off-season; tastings available April–Oct Mon–Fri 9:00–18:00, production, just as the name "Champagne" technically means wines from a specific region of France. Traditionally, farmers and landowners were Portuguese, while the British bought the wine from them, aged it in Porto, and handled the export business. But that arrangement changed in the late 19th century, when an infestation of an American insect called phylloxera (which smuggled itself to the Old World in the humid climate of speedy steamboats) devastated the Portuguese—and European—wine industry.

In the Douro Valley, you'll see lasting evidence of the phylloxera infestations in the "dead" terraces, overgrown with weeds and a smattering of olive trees. During the infestations, these particular terraces were treated with harsh chemicals that contaminated the soil, rendering it suitable only for growing olives, but not grapes. Other terraces were left untouched, as Portuguese vintners simply gave up. Unable to produce usable grapes for over a decade, they sold their land to British companies who were willing to wait until a solution could be found. It was, as phylloxera-resistant American root stock began to be used throughout Europe. Port production resumed, this time on British-owned land.

Today, Porto and the Douro Valley see many British tourists. Though it's largely undiscovered by Americans, this region is a real hot spot among wine-loving Brits.

Sat mornings, none Sun; 1 mile downstream from Pinhão, tel. 254-732-254, fax 254-732-346, www.quintadelarosa.com). Three-course meals paired with their wines cost €25 per person; reserve in advance.

Getting There: This is perhaps the only family *quinta* that is close enough to a town that you can do it without a car (20-min hike from Pinhão). For directions and information on their accommodations, see page 260.

Other Tours and Tastings—Many of the accommodations listed in this chapter also offer tours and tastings.

The finest ports—for serious wine-lovers—are at **Vintage House Hotel**'s Academia do Vinho in Pinhão. They offer three types of "tutored tastings": port introduction (€17.50/person); port wine paired with Belgian Neuhaus chocolate (€26/person); and vintage port paired with gourmet canapés (€28/person). The tastings are generally in the afternoon; call to check the schedule and reserve a spot (shop open daily 10:00–13:00 & 14:00–19:00, tel. 254-730-230, www.cs-hoteis.com, see page 259). In addition they offer three-hour classes on port appreciation (€66/person, four-person minimum, cheaper with six or more people; call for details). They also offer a wine class for the same price. The region's red wines are some of Portugal's fruity finest. Since it's right in the center of Pinhão, this place is an easy choice for non-drivers.

At the other end of the spectrum is the loose, informal, family-run **Quinta de Marrocos** (see page 257), a great place to sample simple ports while chatting with the family that made them (daily 10:00–12:00 & 15:00–18:00). You could hoof it here from Peso da Régua (across the river and about 1.5 miles upstream), but it's not as easy by foot as Quinta de la Rosa, page 250.

The **Solar da Rede** *pousada* runs a *quinta* with tastings, by the river between Peso da Régua and Mesão Frio (drivers only; see page 257). The refined **Solar do Vinho do Porto** (see page 255), in downtown Peso da Régua, is another fine tasting option, especially for those without a car.

Growing—and Stomping— Grapes in the Douro Valley

Port wine can technically only be grown in the Douro Valley, which is unique among European rivers. One glance at those end-

less neat rows of terraces—and the harsh, arid terrain that somehow produces something so flavorful—and visitors can't help but wonder: How do they do it?

The heart of the Douro is characterized by microclimates. A few miles can make a tremendous difference in terms of temperature, precipitation, humidity, and farming conditions. Even within the same vineyard, each parcel of land has its own characteristics. These subtle changes infuse the grapes with completely different aromas and flavors. Over the years, vintners have learned to micromanage their grapes, fine-tuning specific qualities to get the very best port for their conditions.

Near Porto, the Douro has moderate temperatures and a fair amount of precipitation. The vineyards you see north of Porto produce not port, but "green wine" (*vinho verde*—Portugal's refreshing and sprightly light white wine). About 55 miles inland, around Mesão Frio, chains of mountains stretch to the north and south. East of here, the climate changes dramatically, becoming very hot and dry in summer, with heavy rainfall and extreme cold in winter.

Rabelo Boats

Up until the 1970s, when the Douro was tamed by dams, boats called *rabelos* navigated the treacherous waters, carrying

port from the hillsides to the cellars of Porto. It was a three-day trip to cover the 50 to 100 miles. A crew of four loaded the barrels onto the small 20-foot boats. For the downstream trip, the captain stood on a platform to spy rocks and shallows ahead, using the long rudder to guide the flat-bottomed boat through whitewater and hairpin turns. It was dangerous work, and the river was once lined with shrines where superstitious sailors prayed.

At Vila Nova de Gaia, they unloaded their cargo—a mere eight barrels, typically—and headed back. For the slow trip upstream, the tall, square sail helped them ride the prevailing westerly winds. Otherwise, they were pulled by ropes up the worst stretches by men or oxen on towpaths that used to line the riverbank.

Nowadays, the Douro is quiet, port is shipped via tanker trucks, and the few remaining *rabelos* are docked by *quintas* for ambience and advertising.

The terrain around the Douro is dominated by sedimentary rocks that have been buried, heated, and deformed into a meta-

morphic rock called schist *(xisto)*. Thanks to geological processes, the easily fractured layers of schist are tilted beneath the soil at an angle, allowing winter rainfall to easily penetrate the earth and build up in underground reserves. The grapevines' roots plunge deep into the ground—up to 30 feet—in order to reach this water through the long, dry summer.

Douro vineyards are terraced, giving the valley an unusually dramatic look. Building and maintaining these terraces *(geios)* is expensive, and grapes planted there must be cultivated by hand. More recently, some of the bigger companies have attempted different methods: using bulldozers to create larger terraces (called *patamares*) that can be worked by machines; or smoothing out the hillside and planting the vines in vertical rows. (Purists don't like these new methods, which also have their disadvantages—including fewer plants per parcel.) Within the demarcated region, farmers are not allowed to irrigate, except with special permission.

Because the crops here are worked mostly by hand, it can be hard to find good workers (especially for pruning, a delicate task requiring certain skills). Most young people from the Douro move to the cities on the coast. To encourage them to stay, the government offers subsidies and other incentives.

To make the finest port, many *quintas* along the Douro still stomp grapes by foot—not because of quaint tradition, but because it's the best way. Machines would break the grapes' seeds and stems, releasing a bitter flavor—but soft soles don't. During harvest time (late Sept–early Oct), the grapes are poured into big granite tubs called *lagares*. A team of two dozen stompers line up across from each other, put their arms on each other's shoulders, and march, military-style, to crush the grapes. The stomping can last three or four days, and generally devolves into a party atmosphere—with tourists sometimes paying to join in.

Port traditionally stays in the Douro Valley for one winter after it's made, as the cold temperatures encourage the wine and brandy to marry. Then it's taken to Porto, where the more humid, mild climate is ideal for aging. For centuries, port could technically only be aged, marketed, and sold in Porto. But this was deregulated in 1987, and now any Douro *quinta* that offers tours sells its port directly to visitors.

The vineyards along the Douro are traditionally separated by olive trees, many of which produce fine olive oil. The farming demands of olives fit efficiently with those of grapes. There are also almond, orange, apple, and cherry trees, which locals use to make jam.

Peso da Régua

Peso da Régua (PAY-zoo dah RAY-gwah)—or simply "Régua," as it's called by locals—is the administrative capital of the Douro Valley. With 22,000 people, Régua actually feels urban, with modern five- and six-story apartment blocks and hotels that somehow seem out of place in these starkly beautiful surroundings. While the town itself isn't worth the trip, the views and access into the surrounding countryside make it worth considering as a home base—or at least a transportation hub.

ORIENTATION

Peso da Régua consists of basically two bustling streets that run parallel to the Douro. There are three bridges at the east (upriver) end of town.

Tourist Information: The town's TI is at the west (downriver) end of town (July–Sept daily 9:00–12:30 & 14:00–17:30; Oct–June Mon–Fri 9:00–12:30 & 14:00–17:30, closed Sat–Sun; Rua da Ferreirinha, tel. 254-312-846).

Arrival in Peso da Régua: The train station and two recommended hotels are at the edge of the center near the bridges, and the TI is at the west end of the center (downstream). The boat dock is more or less in the middle of town (disembark to the right, walk up the hill for train station and hotels; for the TI, disembark to the left, climb hill, swing right at fountain, and continue straight 3 blocks).

Tours: A cheesy **tourist train** meets arriving boats and does a one-hour circuit (€10, two stops: mountaintop viewpoint and wine cellar for tasting). There are also various informal **boat** trips to villages up and down the Douro (ask TI for details).

SIGHTS

Peso da Régua's sights are few, and most worthwhile for people without cars (who can't get into the countryside, where time is better spent). Downtown, you'll find **Casa do Douro,** the grand headquarters of the local port-wine industry (with pretty stained-glass windows inside).

▲**Douro Museum (Museu do Douro)**—This fine little museum traces the industry and culture of the Douro Valley, with a 3-D relief map of the region, stuffed specimens of local wildlife, models showing the construction of *rabelo* boats, and traditional costumes and musical instruments. You'll also see items relating to port production: tools, casks, barrels, decanters, port-wine bottles and labels, and advertising posters (€1, Tue–Sun 10:00–12:30 & 14:00–18:00, closed Mon, tel. 254-324-320, www.museudodouro .pt). The museum shares the old warehouse with the Solar do Vinho do Porto (at Rua da Alegria 39 in downtown Régua, see below).

▲**Solar do Vinho do Porto**—This facility, run by the Port and Douro Wines Institute, offers tastings and information about the region's products. Atmospherically situated in a renovated old warehouse (Armazém, or #43), with comfy chairs, it's a handy place to sample a variety of ports (Mon–Sat 10:00–13:00 & 14:00–19:00, closed Sun; right downtown at Rua da Ferreirinha, tel. 254-320-960, www.ivp.pt). You'll pay €1–20 per glass; the menu has meats, cheeses, and other delicious, traditional port-tasting snacks.

Quinta de São Domingos—The *quinta*, on a hill just above Peso da Régua, produces port for the big company Castelinho. This is the region's giant, impersonal *quinta*—a standard stop for large tour groups. This corporate experience reminds me of some of the port-wine lodges in Vila Nova de Gaia near Porto—not what you came all the way to the rustic Douro Valley for. The only thing good about it is its convenience for those without a car (free 10-min tour with a short movie and two tastes, daily 9:00–13:00 & 14:00–18:00, tel. 254-320-260). It's just above Régua at the train-station end of town (near the bridges); by foot, walk east (upriver) along the tracks, then cross the tracks through the hard-to-find gate (by the small pink building), and continue uphill to the *quinta* (about 15 min total).

SLEEPING AND EATING

You have two basic options for sleeping in the Douro Valley: Stay in a boring hotel or *residencial* in one of the towns (most likely Peso da Régua or Pinhão), or sleep at a picturesque *quinta* or *pousada* in the countryside. The in-town hotels are handy for those using public transportation, but if you've got a car, the *quintas* offer a better value and a more memorable Douro experience. The fancier places serve meals and have half-board options.

The Douro is extremely crowded during the grape harvest in late September and early October, and good rooms are in short supply to begin with; if visiting during this time, book as far ahead as possible. Simpler places charge the same rates year-round; more expensive hotels charge more for weekends and during the busy season (roughly April–Oct).

In Peso da Régua

You have two options, neither of which is traditional or charming: a tasteful, well-located hotel, and a cheap, basic *residencial*. If you have a car, get out of town!

$$ Hotel Régua Douro is the only classy option in town. With a top-floor panoramic breakfast room and 77 comfortable rooms—many of them with sweeping river views—it's a fine splurge (Sb-€45–62, Db-€60–77, higher prices are for July–Oct, add about €20 for weekends, riverview rooms are a good value at only €2–5 more than cityview rooms, air-con, elevator, expensive Internet in lobby, Largo da Estação da C.P., tel. 254-320-700, fax 254-320-709, www.hotelreguadouro.pt, hotelreguadouro@mail.telepac.pt).

Sleep Code

(€1 = about $1.40, country code: 351)
S = Single, **D** = Double/Twin, **T** = Triple, **Q** = Quad,
b = bathroom, **S** = shower only

To help you easily sort through these listings, I've divided the rooms into three categories, based on the price for a standard double room with bath during high season:

$$$ **Higher Priced**—Most rooms €100 or more.
 $$ **Moderately Priced**—Most rooms between €50–100.
  $ **Lower Priced**—Most rooms €50 or less.

$ Residencial Império has a convenient, central location in a stark tower a block from the station and across the street from Hotel Régua Douro. Its 35 rooms are basic, musty, and surrounded by busy streets, but the price is right (Sb-€30–35, Db-€40–45, Tb-€55–60, air-con, Rua Vasques Osório 8, tel. 254-320-120, fax 254-321-457, www.residencialimperio.com, info@residencialimperio.com).

Near Peso da Régua

$$ Quinta de Marrocos is a wonderful option if you want to stay at a real-life family farm. The Sequeira family farmhouse operates a simple shop and a family vineyard making good ports and table wines. The four rooms include a rustic yet deluxe living room, where the port's always out. Staying here, with the four dogs and farm hands, is a fun, authentic experience. It's a rare opportunity to spend time with locals who really love what they do (Sb-€50, Db-€60, 10 percent discount with this book, on N222 across the river and about 1.5 miles upstream from Peso da Régua, tel. 254-313-012, fax 254-322-680, www.quintademarrocos.com, info @quintademarrocos.com, Rita and her mother, Maria Elisa). They also rent a private two-bedroom family-friendly house on their property (€100). For information on wine tastings, see page 252.

Between Rêde and Mesão Frio

Several places offer rooms in the countryside between these two river towns, about 15 minutes downriver from Peso da Régua.

$$$ Solar da Rede is a destination in itself—a delightful, elegant *pousada* that captures the Douro spirit. This 18th-century manor house, surrounded by vineyards and overlooking a particularly scenic stretch of the Douro, has been converted into a 12-room *pousada* with regal historic furnishings. Throughout the estate, accessed by cobbled paths through the terraced hillsides, are another 17 rooms in various smaller villas with charming country decor. This is a great spot if you're honeymooning—or want to pretend you are. Relax at the swimming pool, stroll through the manicured gardens, feel like a noble in the antique-ridden reading room, or hike up the mountain to a high-altitude picnic table—all with some of the Douro's best views (standard Db-€132–195, deluxe Db-€158–234, two-story suite-€178–263, top prices are weekends April–Oct, lower prices are for weekdays and Nov–March, air-con, tel. 254-890-130, fax 254-890-139, www.pousadas.pt, reservas@cs-solardarede.com). When you reserve, tell them whether you want a room in the more formal manor house or one of the fun-loving villas (with generally better views).

$$ Casa de Canilhas is an old traditional house set among a vineyard that overlooks the river valley (Db-€50–90, Estrada Municipal de Banduja, Mesão Frio, tel. 254-891-181, mobile 917-558-006, fax 254-893-005, www.canilhas.com).

Eating at Solar da Rede: Even if you're not sleeping here, the *pousada* is a fine destination for a fancy dinner—and a chance to wander the grounds and take in the vistas. You'll enjoy crisp but friendly service and fine Portuguese cuisine (main dishes €20–30, half-board for guests costs €26 without wine, open daily 12:30–15:00 & 19:30–22:00, reservations required for non-guests, same contact info as *pousada*). The *pousada* also operates its own *quinta*, with tastings closer to the river (€5 for 3 tastes, call *pousada* for details).

Getting There: Coming by car from Régua, follow the main road west (downstream) towards Mesão Frio; flags mark the road up to the *pousada* on your right after the village of Rêde. If you don't have wheels, the hotel offers a free shuttle service from the train station in Rêde (on the main Porto–Régua line; arrange in advance).

Pinhão

Pinhão (peen-YOW)—known locally as the "heart of the Douro"—feels like a real worka-day small town, where locals go on with their "im-port-ant" business, oblivious to the tourists streaming through their streets. The big white silos are where the wine spends its first winter awaiting shipment downstream to Porto.

ORIENTATION

Pinhão has virtually no sights, but it makes for a handy home base. Even if you don't arrive by train, be sure to check out the **train station**—adorned with tiles illustrating the people and traditions of the countryside. A few accommodations in and near Pinhão don't take credit cards; the lone **ATM** is in the BPI bank, on the left near the west end of town (toward Casal de Loivos).

Arrival in Pinhão: The town has a train station along the main road, and a boat landing down below on the river. The two

*residencial*s are across the street from the station, and the Vintage House Hotel is just upriver, next to the bridge. If you're arriving by **boat,** disembark to the right for the Vintage House; to reach the *residencial*s or the station, leave the boat to the left, then loop up and to the right, around the big concrete wine-storage vats.

Tours: You have various options for **boat trips** on the Douro. Vintage House Hotel organizes river trips on traditional *rabelo* boats for guests and non-guests (€15 for 90-min trip, May–Oct daily at 10:30 and 16:00, Nov–April daily 11:00 and 15:00, call to reserve, tel. 254-730-230). Or try the informal cruise, on a modern boat, offered by Praia Bar down by the dock (€8–15 depending on length, daily in summer, call or show up to ask about today's schedule, tel. 254-731-556).

SLEEPING

In Pinhão

Your in-town options are a plush splurge hotel or two humble *residencial*s. The *residencial*s are next door to each other, across from the train station. Both operate fine restaurants, and both have riverview rooms that don't cost extra but come with some street noise; neither speaks English, but each one sometimes has an English-speaking son available.

$$$ Vintage House Hotel is *the* place if you want to splurge on a fancy, formal hotel on the Douro (as opposed to a hillside *pousada* or manor house). The place is all class, with a wonderfully atmospheric bar (with tree-trunk rafters), a good restaurant with an over-the-top formal interior and riverside terrace outdoor seating, and a wine shop featuring expensive tastings for aficionados (see "*Quintas* Tours and Tastings," page 249). Each of its 43 rooms has a river view and a terrace or balcony, and elegant tile in the bathroom. The halls are lined with baskets of free local oranges and apples, as well as 19th-century photos of the Douro (Sb-€101–145, Db-€114–161, extra bed-€59, child's bed-€30, suites €144–309, weekends in May–June and Aug–Oct are about €20 more, air-con, elevator, between train station and bridge at Lugar da Ponte, tel. 254-730-230, fax 254-730-238, www.cs-hoteis.com).

$ Residencial Douro offers 14 fresh rooms, many with cute riverview balconies (Sb-€30, €35 with breakfast, Db-€45, €50 with breakfast, cash only, air-con, Largo da Estação 39, tel. & fax 254-732-404, Oliveira family, residencialdouro@sapo.pt).

$ Residencial Ponto Grande has 17 comparable rooms with lower prices and older furnishings (Sb-€25, Db-€38, cash only, air-con, Rua António Manuel Saraiva 41A at Largo da Estação, tel. 254-732-456, Vieira family).

Near Pinhão

$$ Quinta de la Rosa, a mile downstream of Pinhão, is a riverside winery offering six comfortable rooms with traditional country furnishings; all but one overlook the river (Sb/Db-€85, a bit less for two nights and off-season, extra bed-€20, Sb costs €70 off-season, optional €25/person half-board includes wine; tel. 254-732-254, fax 254-732-346, www.quintadelarosa.com, sophia@quintadelarosa .com). They also offer in-depth tours and wine tastings (see page 250).

Getting There: Drivers leave Pinhão to the west (downriver) and look for the *quinta* on the left. If walking: from the boat landing, cross the blue pedestrian bridge and continue 20 minutes (or take a €6 taxi from Pinhão station).

Above Pinhão, in Casal de Loivos

$$ Casa de Casal de Loivos hovers on a lofty perch above Pinhão, with perhaps the most dramatic views in all of the Douro Valley. The warm Sampayo family has converted a 17th-century manor house into a six-room hotel with quaintly rustic furnishings and commanding Douro vistas. The family brags that when the BBC filmed a show about the best views in the world, they set up their camera right here (Sb-€70, Db-€95, half-board-€23/person, cash only, swimming pool, closed Jan, tel. & fax 254-732-149, www .casadecasaldeloivos.com, casadecasaldeloivos@ip.pt).

Getting There: The house is in the village of Casal de Loivos, atop the mountain over Pinhão. Leaving Pinhão to the west (downriver), first follow signs for *Alijó,* then for *Casal de Loivos,* and wind your way up the mountain roads. Once in town, look for the poorly marked villa on your right; if you reach the overlook with the white railing, you've gone a block too far. If you don't have wheels, catch a taxi from Pinhão's train station (about €6).

APPENDIX

CONTENTS

PORTUGUESE CAPSULE HISTORY

2000 B.C.–A.D. 500—Prehistory to Rome

Portugal's indigenous race, the Lusiads, was a mix from many migrations and invasions—Neolithic stone builders (2000 B.C.), Phoenician traders (1200 B.C.), northern Celts (700 B.C.), Greek colonists (700 B.C.), and Carthaginian conquerors (500 B.C.).

By the time of Julius Caesar (50 B.C.), rebellious Lusitania (Portugal) was finally under Roman rule, with major cities at Olissipo (Lisbon), Portus Cale (Porto), and Ebora (Évora). The Romans brought laws, wine, the Latin language, and Christianity. When Rome's empire fell (A.D. 476), Portugal was saved from barbarian attacks by Christian Germanic Visigoths ruling distantly from their capital in Toledo.

Eight Dates That Shaped Portugal

1128 "Portucale" separates from Castile.

1498 Vasco da Gama sails Portugal into a century of wealth.

1640 The Spanish are ousted; Portuguese gain their independence.

1755 A massive earthquake rocks Lisbon into poverty.

1822 Portugal loses Brazil as a colony.

1910 The monarchy is deposed, and repressive military regimes rule.

1974 A left-wing revolution brings democracy.

1986 Portugal joins the European Community (the forerunner of the European Union), boosting the economy.

A.D. 711–1400—Muslims vs. Christians, and Nationhood

North African Muslims invaded the Iberian Peninsula, settling in southern Portugal. Christians retreated to the cold, mountainous north, with central Portugal as a buffer zone. For the next five centuries, the Moors made Iberia a beacon of enlightenment in Dark Age Europe, while Christians slowly drove them out, one territory at a time. (Faro was the last Portuguese town to fall, in 1249.) Afonso Henriques, a popular Christian noble who conquered much Muslim land, was proclaimed king of Portugal (1139), creating one of Europe's first modern nation-states. John I solidified Portugal's nationhood by repelling a Spanish invasion (1385) and establishing his family (the House of Avis) as kings.

1400–1600—The Age of Discovery

With royal backing, Portugal built a navy and began exploring the seas—using technology the Arabs had left behind—motivated by spice-trade profit and a desire to Christianize Muslim lands in North Africa. When Vasco da Gama finally inched around the southern tip of Africa and found a sea route to India (1498), suddenly the wealth of all Asia was opened up. Through trade and conquest, tiny Portugal became one of Europe's wealthiest and most powerful nations, with colonies stretching from Brazil to Africa to India to China. Unfortunately, the easy money destroyed the traditional economy. When King Sebastian died, heirless, in a disastrous and draining defeat in Morocco, Portugal was quickly invaded by Spain (1580).

Portuguese Notables

Viriato (d. A.D. 139)—Legendary warrior who (unsuccessfully) resisted the Roman invasion.

Afonso Henriques (1095–1185)—Renowned Muslim-slayer and first king of a united, Christian nation.

Pedro I, the Just (1320–1367)—King and Father of John I, famous for his devotion to his murdered mistress, Inês de Castro.

John I (1358–1433)—King who preserved independence from Spain, launched an overseas expansion, fathered Prince Henry the Navigator, and established the House of Avis as the ruling family.

Henry the Navigator (1394–1460)—Devout, intellectual sponsor of naval expeditions during the Age of Discovery.

Manuel I, the Fortunate (r. 1495–1521)—Promoter of Vasco da Gama's explorations that made Portugal wealthy. Manueline, the decorative art style of that time, is named for him.

Pedro Cabral (1467–1520)—Explorer who found the sea route to Brazil (1500).

Bartolomeu Dias (1450–1500)—Navigator who rounded the tip of Africa in 1488, paving the way for Vasco da Gama.

Vasco da Gama (1460–1524)—Explorer who discovered the sea route to India, opening up Asia's wealth.

Ferdinand Magellan (1480–1521)—Voyager who, sailing for Spain, led the first circumnavigation of the globe (1520).

Luís de Camões (1524–1580)—Swashbuckling adventurer and poet who captured the heroism of Vasco da Gama in his epic poem, *"The Lusiads."*

Marquês de Pombal (1699–1782)—Prime minister who tried to modernize backward Portugal and who rebuilt Lisbon after the 1755 quake.

Fernando Pessoa (1888–1935)—Foremost Portuguese Modernist poet, immortalized in sculpture outside his favorite Lisbon café.

António Salazar (1889–1970)—"Portugal's Franco," a dictator who led Portugal for four decades, slowly modernizing while preserving rule by the traditional upper classes.

1600–1900—Slow Fade

The "Spanish Captivity" (1580–1640) drained Portugal. With a false economy, a rigid class system, and the gradual loss of their profitable colonies, Portugal was no match for the rising powers of Spain, England, Holland, and France. The earthquake of 1755 and Napoleon's invasions (1801–1810) were devastating. While the rest of Europe industrialized and democratized, Portugal lingered as an isolated, rural monarchy living off meager wealth from Brazilian gold and sugar.

1900s—The Military and Democracy

Republican rebels assassinated the king, but democracy was slow to establish itself in Portugal's near-medieval class system. A series of military-backed democracies culminated in four decades of António Salazar's "New State," a right-wing regime benefiting the traditional upper classes. Salazar's repressive tactics and unpopular wars abroad (trying to hang onto Portugal's colonial empire) sparked the Carnation Revolution of 1974. After some initial political and economic chaos, Portugal finally mastered democracy. The tourist industry and subsidies from the European Union have put Portugal on the road to prosperity.

RESOURCES

Tourist Information Offices

In the US

The Portuguese National Tourist Office is a wealth of information. Before your trip, get the free general information packet and request any specifics you want (such as regional and city maps, and festival schedules). Call 800-PORTUGAL, check out www.visitportugal.com, or contact tourism@portugal.org.

In Portugal

The local tourist information office is your best first stop in any new city. In this book, I refer to a tourist information office as a **TI**. Try to arrive, or at least telephone, before it closes. Get a city map and advice on public transportation (including bus and train schedules), special events, and recommendations for nightlife. Many TIs have information on the entire country or at least the region, so try to pick up maps for towns you'll be visiting later in your trip.

While TIs are eager to book you a room, use their room-finding service only as a last resort (bloated prices, fees, no opinions, and they take a cut from your host). You'll get a far better value by using the listings in this book and booking direct.

Resources from Rick

Guidebooks and Online Updates

I've done my best to make sure that the information in this book is up-to-date—but things change. For the latest, visit www.ricksteves.com/update. Also at my website, you'll find a valuable list of reports and experiences—good and bad—from fellow travelers who have used this book (www.ricksteves.com/feedback).

Begin Your Trip at www.ricksteves.com

At our travel website, you'll find a wealth of free information on European destinations, including fresh monthly news and helpful tips from thousands of fellow travelers.

Our **online Travel Store** offers travel bags and accessories specially designed by Rick Steves to help you travel smarter and lighter. These include Rick's popular carry-on bags (wheeled and rucksack versions), money belts, totes, toiletries kits, adapters, other accessories, and a wide selection of guidebooks, planning maps, and DVDs.

Rick Steves' Europe Through the Back Door travel company offers **tours** with more than two dozen itineraries and 450 departures reaching the best destinations in this book... and beyond. We offer a 15-day Spain and Portugal tour that hits the highlights of the Iberian Peninsula. You'll enjoy great guides, a fun bunch of travel partners (with small groups of generally around 25), and plenty of room to spread out in a big, comfy bus. You'll find European adventures to fit every vacation length. For all the details, and to get our Tour Catalog and a free Rick Steves' Tour Experience DVD (filmed on location during an actual tour), visit www.ricksteves.com or call the Tour Department at 425-608-4217.

This book is one of more than 30 titles in my series on European travel, which includes country guidebooks, city and regional guidebooks, and my budget-travel skills handbook, *Rick Steves' Europe Through the Back Door*. My phrase books—for Portuguese, Spanish, German, French, and Italian—are practical and budget-oriented. My other books are *Europe 101* (a crash course on art and history, newly expanded and in full color), *European Christmas* (on traditional and modern-day celebrations), and *Postcards from*

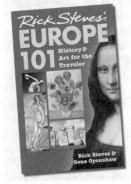

Europe (a fun memoir of my travels over 25 years). For a complete list of my books, see the inside of the last page of this book.

Public Television and Radio Shows

My TV series, *Rick Steves' Europe,* covers European destinations in 70 shows, including two different episodes that explore Portugal. My weekly public radio show, *Travel with Rick Steves,* features interviews with travel experts from around the world. All the TV scripts and radio shows (which are easy and free to download to an MP3 player) are at www.ricksteves.com.

Free Audiotours

If your travels take you beyond Portugal to France or Italy, take advantage of the free self-guided audiotours we offer of the major sights in Paris, Florence, Rome, and Venice. The audiotours, produced by Rick Steves and Gene Openshaw (the co-author of seven books in the Rick Steves' series) are available through iTunes and at www.ricksteves.com. Simply download them onto your computer and transfer them to your iPod or MP3 player. (Remember to bring a Y-jack and extra set of ear buds for your travel partner.)

Maps

The black-and-white maps in this book, designed by my well-traveled staff, are concise and simple. The maps are intended to help you locate recommended places and get to local TIs, where you can pick up a more in-depth map of the city or region (usually free).

Better maps are sold at newsstands and bookstores in Europe—take a look before you buy to make sure it has the level of detail you want. Train travelers can usually manage fine with the freebies they get at the local tourist offices. But drivers shouldn't skimp on maps—get one good overall road map for Portugal (a 1:400,000 map, such as Michelin's *Spain & Portugal Tourist and Motoring Atlas* or *Portugal Map,* is a fine bet). Good regional driving maps are available throughout Portugal. An up-to-date map is essential—it can mean the difference between choosing an old, slow road or saving an hour by finding the brand-new highway.

Other Guidebooks

Especially if you're traveling beyond my recommended destinations, you may want some supplemental information. When you consider the improvements they'll make in your $3,000 vacation, $30 for extra maps and books is money well spent. Particularly for several people traveling by car, the weight and expense of a small trip library are negligible. One budget tip can save the price of an extra guidebook. Note that none of the following books are updated annually; check the publication date before you buy.

Lonely Planet's *Portugal* is thorough, well-researched, and packed with good maps and hotel recommendations for various budgets. The similar *Rough Guide to Portugal* and *Rough Guide Directions Lisbon* are hip and insightful, written by British researchers. (If choosing between these two titles, I buy the one that was published most recently.) Students, backpackers, and nightlife-seekers should consider the Let's Go guides (by Harvard students, has the best hostel listings). *Culture Shock! Portugal* provides insights into the culture, customs, and mentality of the Portuguese people.

Dorling Kindersley publishes snazzy Eyewitness Travel Guides, covering Portugal, Lisbon, and the Algarve. While pretty to look at, these books weigh a ton and are skimpy on actual content.

Older travelers enjoy Frommer's *Portugal* guide, even though it, like the Fodor's guide, ignores alternatives that enable travelers to save money by dirtying their fingers in the local culture. The popular, skinny *Michelin Green Guide: Portugal* is excellent, especially if you're driving. The Green Guides are known for their city and sightseeing maps, dry but concise and helpful information on all major sights, and good cultural and historical background. English editions are sold in Portugal. The encyclopedic *Blue Guide Portugal* is as dry as the sands of the Algarve, but just right for scholarly types. The *Time Out* travel guide provides good, detailed coverage of Lisbon, particularly on arts and entertainment.

Portuguese history is mentioned (but not thoroughly covered) in various guidebooks, such as Cadogan, Eyewitness, and the Michelin Green Guide.

Recommended Books and Movies

For information on Portugal past and present, consider these books and films:

Non-Fiction

For a concise, readable history of this country, pick up *Portugal: A Companion History* (Saraiva), or *The History of Portugal* (Anderson).

For a lively account of the Portuguese sea voyages and discoveries in the 15th and 16th centuries, see *The Portuguese Empire, 1415-1808: A World on the Move* (Russell-Wood). The biography *Prince Henry the Navigator: A Life* (Russell) reveals the man who helped set in motion the Age of Discovery. Other famous Portuguese mariners are described in *Over the Edge of the World: Magellan's Terrifying Circumnavigation of the Globe* (Bergreen) and *Unknown Seas: How Vasco Da Gama Opened the East* (Watkins).

To explore Portugal's cuisine, read *Food of Portugal* (Anderson) or Lonely Planet's *World Food Portugal* (Scott-Aitken and De Macedo Vitorino).

Fiction

The Lusiads (Os Lusíadas) by Luís de Camões is one of the greatest epic poems of the Renaissance, immortalizing Portugal's voyages of discovery; it's considered a national treasure. Also look for the work of Fernando Pessoa, a 20th-century Portuguese poet.

Jose Maria Eça De Queirós, who wrote in part to bring about social reform, is considered by some to be the greatest 19th-century Portuguese novelist. English translations include *The Crime of Father Amaro,* which highlighted the dangers of fanaticism in a provincial Portuguese town.

Nobel prize–winning author Jose Saramago's novel *Baltasar and Blimunda* offers a surrealistic reflection on life in 18th-century Portugal, while his books *Blindness* and *Seeing* are satires on society and politics.

Set in Portugal in 1938 during Salazar's fascist government, *Pereira Declares: A Testimony* (Tabucchi) is the story of the moral resurrection of a newspaper's cautious editor. Another novel by Tabucchi is *Requiem: A Hallucination.*

In *A Small Death in Lisbon* (Wilson), a contemporary police procedural is woven with an espionage story set during World War II, with Portugal's 20-century history as a backdrop. In *Distant Music* (Langley), Catholic Esperanca and Jewish Emmanuel have an affair that lasts through six centuries and multiple incarnations, and describes Portugal's maritime empire, Sephardic Jews, and Portuguese immigrants in London. *The Last Kabbalist of Lisbon* (Zimler), a thriller, illuminates the persecution of the Jews in Portugal in the early 1500s.

Films

Marcello Mastroianni is the namesake in *Pereira Declares* (1996), inspired by the Tabucchi novel mentioned earlier.

Capitães de Abril (2000) relates the 1974 coup that overthrew the right-wing Portuguese dictatorship, from the perspective of two young army captains.

MONEY MATTERS

Damage Control for Lost Cards

If you lose your credit, debit, or ATM card, you can stop people from using it by reporting the loss immediately to the respective global customer-assistance centers. Call these 24-hour US numbers collect: Visa (410/581-9994), MasterCard (636/722-7111), and American Express (623/492-8427).

At a minimum, you'll need to know the name of the financial institution that issued you the card, along with the type of card (classic, platinum, or whatever). Providing the following information will allow for a quicker cancellation of your missing card: full card number, whether you are the primary or secondary cardholder, the cardholder's name exactly as printed on the card, billing address, home phone number, circumstances of the loss or theft, and identification verification (your birth date, your mother's maiden name, or your Social Security number—memorize this, don't carry a copy). If you are the secondary cardholder, you'll also need to provide the primary cardholder's identification-verification details. You can generally receive a temporary card within two or three business days in Europe.

If you promptly report your card lost or stolen, you typically won't be responsible for any unauthorized transactions on your account, although many banks charge a liability fee of $50.

Tipping

Tipping in Portugal isn't as automatic and generous as it is in the US, but for special service, tips are appreciated, if not expected. As in the US, the proper amount depends on your resources, tipping philosophy, and the circumstance, but the following guidelines should help you out.

Restaurants: Tipping is an issue only at restaurants that have table service. If you order your food at a counter, don't tip. In most restaurants, service is included—your menu typically will indicate this by noting *serviço incluido*. Still, if you like to tip and you're pleased with the service, it's customary to leave up to 5 percent. If service is not included *(serviço não incluido)*, tip up to 10 percent. Leave the tip on the table. It's best to tip in cash, even if you pay with your credit card. Otherwise, the tip may never reach your server.

Taxis: To tip the cabbie, round up. For instance, to pay a €13 fare, give €14; for a long ride, to the nearest €5 (for a €37 fare, give €40). If the cabbie hauls your bags and zips you to the airport to help you catch your flight, you might want to toss in a little more. But if you feel like you're being driven in circles or otherwise ripped off, skip the tip.

Special Services: Tour guides at public sites sometimes hold out their hands for tips after they give their spiel. If I've already paid for the tour, I don't tip extra. I don't tip at hotels, but if you do, give the porter a euro or two for carrying bags, and, at the end of your stay, leave a few euros in your room for the maid if the room was kept clean. In general, if someone in the service industry does a super job for you, a small tip (a couple of euros) is appropriate...but not required.

When in doubt, ask: If you're not sure whether (or how much) to tip for a service, ask your hotelier or the TI; they'll fill you in on how it's done on their turf.

VAT Refunds for Shoppers

Wrapped into the purchase price of your souvenirs is a Value Added Tax (VAT, called IVA or *Imposto sobre o Valor Acrescentado* in Portuguese) that's generally 21 percent. If you spend a minimum amount at a store that participates in the VAT refund scheme, you're entitled to get most of that tax back. However, VAT rates fluctuate based on many factors, including what kind of item you are buying. Your refund may be less than the above rate, especially if it's subject to processing fees.

Getting your refund is usually straightforward and, if you buy a substantial amount of souvenirs, well worth the hassle. If you're lucky, the merchant will subtract the tax when you make your purchase. (This is more likely to occur if the store ships the goods to your home). Otherwise, you'll need to:

Get the paperwork. Have the merchant completely fill out the necessary refund document, called a "cheque." You'll have to present your passport at the store.

Get your stamp at the airport or border. Get your cheque(s) stamped at your last stop in the European Union by the customs agent who deals with VAT refunds. It's best to keep your purchases in your carry-on for viewing, but if they're too large or dangerous (such as knives) to carry on, then track down the proper customs agent to inspect them before you check your bag. You're not supposed to use your purchased goods before you leave. If you show up at customs wearing your hand-knit Portuguese sweater, officials might look the other way—or deny you a refund.

Collect your refund. You'll need to return your stamped documents to the retailer or its representative. Many merchants work with a service that has offices at major airports, ports, or border crossings, such as Global Refund (www.globalrefund.com) or Premier Tax Free (www.premiertaxfree.com). These services, which extract a 4 percent fee, usually can refund your money immediately in your currency of choice or credit your card (within two billing cycles). If the retailer handles VAT refunds directly, it's up to you to contact the merchant for your refund. You can mail the documents from home, or quicker, from your point of departure (using a stamped, addressed envelope you've prepared or one that's been provided by the merchant)—and then wait. It could take months.

Customs for American Shoppers

You are allowed to take home $800 worth of items per person duty-free, once every 30 days. The next $1,000 is taxed at a flat 3 percent. After that, you pay the individual item's duty rate. You can also bring in duty-free a liter of alcohol (slightly more than a standard-size bottle of wine; you must be at least 21), 200 cigarettes, and up to 100 non-Cuban cigars. Food in cans or sealed jars is permissible as long as no meat is included. Some, but not all, types of cheese are allowed. Fresh fruits and vegetables are prohibited. Note that you'll need to carefully pack any bottles of wine and other liquid-containing items in your checked luggage, due to the three-ounce limit on liquids in carry-on baggage. To check customs rules and duty rates before you go, visit www.cbp .gov, and click on "Travel," then "Know Before You Go."

TELEPHONES, EMAIL, AND MAIL

Telephones

Smart travelers learn the phone system and use it daily to reserve or reconfirm rooms, get tourist information, reserve restaurants, confirm tour times, or phone home.

Types of Phones

You'll encounter various kinds of phones on your trip.

Card-operated phones—where you insert a locally bought phone card into a public pay phone—are common in Europe.

Coin-operated phones, the original kind of pay phone (but now increasingly rare), require you to have enough change to complete your call.

Hotel room phones are sometimes cheap for local calls (confirm at the front desk first), but can be a rip-off for long-distance calls unless you use an international phone card (described on the next page). But incoming calls are free, making this a cheap way for friends and family to stay in touch, provided they have a good long-distance plan for calls to Europe.

American mobile phones work in Europe if they're GSM-enabled, tri-band, or quad-band, and on a calling plan that includes international calls. They're convenient, but pricey. For example, with a T-Mobile phone, you'll pay $1 per minute for calls.

European mobile phones run about $75 (for the most basic models) and come without contracts. These phones are loaded with prepaid calling time that you can recharge as you use up the minutes. As long as you're not "roaming" outside the phone's home country, incoming calls are free. If you're traveling to multiple countries within Europe, make sure the phone is electronically "unlocked," so that you can swap out its SIM card (a fingernail-sized chip that holds the phone's information) for a new one in other countries. For more information on mobile phones, see www.ricksteves.com /plan/tips/mobilephones.htm.

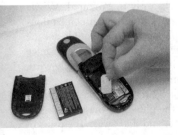

The Portuguese Language Barrier

Portugal can surprise English-speaking travelers with one of the biggest language barriers in Western Europe. Locals visibly brighten when you know and use some key Portuguese words (see "Portuguese Survival Phrases" later in the appendix). Travel with a phrase book, particularly if you want to interact with local people. You'll find that doors open quicker and with more smiles when you can speak a few words of the language.

If you speak intermediate Spanish, you'll be able to stumble through newspapers and read road signs, even if you can't pronounce the words. (Accent marks are keys to pronunciation, but nothing more.)

Surprisingly, English speakers do much better speaking Portuguese than the Spanish do, because we have roughly the same amount of vowel sounds. Spoken Portuguese sounds like a mix of a Slavic language and Spanish. If you want to take a Portuguese language course before your trip here, make sure your professor is Portuguese, not Brazilian—the accents are very distinct.

If you're having trouble communicating in Portuguese, try English, French, and Spanish, in that order (because some locals give Spanish-speakers the cold shoulder). The Portuguese do, however, speak more English than their Spanish neighbors, since English is required in school. (Their American movies are also subtitled, while the Spanish get their Hollywood flicks dubbed.)

Considering how fun it is to eat local dishes, the food phrase list in this book is particularly helpful (see "Typical Portuguese Foods," page 18). Use it, and you'll eat much better than the average tourist.

Using Phone Cards

Get a phone card for your calls. Prepaid cards come in two types: insertable phone cards (usable only in pay phones) and international phone cards (usable from any phone). Both are described below. Look for these cards at any post office and most newsstands and tobacco shops, including at train stations and airports.

Either type of phone card works only in Portugal. While traveling, you can share either type of card with your companions (and, in the case of an international phone card, your buddy doesn't even need the actual card—just the numbers on it). If you have time left on a card when you leave the country (as you likely will), simply give it to another traveler—anyone can use it.

An **insertable phone card,** called a *cartão telefónico,* can only be used at pay phones. Simply take the phone off the hook, insert the prepaid card, wait for a dial tone, and dial away. The price of the call (local or international) is automatically deducted from your card. The phone doesn't beep to remind you that you've left the card in, so don't forget to remove it when you're done. Insertable phone cards are a good deal for calling within Europe, but calling the US can be more expensive (at least 50 cents/min) than if you use an international phone card.

Prepaid **international phone cards,** called a *cartão telefónico com código pessoal,* are popular and easy to buy. Look for fliers advertising long-distance rates, or ask about the cards at Internet cafés, newsstands, souvenir shops, youth hostels, and post offices. With one of these cards, your calls to the US will generally cost around 25–50 cents per minute (and they also work for domestic calls).

Before buying a card, make sure the access number you dial is toll-free, not a local number (or else you'll be paying for a local call *and* deducting time from your calling card). These cards usually work only in the country where you buy them, but some brands work internationally. Buy a lower denomination in case the card is a dud.

To use a card, scratch off the back to reveal your code. After you dial the access phone number, the message tells you to enter your code and then dial the phone number you want to call. A voice may announce how much is left in your account before you dial. Usually you can select English, but if the prompts are in another language, experiment: Dial your code, followed by the pound sign (#), then the number, then pound again, and so on, until it works. To call the US, see "Dialing Internationally," page 276.

Using Hotel-Room Phones, VoIP, or US Calling Cards

The best way to call home is using an international phone card, but here are some other alternatives.

The phone in your **hotel room** is convenient...but expensive. While incoming calls (made by folks back home) can be an affordable way to keep in touch, charges for *outgoing* calls can be a very unpleasant surprise. Always ask first how much you'll be charged, even for local and (supposedly) toll-free calls.

Dialing direct from your hotel room—without using an international phone card (described above)—is usually quite pricey for international calls.

If your family has an inexpensive way to call Europe, either through a long-distance plan or prepaid calling card, have them call you in your hotel room. Give them a list of your hotels' phone numbers before you go. Then, as you travel, send them an email or make a quick pay-phone call to set up a time for them to give you a ring.

Metered phones are available in phone offices and sometimes in bigger post offices. You can talk all you want, then pay the bill when you leave—but be sure you know the rates before you have a lengthy conversation.

European Calling Chart

Just smile and dial, using this key:
AC = Area Code, LN = Local Number.

European Country	Calling long distance within...	Calling from the US or Canada to...	Calling from a European country to...
Austria	AC + LN	011 + 43 + AC (without the initial zero) + LN	00 + 43 + AC (without the initial zero) + LN
Belgium	LN	011 + 32 + LN (without initial zero)	00 + 32 + LN (without initial zero)
Bosnia-Herzegovina	AC + LN	011 + 387 + AC (without initial zero) + LN	00 + 387 + AC (without initial zero) + LN
Britain	AC + LN	011 + 44 + AC (without initial zero) + LN	00 + 44 + AC (without initial zero) + LN
Croatia	AC + LN	011 + 385 + AC (without initial zero) + LN	00 + 385 + AC (without initial zero) + LN
Czech Republic	LN	011 + 420 + LN	00 + 420 + LN
Denmark	LN	011 + 45 + LN	00 + 45 + LN
Estonia	LN	011 + 372 + LN	00 + 372 + LN
Finland	AC + LN	011 + 358 + AC (without initial zero) + LN	999 + 358 + AC (without initial zero) + LN
France	LN	011 + 33 + LN (without initial zero)	00 + 33 + LN (without initial zero)
Germany	AC + LN	011 + 49 + AC (without initial zero) + LN	00 + 49 + AC (without initial zero) + LN
Greece	LN	011 + 30 + LN	00 + 30 + LN
Hungary	06 + AC + LN	011 + 36 + AC + LN	00 + 36 + AC + LN
Ireland	AC + LN	011 + 353 + AC (without initial zero) + LN	00 + 353 + AC (without initial zero) + LN

European Country	Calling long distance within...	Calling from the US or Canada to...	Calling from a European country to...
Italy	LN	011 + 39 + LN	00 + 39 + LN
Montenegro	AC + LN	011 + 382 + AC (without initial zero) + LN	00 + 382 + AC (without initial zero) + LN
Netherlands	AC + LN	011 + 31 + AC (without initial zero) + LN	00 + 31 + AC (without initial zero) + LN
Norway	LN	011 + 47 + LN	00 + 47 + LN
Poland	LN	011 + 48 + LN (without initial zero)	00 + 48 + LN (without initial zero)
Portugal	LN	011 + 351 + LN	00 + 351 + LN
Slovakia	AC + LN	011 + 421 + AC (without initial zero) + LN	00 + 421 + AC (without initial zero) + LN
Slovenia	AC + LN	011 + 386 + AC (without initial zero) + LN	00 + 386 + AC (without initial zero) + LN
Spain	LN	011 + 34 + LN	00 + 34 + LN
Sweden	AC + LN	011 + 46 + AC (without initial zero) + LN	00 + 46 + AC (without initial zero) + LN
Switzerland	LN	011 + 41 + LN (without initial zero)	00 + 41 + LN (without initial zero)
Turkey	AC (if no initial zero is included, add one) + LN	011 + 90 + AC (without initial zero) + LN	00 + 90 + AC (without initial zero) + LN

- The instructions above apply whether you're calling a land line or mobile phone.
- The international access codes (the first numbers you dial when making an international call) are 011 if you're calling from the US or Canada, or 00 if you're calling from virtually anywhere in Europe (except Finland, where it's 999).
- To call the US or Canada from Europe, dial 00, then 1 (the country code for the US and Canada), then the area code and number. In short, 00 + 1 + AC + LN = Hi, Mom!

If you're traveling with a laptop, consider trying **VoIP (Voice over Internet Protocol).** With VoIP, two computers act as phones, allowing for a free Internet-based call. The major providers are Skype (www.skype.com) and Google Talk (www.google.com/talk).

US Calling Cards (such as the ones offered by AT&T, MCI, or Sprint) are the worst option. You'll nearly always save a lot of money by paying with a phone card (see above).

How to Dial

Calling from the US to Europe, or vice versa, is simple—once you break the code. The European calling chart on page 274 will walk you through it.

Dialing Within Portugal

Portugal has a direct-dial nine-digit phone system (no area codes). To call anywhere within Portugal, just dial the number. For example, to call one of my recommended Lisbon hotels from Salema, simply dial its local number (213-219-030).

Dialing Internationally

If you want to make an international call, follow these three steps:

1.) Dial the international access code (00 if you're calling from Europe, 011 from the US or Canada).

2.) Dial the country code of the country you're calling (351 for Portugal, or 1 for the US or Canada).

3.) Dial the nine-digit local number.

For example, to call the recommended Lisbon hotel from the US, dial 011 (the US international access code), 351 (Portugal's country code), then 213-219-030.

To call my office in Edmonds from anywhere in Europe, I dial 00 (Europe's international access code), 1 (the US country code), 425 (Edmonds' area code), and 771-8303.

Useful Phone Numbers

Emergency: Dial 112.

Directory Assistance: Dial 118 for local numbers and 177 for international numbers.

US Embassy: Tel. 217-273-300, Avenida das Forças Armadas, Lisbon, www.american-embassy.pt.

Email and Mail

Email: Many travelers set up a free Web-based email account with Yahoo, Microsoft (Hotmail), or Google (Gmail). Internet cafés are easy to find in big cities. Most of the towns for which I've listed accommodations in this book also have Internet cafés. Look for the places listed in this book, or ask the local TI, computer store, or your hotelier. Some hotels have a dedicated computer for guests' email needs—sometimes free, sometimes for a fee. Small places are accustomed to letting clients (who've asked politely) sit at their desk for a few minutes just to check their email.

Internet access for laptop users is becoming more common at hotels and B&Bs. Most hotels that offer this do so for free, but some (especially fancier chain hotels) charge by the minute. You'll either access the hotel's wireless Internet (Wi-Fi, sometimes called "WLAN" in Europe), sometimes using a password provided by the hotelier; or plug your computer directly into an Internet wall socket (they can usually loan you a cable).

Mail: Get stamps at the neighborhood post office, newsstands within fancy hotels, and some mini-marts and card shops. While you can arrange for mail delivery to your hotel (allow 10 days for a letter to arrive), phoning and emailing are so easy that I've dispensed with mail stops altogether.

TRANSPORTATION

By Car or Public Transportation?

Cars are best for three or more traveling together (especially families with small kids), those packing heavy, and those scouring the countryside. Trains and buses are best for solo travelers, blitz tourists, and city-to-city travelers.

Overview of Trains and Buses

Portugal straggles behind the rest of Europe in train service, but offers excellent bus transportation. Off the main Lisbon–Porto–Coimbra train lines, buses are usually a better bet. In cases where buses and trains serve the same destination, the bus is often more efficient, offering more frequent connections and sometimes a more central station. If schedules are similar, use the maps in this book to determine which station is closest to your hotel.

The best public transportation option is to mix bus and train travel. Always verify bus or train schedules before your departure, and never leave a station without the next day's schedule options in hand. To ask for a schedule at an information window, say, *"Horario para* (fill in names of cities), *faz favor."* (The local TI will sometimes have schedules available for you to take or copy.) To study train schedules in advance, see www.cp.pt for all domestic and Spain/France routes (schedules are downloadable PDFs) or Germany's handy all-Europe website (http://bahn.hafas.de/bin /query.exe/en) for long-distance international connections.

Departures and arrivals are *partidas* and *chegadas,* respectively. These key Portuguese "fine print" words may also come in handy in your travels: Both *as* and *aos* mean "on"; *de* means "from," as in "from this date to that date"; *só* means "only," as in "only effective on..."; *não* means "not"; and *feriado* means "holiday." On schedules, exceptions are noted, like in this typical qualifier: *"Não se efectua aos sábados, domingos, e feriados oficiais"* ("Not effective on Saturdays, Sundays, and official holidays").

Trains (Comboios)

Portugal has a mix of slow milk-run trains and an occasional Expresso. On Portuguese train schedules, *diario* means "daily" and *mudança de comboio* means "change trains."

Because you'll use a mix of trains and buses on your trip, a Portuguese Flexipass is generally not a good value. If you're traveling beyond Portugal, the Iberic Flexipass (which includes Spain) or Eurail Selectpass can make sense, but use the pass wisely, only for your long train trips. These passes are sold outside of Europe only. For prices and specifics, visit www.ricksteves.com/rail. Even if you have a railpass, use buses when they're more convenient and direct than the trains.

Overnight Trains: If you'll be going to Madrid, book ahead for the overnight train to ensure you get a berth and/or seat. It's a pricey Hotel Train called the "Lusitânia" (prices listed on top of page 95; railpass accepted if you pay extra sleeper fee). No cheaper rail option exists between these two capital cities. You can save money by taking a bus (€44, Intercentro Lines service using an Alsa bus), or save time by taking a plane (see "Cheap Flights," later in this chapter).

Buses (Autocarros)

Portugal has a number of different bus companies, sometimes running buses to the same destinations and using the same transfer points. If you have to transfer, make sure to look for a bus with the same name/logo as the company you bought the ticket from. The largest national company is Rede Expressos (www.rede-expressos.pt). You can pre-plan bus trips between cities online, but you should always confirm the schedule in person.

Long-distance (and most short-distance) buses are now officially non-smoking. Some passengers may ignore the signs, but it rarely happens these days.

If the bus station is not central, ask at the TI about travel agencies near your hotel that sell bus tickets. Don't leave a bus station to explore a city without checking your departure options and buying a ticket in advance if necessary (and possible). Bus service on holidays, Saturdays, and especially Sundays can be dismal.

You can (and most likely will be required to) stow your luggage under the bus. For longer rides, give some thought to which

Portugal's Public Transportation

side of the bus will get the most sun, and sit on the opposite side. Even if a bus is air-conditioned and has curtains, direct sunlight can still heat up your seat.

Drivers and station personnel rarely speak English. Buses usually lack WCs but stop every two hours or so for a break (usually 15 min, but can be up to 30). Ask the driver, "How many minutes here?" *("Quántos minutos aqui?")* so you know if you have time to get out. Bus stations have WCs (rarely with toilet paper) and cafés offering quick and cheap food.

Your ride will likely come with a soundtrack: taped music (usually American pop), a radio, or sometimes videos. If you prefer silence, bring earplugs.

Bus schedules in Portugal are clearly posted at each major

station. *Directo* is "direct." *Ruta* buses are slower because they make many stops en route. Posted schedules list most, but not all, destinations. If your intended destination isn't listed, check at the ticket/information window for the most complete schedule information. For long trips, your ticket might include an assigned seat.

Taxis *(Táxis)*

Most taxis are reliable and cheap. Drivers generally respond kindly to the request, "How much is it to (destination), more or less?" *("Quanto é para* (destination) *mais ou menos?")* Rounding the fare up to the nearest large coin (maximum of 10 percent) is adequate for a tip. City rides cost $4 to $8. Keep a map in your hand so the cabbie knows (or thinks) you know where you're going. Big cities have plenty of taxis. In many cases, couples can travel by cab for little more than two bus or subway tickets.

Renting a Car

You can drive in Portugal with a valid US drivers license for up to six months.

Drivers under the age of 25 may incur a young-driver surcharge, and some rental companies do not rent to anyone 75 or over. If you're considered too young or old, look into leasing, which has less-stringent age restrictions (see "Leasing").

Research car rentals before you go. It's cheaper to arrange most car rentals from the US. Call several companies and look online to compare rates, or arrange a rental through your hometown travel agent. Two reputable companies among many are Auto Europe (www.autoeurope.com) and Europe by Car (www.europebycar.com). Rent by the week with unlimited mileage. I normally rent the smallest, least-expensive model with a stick-shift (cheaper than an automatic). If you want an automatic, reserve the car at least a month in advance and specifically request an automatic.

For a two-week rental, allow $600 per person (based on two people sharing a car), including insurance, tolls, gas, and parking. Always keep your receipts in case any questions arise about your billing. For longer trips, consider leasing; you'll save money on insurance and taxes. Compare pick-up costs (downtown can be cheaper than the airport) and explore drop-off options.

When you pick up the car, check it thoroughly and make sure any damage is noted on your rental agreement. Find out how your car's lights, turn signals, wipers, and gas cap function.

Returning a car at a big-city train station can be tricky; get precise details on the car drop-off location and hours. Note that rental offices may close from midday Saturday until Monday. When you return the car, make sure the agent verifies its condition with you.

Appendix

Car Insurance Options

When you rent a car, you are liable for a very high deductible, sometimes equal to the entire value of the car. There are various ways you can limit your financial risk in case of an accident. For Portugal, you have three options: buy Collision Damage Waiver (CDW) coverage from the car-rental company, get coverage through your credit card (free, if your card automatically includes zero-deductible coverage), or buy coverage through Travel Guard.

CDW includes a very high deductible (typically $1,000–1,500). When you pick up the car, you'll be offered the chance to "buy down" the deductible to zero (for $10–30/day; this is often called "super CDW").

If you opt for credit-card coverage, there's a catch. You'll technically have to decline all coverage offered by the car-rental company, which means they can place a hold on your card for the full deductible amount. In case of damage, it can be time-consuming to resolve the charges with your credit-card company. Before you decide on this option, quiz your credit-card company about how it works and ask them to explain the worst-case scenario.

Buying CDW insurance (plus "super CDW") is the easier but pricier option. Using the coverage that comes with your credit card saves money, but can involve more hassle.

Finally, you can buy CDW insurance from Travel Guard ($9/day plus a one-time $3 service fee covers you up to $35,000, $250 deductible, tel. 800-826-4919, www.travelguard.com). It's valid throughout Europe, but some car-rental companies refuse to honor it (especially in Italy and the Republic of Ireland). Oddly, residents of Washington State aren't allowed to buy this coverage.

For more fine print about car-rental insurance, see www.ricksteves.com/cdw.

Leasing

For trips of two and a half weeks or more, leasing (which automatically includes CDW-like insurance) is the best way to go. By technically buying and then selling back the car, you save lots of money on tax and insurance. Leasing provides you a brand-new car with unlimited mileage and a 24-hour emergency assistance program. You can lease for little as 17 days to as long as 6 months. Car leases must be arranged from the US. One of many reliable companies offering affordable lease packages is Europe by Car (US tel. 800-223-1516, www.europebycar.com or Auto Europe (www.autoeurope.com).

Driving

Drivers in Portugal encounter sparse traffic and very good roads connecting larger cities. You can pick up a Michelin map in the

US or buy one of the good, inexpensive maps available throughout Portugal. Freeways come with tolls (about $5/hr), but save huge amounts of time. Always pick up a ticket as you enter a toll freeway, and then pick up tickets at each opportunity along the way (or risk a fine). Don't use the no-stop-necessary speed lane (labeled *Reservada a Aderentes,* reserved for locals with a monthly pass), or you'll pay for a trip across the country in order to exit—a lesson I learned the expensive way. On freeways, navigate by direction (*norte* = north, *oeste* = west, *sul* = south, *este* = east). Also, since road numbers can be confusing and inconsistent, navigate by city names.

Portugal, statistically one of Europe's most dangerous places to drive, has lots of ambulances on the road. Drive defensively. If you're involved in an accident, expect a monumental headache—you will be blamed. Seat belts are required by law. Expect to be stopped for a routine check by the police (be sure your car insurance form is up-to-date). Small towns come with speed traps and corruption. Tickets, especially for foreigners, are issued and paid for on the spot. Insist on a receipt, so the money is less likely to end up in the cop's pocket.

Gas and diesel prices are controlled and the same everywhere—around $6 a gallon for gas *(gasolina)*, and less for diesel *(diesel)*.

AND LEARN THESE ROAD SIGNS

STOP

Speed Limit (km/hr) · Yield · No Passing · End of No Passing Zone

One Way · Intersection · Main Road · Freeway

Danger · No Entry · No Entry for cars · All Vehicle Prohibited

Parking · No Parking · Customs · Peace

Choose parking places carefully. Parking areas in cities generally have a large white "P" on a blue background. Don't assume it's free—check around for meters or ticketing machines. Keep your valuables in your hotel room, or, if you're between destinations, covered in your trunk. Leave nothing worth stealing in the car, especially overnight. If your car's a hatchback, take the trunk cover off at night so thieves can look in without breaking in. Try to make your car look locally owned by hiding the "tourist-owned" rental-company decals and putting a local newspaper in your front or back window. Ask your hotelier for advice on parking. In cities you can park safely but expensively in guarded lots. While you should avoid parking lots with twinkly asphalt, thieves break car windows anywhere, even at stoplights.

Driving in Portugal: Distance and Time

To Santiago de Compostela
450m • 8.5h

m = miles
h = hours

Porto
55m•1h
70m•1h
100m•2h

Peso da Régua
155m • 3.75h
Pinhão
15m .5h
165m•3h
Salamanca
60m•1h

Coimbra
135m • 2.75h
Ciudad Rodrigo

30m•.75h
Nazaré
25m•.5h
50m•.75h
Óbidos
50m•.75h
240m • 4h
Sintra
20m•.5h

Fátima
125m • 2.5h
75m•1.25h

Lisbon
85m•1.5h
315m • 4.75h (via Badajoz)
To Madrid

Évora

175m•3h
145m•3h
185m•3h
155m•2.75h
250m • 4.75h (via Beja)

13m•.5h
13m•.5h
Sagres
Salema
Lagos
65m•1h
100m•1.5h
Sevilla
Tavira

Note: Your times may vary based on traffic, construction, and road conditions.

Cheap Flights

If you're visiting one or more cities on a longer European trip, you might want to look into the affordable intra-European airlines. While trains are still the best way to connect places that are close together, a flight can save both time and money on long journeys.

One of the best websites for comparing inexpensive flights is www.skyscanner.net. Other comparison search engines include www.kayak.com, www.mobissimo.com, www.sidestep.com, and www.wegolo.com.

For flights within Portugal, the country's national carrier is **TAP** (www.flytap.com). For flights between Lisbon and other cities in Europe, also try **Iberia** (www.iberia.com), **Vueling Airlines** (www.vueling.com), **Spanair** (www.spanair.com), and **easyJet** (www.easyjet.com). Be aware of the potential drawbacks of flying on the cheap: nonrefundable and nonchangeable tickets, rigid baggage restrictions (and fees if you have more than what's officially allowed), use of airports far outside town, tight schedules that can mean more delays, little in the way of customer assistance if problems arise, and, of course, no frills. To avoid unpleasant surprises, read the small print—especially baggage policies—before you book.

HOLIDAYS AND FESTIVALS

This is a partial list of holidays and festivals. For specifics, contact the Portuguese National Tourist Office in the US (tel. 800-PORTUGAL, www.visitportugal.com, tourism@portugal.org).

Jan 1	New Year's Day
Mardi Gras Carnival	(Feb 5 in 2008, Feb 24 in 2009)
Holy Week	(week before Easter)
Easter	(March 23 in 2008, April 12 in 2009)
April 25	Liberty Day (parades, fireworks)
May–June	Algarve Music Festival, Algarve
May 1	Labor Day (closures)
May 13	Pilgrimage to Fátima
Corpus Christi	(May 22 in 2008, June 11 in 2009)
June	Lisbon's Festival, Lisbon
June 10	Portuguese National Day
June 13	St. Anthony's Day, Lisbon; Pilgrimage to Fátima
June 29	St. Peter's Day, Lisbon
July 13	Pilgrimage to Fátima
Aug 13	Pilgrimage to Fátima
Aug 15	Assumption (religious festival)
Aug 19	Pilgrimage to Fátima
Sept 13	Pilgrimage to Fátima
Mid-Sept	Our Lady of Nazaré Festival, Nazaré
Oct 5	Republic Day (businesses closed)
Oct 13	Pilgrimage to Fátima
Nov 1	All Saints' Day
Dec 1	Independence Restoration Day
Dec 8	Feast of the Immaculate Conception
Dec 25	Christmas
Dec 31	New Year's Eve

CONVERSIONS AND CLIMATE

Numbers and Stumblers

- Europeans write a few of their numbers differently than we do. 1 = 1, 4 = 4, 7 = 7.
- In Europe, dates appear as day/month/year, so Christmas is 25/12/09.
- Commas are decimal points and decimals commas. A dollar and a half is 1,50, and there are 5.280 feet in a mile.
- When counting with fingers, start with your thumb. If you hold up your first finger to request one item, you'll probably get two.
- What Americans call the second floor of a building is the first floor in Europe.
- On escalators and moving sidewalks, Europeans keep the left "lane" open for passing. Keep to the right.

Metric Conversions (approximate)

1 foot = 0.3 meter	1 square yard = 0.8 square meter
1 yard = 0.9 meter	1 square mile = 2.6 square kilometers
1 mile = 1.6 kilometers	1 ounce = 28 grams
1 centimeter = 0.4 inch	1 quart = 0.95 liter
1 meter = 39.4 inches	1 kilogram = 2.2 pounds
1 kilometer = 0.62 mile	32°F = 0°C

Climate

The first line is the average daily high; the second line, the average daily low. The third line shows the average number of days without rain. For more detailed weather statistics for destinations in this book (as well as the rest of the world), check www.worldclimate .com.

	J	F	M	A	M	J	J	A	S	O	N	D
Lisbon												
	57°	59°	63°	67°	71°	77°	81°	82°	79°	72°	63°	58°
	46°	47°	50°	53°	55°	60°	63°	63°	62°	58°	52°	47°
	16	16	17	20	21	25	29	29	24	22	17	16
Faro (Algarve)												
	60°	61°	64°	67°	71°	77°	83°	83°	78°	72°	66°	61°
	48°	49°	52°	55°	58°	64°	67°	68°	65°	60°	55°	50°
	22	21	21	24	27	29	31	31	29	25	22	22

Temperature Conversion: Fahrenheit and Celsius

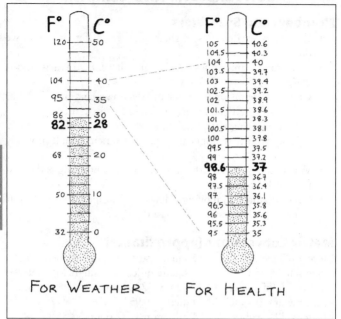

Europe takes its temperature using the Celsius scale, while we opt for Fahrenheit. For a rough conversion from Celsius to Fahrenheit, double the number and add 30. For weather, remember that 28°C is 82°F—perfect. For health, 37°C is just right.

Essential Packing Checklist

Whether you're traveling for five days or five weeks, here's what you'll need to bring. Remember to pack light to enjoy the sweet freedom of true mobility. Happy travels!

- ❑ 5 shirts
- ❑ 1 sweater or lightweight fleece jacket
- ❑ 2 pairs pants
- ❑ 1 pair shorts
- ❑ 1 swimsuit (women only—men can use shorts)
- ❑ 5 pairs underwear and socks
- ❑ 1 pair shoes
- ❑ 1 rainproof jacket
- ❑ Tie or scarf
- ❑ Money belt
- ❑ Money—your mix of:
  - ❑ Debit card for ATM withdrawals
  - ❑ Credit card
  - ❑ Hard cash in US dollars
- ❑ Documents (and backup photocopies)
- ❑ Passport
- ❑ Airplane ticket
- ❑ Driver's license
- ❑ Student ID and hostel card
- ❑ Railpass/car-rental voucher
- ❑ Insurance details
- ❑ Daypack
- ❑ Sealable plastic baggies
- ❑ Camera and related gear
- ❑ Empty water bottle
- ❑ Wristwatch and alarm clock
- ❑ Earplugs
- ❑ First-aid kit
- ❑ Medicine (labeled)
- ❑ Extra glasses/contacts and prescriptions
- ❑ Sunscreen and sunglasses
- ❑ Toiletries kit
- ❑ Soap
- ❑ Laundry soap (if liquid and carry-on, limit to 3 oz.)
- ❑ Clothesline
- ❑ Small towel
- ❑ Sewing kit
- ❑ Travel information
- ❑ Necessary map(s)
- ❑ Address list (email and mailing addresses)
- ❑ Postcards and photos from home
- ❑ Notepad and pen
- ❑ Journal

Hotel Reservation

To: _____ _____
  hotel   *email or fax*

From: _____ _____
  name   *email or fax*

Today's date: _____ / _____ / _____
  day   *month*   *year*

Dear Hotel _____ ,

Please make this reservation for me:

Name: _____

Total # of people: _____ # of rooms: _____ # of nights: _____

Arriving: _____ / _____ / _____ My time of arrival (24-hr clock): _____
  day *month* *year*   (I will telephone if I will be late)

Departing: ____ / ____ / ____
  day *month* *year*

Room(s): Single___ Double ___ Twin ___ Triple ___ Quad___

With: Toilet ____ Shower ____ Bath ____ Sink only___

Special needs: View___ Quiet___ Cheapest ___ Ground Floor___

Please email or fax confirmation of my reservation, along with the type of room reserved and the price. Please also inform me of your cancellation policy. After I hear from you, I will quickly send my credit-card information as a deposit to hold the room. Thank you.

_____
Name

_____
Address

_____
City   *State*   *Zip Code*   *Country*

Before hoteliers can make your reservation, they want to know the information listed above. You can use this form as the basis for your email, or you can photocopy this page, fill in the information, and send it as a fax (also available online at www.ricksteves.com/reservation).

Portuguese Survival Phrases

In the phonetics, nasalized vowels are indicated by an underlined **n** or **w**. As you say the vowel, let its sound come through your nose as well as your mouth. The character **ī** sounds like the letter I in "light."

Good day.	**Bom dia.**	bohn **dee**-ah
Do you speak English?	**Fala inglês?**	**fah**-lah een-**glaysh**
Yes. / No.	**Sim. / Não.**	seeng / no<u>w</u>
I (don't) understand.	**(Não) compreendo.**	(no<u>w</u>) koh<u>n</u>-pree-**ayn**-doo
Please.	**Por favor.**	poor fah-**vor**
Thank you. (said by male)	**Obrigado.**	oh-bree-**gah**-doo
Thank you. (said by female)	**Obrigada.**	oh-bree-**gah**-dah
I'm sorry.	**Desculpe.**	dish-**kool**-peh
Excuse me (to pass).	**Com licença.**	koh<u>n</u> li-**sehn**-sah
(No) problem.	**(Não) á problema.**	(no<u>w</u>) ah proo-**blay**-mah
Good.	**Bom.**	boh<u>n</u>
Goodbye.	**Adeus.**	ah-**deh**-oosh
one / two	**um / dois**	oo<u>n</u> / doysh
three / four	**três / quarto**	traysh / **kwah**-troo
five / six	**cinco / seis**	**seeng**-koo / saysh
seven / eight	**sete / oito**	**seh**-teh / **oy**-too
nine / ten	**nove / dez**	**naw**-veh / dehsh
How much is it?	**Quanto custa?**	**kwahn**-too **koosh**-tah
Write it?	**Escreva?**	ish-**kray**-vah
Is it free?	**É gratis?**	eh **grah**-teesh
Is it included?	**Está incluido?**	ish-**tah** een-kloo-**ee**-doo
Where can I find / buy...?	**Onde posso encontrar / comprar...?**	**ohn**-deh **paw**-soo ayn-kohn-**trar** / kohn-**prar**
I'd like / We'd like...	**Gostaria / Gostaríamos...**	goosh-tah-**ree**-ah / goosh-tah-**ree**-ah-moosh
...a room.	**...um quarto.**	oo<u>n</u> **kwar**-too
...a ticket to ___.	**...um bilhete para ___.**	oo<u>n</u> beel-**yeh**-teh **pah**-rah
Is it possible?	**É possível?**	eh poo-**see**-vehl
Where is...?	**Onde é que é...?**	**ohn**-deh eh keh eh
...the train station	**...a estação de comboio**	ah ish-tah-**sow** deh kohn-**boy**-yoo
...the bus station	**...a terminal das camionetas**	ah tehr-mee-**nahl** dahsh kahm-yoo-**neh**-tahsh
...the tourist information office	**...a informação turistica**	ah een-for-mah-**sow** too-**reesh**-tee-kah
...the toilet	**...a casa de banho**	ah **kah**-zah deh **bahn**-yoo
men	**homens**	**aw**-may<u>n</u>sh
women	**mulheres**	mool-**yeh**-rish
left / right	**esquerda / direita**	ish-**kehr**-dah / dee-**ray**-tah
straight	**em frente**	ay<u>n</u> **frayn**-teh
What time does this open / close?	**A que horas é que abre / fecha?**	ah keh **aw**-rahsh eh keh **ah**-breh / **feh**-shah
At what time?	**A que horas?**	ah keh **aw**-rahsh
Just a moment.	**Um momento.**	oo<u>n</u> moo-**mayn**-too
now / soon / later	**agora / em breve / mais tarde**	ah-**goh**-rah / ay<u>n</u> **bray**-veh / mīsh **tar**-deh
today / tomorrow	**hoje / amanhã**	**oh**-zheh / ah-ming-**yah**

In the Restaurant

English	Portuguese	Pronunciation
I'd like / We'd like...	Gostaria / Gostaríamos...	goosh-tah-**ree**-ah / goosh-tah-**ree**-ah-moosh
...to reserve...	...de reservar...	deh reh-zehr-**var**
...a table for one / two.	...uma mesa para uma / duas.	oo-mah **may**-zah **pah**-rah oo-mah / **doo**-ahsh
Non-smoking.	Não fumar.	no<u>w</u> foo-**mar**
Is this table free?	Esta mesa está livre?	ehsh-tah meh-zah ish-**tah** lee-vreh
The menu (in English), please.	A ementa (em inglês), por favor.	ah eh-**mayn**-tah (ay<u>n</u> een-**glaysh**) poor fah-**vor**
service (not) included	serviço (não) incluído	sehr-**vee**-soo (no<u>w</u>) een-kloo-**ee**-doo
cover charge	tixa aplicada	tī-shah ah-plee-**kah**-dah
to go	para o caminho	**pah**-rah oo kah-**meen**-yoo
with / without	com / sem	koh<u>n</u> / say<u>n</u>
and / or	e / ou	ee / oh
menu (of the day)	ementa (do dia)	eh-**mayn**-tah (doo **dee**-ah)
specialty of the house	especialidade da casa	ish-peh-see-ah-lee-**dah**-deh dah **kah**-zah
half portion	meia dose	**may**-ah **doh**-zeh
daily special	prato do dia	**prah**-too doo **dee**-ah
tourist menu	ementa turistica	eh-**mayn**-tah too-**reesh**-tee-kah
appetizers	entradas	ay<u>n</u>-**trah**-dahsh
bread	pão	po<u>w</u>
cheese	queijo	**kay**-zhoo
sandwich	sanduíche	sahnd-**weesh**-eh
soup	sopa	**soh**-pah
salad	salada	sah-**lah**-dah
meat	carne	**kar**-neh
poultry	aves	**ah**-vish
fish	peixes	**pay**-sheesh
seafood	marisco	mah-**reesh**-koo
fruit	fruta	**froo**-tah
vegetables	legumes	lay-**goo**-mish
dessert	sobremesa	soo-breh-**may**-zah
tap water	água da torneira	**ah**-gwah dah tor-**nay**-rah
mineral water	água mineral	**ah**-gwah mee-neh-**rahl**
milk	leite	**lay**-teh
(orange) juice	sumo (de laranja)	**soo**-moo (deh lah-**rah<u>n</u>**-zhah)
coffee	café	kah-**feh**
tea	chá	shah
wine	vinho	**veen**-yoo
red / white	tinto / branco	**teen**-too / **brang**-koo
glass / bottle	copo / garrafa	**koh**-poo / gah-**rah**-fah
beer	cerveja	sehr-**vay**-zhah
Cheers!	Saúde!	sah-**oo**-deh
More. / Another.	Mais. / Outro.	mīsh / **oh**-troo
The same.	O mesmo.	oo **mehsh**-moo
Bill, please.	Conta, por favor.	**koh<u>n</u>**-tah poor fah-**vor**
tip	gorjeta	gor-**zheh**-tah
Delicious!	Delicioso!	deh-lee-see-**oh**-zoo

For hundreds more pages of survival phrases for your trip to Portugal, check out *Rick Steves' Portuguese Phrase Book.*

INDEX

Travel smart…carry on!

The latest generation of Rick Steves' carry-on travel bags is easily the best—benefiting from two decades of on-the-road attention to what really matters: maximum quality and strength; practical, flexible features; and no unnecessary frills. You won't find a better value anywhere!

Rick Steves' Convertible Carry-On $99.95

Our roomy, versatile 9" x 21" x 14" carry-on has a large 2600 cubic-inch main compartment, plus four outside pockets (small, medium and huge) that are perfect for often-used items. Wish you had even more room to bring home souvenirs? Pull open the full-perimeter expando-zipper and its capacity jumps from 2600 to 3000 cubic inches. When you want to use it as a suitcase or check it as luggage (required when "expanded"), the straps and belt hide away in a zippered compartment in the back. It weighs just 3 lbs.

Rick Steves' Classic Back Door Bag $79.95

This ultra-light (1½ lbs.) version of our Convertible Carry-On features the same 9" x 21" x 14" dimensions and hideaway straps, but does not include a waistbelt or expandability. This is the bag that Rick lives out of for three months a year!

Rick Steves' 21" Roll-Aboard $139.95

Our sturdy 21" Roll-Aboard is rucksack-soft in front, but the rest is lined with a hard ABS-lexan shell to give maximum protection to your belongings. We've spared no expense on moving parts, splurging on an extra-long button-release handle and big, tough inline skate wheels for easy rolling on rough surfaces. It features the same 9" x 21" x 14" carry-on dimensions, pocket configuration and expandability as our Convertible Carry-On—and at 7 lbs. it's the lightest roll-aboard in its class.

Prices and features are subject to change.

For great deals on a wide selection of travel goodies, begin your next trip at the Rick Steves Travel Store!

Visit the Rick Steves Travel Store at
www.ricksteves.com

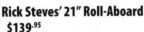

Start your trip at
www.ricksteves.com

Rick Steves' website is packed with over 3,000 pages of timely travel information. It's also your gateway to getting FREE monthly travel news from Rick—and more!

Free Monthly Travel News

Fresh articles on Europe's most interesting destinations and happenings. Rick will even send you an email every month (often direct from Europe) with his latest discoveries!

Timely Travel Tips

Rick Steves' best money-and-stress-saving tips on trip planning, packing, transportation, hotels, health, safety, finances, hurdling the language barrier...and more.

Travelers' Graffiti Wall

Candid advice and opinions from thousands of travelers on everything listed above, plus whatever topics are hot at the moment (discount flights, politics, nude beaches, scams...you name it).

Rick's Guide to Eurail Passes

The clearest, most comprehensive guide to the confusing array of railpass options out there, and how to choo-choose the railpass that best fits your itinerary and budget.

Great Gear at Our Travel Store

In the past year alone, more than 50,000 travelers have enjoyed great online deals on Rick's guidebooks, maps, DVDs—and his custom-designed carry-on bags, day packs, and light-packing accessories.

Rick Steves Tours

This year, 12,000 lucky travelers will explore Europe on a Rick Steves tour. Learn about our 28 different one- to three-week itineraries, read uncensored feedback from our tour alums, and get our free Tour Experience DVD.

Rick on TV, Radio and Podcasts

Read the scripts from the popular Rick Steves' Europe TV series, and listen to or download your choice of over 100 hours of our Travel with Rick Steves radio show.

Respect for Your Privacy

Whether you buy something from us or subscribe to Rick's monthly Travel News emails, we'll never share your name or email address with anyone else. You won't be spammed!

Have fun raising your Travel I.Q. at
www.ricksteves.com

Rick Steves®

More *Savvy*. More *Surprising*. More *Fun*.

COUNTRY GUIDES

Croatia & Slovenia
England
France
Germany & Austria
Great Britain
Ireland
Italy
Portugal
Scandinavia
Spain
Switzerland

CITY GUIDES

Amsterdam, Bruges & Brussels
Florence & Tuscany
Istanbul
London
Paris
Prague & The Czech Republic
Provence & The French Riviera
Rome
Venice

BEST OF GUIDES

Eastern Europe
Best of Europe

As the #1 authority on European travel, Rick gives you inside information on what to visit, where to stay, and how to get there—economically and hassle-free.

www.ricksteves.com

PHRASE BOOKS & DICTIONARIES

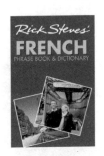

French
French, Italian & German
German
Italian
Portuguese
Spanish

MORE EUROPE FROM RICK STEVES

Europe 101
Europe Through the Back Door
Postcards from Europe

RICK STEVES' EUROPE DVDs

All 70 Shows 2000–2007
Britain
Eastern Europe
France & Benelux
Germany, The Swiss Alps & Travel Skills
Ireland
Italy
Spain & Portugal

PLANNING MAPS

Britain & Ireland
Europe
France
Germany, Austria & Switzerland
Italy
Spain & Portugal

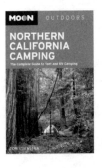

CREDITS

Researcher

To help update this book, Rick relied on…

Robert Wright

Robert was raised in Memphis, but now lives a bit farther south—in Buenos Aires, Argentina. A long-time Iberophile and a guide for Rick Steves tours, Robert spends his free time in Portugal searching for the best *salame de chocolate* and *vinho verde*. You can see his photos of Portugal at www.wrighton.com.ar/portugal.

IMAGES

Location	Photographer
Lisbon: View from Largo Santa Luzia	Rick Steves
Sintra: National Palace	Robert Wright
The Algarve: Algarve Beach	Rick Steves
Évora: Roman Temple	Rick Steves
Nazaré and Nearby:	
View of Nazaré from Sítio	David C. Hoerlein
Coimbra: Street Scene	Rick Steves
Porto: Ponte Dom Luís I	Cameron Hewitt
Douro Valley: Valley View	Cameron Hewitt

Rick Steves' Guidebook Series

Country Guides

Rick Steves' Best of Europe
Rick Steves' Croatia & Slovenia
Rick Steves' Eastern Europe
Rick Steves' England
Rick Steves' France
Rick Steves' Germany & Austria
Rick Steves' Great Britain
Rick Steves' Ireland
Rick Steves' Italy
Rick Steves' Portugal
Rick Steves' Scandinavia
Rick Steves' Spain
Rick Steves' Switzerland

City and Regional Guides

Rick Steves' Amsterdam, Bruges & Brussels
Rick Steves' Florence & Tuscany
Rick Steves' Istanbul
Rick Steves' London
Rick Steves' Paris
Rick Steves' Prague & the Czech Republic
Rick Steves' Provence & the French Riviera
Rick Steves' Rome
Rick Steves' Venice

Rick Steves' Phrase Books

French
German
Italian
Spanish
Portuguese
French/Italian/German

Other Books

Rick Steves' Europe Through the Back Door
Rick Steves' Europe 101: History and Art for the Traveler
Rick Steves' Postcards from Europe
Rick Steves' European Christmas

(Avalon Travel)

Avalon Travel
a member of the Perseus Books Group
1700 Fourth Street
Berkeley, CA 94710, USA

Thanks to Cameron Hewitt for writing the original versions of the Porto and Douro Valley chapters.

Portions of this book were originally published in *Rick Steves' Spain & Portugal* © 2005, 2004, 2003, 2002, 2001, 2000, 1999, 1998, 1997, 1996 by Rick Steves.

For the latest on Rick Steves' lectures, guidebooks, tours, public radio show, and public television series, contact Europe Through the Back Door, Box 2009, Edmonds, WA 98020, tel. 425/771-8303, fax 425/771-0833, www.ricksteves.com, rick@ricksteves.com.

ISBN(10): 1-56691-966-5
ISBN(13): 978-1-56691-966-1
ISSN 1551-837X

Europe Through the Back Door Managing Editor: Risa Laib
ETBD Editors: Cathy McDonald, Cameron Hewitt (Senior Editor)
Avalon Travel Senior Editor and Series Manager: Madhu Prasher
Avalon Travel Project Editor: Kelly Lydick
Avalon Travel Editorial Assistant: Jamie Andrade
Copy Editor: Amy Scott
Proofreader: Janet Walden
Indexer: Clare Splan
Production and Typesetting: McGuire Barber Design
Research Assistance: Robert Wright
Cover Design: Kari Gim, Laura Mazer
Cover Art Manager: Laura VanDeventer
Maps and Graphics: David C. Hoerlein, Lauren Mills, Laura VanDeventer, Mike Morgenfeld, Brice Ticen, Chris Markiewicz
Front Matter Color Photos: Lisbon Street © Robert Wright
Front Cover Images: front image, Belém Tower, Lisbon © Robyn Stencil; back image: Salema Beach © David C. Hoerlein
Photography: Robert Wright, Cameron Hewitt, David C. Hoerlein, Carol Reis, Rick Steves, and others

Distributed to the book trade by Publishers Group West, Berkeley, California.